Contributions to Finance and Accounting

The book series 'Contributions to Finance and Accounting' features the latest research from research areas like financial management, investment, capital markets, financial institutions, FinTech and financial innovation, accounting methods and standards, reporting, and corporate governance, among others. Books published in this series are primarily monographs and edited volumes that present new research results, both theoretical and empirical, on a clearly defined topic. All books are published in print and digital formats and disseminated globally. This book series is indexed in Scopus.

Sinem Derindere Köseoğlu • Adam Patterson
Editors

Valuation in Emerging Markets

Challenges, Approaches and Strategies

Springer

Editors
Sinem Derindere Köseoğlu
Transportation and Logistics Faculty
Istanbul University
Istanbul, Türkiye

Adam Patterson
Redirection
Curitiba, Paraná, Brazil

ISSN 2730-6038 ISSN 2730-6046 (electronic)
Contributions to Finance and Accounting
ISBN 978-3-031-93525-1 ISBN 978-3-031-93526-8 (eBook)
https://doi.org/10.1007/978-3-031-93526-8

This Springer imprint is published by the registered company Springer Nature Switzerland AG
The registered company address is: Gewerbestrasse 11, 6330 Cham, Switzerland

Contents

Contributors

Kivilcim Cayli Ankara, Turkey

Sinem Derindere Köseoğlu Finance (Transportation and Logistic Faculty), Istanbul University, Istanbul, Turkey

Michael Frigatti Nimber Capital Founder, Curitiba, Brazil

Kelvin Leong University of Chester, Chester, UK

Mauricio Ribeiro Maciel Marins Bertoldi Law Firm, Curitiba, Brazil

Malcolm McLelland McLelland Financial Economics LLC, Saint Petersburg, FL, USA

Adam Patterson Redirection Corporate Advisory, London, UK

Breno Pavao Curitiba, Brazil

Alexandre M. Scherer Borborema Investment Banking, Apex Partners, Vitoria, Brazil

Anna Sung University of Chester, Chester, UK

Jesus Cuauhtemoc Tellez Tecnologico de Monterrey, Business School, Monterrey, Mexico

Guilherme Vanzin Nob Hill Consultoria Ltda., Curitiba, Brazil

List of Figures

Valuation Methods and Techniques: Fundamental Principles of Valuation Theory in Emerging Markets

Public Company Valuation in Emerging Markets: A Simplified and Practical Step-by-Step Approach via DCF

Emerging Market Valuation Multiples

High Stakes, Higher Rates: An Overview and Step-by-Step Approach to Calculating the Cost of Capital in Emerging Market firms

Estimating Privately Held Capital Asset Values in Emerging Markets Using Certainty-Equivalent Risk Pricing

The Practical Application of Discounted Cash Flow in Emerging Markets: A Case Study of a Brazilian Privately Held Company

The Art of (Valuing) the Deal: Valuation Best Practices in Emerging Markets M&A

List of Tables

Emerging Market Valuation Multiples

Startup Valuation Based on a Multivariate Real Options Approach: When the Type of Market Matters

Introduction: Presenting Conceptual and Practical Approaches to Emerging Market Valuation

Sinem Derindere Köseoğlu and Adam Patterson

> *[Annual consumption in emerging markets]—the biggest growth opportunity in the history of capitalism.*
> *—McKinsey & Company (2021)*
> *There's no denying the appeal of investing in emerging markets. But there's no sugarcoating the uncertainties, either.*
> *—Guimaraes and Koller (2021)*

Abstract Emerging markets are no longer an afterthought in international finance—they now account for more than half of global GDP and create the majority of global economic growth. But while the opportunity in these markets is vast, so too are the challenges from a valuation perspective. Or in other words, how to best quantify emerging market opportunities. Political, economic, currency and regulatory risks, and less developed financial markets all add additional layers of complexity that robust valuation models need to capture. "Valuation in Emerging Markets: Challenges, Opportunities, and Strategies" provides a comprehensive framework for understanding the nuances of valuation in these economies. It bridges theory and practice, covering key topics such as forecasting, the cost of capital, liquidity constraints, adjustments, valuation multiples, M&A dynamics, and startup valuation—each examined through the lens of emerging market realities. Whether you're valuing a startup, private business, or public company, this book provides the tools and techniques required to address the unique challenges of emerging markets. In short, this book demystifies emerging market valuation, providing a practical and essential guide for anyone operating or interested in these high growth but complex environments.

S. D. Köseoğlu (✉)
Finance (Transportation and Logistic Faculty), Istanbul University, Istanbul, Turkey
e-mail: sderin@istanbul.edu.tr

A. Patterson
Redirection Corporate Advisory, London, UK
e-mail: adam@redirection.com.br

S. Derindere Köseoğlu, A. Patterson (eds.), *Valuation in Emerging Markets*, Contributions to Finance and Accounting,
https://doi.org/10.1007/978-3-031-93526-8_1

Keywords Approaches · Growth · Opportunity · Investment · Economics · Finance · Assets · Value · Knowledge · Practical skills

The global economy is increasingly being influenced by Emerging Markets (EMs). Over the past two decades, these countries have witnessed significant growth, economic development, and integration into global markets. Moreover, despite only being recognized as a distinct asset class in the 1980s, the EM universe now represents a substantial component of a well-diversified global investment portfolio.

The numbers highlighting this dynamic are astounding. Emerging markets represented 50.4% of Global GDP in 2024, and 65.9% of global GDP growth in the past 10 years to 2024 (World Economics 2025). Indeed, the total portion of global GDP made up of the 10 largest emerging markets more than doubled between 2000 and 2023, growing from 13% to 31% based on S&P data. EMs have, without doubt, become important engines of the world economy: Moreover, "Between 2000 and 2019, the share of emerging markets as recipients of global foreign direct investment increased from 15% to 46%" (OECD 2025). Most economists would suggest that economic growth in EMs should continue to surpass developed markets over the medium term.

In addition, as of the time of writing, the population of EMs was put at 6.9 billion, over 85% of the world's total population (IMF 2025). They are, or have been, experiencing rapid industrialization, urbanization, technological development, and a growing middle class. Incredibly, and looking in future workforces, the United Nations also estimate that around 90% of the world's young people between the ages of 10 and 24 already live in developing markets.

But while the appeal of emerging economies is self-explanatory, so too are the challenges that they present from a business, investment and market standpoint. Investing in emerging economies has always been synonymous with a high-risk, high-reward framework. In a nutshell, these risk factors typically entail—or are perceived to entail—political or geopolitical instability, economic, and forex volatility—prone to crises—less solid regulation, reduced liquidity and at the corporate level, limitations on governance and data quality.

However, is this view on EM risk somewhat dated? Have EMs turned a conceptual corner? Furthermore, with such diverse economies in the EM universe, can we even classify them all as a homogenous construct? Do we need new terms in our vocabulary?

Nonetheless, it does seem that EMs ceteris paribus, can present additional risk factors that can create uncertainty and complexity which in turn can pose challenges for corporate finance strategies, or in other words, a company's funding, capital structuring, and investment decisions. And within this nexus valuation is a fundamental element, helping underpin and quantify capital allocation projects, M&A, and financial planning for instance. As such, valuation in emerging markets presents unique challenges, including country risk and sovereign uncertainty, differing accounting standards and financial transparency, cost of capital adjustments, less developed equity markets, and often more complex ownership structures and company liabilities. And that is far from an exhaustive list, as we shall see throughout this volume. All these considerations may require additional technical calibration, statistical analysis, and enhanced awareness of regional market dynamics in order to produce meaningful estimates of value.

In the integrated global financial system, the necessity of business valuation has now extended far beyond portfolio management. There are dozens of reasons why valuation is needed. Additionally, at every stage of a company's life cycle, this need arises for different reasons. These reasons can include initial public offerings (IPOs), fundraising, mergers and acquisitions, foreign direct investments, bringing in new partners, exiting a partnership, determining the value of shares for creditors, share pledges, and value-oriented management. Additionally, other reasons may include tax planning and compliance, litigation or dispute resolution, financial reporting and auditing, Strategic sucession planning, strategic decision-making, regulatory compliance, efficient resource allocation, and performance evaluation (Pereiro 2002; Sivitska 2015; Lukanima 2023; Gavrilova and Hasjanova 2024). Toll and Hering (2025) even acknowledges that the same company can have different values depending on the defined purpose of the valuation. As such, valuation conducted for multiple purposes, considering the complexities of real-world valuation processes, becomes even more important in emerging markets due to their unique characteristics in the business valuation process.

Several authors have previously contributed to the discussion. Business valuation in emerging markets present unique challenges due to generally greater economic volatility, regulatory differences, market inefficiencies, lack of accounting transparency, data unavailability and reduced quality, lack of corporate governance, liquidity constraints, currency risks, and many others (see Bekaert et al. 2007; Damodaran 2012; Atwi et al. 2017; Shahid 2017; Claessens and Yurtoglu 2012; Abuamsha 2021; Basiru et al. 2023).

Liquidity is crucial for asset pricing, as it allows for the efficient sale of stocks at fair value. A lack of liquidity can lead to increased costs of trading, negatively impacting equity returns. Firms with better internal liquidity can better capitalize on investment opportunities, whilst those facing liquidity constraints struggle to finance growth, affecting their valuation negatively (Shahid 2017). Therefore, liquidity is a critical factor in emerging markets, affecting both stock market development and individual firm valuations. The impact of liquidity on expected returns in emerging markets is significant, with local market liquidity being an important driver (Bekaert et al. 2007). Furthermore, the internationalization of firms—and specifically local firms 'IPOing' in foreign stock exchanges—can negatively affect the liquidity of firms opting to remain in domestic markets through migration effects and liquidity spillovers (Levine and Schmukler 2006). These findings underscore the importance of considering liquidity when evaluating businesses and markets in emerging economies.

Understanding country-level determinants of liquidity synchronization is crucial, as higher synchronicity is associated with weaker economic and financial environments (Zaidi and Rupeika-Apoga 2021). This concept can help in adjusting valuation models to account for systemic illiquidity risks. In addition, incorporating liquidity as a priced factor in asset pricing models, particularly for segmented markets, can improve valuation accuracy (Bekaert et al. 2007). Moreover, considering alternative liquidity measures, such as the proportion of zero daily firm returns, may provide more accurate predictors of future returns in emerging markets compared to traditional measures like turnover (Ahn et al. 2018; Bekaert et al. 2007).

While conventional wisdom suggests that illiquidity should negatively affect asset values, some studies have found potentially surprising results. For instance, research on frontier markets revealed no evidence of an illiquidity premium in equities, contrary to typical relationships in developed and emerging markets (Stereńczak et al. 2019). This suggests that for countries not fully integrated with the global economy, diversification benefits may offset illiquidity concerns. Either way, each valuation exercise, depending on its basis of value, should contemplate such factors as part of the analysis.

Currency risk also significantly impacts the valuation of businesses in emerging markets, primarily through exchange rate fluctuations that affect cash flows and the cost of equity. The sensitivity of firms to currency changes varies, with some experiencing adverse effects while others may benefit. Understanding these dynamics is crucial for accurate business valuation in these regions. Exchange rate fluctuations can significantly affect the value of emerging market firms. Indeed, data suggests that approximately 25% of firms experience a decline in share prices due to currency depreciation, while 15% see a positive impact. Businesses with higher indebtedness are more adversely affected by currency depreciation, highlighting the importance of managing foreign currency-denominated debts (Windsor 2016). Empirical tests across developed and emerging markets have shown that emerging market currency risk is priced separately from other local risk factors and represents a significant component of equity returns in both developed and emerging markets (Carrieri et al. 2006). Currency risk is a major factor influencing the cost of equity in BRICS nations, with firms reporting substantial currency losses facing higher required returns. In contrast, firms in Brazil, India, and South Africa with notable currency gains may experience lower required returns compared to those with minimal currency fluctuations (Kuchin et al. 2019). Almeida and Fernández (2009) developed a modified CAPM to incorporate foreign exchange risk, which is particularly relevant in Latin American markets. This model has shown improved predictive accuracy compared to traditional approaches.

The choice of currency for valuation is also a critical issue, as firms, especially those with international operations or investors, also seek to express cash flows in a stable currency, typically the US dollar. Forecasting exchange rates is essential for accurate valuation, with models suggesting that the real exchange rate's evolution can significantly impact economic value (Dumrauf 2014).

Data unavailability and quality issues also significantly hinder business valuation in emerging markets. These challenges stem from unreliable input data, lack of standardization, and external influences that can distort valuation accuracy. Accounting and financial data in emerging markets often lack consistency and reliability. In Malaysia, differences between databases can lead to discrepancies in financial research, making valuations more challenging (Suret et al. 1996, 1998). Similarly, in Tanzania, even with greater digital access to data, professionals still face difficulties in ensuring the credibility of their assessments due to limited trustworthy sources. Valuers frequently rely on government guidelines, which may not reflect actual market conditions, leading to discrepancies in property valuations, for instance. Limited professional training and adherence to outdated guidelines contribute to valuation inaccuracies, as valuers may not fully understand market dynamics. The lack of robust professional valuation boards exacerbates these issues, as they fail to keep members updated on best practices (Komu 2018).

Addressing data availability and quality issues in emerging market valuations requires requires a multifaceted approach. Utilizing open data can improve transparency and accessibility of market information, allowing valuers to triangulate data sources for better accuracy (McDermott 2015). Systematic evaluation of existing financial databases can also help identify discrepancies and improve the reliability of data used in valuations (Suret et al. 1996). Encouraging firms to adopt standardized accounting and governance practices can enhance the quality and comparability of financial data. Employing robust valuation methodologies, such as discounted cash flow analysis, can help navigate complexities like inflation and tax implications (Velez-Pareja and Tham 2010). Furthermore, providing training for valuers on the unique challenges of emerging markets can reduce variability in valuation outcomes (Kucharska-Stasiak 2005). Arguably, advancements in technology and data analytics could improve data availability and quality in emerging markets, potentially enhancing valuation practices in the future.

It is necessary to reflect on these characteristics in emerging markets in business valuations. These can be in the form of modifications or risk premiums. The country risk premium is an additional return demanded by investors for investing in a country with higher risk compared to a more stable country. On average, higher geopolitical risk increases the cost of equity capital (Carney et al. 2024). This premium is often added to the cost of equity in valuation models. For instance, adding to the CAPM-derived cost of equity to account for these country-specific risks. This practice is based on the assumption that emerging markets are less integrated into global capital markets and therefore require an additional premium (Sanvicente 2021; Sanvicente et al. 2017). However, adding a country risk premium to the CAPM may be redundant if the local market index already reflects the country risk. For example, in the Brazilian market, the Ibovespa index already incorporates the country risk premium, making the addition of an extra premium redundant and potentially leading to pricing errors (Sanvicente 2021). In addition, some argue that focusing solely on this aspect may overlook other critical factors such as market potential and growth opportunities, which can also significantly impact investment decisions in emerging markets (Roggi et al. 2016). This premium can also be expressed as a company-specific risk premium that measures the effective exposure of a company to country risk. This method considers the company's specific characteristics, such as its industry, size, and geographic diversification, to estimate the premium (Roggi et al. 2016). Shepeleva (2016) proposed a new approach to evaluating company-specific risk premiums in emerging markets, allowing for more accurate estimation of enterprise value. This method is adaptable and can be modified to suit changing economic conditions, providing a more objective assessment of equity returns.

Emerging markets often exhibit countercyclical interest rates, which can complicate valuation processes. Fernández and Gulan (2015) provide a micro-level rationale for this pattern by linking interest rate spreads to corporate leverage dynamics. This relationship between interest rates and leverage could thus be considered when valuing businesses in these markets, as it can significantly impact a company's cost of capital and overall financial structure.

In addition, modifications can be made to multipliers in practical applications. Adjustments to global market multiples are also essential to reflect operational efficiencies specific to emerging markets. This includes refining the selection of comparable companies to ensure they share similar operational characteristics. Recent studies propose improved methods for adjusting market multiples, removing inherent restrictions to better reflect the realities of emerging markets (Kanaryan 2019). As seen in the literature, business valuation in emerging markets presents numerous challenges and has been the subject of extensive research. Various studies have addressed these challenges.

And yet despite the increasing importance of emerging markets in the global economy, there is seemingly a gap in academic contributions which address these issues in a practical 'how to' manner, going beyond mere theoretical treatments. What is more, we note that to date, academic articles focused on EM valuation make up just a small part of the total literature related to company valuation.

This book *Valuation in Emerging Markets: Challenges, Opportunities, and Strategies* offers an in-depth exploration of the unique landscape of emerging markets as well as the methodologies employed in valuing businesses within these environments. It therefore seeks to provide insight around the 'what', 'why', and 'how' to value and invest in assets in these markets.

The book's primary aim is to equip practitioners, academics, and students with a robust framework for understanding the EM environment, and performing valuations in emerging markets, in a dual holistic theoretical and practical approach. In doing so, the authors seek to calibrate existing value principles and best practices to ensure compliance with the specific characteristics of EMs. After all, the same principles of traditional company valuation apply.

The volume starts by looking at the history, trends, and drivers of the EM valuation universe before advancing to look at step-by-step valuation approaches for public and private companies and startups, touching on a broad range of applicable themes such as value in M&A, liquidity risk pricing and real options analysis, and in an exclusive section, practical real-world contributions from academic experts and corporate advisors from the emerging market ecosystem.

Consequently, by incorporating real-world examples and case studies, the book will give not only theoretical guidance but also actionable and comprehensive insights. This practical focus, coupled with a holistic look at some of the economic, legal, and accounting fundamentals, renders the book simultaneously a learning tool and a functional handbook for professionals and subject matter practitioners dealing with the valuation of emerging market companies and a go-to guide for understanding and manoeuvring the nuances of these important yet arguably under-researched markets.

This book is divided up into 17 chapters, each of which explores a different aspect of emerging market valuation.

In our second chapter, *The Emerging Markets Investment Landscape: Past, Present and Future,* the authors' trace the evolution of emerging market investments, from early trade routes and colonial expansion to the modern context of acute growth, financial liberalization, and technological transformation. It explores how these markets have developed alongside persistent challenges such as economic volatility, regulatory uncertainty, and geopolitical risks. The chapter provides a foundational understanding of what defines an emerging market and examines investment strategies, including public equities, FDI, and M&A. Case studies highlight historical EM investments in the European Exploration Age, while discussions on valuation challenges and solutions, as well as anticipated market drivers, set the stage for deeper analysis in later chapters. By bridging theoretical frameworks with real-world applications, the chapter equips readers with essential comprehension insights into the dynamic nature of EM investing.

Chapter 3, *Key Drivers of Valuation and Returns in Emerging Markets: An Investment Advisor's View* analyses the fundamental determinants of equity valuations and returns of emerging markets, providing theoretical considerations and empirical insights. It begins with an overview of EM equity indexes, their historical evolution and their position in global finance. The symposium proceeds to bring into focus major explanatory drivers of EM performance, distinguishing between exogenous drivers—macroeconomic patterns and market volatility—and endogenous drivers like corporate governance and institutional quality. Moving from the theoretical to practical analytics, a bespoke regression model establishes revenue growth, debt, and innovation spending as primary valuation drivers for EM equity sectors. The chapter concludes with the author drawing on his practical experience in looking at how investment strategies such as diversification, long-term investment horizons, style investing, and leveraging local know-how can help take advantage of EM opportunities.

The fourth chapter contribution, *Understanding the Unique Characteristics of Emerging Markets*, explores the process of valuation, which determines the value of assets, companies, and investments, emphasizing its importance in financial decisions and economic development. It provides a historical overview of valuation, discusses core principles like the time value of money and risk-return trade-off, and explains key methods, such as discounted cash flow (DCF) and market comparisons. The chapter highlights the challenges of valuation in emerging markets, including economic instability, currency fluctuations, and limited access to reliable financial data. It also discusses how modern technologies, like artificial intelligence and data mining, enhance valuation accuracy by providing real-time insights. This chapter underscores valuation's critical role in efficient resource allocation, supporting investment, and fostering financial stability, especially in the dynamic context of emerging markets.

Chapter 5 entitled *Valuation Methods and Techniques: Fundamental principles of valuation theory in emerging markets*, examines enterprise valuation techniques in emerging markets, focusing on the core methods and the adjustments required to address the unique risks and opportunities inherent in these economies. It provides a comprehensive overview of valuation approaches, emphasizing the key distinctions between emerging and developed markets. A detailed case study from Turkey, conducted in Turkish Lira (TL), illustrates the practical application of three core valuation methods, guiding readers through the entire process from start to finish. By highlighting the challenges of valuing enterprises in a volatile and unpredictable environment, this chapter offers critical insights and equips readers with the tools to navigate the complexities of valuation in emerging markets. Given the scarcity of practical applications in the literature, this study serves as a valuable resource for understanding and applying core valuation methods in such contexts.

The following chapter, Chap. 6, *Public Company Valuation in Emerging Markets: A simplified and practical step-by-step approach* via *DCF*, presents a step-by-step guide to listed emerging market company valuation and integrates corporate finance theory and real-world techniques. The chapter outlines the key valuation issues and theory-based solutions, offering step-by-step procedures to estimate fundamental company value. Using the work of multiple authors in the space as a foundation, readers can gain practical knowledge of financial forecasting, computing cost of capital and reconcile the FCFF and FCFE models to intrinsic company valuation.

In our seventh chapter, *Emerging Market Valuation Multiples: 'It's all relative'*, the author explores the fundamentals of relative valuation, emphasizing its applications, advantages, and limitations, with a special focus on the challenges of applying the methodology to emerging market contexts. It examines practical solutions, such as cross-border adjustments and clustering benchmarks by value drivers, while highlighting the restrictions and lessons learned of these techniques. The chapter concludes with a step-by-step guide and a practical example to demonstrate the approach in action.

High Stakes, Higher Rates: An overview and step-by-step approach to calculating the Cost of Capital in Emerging Market firms, chapter number eight, explores the complexities of estimating the cost of capital in emerging markets, a key pillar of valuation processes which directly affects not only results but also investment decisions. The chapter begins with a survey of the literature on the evolution of cost of capital models before exploring the unique challenges of applying the models in emerging economies, such as increased risk premiums, currency volatility, and limited financial data. The chapter then offers a step-by-step, detailed manual on how to estimate the weighted average cost of capital (WACC) of a privately held emerging market firm, including breaking down the principal inputs, financial assumptions, and best practices. The chapter seeks to demystify the WACC calculation, allowing valuation professionals a clear and effective framework to navigate the higher risks and complexities of emerging market firm and their opportunity costs.

Valuation of privately held enterprises in emerging markets is widely regarded as being problematic due to a lack of relevant valuation data and the common use of unsupported valuation assumptions. That being so, Chap. 9, *Estimating privately held capital asset values in emerging markets using certainty-equivalent risk pricing*, presents a theory and method for developing enterprise valuation estimates that are objective and have demonstrable accuracy and reliability in any market. Such theory and method are especially relevant and applicable to emerging market valuation estimates where transparency and objectivity are critical, among other uses, for capital asset transaction negotiations.

In *The Practical Application of Discounted Cash Flow in Emerging Markets: A Case Study of a Brazilian Privately Held Company*, our book's tenth chapter, the author presents a comprehensive valuation for a fictitious Brazilian company and offers a simple and practical financial modelling perspective on private enterprise value in an emerging market setting that is useful for both corporate finance students and valuation professionals. The chapter integrates macroeconomic factors and uses Discounted Cash Flow (DCF) to estimate the firm's intrinsic value. Scenario analyses and market multiples are employed to validate the result and evaluate the risks related to fundamental valuation.

Chapter 11, *The Art of (Valuing) The Deal: Valuation best practices in Emerging Markets M&A*, discusses the central role of valuation in M&A deals, particularly in the complex dynamics of emerging markets. It discusses challenges like regulatory uncertainty, currency risk, information asymmetry, and corporate governance, which may complicate deal structuring and value approximation. It touches on the differing dynamics of value and pricing. The chapter summarizes theoretical valuation approaches, discusses practical approaches to quantifying synergies, and offers real-world M&A valuation models such accretion/dilution analysis and synergy valuation. It closes out by highlighting solutions like earn-outs to bridge valuation gaps, giving a combination of theory and practice for effective handling of EM M&A deals.

Building on the previous discussion, *Beyond Valuation: Legal, Regulatory & Corporate Governance Issues in Emerging Market M&A*, our twelfth chapter addresses literature gaps in emerging market M&A in terms of a lack of practitioner insights for acquirers, advisers, and students. It combines literature review with the author's practice experience as a Brazilian lawyer and addresses key legal, regulatory, corruption, rule of law and corporate governance issues in due diligence, share purchase agreements, and shareholder agreements, and the impact of these unique characteristics on M&A risks. The chapter focuses on EMs' special legal and ownership structures compared with developed markets, as well as the necessity for disciplined due diligence, contractual protection, and risk analysis in determining transaction prices.

With an emphasis on liquidity effects, Chap. 13, *Liquidity in Equity Markets: Theory and Practice for Emerging Markets*, examines liquidity differentials across various markets and asset classes, with a particular focus on emerging versus developed markets and private versus public equities. Recognizing the abstract nature of liquidity, the chapter includes a literature review to explore the definition of liquidity in a valuation context, its influence on asset prices, and its implications for valuation frameworks. The intrinsic relationship between liquidity risk and other risk factors poses challenges in isolating the specific price impact attributable to liquidity differentials. To address this, the chapter introduces a theoretical framework that isolates the liquidity premium by analysing yields implied by observed market prices and dividends or cash flows from assets that have similar risk-return characteristics but are traded in different markets. This approach highlights that liquidity is inherently a relative concept, allowing for the comparison of liquidity premiums across different markets, both developed and emerging.

To deepen our understanding of the topic, our fourteenth chapter, *Estimating liquidity risk pricing and transaction costs in the valuation of privately held capital assets in emerging markets*, essentially addresses so-called "discounts for lack of marketability," which is one of the most subjective and problematic issues in privately held enterprise valuation. The chapter presents theory demonstrating such discounts essentially represent differences in transaction costs between public and private market capital asset transactions and then presents a method for applying the theory to an emerging market valuation example. It is shown that the method is transparent and objective, which is particularly critical in emerging market private firm valuations.

Technology and Financial Innovation in Emerging Markets: Impacts on Value creation, our fifteenth contribution, which highlights how financial technology (FinTech) is transforming emerging markets by improving financial inclusion, efficiency, and sustainability. It traces FinTech's evolution through three phases, from early technologies like ATMs to modern innovations such as blockchain, mobile payments, and AI. These advancements address challenges in underbanked regions, exemplified by platforms like Kenya's M-Pesa and AI-driven agricultural solutions in India. Despite barriers like regulatory issues and limited digital literacy, the chapter emphasizes future trends, including quantum computing and decentralized finance, which have the potential to reshape global financial systems. Ultimately, it showcases FinTech as a key driver of economic growth and innovation in developing economies.

Continuing the emphasis on early-stage firms, Chap. 16, *Startup Valuations in Emerging Markets*, addresses the unique challenges of startup valuations in emerging markets, in which macroeconomic conditions like inflation, currency exchange rate volatility, political instability can add further complexity to valuation for such already volatile early-stage businesses. The author lists ten startup valuation methods and proposes strong adaptations and accommodations, with the goal of incorporating them in a startup-specific but still reasonable methodology in the broader framework of emerging markets. Moreover, the chapter also analyses the investor perspective of the startup industry and argues that valuation is utilized in order to enable effective investment decisions and understanding of financial performance and outlook, and thus not as an end per se. Key components of the valuation process such as due diligence, performance metrics, regulatory concerns, and exit strategies are addressed to develop an overall framework to value startups in the rapidly evolving environments of emerging market economies.

Picking up on advanced valuation approaches within the startup space, we close out this volume with "*Startup Valuation based on a Multivariate Real Options Approach: When the type of market matters*", our final chapter. For the author, since emerging markets are described by common economic factors like high levels of risk, exchange rate fluctuations, inflation, and economic growth rates often more volatile than developed economies, it would be reasonable to compensate investors with a higher premium than that in a developed market. Furthermore, if any startup is a "high uncertainty venture", its uncertainty could be magnified because of its EM origins, and as such a valuation approach could reasonably be required that captures this double-edged sword: uncertainty and country origins. For this reason, the chapter applies an Equity-Linked Exchange Rate Option which is an extension of the Black-Scholes option pricing framework that simultaneously captures the volatility of the main underlying uncertainty factors such as the expected revenues and the co-movement with other risk factors. The proposed Multivariate Real Options (MVRO) approach shows that even in the worst-case scenario, it is possible to create value when investing in an emerging-based startup. Also, it is shown that the startup value increases at a diminishing rate as the volatility of the risk factor increases. Nevertheless, the chapter closes out by emphasizing that the MVRO approach should be complementary to other valuation methods in the investment decision-making.

In conclusion, emerging markets are therefore an increasingly important economic, political, and investment paradigm. "Valuation in Emerging Markets: Challenges, Opportunities, and Strategies" addresses a vital need in the literature and practice of financial valuation in these markets and in doing so can function as one-stop-shop for both broad market context and applied approaches in the EM space, for business and finance professionals, and for those simply interested in the developing economy nexus. The chapters can be read sequentially or as stand-alone chapters on specific topics. With all of them, we endeavour to demystify and democratize knowledge of EM valuation to a broader audience. By the end, we are optimistic that readers will be better equipped to value—with both intrinsic and relative approaches—not only EM listed equities but also SMEs, startups, and better understand how to resolve the myriad valuation challenges these firms can present. We hope you enjoy reading as much as we enjoyed writing. Now, as Plato once said, "the beginning is the most important part of the work", so let us start on our emerging market valuation endeavour.

References

Abuamsha MK (2021) Valuation methods in emerging financial markets: literature review study. Acad Strateg Manag J 20:1–27. https://www.abacademies.org/articles/valuation-methods-in-emerging-financial-markets-literature-review-study.pdf

Ahn H-J, Cai J, Yang C-W (2018) Which liquidity proxy measures liquidity best in emerging markets? Economies 6(4):67. https://doi.org/10.3390/economies6040067

Almeida AH, Fernández PL (2009) A modified CAPM valuation model for Latin American emerging markets. *Documentos de trabajo en finanzas de empresas* 1:1. https://dialnet.unirioja.es/servlet/articulo?codigo=2957154

Atwi L, Safieddine A, Titman S (2017) Investor protection and governance in the valuation of emerging markets investments. J Appl Corp Financ 29(3):89–100. https://doi.org/10.1111/JACF.12253

Basiru JO, Ejiofor CL, Onukwulu EC, Attah RU (2023) Financial management strategies in emerging markets: a review of theoretical models and practical applications. Magna Scientia Adv Res Rev 7(2):123–140. https://doi.org/10.30574/msarr.2023.7.2.0054

Bekaert G, Harvey CR, Lundblad C (2007) Liquidity and expected returns: lessons from emerging markets. Rev Financ Stud 20(6):1783–1831. https://doi.org/10.1093/rfs/hhm030

Carney RW, El Ghoul S, Guedhami O, Wang HH (2024) Geopolitical risk and the cost of capital in emerging economies. Emerg Mark Rev 61:101149. https://doi.org/10.1016/j.ememar.2024.101149

Carrieri F, Majerbi B, Errunza V (2006) Does emerging market exchange risk affect global equity prices? J Financ Quant Anal 41(3):511–540. https://doi.org/10.1017/s0022109000002520

Claessens S, Yurtoglu BB (2012) Corporate governance in emerging markets: a survey. Available at SSRN: https://ssrn.com/abstract=1988880 or https://doi.org/10.2139/ssrn.1988880

Damodaran A (2012) Investment valuation: tools and techniques for determining the value of any asset. 3rd Edition, Wiley, Hoboken

Dumrauf GL (2014) Currency choices in valuation: an approach for emerging markets. Soc Sci Res Netw. https://doi.org/10.2139/SSRN.2006502

Fernández A, Gulan A (2015) Interest rates, leverage, and business cycles in emerging economies: the role of financial frictions. Am Econ J Macroecon 7(3):153–188. https://doi.org/10.1257/mac.20120141

Gavrilova EN, Hasjanova DN (2024) Comparative analysis of approaches to assessing the market cost of business in domestic and foreign practice. Вестник Университета 3:130–141. https://doi.org/10.26425/1816-4277-2024-3-130-141

Guimaraes P, Koller T (2021) Don't overthink your approach to valuation in emerging markets, McKinsey & Company, Article online. Available at: How to value a company in an emerging market | McKinsey

International Monetary Fund (IMF) (2025) DataMapper: labour productivity. IMF World Economic Outlook. Available at: https://www.imf.org/external/datamapper/LP@WEO/OEMDC/ADVEC/WEOWORLD. Accessed 06 Mar 2025

Kanaryan N (2019) Enhancing the adjustments of market multiples for better operating efficiency. 3–20. https://ideas.repec.org/a/dat/earchi/y2019i4p3-20.html

Komu FJ (2018) Valuation accuracy and certainty in developing countries- a socio-political analysis. RELAND: Int J Real Estate Land Planning 1:67–76

Kucharska-Stasiak IIE (2005) Uncertainty of valuation in the emerging markets. The polish case. Research papers in Economics. https://EconPapers.repec.org/RePEc:arz:wpaper:eres2005_233

Kuchin I, Elkina M, Dranev Y (2019) The impact of currency risk on firm's value in emerging countries. *Корпоративные финансы* 13(1):7–27. https://doi.org/10.17323/J.JCFR.2073-0438.13.1.2019.7-27

Levine R, Schmukler SL (2006) Internationalization and stock market liquidity*. Rev Finance 10(1):153–187. https://doi.org/10.1007/s10679-006-6981-7

Lukanima BK (2023) An overview of corporate valuation. Springer International Publishing, pp 3–24. https://doi.org/10.1007/978-3-031-28267-6_1

McDermott A (2015) Harnessing the potential of open data for valuation transparency in the developing world. https://opus.lib.uts.edu.au/bitstream/10453/43676/1/McDermott-718-718_paper.pdf

Organisation for Economic Co-operation and Development (OECD) (2025) Emerging markets network. OECD. https://www.oecd.org/en/networks/emerging-markets-network.html#:~:text=Between%202000%20and%202019%2C%20the,growth%20occurs%20in%20those%20markets. Accessed 06 Mar 2025

Pereiro LE (2002) Valuation of companies in emerging markets: a practical approach. John Wiley & Sons

Roggi O, Giannozzi A, Baglioni T (2016) Firm valuation in emerging markets and the exposure to country risk. Glob J Manag Bus Res 16(1):10–30. https://globaljournals.org/GJMBR_Volume16/1-Firm-Valuation-in-Emerging.pdf
Sanvicente AZ (2021) Relevance of country risk premium in cost of equity estimation. J Contemp Adm 19(spe1):38–52. https://doi.org/10.6084/m9.figshare.14320826
Sanvicente AZ, Sheng HH, Sheng HH, Guanais LFP (2017) Are country and size risks priced in the Brazilian stock market. Bar Brazilian Adm Rev 14(1):e160076. https://doi.org/10.1590/1807-7692BAR2017160076
Shahid MS (2017) Investment opportunities & liquidity constraints: evidence from two emerging markets, India and Pakistan. JISR Manag Soc Sci Econ 15(1):69–83. https://doi.org/10.31384/JISRMSSE/2017.15.1.5
Shepeleva A (2016) Evaluation of a company-specific risk premium on emerging markets: a new approach. Int J Arts Sci, Forthcoming, Available at SSRN: https://ssrn.com/abstract=2717618
Sivitska Y (2015) The role of business valuation in strategic planning of activity of the company. Int J Finance Account 4(2):140–143. http://article.sapub.org/10.5923.j.ijfa.20150402.04.html
Stereńczak S, Zaremba A, Umar Z (2019) Is there an illiquidity premium in frontier markets? Emerg Mark Rev 42(42):100673. https://doi.org/10.1016/j.ememar.2019.100673
Suret J-M, Morrill CKJ, Morrill J (1996) Availability and accuracy of accounting and financial data in emerging markets. Research Papers in Economics. https://ideas.repec.org/p/fth/lavadm/96-49.html
Suret J-M, Morrill CKJ, Morrill J (1998) Availability and accuracy of accounting and financial data in an emerging market: the case of Malaysia. Asia-Pac J Account 5(1):95–126. https://doi.org/10.1080/10293574.1998.10510532
Toll C, Hering T (2025) Functional business valuation – purpose is king! Manag Econ 25(2):159. https://doi.org/10.7494/manage.2024.25.2.159
Velez-Pareja I, Tham J (2010) Company's valuation in an emerging economy – case study TIMANCO S.A. Valuat J 5(2):4–45. https://ideas.repec.org/a/vaj/journl/v5y2010i2p4-45.html
Windsor C (2016) Currency risk at emerging market firms. 59–70. https://ideas.repec.org/a/rba/rbabul/jun2016-08.htm
World Economics (2025) Emerging markets. World Economics. https://www.worldeconomics.com/Regions/Emerging-Markets/. Accessed 06 Mar 2025
Zaidi SH, Rupeika-Apoga R (2021) Liquidity synchronization, its determinants and outcomes under economic growth volatility: evidence from emerging Asian economies. Risks 9(2):43. https://doi.org/10.3390/risks9020043

The Emerging Markets Investment Landscape: Past, Present, and Future

Adam Patterson and Sinem Derindere Köseoğlu

> *emerging market*
> *noun.*
> *an economy that has some features of a developed market economy such as those of the US, Japan, and western Europe, but not all.*
> *—Cambridge Dictionary*
> *The world economy is shifting. We will see a restructuring of the global economy. The economic influence of the G7 countries will shift to the Emerging 7, fuelling the rise of a newly affluent community and a different breed of corporations.*
> *—Sydney Business Insights*
> *An ongoing shift in global economic activity from developed to developing economies, accompanied by growth in the number of consumers in emerging markets, are the global developments that executives around the world view as the most important for business…over the next five years. We're looking at the challenges in [emerging] markets and making sure that we stay close to them to understand what those challenges are.*
> *—McKinsey & Company*

Abstract The role of emerging markets (EM) has increased exponentially in global financial markets during the last few decades, creating a vibrant space of economic development and varied investment opportunities. This chapter explores the history of EM investments, approaches and the various challenges and solutions that valuation professionals usually encounter in this milieu. Its objective is to give a

A. Patterson
Redirection Corporate Advisory, London, UK
e-mail: adam@redirection.com

S. D. Köseoğlu (✉)
Finance (Transportation and Logistic Faculty), Istanbul University, Istanbul, Turkey
e-mail: sderin@istanbul.edu.tr

S. Derindere Köseoğlu, A. Patterson (eds.), *Valuation in Emerging Markets*, Contributions to Finance and Accounting,
https://doi.org/10.1007/978-3-031-93526-8_2

historical, illustrative, and introductory context to contribute to readers' general knowledge as they read the book. By highlighting the evolution of EM investments through time, the modern-day outlook combined with practical valuator concerns, the chapter attempts to lay the foundation for the additional development of emerging market valuation principles in subsequent chapters, ranging from theoretical underpinnings to real-world practical examples.

Keywords History · Growth · Globalization · Frontier economies · Trends · Challenges · Strategies · Opportunities · Risks

Introduction

The shift in the importance of Emerging Markets (EMs) over the last few decades is often considered a "mega" trend in global financial markets. The landscape of emerging markets investment represents a dynamic intersection of economic growth, global integration, and diverse investment opportunities. Emerging market investments can be traced from the first exploration of ancient trading routes through colonial expansion and the post–World War II reforms. EMs have gone through decades of development with major changes in political regimes, economic liberalization and technological advancements to deeply transform their business and financial market environments. Nonetheless, alongside these opportunities, such developments also include significant challenges including economic volatility, regulatory uncertainties, financial crises, and geopolitical risks. As such, valuation—in other words, the process for determining the present worth of a company or asset—is increasingly an important activity within emerging markets. Hence, this chapter aims to explore the multifaceted nature of the emerging markets investment landscape, analyse historical trajectories, contemporary challenges and emerging trends that shape the valuation and strategic considerations for investors and corporate finance professionals in these dynamic economies. It then serves as a comprehensive historical introduction to the more theoretical and technical valuation approaches presented later in this book. In other words, before we dig deeper into approaches, challenges and main trends to emerging market valuation, we should understand the macro landscape of the development of such economies to provide context and help set the scene.

Lexicology and the Current Milieu

Let us begin with some definitions as, to paraphrase Socrates, "the beginning of wisdom is the definition of terms" (n.d., in Hollingsworth 2015). In academic literature, definitions serve as conceptual tools that not only define the scope but also facilitate rigorous analysis and systematic inquiry. Defining terms is not only an exercise in semantic precision but also foundational constructs that provide clarity and precision to our discourse.

Nonetheless, the task of defining emerging markets is fraught with complexity, as these economies exhibit heterogeneous characteristics ranging from rapid industrialization and demographic shifts to varying levels of institutional development and market integration (UNIDO 2020). And yet, define we must as before we endeavour to tackle valuation theory, applications and practical case studies in emerging markets, we must endeavour to understand the broader EM context and past trajectories.

The distinction between "economy" and "market" is often delineated by their respective scopes: the economy encompasses broader social interactions that occur through production, trade, investment or consumption in a specific area or areas. Here, we recall Econ101 and the key elements in the Gross Domestic Product formula: $GDP = C + I + G + (X\text{-}M)$. Markets on the other hand, refer to the space where those activities are negotiated, exchanged or spent: the microeconomic interactions within specific sectors. However, in this chapter, these terms will be used interchangeably.

According to the International Monetary Fund, there is no official definition of an emerging market (IMF 2023). The IMF does however classify 39 economies as "advanced," considering criteria like high per capita income, diverse exports and strong integration into the global financial system. Other countries fall into the category of "emerging market and developing economies", characterized by volatility, promising growth prospects and opportunities for substantial macroeconomic reforms (IMF 2023). Indeed, the World Bank classes economies based on their GNI per capita (computed using the "Atlas" method), without entering into normative judgements "concerning the development status of any country or territory" (World Bank 2021). To the Economist (2017), in broad brush strokes they are an economy that is "not too rich, not too poor and not too closed to foreign capital".

Their distinct characteristics set them apart from developed markets, primarily due to lower per capita income, evolving financial systems, and higher susceptibility to economic shocks (Bekaert and Harvey 2014). Emerging markets are nonetheless important for global economic growth and although they can be characterized by diverse economic structures, legal frameworks, and growth trajectories, reflecting their varied stages of development and regional contexts (Krugman 1994; Rodrik 2008), there are no one-size-fits-all terms. For instance, countries like Brazil and Russia depend heavily on commodities such as energy, minerals, and agribusiness production. Conversely, emerging giants like China and India combine robust manufacturing sectors with burgeoning consumer bases, driving both export-oriented growth and domestic consumption-led expansion in their substantial populations. And yet there are extensive economic, political, and social differences—and similarities—between even these examples. The Brazilian and Indian economies may have separate economic structures, but they are both nevertheless representative democracies after all. Thus, besides the unifying characteristic of being emerging markets, all the underlying countries have their own currency, economic policy, and a set of companies representing their major sectors, which makes broad comparison across markets challenging. No two EMs or their respective investment profiles are identical but as we will see throughout this book, approaches to better quantify risk and value in these markets certainly borrow key characteristics.

Moreover, emerging economies undergo dynamic transformations over time, exemplified by the evolution of Eastern European nations in the post-Soviet era (Gros 2017), Japan's rapid industrialization in the 1960s (Johnson 1982), and South Korea's economic ascent in subsequent decades (Amsden 1989). These historical examples underscore the fluidity and complexity inherent in assessing and valuing emerging market economies. Pre-1980s, a lot of market discourse was coloured by Cold War terminology and subsequent world groupings via "blocs". The First World consisted of the United States, Western Europe, and their allies. The Second World was the Communist Bloc of the Soviet Union, China, Cuba, and aligned countries. The remaining nations, often in the global south and without formal alignment were assigned to the Third World. The end of the Cold War would soon change this dichotomy and arguably its simplified vocabulary.

The term "emerging markets" (or abbreviated to "EMs") was first coined by economist Antoine W. Van Agtmael in the early 1980s to describe economies transitioning from low-income to middle-income status through structural reforms and economic liberalization whilst promoting global listed equity investment vehicles for such countries (Van Agtmael 2007). The story goes that whilst working for the International Finance Corporation (IFC) Agtmael "pitched an idea for a listed company investment fund focused on the developing world. The idea was good, but the name wasn't. 'Third World Equity Fund', van Agtmael later admitted, implied backwardness, poverty, and stagnation" (EQT 2024). This was soon optimized to "Emerging Markets", which, of course, soon caught on. According to the same author, emerging markets are economies that are gaining significance in the world and whose contribution to future economic growth was expected to be high. This shift is usually characterized by increased industrialization, improved infrastructure, and developing human capital. These elements combine to create an enabling environment for acute economic development and integration into the global economy.

Emerging markets now play a crucial role in global economic growth, acting as engines of expansion that significantly contribute to the overall increase in global GDP. Or as a Forbes article in 2010 contended: "The opening of these large economies to global capital, technology, and talent over the past two decades has fundamentally changed their economic and business environments. As a result, the GDP growth rates of these countries have dramatically outpaced those of more developed economies, lifting millions out of poverty and creating new middle classes—and vast new markets for consumer products and services". These markets provide fertile ground for innovation and entrepreneurship, further enhancing their economic prospects and global significance.

The rapid growth of countries such as China, India, and Brazil has accelerated a paradigm shift in economic power from developed economies. This shift is underlined by the increased share of global GDP contributed by these markets and their increasing voice in international economic forums and institutions. Moreover, the adjacent growth in multinational corporations from these economies—"-emerging market multinationals" —helps convey the dynamism and global competitiveness of those emerging economies (Cuervo-Cazurra and Genc 2008). Indeed, several of these EM MNCs are now not only well-known brand names in developed economies in their own right—think of the popularity of Mexican beer Corona or Brazilian Havaianas fashion apparel in the Western world—but they have also been active in corporate M&A strategies purchasing well-known Western firms, such as the Brazilian-Belgian brewer InBev acquiring Anheuser-Busch for $52 billion in 2008 or India's Mittal Steel purchasing Arcelor for $33.1 billion in 2006, forming ArcelorMittal. These acquisitions, and the leading sector groups they created, help showcase the economic power of EM firms.

The evolving economic landscape of emerging markets offers significant opportunities for investors and businesses. According to Morningstar (2014), an American financial services firm, "in 1988 there were just 10 emerging markets – representing 1% of the total value of shares available to private investors. By 2014 there [were] 23, representing 11% of the investable market". In the decade from 2003, emerging markets went from making up 24% of worldwide GDP to 43%. By 2022, EMs represented around 27% of total global market cap (Goldman Sachs 2023).

A Brief History of Emerging Market Trade and Investment

The concept of emerging markets, though modern in terminology, has its roots in ancient times when civilizations engaged in trade and investment both between each other and in less developed regions. History provides many examples, or to paraphrase Thucydides: history is philosophy learned from examples. While there is a common belief that many countries now classified as emerging markets lacked global significance until the late twentieth century, historical evidence shows that China, Egypt, India, Mexico, Peru, and others were influential regional powers long before and even after the age of European exploration from the fifteenth century (University of Oxford 2018). In the seventeenth and early eighteenth centuries, for instance, it has been estimated that Mughal India was responsible for 25% of the world's industrial output (Times of India 2008).

By around 3000 BCE during the Sumerian period, city-states like Ur and Uruk traded with far-off regions such as the Indus Valley and parts of Anatolia. For these countries, trade included export of textiles and surplus crops in exchange for metals and semi-precious stones et al. Such forms of trade were often characterized by the establishment of trading outposts and commercial arrangements with local rulers. From around 900 BC, the famous ancient seafaring nation the Phoenicians began navigating systematically through the Mediterranean and constructed an extensive trade network (LSE 2019). The Achaemenid Empire of the Persians (550 to 330 BCE) also sought to connect territories to boost trade. The objective of the Royal Road, an ancient highway reorganized and rebuilt for trade by Darius the Great, was to link less developed areas such as parts of Central Asia into central trade networks (Briant 2002). The Persian rulers made infrastructure investments in the newly conquered territories like Mesopotamia and Egypt aiming to merge them into their vast empire. These were aimed at building new roads, irrigation networks, and administrative centres to encourage agricultural produce and trade productivity to boost future taxation revenues (ibid.).

At around the same time, the early fifth century BCE, the Greek city-states, and especially Athens, expanded their international investments in the Black Sea region to secure vital resources such as grain, fish, and timber. Perhaps even more well known, the Chinese Silk Road, was established during the Han Dynasty (206 BCE–220 CE) to promote the exchange of goods, culture, and ideas (Whitfield 2000) and helped embody early trade and investment in emerging markets. The Roman Empire also invested heavily in infrastructure, mining, and agricultural ventures in its provinces, particularly in North Africa and the Iberian Peninsula, to extract resources for the core economy and amplify empire-wide trade (Scheidel 2009). Roman imperial investments in its provinces during both the Republic and the Empire periods can also be conceptualized as an early form of investment in emerging markets. The Roman elite and public institutions helped finance and build aqueducts, amphitheatres, and roads in frontier provinces such as Gaul, Britain, the Balkans, and elsewhere. This investment sought to ensure the incorporation of such territories into Rome's proto common market in addition to assimilation and control factors (Mattingly 2011). Such investments were driven by the expectation of economic returns from the enhanced productivity and trade facilitated by improved infrastructure and commercial projects. While these examples were in part state-driven and intertwined with imperial expansion, they set a historical precedent for viewing regions with untapped economic potential as destinations for resource allocation—an early form of emerging market investment.

The common theme in these historical examples, which is mirrored in modern times, was that investment and trade development as well as joint ventures with local rulers in distant geographics benefited both the core economy and domestic corporate interests (Abulafia 2011). *Plus ça change, plus c'est la même chose*? In medieval Europe, the Haneseatic League, a commercial and defensive network of merchant and market communities, centred on modern Germany, facilitated trade and investment in the regional emerging markets on the eastern fringes of Europe, such as the Baltic Sea and Novgorod in present-day Russia (Dollinger 1970).

The Age of Exploration, spanning between the fifteenth and seventeenth centuries, marked a significant shift in investment in emerging markets as European powers sought new trade routes and colonial territories. The Spanish and Portuguese empires were the initial "market disruptors," to use current terminology. In Spanish America, significant investments were directed towards mining operations, particularly the Potosí silver mines located in what is now Bolivia. This was accompanied by the establishment of solid infrastructure, including roads, mule trails, and labour systems to ensure a steady supply of precious metals to Europe (Bakewell 1971). The Portuguese also made substantial investments in sugarcane plantations in Brazil during the sixteenth and seventeenth centuries, which also demanded on-going infrastructure development and labour resources.

In a link-up to modern corporate activity, the 1600s saw the emergence of joint-stock companies, like the British East India Company (founded in 1600) and the Dutch East India Company (1602), which played pivotal roles in investing in emerging markets and laid the groundwork for corporate and non-state led investment activity. These companies were granted monopolies from their respective governments to trade in certain areas allowing them to set up colonies, build infrastructure, and run trade routes (Robins 2012). The British East India Company, for instance, invested heavily into India, taking over huge tracts of land and (re)-connecting the Indian economy to the global market (Dalrymple 2002). By the 1880s, the British East India Company had spent £270 million on irrigation, industry, and infrastructure in India, according to estimates from historian Niall Ferguson (History Extra 2020).

Similarly, the Dutch East India Company became a leading force in Southeast Asia in Indonesia where it ran the profitable spice trade (Boxer 1965). It has even been estimated that the company was one of the most valuable of all time, with a valuation in today's money of approximately $7.9 trillion (Fig. 1).

We summarize historical cases of investment and returns in emerging markets in figure one above. In the Americas, the eighteenth century saw major investments in new markets as European colonies expanded. The British and French allocated resources into North American colonies setting up farms and businesses that paved the way for future economic growth (Middleton 2002). The influx of European capital and technology transformed these regions, integrating them into the global economy, initially as sources of raw materials and markets for home economy finished goods.

British investment into the North American colonies was significant, encompassing both private and public expenditures. These investments were directed primarily toward land acquisition, infrastructure, and economic activities such as agriculture, trade, and resource extraction. Military outlays to protect colonies and fund wars like the French and Indian War (1754–1763) can also be classed as financial commitments to the region. When the colonial era ended, centuries of investment in both physical infrastructure and (potentially even more important) institutional development helped set the stage for future economic growth in many new markets (Acemoglu et al. 2001).

Into Modern Times

The concept of formalizing emerging markets arguably has its beginnings in the years after World War II and the 1944 Bretton Woods system, when decolonization transformed numerous developing countries into potential investment destinations from new players. State- led EM investment had given way to corporate investment. In the 1950s and 1960s, countries in Asia, Africa, and Latin America that had recently become independent embarked on ambitious development programs

Historical Case	*Investment & Terms*	*Investment Returns*	*Principal Investors*
The Spanish Crown and Christopher Columbus	*In 1492, the Spanish Crown funded Christopher Columbus's expedition to the "Indies". Multiple scholars have projected a wide variety of estimates about the cost in terms of modern currency of the first voyage to the new world. (Pickering, 2000). The voyage cost approximately 2 million Spanish maravedis or around one million US Dollars according to a paper from Follett & Vacchiano (2018). Columbus was also promised 10% of all the revenues from the new lands in perpetuity if he was successful.*	*ROI greatly exceeded the original cost of investing in Columbus' voyage. Specifically, Columbus' discovery of the New World had subsequently created further colonization and the extraction of extensive resources – mainly, silver and gold – from the Americas that eventually created immense wealth for the Spanish Empire during that period (Elliott 2006), in addition to the growth in territories and global influence. It has been estimated that between 1492-1600 the Spanish extracted around 25,000 tonnes of silver and 100 tonnes of gold (Cartright, 2022), worth around $1.6 billion dollars in today's money.*	*King Ferdinand and Queen Isabella of Spain, who provided financial backing and royal support for Columbus's voyages.*
The Portuguese Crown and Vasco da Gama	*Vasco da Gama's expedition to India in 1497 was funded by the Portuguese Crown together with significant logistical support, including ships, crews, and provisions, estimated at around 500,000 cruzados or approximately $100 million dollars (Boxer, 1969).*	*The successful voyage of Vasco da Gama opened up the sea route to India, which developed into a lucrative spice trade that brought an immense amount of wealth into Portugal, yielding returns many times over the initial investment (Subrahmanyam, 1997). It has been argued that the two ships that returned to Portugal were laden with enough spices to yield a 60x ROI on the funds invested in the expedition (WONKA, 2013).*	*King Manuel I of Portugal, who aimed to establish a direct trade route to India to bypass the overland routes controlled at the time by Islamic powers (Boxer, 1969).*
The Dutch East India Company and the Spice Islands	*The Dutch East India Company (VOC) invested heavily in establishing a monopoly over the spice trade in Asia from the early 17th century, with initial raised capital estimated at around 6.5 million guilders, estimated at over $1 billion today (Boxer, 1965).*	*The VOC recorded significant profits from its spice monopoly and slave trading activities throughout most of the 17th century. The company "remained an important trading concern and paid annual dividends that averaged about 18% of the capital for almost 200 years" (Taylor, 2024)). As a comparison, long-term historical dividend yields for the S&P 500 have typically ranged from between 3% to 5% based on data from Investopedia.*	*Mostly Dutch merchants and investors bought shares in the VOC, the first joint-stock company with publicly traded shares (Gaastra, 2003). The VOC's initial public offering (IPO) in August 1602 had over a thousand investors.*
The British East India Company	*Most of the investments by the British East India Company were in Bengal during the 18th century and have been estimated at £1 million, or roughly about £150 million today, including military and administrative expenditure (Dalrymple, 2002).*	*Between 1600 and 1874, the East India Company built one of the most powerful corporations of all time, complete with its own army, its own territory, and a near-total monopoly on the tea trade. The company's return far exceeded its investments (Marshall, 1996). It has been estimated that it provided investors with returns as high as 30% (History.com, 2020).*	*Mostly British shareholders who purchased stock in the Company, which was granted a royal charter to trade in India (Robins, 2012). The EIC's investors came from a variety of backgrounds.*

Fig. 1 Historical examples of Emerging Market investment during the European Exploration Age (15th–17th centuries). Source: Author's own elaboration based on multiple sources

aimed at industrialization and modernization. These efforts were initially supported by multinational organizations like the World Bank and the International Monetary Fund (IMF) in the form of financing and expert advice (Rostow 1960) but increasingly opened opportunities for Western firms, especially in key sectors such as energy, mining, and transport.

The 1990s were a pivotal decade for emerging markets, characterized by significant economic reforms and increased integration into a newly opened global economy. The collapse of the Soviet Union and the subsequent liberalization of Eastern Europe created new frontiers for investment and the so-called "end of history" economic moment. At the same time, Asia and Latin America were also implementing market reforms, deregulating industries and privatizing state-owned enterprises (Williamson 1990). This attracted extensive foreign direct investment (FDI) flows and portfolio capital into these regions and helped make emerging markets more attractive as investment destinations (Stiglitz 2002). The old Cold War blocs had thus given away to a single and increasingly globalized market.

Fast forward a decade or so and one of the milestone developments of this era was the formation of the BRIC (Brazil, Russia, India,and China) grouping which highlighted the growing importance of these large emerging economies. The then Goldman Sachs chief economist, Jim O'Neill coined the BRICs term in a landmark 2001 paper—"Building Better Global Economic BRICs" —and forecast that these four countries would be some of the dominant suppliers of raw materials, manufactured goods, services and subsequently overtake the G-6 economies (US, Japan, UK, Germany, France, and Italy) in US dollar terms by the middle of the twenty-first century (O'Neill 2001). The BRICs framework demonstrated the strategic (and marketing) significance of investing in emerging markets. This "rise of the rest" can be interpreted not only as a seismic change in the balance of economic power in the world, to paraphrase author Fareed Zakaria (2008), but also could hold the key to growth for developed market firms in the face of macroeconomic challenges in their home economies.

The turn of the twenty-first century saw further growth and diversification in emerging markets, with the likes of Turkey and Indonesia joining the ranks of key evolving investment destinations. The advent of the internet, mobile technology, and greater access to financial information greatly brought the so-called emerging markets into the global financial system (Prahalad 2004). This period also saw the emergence of sovereign wealth funds from EMs (for instance, from the Middle East) become major players in international investment, further exemplifying the shifting economic power of these regions. A brave new world indeed.

All the same, investment in these emerging markets has not been positively linear or devoid of challenges. The Asian financial crisis of 1997–1998, the Russian financial crisis of 1998, and the Argentine economic crisis of 2001 all demonstrated some of the weaknesses that are often part and parcel of such economies: political instability, currency volatility, and weak regulatory frameworks. These crises highlighted the need for stringent risk management practices. Nonetheless, the velocity at which many emerging markets recovered has underlined their long-term investment potential. This trend became even more evident in the wake of the 2008 global financial crisis which had significant adverse impacts in the United States and Europe. Despite economic corrections, EMs such as China and India weathered the crisis well with growth rates remaining above the 5% mark (IMF 2023). South-South investment flows also increased at this time, as emerging markets enhanced their own investments in their less developed neighbours, helping to promote economic cooperation and regional integration (UNCTAD 2023).

Today, emerging markets are some of the leading engines of global growth. Diversification of these economies plus on-going structural reforms and technological innovations create new investment universes. As Khanna and Palepu (2010) contend, understanding the institutional context and developmental path of emerging markets is key to making good investment decisions. Secular trends such as urbanization, growing middle classes, and increasing innovation ensure that emerging markets will be at the forefront of investment opportunities for the foreseeable future. This is especially the case when we consider the often-stagnant growth in developed markets over the last few years driven by the pandemic, geopolitical stress, and the cost-of-living crisis of 2021–2022. Nevertheless, investors in emerging markets have to wade through complex emerging issues relating to political risk, regulatory environment, and economic volatility. Similarly, we would argue that there should be an integrative approach which considers these different factors and how they relate to each other on investment valuation and return maximization in emerging economies. We have discussed how emerging markets have not only a rich history but present extensive opportunities in modern markets and will now examine specific ways to invest in the EM assets universe.

The Emerging Market Investment Nexus

Investments in emerging economies are today witnessing a cohesive interplay between public equity markets, mergers and acquisitions (M&A), and foreign direct investment (FDI). These are three of the major economic pathways for investors to gain exposure to emerging markets. By examining these pathways, with a particular focus on valuation concerns and recent developments, we aim to provide a comprehensive understanding of the mechanisms and trends that underpin the valuation of investments in emerging markets.

Public Equity Markets and Indexes

Public equity markets in emerging economies have witnessed substantial growth over the past few decades driven by higher economic growth, technological advancement, and improved corporate earnings and governance, leading to a more diverse and higher quality asset class. Multiple listed indexes, such as the MSCI Emerging Markets Index, which was launched in 1987, now offer broad exposure to the space. The MSCI index includes a diversified range of over 1200 large and mid-cap companies across 24 emerging economies. As of 2024, the index represents approximately 13% of the world's market capitalization and has grown from 10 countries with an equity market capitalization of $15 billion in 1988 to a current size of $7.7 trillion which underscores the significant role of these markets in the global financial ecosystem and covers "approximately 85% of the free float-adjusted market capitalization in each country" (MSCI 2023). Other major EM equity indices include the Dow Jones Emerging Markets Index, the iShares MSCI Emerging Markets ETF, and The STOXX Emerging Markets Index.

Thirty years ago, emerging market economies were a conglomerate of low-cost manufacturers and commodity exporters. As a reflection of the economic transformation since then, companies in the information technology, consumer discretionary, financial, and communication services sectors—all of which are fuelled by either high value-added exports or domestic consumption—now make up the majority of the MSCI EM index (Hymans 2024).

Price-to-earnings (P/E) ratios, price-to-book (P/B) ratios, and other common relative valuation measures generally indicate more volatility and higher risk than developed markets. This volatility, although arguably decreasing over time, is driven by relatively increased political instability, economic volatility, and greater uncertainty in regulatory landscapes. For instance, the behaviour of equity markets in countries such as Brazil (2015–2016) and Turkey (2018–2023) has been strongly affected by political events as well by macroeconomic conditions over recent periods. Investors must carefully weigh risk-reward factors (Griffin et al. 2010). Furthermore, currency fluctuations can have an acute influence on returns and thus strategies for mitigating foreign exchange risk, such as hedging or risk-adjusted discount rates, are fundamental.

For example, let's say a stock investor purchases shares in Company X, a fast-growing consumer goods firm in an emerging market, at 100 local currency units (LCU) per share in Year 1. Over the next 3 years, the company's strong earnings growth and innovative product offering drive its stock price up by 150%, reaching 250 LCU per share in Year 3.

However, during the same period, the local currency depreciates by 50% against the investor's home currency (the USD in this case). The exchange rate moves from 5 LCU/USD to 10 LCU/USD, or:

Year 1: 100 LCU per share → USD 20 per share (100 ÷ 5)
Year 3: 250 LCU per share → USD 25 per share (250 ÷ 10)

As such, despite the stock price increasing by 150% in local currency terms, the actual return in USD is only 25% instead of 150% due to currency depreciation.

Indeed, at the time of writing, we can observe that based on MSCI data, emerging markets, over the last 10 years, have seen lower annual returns, higher risk, and subsequently a lower Sharpe ratio than the broader global equity benchmark which also includes developed firms. This has translated into a heavy valuation discount—often explained by emerging markets' price volatility, political instability and sensitivity to commodity prices, and other external shocks—which underscores

Index	Annualized 10yr Net Returns (%)	Annualized 10yr Std.Dev. (%)	Annualized 10yr Sharpe Ratio	P/E Multiple
MSCI Emerging Markets	3.16	18.78	0.16	15.34
MSCI World	10.06	17.85	0.60	23.54

Fig. 2 Comparing developed and emerging market equity indexes. Source: MSCI, 29/11/24

inherent risks in these markets. Figure 2 denotes approximately a 65% discount based on the relative P/E ratios. As other authors will address throughout this book, emerging market assets provide significant opportunities but valuation and a critical understanding of risk and return factors are essential.

Recent developments in public equity markets in emerging economies have seen increased participation from both domestic and international investors. This participation is facilitated by improved regulatory frameworks and financial infrastructure in many emerging markets. Furthermore, growth in brokers and technological advancements, such as the adoption of electronic trading platforms, smart phones, and new payment solutions have reduced transaction costs and increased market efficiency, making it easier for investors to engage with these markets, including a broad universe of mutual funds, exchange-traded funds (ETFs), American Depositary Receipts (ADRs), and bond indices which provide wider exposure to EM assets while managing risk through active or passive strategies.

Mergers and Acquisitions (M&A)

M&A activity in emerging markets has gained momentum over the last few decades as firms have sought to expand their global footprint, access new markets, and acquire strategic assets. The value of M&A transactions in emerging markets has shown a robust upward trend (if not always linear), with notable deals in sectors such as technology, financial services, energy, and consumer goods. M&A activity with emerging markets involvement reached US$677.5 billion in deal value in 2023—approximately 22% of the total—with China and India accounting for around half of all transactions (LSEG 2024) (see Fig. 3 below).

Emerging market M&A dealmaking is driven by several factors, including the pursuit for market entry, economies of scale, and diversification. Multiple emerging markets have substantial populations and internal markets and thus offer significant demand for developed firms' products, services, and technology offerings. Emerging market deals can be attractive strategies, especially if the alternative is endless product launches in home markets. Price points are often higher as well. For instance, in Brazil, an iPhone which costs around a thousand dollars in the United States can retail for close to double that value (and that is despite much lower per capita income). Multinational corporations therefore often pursue acquisitions in

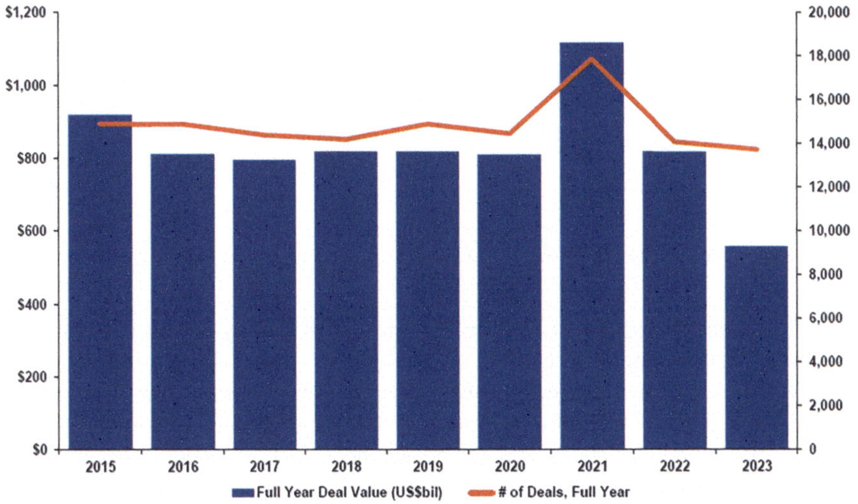

Fig. 3 Emerging markets announced M&A. Source: LSEG, 2024

emerging markets to capitalize on growing discretionary consumer spending, favourable demographic trends, and the lack of domestic product competition. Western firms have also been active in developing joint ventures and strategic alliances as a cost-effective corporate development strategy and frequently as an initial step before explicit acquisitions. The sheer size of growing middle-class populations in countries like China, India, and Brazil —approximately 500, 400, and 100 million, respectively—in particular presents significant opportunities for developed firms' companies in multiple sectors ranging from retail to health care (Kearney 2019). In parallel, emerging market firms themselves are increasingly engaging in cross-border M&A, seeking to acquire technology and expertise to enhance their competitive positioning and move into new markets. Moreover, there is broad access to corporate and real estate assets via multiple emerging market focused private equity (PE), venture capital (VC), and special purpose vehicles. According to EQT Group (2024), $93.6 billion of investment was allocated in emerging markets in 2023 and yet after a decade of falling returns, private equity remains acutely underexposed to EMs.

Valuation in M&A transactions within emerging markets exhibits additional challenges. First, the availability and reliability of financial information can be limited, making data capture, due diligence, and accurate valuation challenging. It is common to see tax-driven accounting rather than focus on robust financial controls and accounting standards. Higher corruption, lower standards of governance, and lax reporting on intercompany liabilities can also amplify uncertainty. A key question is often around the quality of earnings and the required guarantees around potential future liabilities. Multiple adjustments to operating profit are common. As such, occasionally, the focus is not so much on an appropriate valuation multiple but the level of effective profitability which should be considered. Second, market conditions and economic indicators may be more volatile, especially inflation, affecting the perceived value of target companies. Regulatory environments can also be unpredictable, with changes in laws and policies potentially impacting the valuation and consequent success of M&A deals. Regulatory restrictions can also have an impact on what foreign investors can purchase and on what terms.

Foreign Direct Investment (FDI)

According to the World Bank (2024), FDI is the sum of "equity capital, reinvestment of earnings, other long-term capital, and short-term capital. It's measured as net inflows, which is the difference between new investment inflows and disinvestment". FDI remains a crucial component of emerging market investment, driving economic development, technological advancement, and job creation in emerging countries, and providing future economic gains for developed corporates. According to the IMF, FDI inflows to emerging markets reached $916 billion, or more than 70% of global flows in 2023 (IMF 2023). These investments are particularly significant in sectors such as manufacturing, infrastructure, agrifood systems, and energy, which require substantial capital and contribute to long-term economic growth, productivity increases, and progress towards sustainability goals.

Valuation concerns in FDI are multifaceted. The political risk associated with emerging markets can significantly influence the perceived value of investments. Changes in government policy frameworks, expropriation risks, definitions of "strategic sectors", and economic instability can impact the investment environment. Investors often employ strategies, such as political risk insurance and hedging to mitigate these risks (Jensen 2008). Legal and regulatory stability, together with public-private dialogue, could be a way of alleviating perceptions of risk and attracting more FDI into emerging markets. The use of international statistical standards are supportive of an improved analysis of FDI and subsequent value creation. In turn, the ability to analyse granular data on local economies and sectors can help improve estimates of the project viability their return on investment (OECD 2021). Different types of FDI are driven by different sets of factors. Jadhav et al. argued that variables such as market size, the openness of the country, inflation, exchange, and tax rates are important determinants of FDI. Data from the Kearney FDI Confidence Index (2023) accentuates the optimistic outlook of investors towards emerging economies. Middle Eastern countries such as the UAE and Quatar, together with East Asian and Latam nations (Brazil & Mexico), were seen as the most attractive destinations for FDI into EMs.

EMs help attract FDI by often offering a basket of incentives that include tax breaks, reduced regulatory environments, land grants, and creating special economic zones. Major successful case studies exist in several countries like Brazil's Manaus Free Trade Zone, or MFTZ, created in the 1960s; India, which, through its liberalization policies in the 1990s, paved the way for increased FDI inflows, especially within the information technology and automotive sectors (Basu and Srinivasan

2002); and China, in key cities like Shenzhen, Zhuhai, and Xiamen in the late twentieth century (Chen 2020). These SEZs positively impacted industrial production, income, and integration into global supply chains.

Key trends and developments in FDI include a growing emphasis on sustainable investment, green tech and ESG concerns, a shift from manufacturing to services investment, growing focus of FDI allocation in major EMs rather than smaller countries UNCTAD, 2023), and friend and near-shoring investment led in part by geopolitical stresses, US trade policy, and the aim to develop simplified and less fragile supply chains.

The complex interaction amongst public equity capital markets, M&A activities, and FDI flows underlies the broad environment of investment in emerging markets. Each one of these investment channels comprises a unique set of challenges and opportunities for asset and project valuation; each therefore demands nuanced strategies, underpinned by deep market insight and fundamental quantitative analysis.

Anticipated Drivers in Emerging Market Valuations and Strategies for Adapting to Evolving Market Dynamics

As emerging markets continue to integrate into the global economy, the valuation of assets within these markets present both promising opportunities and significant challenges. Emerging markets are poised to witness a range of developments that will significantly impact asset valuations. These developments include:

- **Will EM's start closing the valuation "gap"?** According to a research paper from Northern Trust (2024), "Emerging market equity valuations, as represented by the price-to-book ratio, are about 40% lower than that of developed markets (3.2x for developed markets versus 1.8x for emerging markets as of 31 March 2024), well over the historical average [of around 17%]. From a macroeconomic perspective, these markets continue to contribute substantially to the global economy and exhibit robust growth potential. Analysts project emerging market companies to achieve significantly higher earnings growth compared to their developed markets peers, particularly in countries such as Taiwan, India, and Korea [see Fig. 4]. We think this growth potential, combined with attractive valuations, makes emerging markets a compelling investment opportunity". The paper goes on to contend that "factor" investing can add value by selecting in EM stocks with specific characteristics such as "the resilient performance of style factors such as quality, value, momentum and low volatility over time

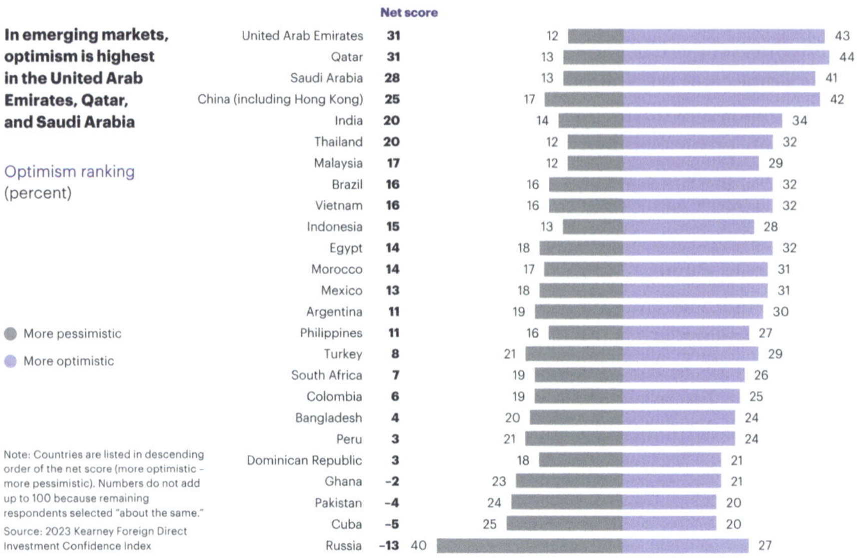

Fig. 4 Kearney emerging market FDI Confidence Index 2023. Source: Investment Monitor, 2024

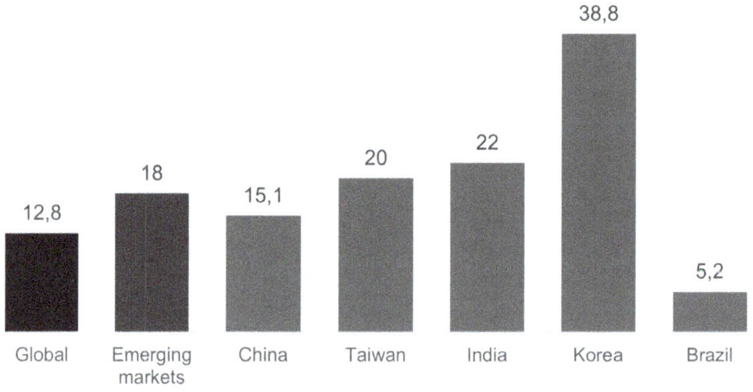

Fig. 5 5-year earnings growth forecasts (%): global vs. emerging countries. Source: Northern Trust 2024, citing data from MSCI

underscores the potential of factor investing as a powerful solution to capture alpha in emerging markets and to make the most out of the current opportunity. Style factors have historically delivered consistent sources of excess and risk-adjusted returns in emerging markets; paralleling trends seen in developed markets" (Fig. 5).

- **Technological Advancements:** The rise of digital technologies is leading to major changes in emerging markets by boosting productivity, encouraging innovation, and opening new investment avenues. The integration of artificial intelligence (AI), blockchain, and financial technologies (fintech) is transforming industries and enhancing market efficiencies. For instance, mobile banking and digital payment systems have dramatically improved financial inclusion in countries like Kenya, India, and Brazil (Demirgüç-Kunt et al. 2018). Health care and education should also increasingly be impacted by technological shifts. These technological developments also require adjusted valuation models to incorporate the intangible assets and growth potential they create as well as exponential disruption potential. Moreover, EMs shifting to high-tech economies and develop leading firms and ecosystems (for example, we can cite Singapore, Israel and UAE,etc.) could help raise valuation convergence to global averages. What is more, key components in technological development and modern computing, such as semiconductors, are often produced by firms in developing markets, including Samsung (South Korea) and TSMC (Taiwan). In summary, a paper by Robeco (2024), a global asset manager, proposes that EMs exhibit three marked advantages associated with new technology adoption, which we quote in full here:

    (a) *They likely won't have to upend existing costly infrastructure or deeply embedded legacy systems.*
    (b) *They have young populations that are digitally savvy, have a real thirst to embrace change, and are open to experiment and implement these technologies.*
    (c) *Their governments play a key role. While the private sector in mature markets tends to drive innovation, governments in some of the larger emerging markets are actively partnering and supporting entrepreneurial efforts in new technologies as a way to nurture local talent and skills.*

- **Demographic Shifts:** As previously highlighted, Emerging Markets are going through striking demographic changes such as urbanization and growth of the middle class. For example, by 2030, it is estimated that more than two-thirds of the world's middle class will be in Asia (Kharas 2017). This helps fuel consumer demand and economic growth that should have an impact on asset pricing across sectors such as retail, health care, and real estate. Additionally, it has been estimated that over 80% of the world's megacities are in emerging markets (Robeco 2024). Investors should take these demographic and urban trends into account and consider their effects on future revenue streams and market opportunities. On the regulatory side, policies that enhance sustainable development, infrastructure resilience, and environment conservation will be critical to ensure EMs s continue to amplify their economic growth prospects.
- **Increased Policy Reforms and Market Liberalization:** The nature of improvements in the business environment, reforms in the regulatory framework, and deregulation help drive asset valuation in developing markets. In this regard, your

authors would note developments in Argentina by the Milei government (2023–). For instance, in the first full year of his administration the principal domestic stock index, the Merval, nearly tripled in value. At the time of writing, it is early days of course but if deregulation and promoting more business-friendly environments are successful, other EMs will take note. Such changes can lower risk premiums and bolster investor confidence, resulting in increased asset valuations. In general, we can argue that countries with greater economic freedoms and ease of doing business possess higher average valuations. For example, research from Boateng et al. argued that in the M&A space, acquirers from countries with higher economic freedom tend to achieve better valuation outcomes in cross-border deals.

- **Increased Focus on Sustainability:** Emerging markets will be essential to reaching global net-zero targets, not only because of relative scale of their emissions but also the natural resources and technologies which are fundamental in the energy transition. For instance, Latin America and Africa boast large supplies of copper, cobalt, and rare metals while Southern Asia takes the lead in the production of electric batteries and solar panels. Commodity-producing EM countries, such as China, Brazil, Indonesia, Chile, and South Africa, are likely to benefit positively from the energy transition. Thus, companies with competitive advantages and strong market positioning in some of the key sectors of the green economy may attract valuation premiums. In fact, several studies have documented the growth expectations and consequent valuation effects of green technology investments in emerging market firms (such as Takacs 2023). Indeed, Sinha et al. also found that EM firms prioritizing sustainability initiatives are more likely to drive innovation and enhance long-term value creation, making them more resilient in dynamic markets, which helps reinforce the positive link exists between strong ESG profiles and higher firm valuations in these countries.

Macro Challenges and Solutions in Emerging Market Valuations

With 50% of the world's people and nearly half its economy, emerging markets expect to be increasingly powerful actors on the world stage. But in varying degrees, their prospects for sustained growth, social cohesion, and political stability are menaced by: eroding competitive advantages; environmental degradation, depletion and destruction; corruption and other weaknesses in national, local and corporate governance; and unresolved issues of human welfare associated with urbanization, population ageing, nutrition, health, housing, employment, social care, and the coordination of action within governments and between governments, businesses, and civil societies.

Challenges to emerging markets range from creating and sustaining economic environments that promote and enable growth, to contending with their physical environments, to managing the determinants of human welfare. Many of these challenges were addressed by today's rich countries as they developed economic, social, and political systems that improved productivity, incomes, health, education, and social care in the nineteenth and twentieth centuries. Those countries have not finished the job (Oxford University, 2018*).*

Therefore, despite broad-based promising developments, a myriad basket of challenges can complicate the valuation of assets in emerging markets. As always, with opportunities comes the associated risk. Multiple authors have developed bodies of work on the major risk factors present in EMs. Such aspects include economic volatility (see for instance Loayza et al. 2007), political risk (Jensen 2008), forex risk (Robeco 2024), a lack of financial development and data transparency (King and Levine 1993), and market inefficiencies (Bekaert and Harvey 2003). There is also the potential for the so called "middle-income" trap in emerging markets, which could limit long-term growth prospects and therefore limit the potential for these countries to reach U.S. or European levels of development (EQT 2024). Geopolitical stress and trade conflicts could also be negative factors. Nonetheless, whisper it, but perhaps this viewpoint on universal, across the board EM risk, is to a certain extent in the rearview mirror. Afterall, investment returns in EMs have recently been relatively closer to those of developed markets. For instance, "Since 2000, according to Bloomberg data, Asian small-caps have comfortably outperformed DM large-caps [and have] have experienced notably less volatility over the past six years". There also seems to have been an effective and relative reduction in EM crises over the last decade as well. We have also seen that developed markets have not been free of political crises, high inflation, and economic worries over the last few decades.

That being said, to navigate the complexities of emerging market valuations, capitalize on the evolving market dynamics, and reduce the impact of the risk elements flagged up above, investors can employ several strategies, which can incorporate:

- **Enhanced Due Diligence and Local Expertise:** Due to analytical challenges posed by governance issues, lack of robust financial controls, data transparency, and reporting standards, it is essential to conduct comprehensive due diligence and local expertise in order to assess and validate the key assumptions and accounting numbers which underpin valuation estimates. Understanding the local landscape can offer critical insights into market dynamics, regulatory frameworks, and potential risks. Partnering with local professionals can also improve the accuracy of valuations and guide investment decisions (Khanna and Palepu 2010). Heightened due diligence can also help reconcile differences in Fair Market Value and transaction prices (Horvath and Conte 2010).
- **Diversification and Risk Management:** Spreading investments across various regions, sectors, and asset classes can help mitigate the risks linked to economic fluctuations and political uncertainty. By diversifying, investors can lessen their

exposure to specific country risks and bolster the resilience of their portfolios. Additionally, the implementation of risk management strategies, such as insurance instruments, warrants, and currency hedging, can help provide protections against adverse events and stabilization of returns, both in private and public investment.

- **Adopting Advanced Valuation Techniques:** Valuation professionals can employ advanced valuation techniques, such as real options analysis (ROA), sensitivity and scenario and analysis, expected value models and Monte Carlo simulations, which provide more robust and dynamic assessments of not only asset values but also value drivers and uncertainty factors such as regarding external macroeconomic variables. Some of these techniques will be addressed later in this volume.
- **Continuous Monitoring and Adaptation:** The ever-changing landscape of emerging markets requires investors to regularly track and optimize their investment strategies. To your authors, valuation should always be conceived as a dynamic and not static process, an analytical "mind-set" if you will. It is therefore essential for investors to frequently reevaluate their valuations and modify their portfolios based on shifts in market conditions, regulatory changes, and macroeconomic trends. Such a concept can also contribute to Value-Based Management (VBM) approaches.

Closing Thoughts

Emerging markets have presented a rich and attractive frontier of opportunity since ancient times and are now at the forefront of the global economic transformation. Your authors would note that at one point, even the economies of Europe and the United States were "emerging". Today, the EM investing universe is huge with extensive economic activity in equity investment, FDI, and M&A. Anticipated developments such as technological advancements, demographic shifts, policy reforms, and increased focus on sustainability offer significant opportunities for value creation. And yet, we highlight that first, these markets combine unique risk factors and that second, valuing assets in these markets brings additional challenges which our valuation toolkits must be ready to deal with. These hurdles, however, are not insurmountable, as we shall see in other contributions in this book. However, investors must navigate challenges including economic volatility, political risk, data transparency, and market inefficiencies. Tailored strategies and approaches such as enhanced due diligence, diversification, and adoption of advanced valuation techniques can help unlock significant value. The valuation of assets in emerging markets presents a complex but rewarding challenge for investors, and as we have seen this has been the case for at least the last 5000 years.

References

Abulafia D (2011) The discovery of mankind: Atlantic encounters in the age of Columbus. Yale University Press

Acemoglu D, Johnson S, Robinson JA (2001) The colonial origins of comparative development: an empirical investigation. Am Econ Rev 91(5):1369–1401

Amsden AH (1989) Asia's next Giant: South Korea and late industrialization. Oxford University Press

Bakewell PJ (1971) Silver Mining and Society in Colonial Mexico: Zacatecas 1546–1700. Cambridge University Press

Basu P, Srinivasan N (2002) Foreign direct investment in Africa: some case studies. IMF Working Paper No. 02/61. International Monetary Fund

Bekaert G, Harvey CR (2003) Emerging markets finance. J Empir Financ 10(1–2):3–55

Bekaert G, Harvey CR (2014) Emerging equity markets in a globalizing world. Princeton University Press

Boxer CR (1965) The Dutch seaborne empire 1600–1800. Hutchinson

Briant P (2002) The Persian empire: a historical encyclopedia. ABC-CLIO

Chen J (2020) The impact of COVID-19 on emerging markets. J Emerg Mark Econ 12(3):215–233

Cuervo-Cazurra A, Genc M (2008) Transforming disadvantages into advantages: developing-country MNEs in the least developed countries. J Int Bus Stud 39(6):957–979

Dalrymple W (2002) White Mughals: love and betrayal in eighteenth-century India. HarperCollins

Demirgüç-Kunt A, Klapper L, Singer D, Ansar S, Hess J (2018) The global Findex database 2017: measuring financial inclusion and the Fintech revolution. World Bank Group

Dollinger M (1970) Institutional theory and organizational change. Northwestern University Press

EQT Group (2024) "Emerging markets: still the future of private equity." From EQT Group. https://pw.eqtgroup.com/thinq/emerging-markets/emerging-markets-still-the-future-of-private-equity. Accessed December 2024

Goldman Sachs (2023) Emerging stock markets projected to overtake the US by 2030. https://www.goldmansachs.com/intelligence/pages/emerging-stock-markets-projected-to-overtake-the-us-by-2030.html. Accessed 16 July 2024

Griffin JM, Kelly PJ, Nardari F (2010) Do market efficiency measures yield correct inferences? A comparison of developed and emerging markets. Rev Financ Stud 23(8):3225–3277

Gros D (2017) The lost decade: the making of America's debt crisis and the long recovery. Brookings Institution Press

History Extra (2020) "The East India Company: how a trading corporation became an imperial ruler." From History Extra. https://www.historyextra.com/period/tudor/the-east-india-company-how-a-trading-corporation-became-an-imperial-ruler/. Accessed December 2024

Ferguson, Neil in History.com (2020) How the East India company became the world's most powerful corporation. https://www.history.com/news. Accessed January 2025

Horvath JL, Conte V (2010) Conventional valuation methodologies in unconventional markets. In: Horvath J (ed) Valuing a business in volatile markets, Chapter, p 835. Jim Horvath

Hymans Robertson (2024) "Emerging market equity." From Hymans Robertson. https://www.hymans.co.uk/media/uploads/Emerging_market_equity.pdf. Accessed December 2024

International Monetary Fund (2023) "Balance of payments Statistics yearbook 2023." From IMF. https://www.imf.org/external/pubs/ft/bop/2023/pdf/42/23-21.pdf. Accessed December 2024

Investment Monitor (2024) "FDI in emerging economies." From Investment Monitor. https://www.investmentmonitor.ai/sponsored/fdi-emerging-economies/. Accessed December 2024

Jensen MC (2008) The agency costs of overvalued equity and the current state of corporate finance. Harvard NOM Research Paper No. 04–26

Johnson C (1982) MITI and the Japanese miracle: the growth of industrial policy, 1925–1975. Stanford University Press

Kearney AT (2019) The 2019 global retail development index: global retail expansion at a crossroads. A.T. Kearney

Khanna T, Palepu K (2010) Winning in emerging markets: a road map for strategy and execution. Harvard Business Review Press
Kharas H (2017) The unprecedented expansion of the global middle class: an update. Brookings Institution
King RG, Levine R (1993) Finance and growth: Schumpeter might be right. Q J Econ 108(3): 717–737
Krugman P (1994) Competitiveness: a dangerous obsession. W. W. Norton & Company
Loayza NV, Rancière R, Serven L, Ventura J (2007) Macroeconomic volatility and welfare in developing countries: an introduction. J Econ Growth 12(4) https://link.springer.com/article/10.1007/s10887-007-9012-5. Accessed December 2024
London Stock Exchange Group (2024) "Emerging markets investment trends." From the Source. https://thesource.lseg.com/TheSource/getfile/download/ed6f6cd5-8dc6-4335-859f-3c2712441571. Accessed January 2025
LSE Business Review (2019) As the Phoenicians sailed across the Mediterranean, they spread mice and growth." From LSE Business Review. https://blogs.lse.ac.uk/businessreview/2019/04/04/as-the-phoenicians-sailed-across-the-mediterranean-they-spread-mice-and-growth/. Accessed December 2024
Mattingly D (2011) Imperialism, power, and identity: experiencing the Roman empire. Princeton University Press
Middleton R (2002) The world of the American west. Routledge
Morningstar (2014) What is an emerging market? https://my.morningstar.com/my/news/131613/what-is-an-emerging-market.aspx. Accessed 16 July 2024
MSCI (2023) "Emerging markets insight." From MSCI. https://www.msci.com/documents/10199/c0db0a48-01f2-4ba9-ad01-226fd5678111. Accessed January 2025
Northern Trust (2024) "Seizing opportunity in emerging markets." From Northern Trust. https://www.northerntrust.com/middle-east/insights-research/2024/point-of-view/seizing-opportunity-emerging-markets. Accessed December 2024
O'Neill J (2001) Building better global economic BRICs. Global Economics Paper No. 66. Goldman Sachs
OECD (2021) FDI qualities indicators: measuring the sustainable development impacts of investment. OECD Publishing
Prahalad CK (2004) The fortune at the bottom of the pyramid: eradicating poverty through profits. Wharton School Publishing
Robeco (2024) "Three emerging markets trends for the next decade". https://www.robeco.com/en-latam/insights/2024/05/three-emerging-markets-trends-for-the-next-decade. Accessed January 2025. Authors: Pals, WII & Bruijn, J
Robins N (2012) The corporation that changed the world: how the East India company shaped the modern multinational, 2nd edn. Pluto Press
Rodrik D (2008) One economics, many recipes: globalization, institutions, and economic growth. Princeton University Press
Rostow WW (1960) The stages of economic growth: a non-communist manifesto. Cambridge University Press
Scheidel W (2009) The Oxford handbook of the state in the ancient near East and Mediterranean. Oxford University Press
Socrates (n.d.) "The beginning of wisdom is the definition of terms", quoted in Hollingsworth, Alan. (2015). "The beginning of wisdom is the definition of terms"—Socrates. Breast J 21:119–120. https://doi.org/10.1111/tbj.12370
Stiglitz JE (2002) Globalization and its discontents. W. W. Norton & Company
Takacs A (2023) "The positive effects of green technology investments on growth expectations." Technology in Society, Volume 75. https://www.journals.elsevier.com/technology-in-society. Accessed December 2024
The Economist (2017) Defining emerging markets. https://www.economist.com/special-report/2017/10/05/defining-emerging-markets. Accessed 16 July 2024

Times of India (2008) "India to reclaim Mughal-age economic aura." From Times of India. https://timesofindia.indiatimes.com/business/india-business/india-to-reclaim-mughal-age-economic-aura/articleshow/3408144.cms. Accessed December 2024

UNCTAD (2023) World investment report 2023: investing in sustainable recovery. United Nations Conference on Trade and Development

United Nations Industrial Development Organization (UNIDO) (2020) Industrial development report 2020. UNIDO, Vienna

University of Oxford (2018) Why are emerging markets important? https://www.gtc.ox.ac.uk/academic/emerging-markets-symposium/about/why-are-emerging-markets-important/. Accessed 16 July 2024

Van Agtmael A (2007) The emerging markets century: how a new breed of world-class companies is overtaking the world. Free Press

Whitfield J (2000) Fungi: the great decomposers. Nature 404(6775):551–552

Williamson J (1990) What Washington means by policy reform. In: Williamson J (ed) Latin American adjustment: how much has happened? Institute for International Economics, Washington, DC, pp 5–20

World Bank (2021) What are emerging markets? https://datahelpdesk.worldbank.org/knowledgebase/articles/114958-what-are-emerging-markets. Accessed: 16 July 2024

World Bank (2024) "Foreign Direct Investment." From World Bank Data Bank. https://databank.worldbank.org/metadataglossary/africa-development-indicators/series/BN.KLT.DINV.CD.ZS#:~:text=Foreign%20direct%20investment%20is%20net,are%20in%20current%20U.S.%20dollars. Accessed December 2024

Zakaria F (2008) 'The rise of the rest', Fareed Zakaria, 12 May. https://fareedzakaria.com/columns/2008/05/12/the-rise-of-the-rest. Accessed January 2025

Key Drivers of Valuation and Returns in Emerging Markets: An Investment Advisor's View

Michael Frigatti

> *Emerging equity markets differ in a statistically significant fashion from developed markets, featuring much lower levels of GDP per capita and equity integration. They also have significantly lower stock market development levels and, on average, feature lower valuation ratios.*
> —*Bekaert et al. (2023)*
> *The drivers of emerging market equity returns are evolving as innovation and economic decoupling join favourable demographics as future sources of excess returns.*
> —*Janus Henderson Investors (2024)*

Abstract This chapter provides a broad discussion on the Emerging Market equity indices, highlighting their historical background and development, as well as their importance in the global financial perspective. Furthermore, the chapter reviews the existing literature on some of the important exogenous and endogenous value drivers of equity valuations in EM, including the theoretical underpinnings of such concepts. The chapter then applies regression analysis to empirically understand certain valuation drivers and finds that expected revenue growth, levels of debt, and the spending on innovation are the significant contributors to EM valuations, in accordance with intrinsic valuation principles related to risk and return as they are key building blocks of economic value. It concludes with practical insights and strategies on how to improve investment strategies in EM equities using the personal experiences of the author.

Keywords Growth · Equities · ETFs · Shares · Risk · Regression · Value drivers · Fundamentals

M. Frigatti (✉)
Nimber Capital Founder, Curitiba, Brazil
e-mail: michael.frigatti@nimbercapital.com.br

S. Derindere Köseoğlu, A. Patterson (eds.), *Valuation in Emerging Markets*, Contributions to Finance and Accounting,
https://doi.org/10.1007/978-3-031-93526-8_3

Introduction

Since the start of the century, globalization has increased the connectivity of the world's financial markets. It has also led to a shift in how and why people invest in stocks in different countries, including emerging markets. EMs have undergone a profound transformation over the same period, driven by sweeping geopolitical, economic, and demographic evolutions. Emerging markets encompass a diverse range of nations and definitions but are generally characterized by strong potential for economic growth and, consequently, promising investment returns, often tied to the expansion of a burgeoning middle class, increasing per capita wealth, favourable demographic trends, and higher savings rates. The prominence of EM companies within global markets has also subsequently risen considerably, with their share of the MSCI All Country World Index growing from just 4% in 1998 to around 13% today, underscoring their increasing influence on the global investment landscape. And yet it is often said that EM stock markets are more unstable and riskier compared to those in well-established developed economies due to political instability, changing economic rules, rudimentary financial and physical infrastructure, and a greater risk of being affected by global crises. As such, the stock markets in these countries present valuation discounts. However, as these economies are increasingly a key motor of global economic growth and global diversified investment portfolios, it is essential to understand at a fundamental level what drives valuations and returns in the EM universe. This chapter then offers a broad overview by reviewing existing literature of which factors impact stock valuations and examines the interlinkages between financial, economic, and behavioural dimensions in EM stock markets. A key focus of this book is on "how" to value EM assets, but in this contribution, the author seeks to explain and drill down into the "why" of EM valuations based on a robust review of the literature before constructing a practical regression model to conduct our own investigations into value drivers. We close out with some high-level data backed insights on conceptual approaches to maximize EM equity returns.

The Beginnings of the EM Equity Nexus

Emerging markets offer portfolio diversification, higher returns, and geographic risk reduction. Globalization has helped these economies grow by attracting foreign investment. Thus, as developing countries started to join the global economy and attracted the attention of principal institutional investors, there was a need to track how well they were doing overall. This is important for our discussion, as before we can analyse returns and valuation metrics, it is crucial to start to construct the EM equity universe. That being so, the introduction of regional stock market indices was a major step forward, offering clear and consistent ways to measure performance. It was in 1988 that the MSCI launched the first comprehensive emerging markets index (known as the 'Morgan Stanley Capital International' at that time). The MSCI Emerging Markets Index started with only 10 countries included, which represented about 1% of the global stock market's total market capitalization (MSCI 2022a, 2022b). This index became a benchmark for institutional investors and was widely used to track funds focused on emerging markets. It also helped popularize ETFs (Exchange Traded Funds) so retail investors could start to access this asset class (Kruger 2021).

Such financial innovation came at a similar time as many emerging markets underwent significant reforms in the 1980s and 1990s, especially at the macroeconomic, financial, and political levels. Generally, such reforms involved the liberalization of trade, industry deregulation, privatization of state-owned enterprises, and financial market modernization. With a greater positioning towards global trade and investment, such markets began to attract foreign capital and improved liquidity which boosted investor confidence. For instance, the liberalization of India's economy in the early 1990s was followed by acute growth in its equity market as reforms generated investment from both domestic and international investors (Sharma 2000). Similarly, policies which led to greater market access in Latin America and Eastern Europe, together with privatization of state assets, made these countries attractive investment destinations and ultimately helped lead to equity market gains seen over the following decades (Eichengreen 2001a, 2001b).

These changes not only improved the risk-return profiles of these equity markets but also better integrated those economies into the global financial system, allowing for increased efficiency in capital allocation. Emerging market equities proved to be key complementary assets to developed market equities, with higher potential returns despite their associated risks (Bekaert and Harvey 2003). These reforms, including democratization and deregulation, have also contributed to the stability of the investment environment and further improved the attractiveness of these markets for global investors.

For example, in the Latin American region, where your author is based, the introduction of Brady Bonds, a collaborative effort proposed by US Treasury Secretary Brady in 1989, to help emerging economies strengthen their financial markets, helped address issues around sovereign debt volatility. These bonds, collateralized by US Treasury securities, allowed debtor countries to restructure their outstanding debt, reduce their debt service burdens, and restore investor confidence. This restructuring contributed to the stabilization of the macroeconomy, while at the same time attracting foreign investment and increasing the creditworthiness of Latin American countries to boost local financial markets and asset valuations (Eichengreen 2001a, 2001b; Reinhart and Rogoff 2004). We can extend this framework for individual countries in the region.

Brazil's "Real Plan" of 1994 was an economic milestone and helped reduce inflation, stabilize the currency, improve purchasing power, and lay the groundwork for future economic development and annual GDP growth of around 4%. One of the additional impacts was that companies and investors started to trust Brazil's economic institutions and potential (Bacha 2020). Within a period of only 6 years, to the year 2000, over U$119 billion in capital flows entered the country. In short then, since the 1980s, many emerging countries have implemented policies to strengthen their institutions, reduce trade barriers, and enhance foreign direct investment (Prasad 2014). Moreover, access to technology and communication infrastructure has boosted productivity and innovation in these markets (Kumar and Waheed 2020). We close out this section by quoting in full an interesting analysis from global asset manager Dimensional (2022):

> *The size and composition of the investible universe in emerging markets have steadily evolved since the late 1980s, when most comprehensive data sets and benchmarks for emerging markets begin. At the beginning of 1990, emerging markets represented $63 billion, and by the end of 2021, over $10 trillion, a staggering increase of well over a hundredfold. In the same period, developed markets grew by less than 10 times their value.*

Digging into EM Equity Performance

Emerging markets have been crucial components of global financial market growth since the start of the new millennium. And yet a common refrain is that emerging markets are much more volatile and that over the last decade, in particular, EM stock performance has lagged that of developed markets. Analysis from Morgan Stanley (2024) highlights that: "in the 2010s, emerging market (EM) equities suffered their worst performance as an asset class since the 1930s. They returned a mere +49%, compared to an average of +203% in the previous seven decades". Indeed, if we look at MSCI data (below in Fig. 1) we can see that in the 10 years to the end of 2024, the MSCI Emerging Markets index, which follows the performance of the main stock markets in these countries, returned 3.64% compared to 9.23% for the MSCI World. We also note that annualized volatility over the last 10 years, as measured by standard deviation, was higher (17.13% against 15.06%) and the Sharpe Ratio was lower (0.19 against 0.59) since the year 2000. Explicitly then, the return and risk profile in EMs is often self-evidently less attractive than developed market equities (Fig. 1).

INDEX PERFORMANCE – NET RETURNS (%) (DEC 31, 2024)

					ANNUALIZED			
	1 Mo	3 Mo	1 Yr	YTD	3 Yr	5 Yr	10 Yr	Since Dec 29, 2000
MSCI Emerging Markets	-0.14	-8.01	7.50	7.50	-1.92	1.70	3.64	7.54
MSCI World	-2.61	-0.16	18.67	18.67	6.34	11.17	9.95	6.67

FUNDAMENTALS (DEC 31, 2024)

	Div Yld (%)	P/E	P/E Fwd	P/BV
MSCI Emerging Markets	2.64	15.43	11.91	1.80
MSCI World	1.73	23.04	19.06	3.57

INDEX RISK AND RETURN CHARACTERISTICS (DEC 31, 2024)

		ANNUALIZED STD DEV (%)[2]			ANNUALIZED STD DEV (%)[2 3]			
Index	Turnover (%)[1]	3 Yr STD Dev (%)	5 Yr STD Dev (%)	10 Yr STD Dev (%)	3 Yr Sharpe	5 Yr Sharpe	10 Yr Sharpe	Sharpe Since Dec 29, 2000
MSCI Emerging Markets	5.64	17.75	18.50	17.13	-0.24	0.05	0.19	0.37
MSCI World	2.36	16.88	17.91	15.06	0.22	0.55	0.59	0.37

Notes:

[1] Last 12 months

[2] Based on monthly net returns data

[3] Based on NY FED Overnight SOFR from Sep 1 2021 & on ICE LIBOR 1M prior that date

Fig. 1 MSCI index performances: EM x World. Source: MSCI, Dec/24

Total Market (without financials)	Number of Firms	Net Margin	ROE	(ROE - COE)	Dividend Payout	Dividend Yield	Cash Return as % of Net Income
US Equities	4935	7.33%	16.41%	7.13%	39.68%	1.13%	93.68%
Global Equities	42750	5.77%	11.12%	0.56%	53.54%	1.98%	81.93%
EM Equities	23970	5.1%	8.74%	-3.02%	69.85%	3.02%	105.73%

Fig. 2 Equity market performance: a comparative view. *Source*: Damodaran, Jan/25

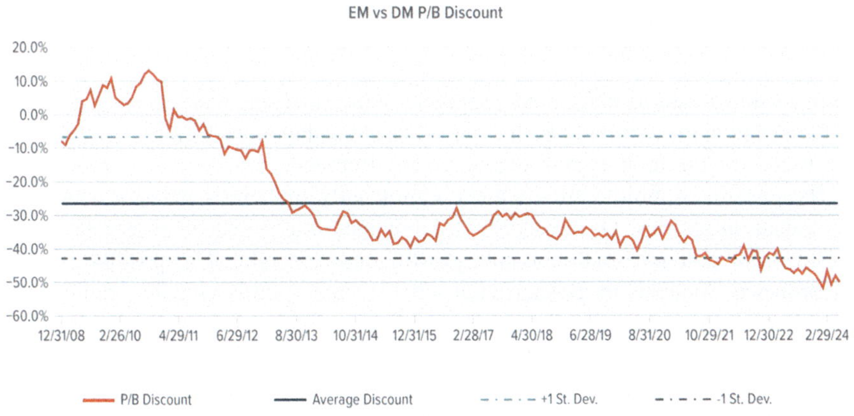

Fig. 3 P/B discount in Emerging Markets x Developed Markets. *Source*: Bloomberg, MSCI data, May 2024

And yet the analytical picture depends on where you start and end the narrative frame. The author would opine that EMs are a long-term game. Returns require patience (and a healthy dose of composure!). For example, as the above table illustrates, if we extend out timeframe, we see that since the end of the year 2000, EM equities have grown by 7.54% per year, superior returns than the MSCI World's 6.67%. Over the same period, both indices also share an identical Sharpe Ratio of 0.37. Moreover, data from Damodaran (2025) shows that the EM equity universe has on aggregate, a greater dividend payout ratio, dividend yield, and cash return as a percentage of earnings. However, profitability and return on equity are certainly inferior (Fig. 2).

Putting all this together in terms of valuation, despite at times delivering greater returns and less risk over the long-term, emerging market (EM) stocks are currently and historically priced much lower compared to developed market stocks. Figure 1 clearly shows a P/E multiple divergence of 15.43 and 23.04 for the MSCI EM and MSCI World, respectively, a discount of 33%. Other valuations multiples support this view. Since 2018, Price/Book ratios have averaged a discount of around 25% between EM and developed market assets. On the same metric over a longer period of 20 years, the average discount has been estimated at 17% (Northern Trust 2024). As of 2024, the discount exceeds 40%, more than one standard deviation below its historical average (Fig. 3).

The valuation discount between emerging market and developed market equities has been widely discussed in the academic and financial literature. This persistent valuation gap underscores the importance of understanding the nuances of EM markets and as such, let us now explore some of the key drivers that are responsible for emerging market equity returns and valuations. And of course, how to benefit from value opportunities.

Explanatory Factors Behind EM Returns

Returns and valuations in the equity segment of the emerging market are determined by the dynamic interaction of both exogenous and endogenous factors. We will start our discussion on the impact of the macro environment.

The general economic environment significantly influences investor sentiment and valuation metrics. Ocampo (2015) maintained that stable inflation rates, controlled fiscal policies, and economic growth rates are related to positive market performance. Analysis by Bekaert et al. (2015) supports this view by arguing that there is a strong correlation between growth rates with stock market returns for various emerging economies. There is no need to reiterate the rapid economic growth of EMs over the last 30 years, needless to say that the combined share of GDP of 10 largest emerging markets has more than doubled since 2000 and is now catching up with the top 10 DMs. And yet, the author is aware of Ritter's study which conversely demonstrated a negative correlation between equity returns and GDP growth for a basket of countries over more than 100 years. Klement (2014) adds to this hypothesis by claiming that there is no discernible relationship between real GDP growth and real stock market returns (for large, mid, or small cap companies) looking at 22 developed and 22 developing market nations (Fig. 4).

Nevertheless, a country's stock market development is a key part of broader financial development which subsequently is intrinsically linked to economic growth. This occurs as financial deepening promotes economic growth which in turn stimulates financial development. The macroeconomic context is important in other ways as well. Research indicates that CDS premiums, oil, and gold prices negatively influence long-term emerging market stock indices, while higher VIX and MSCI values exert positive effects. These dynamics underscore the dual role of risk sentiment and macroeconomic factors in shaping stock performance (Efe 2021a, 2021b). As emerging markets integrate more and more into the current global financial architecture, their correlated movement has increased with the developed economies. This means, however, that these markets are now increasingly exposed to exogenous shocks of global financial crises or geopolitical events. As such, Chang et al. (2022) argue that these external shocks render the EMs overly sensitive to global risk sentiment; thus, it has become crucial to consider these fluctuations in assessing EM returns.

While EMs have gained resilience over time, their dependence on foreign investment and export revenues keeps them highly vulnerable to external fluctuations. In addition, variance decomposition analysis by Kwon 2022 depicts that global uncertainty accounts for more than 30% of the fluctuation in short-term returns, whilst US

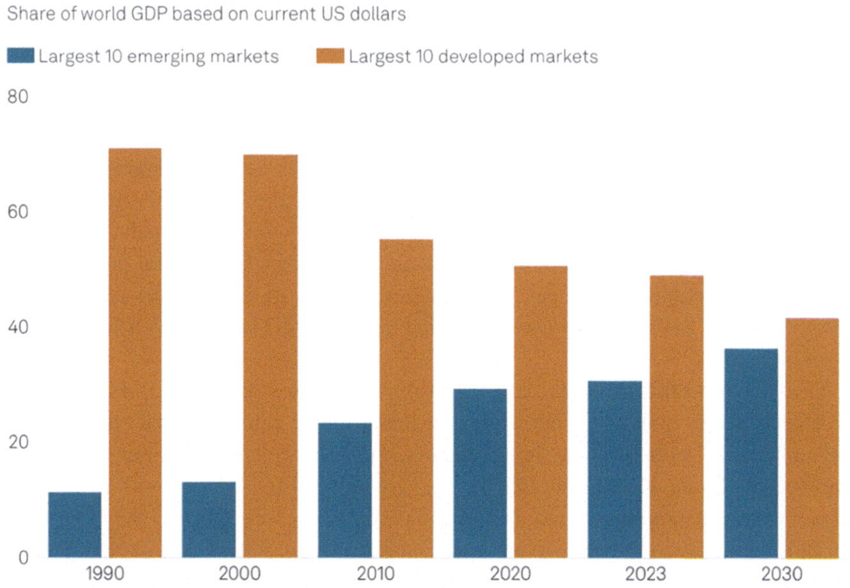

Fig. 4 Emerging markets' GDP catching up to developed markets (%). *Source*: International Labour Organization, World Bank, S&P Global, 2024

dollar shocks dominate the long-term impacts and explain over 40% of the variability. These results have key implications for investors and policymakers in emerging markets. Globalization, a positive factor that it may be, has nonetheless amplified the impact of external factors, such as capital flows and commodity prices, on EM valuations.

The literature has also widely proposed that the quality of a country's institutions is also a key factor in supporting EM equity market performance. Your author argues that the stronger institutional frameworks are, the more resilient returns are likely to be. Academic consensus broadly supports this opinion by illustrating the importance of political stability, good governance, and a sound institutional framework in facilitating investor confidence in the EM markets. Or, in other words, a stable political environment with a high level of institutional development should therefore face lower risk premia and thus better stock market performance and valuations. In politically unsteady markets, an investor will demand higher returns to compensate for increased uncertainty, which itself can depress valuations significantly. Nguyen et al. (2020a, 2020b) go further and suggest that surplus liquidity positively impacts stock market returns in emerging economies, with this effect amplified by the presence of robust institutional frameworks, which highlight the synergy between market liquidity and governance in driving sustainable market growth. As Lesmond (2008) suggests, low liquidity normally leads to high volatility of prices, negatively impacting returns and valuation for the EMs. Moreover, over the last decade, there has been an evolution of trading mechanisms and access to markets that has made trading more efficient and liquid in EMs. Barriers have fallen for institutional investors, with lower costs and increased transparency. We would flag that when there is substantial trading activity and a large supply and demand for an asset, high levels of liquidity result.

In addition, as EMs develop, they also develop key economic sectors which historically have higher valuations such as the fintech sector, e-commerce, and renewable energy. These industries have transformed the economic landscape of emerging markets by moving away from dependency on traditional commodity exports and into a more diversified economic base. In fact, as digital connectivity and technological development gain pace, valuation in EM stocks increasingly becomes linked to the pace of innovation and quality of the local ecosystem fostering those industries.

Picking up on this point, the growth of new economic sectors in EMs has led to the emergence of domestic MNCs who are increasingly gaining global market share and enhancing technological innovation. Companies such as Ambev in Brazil, Samsung in South Korea, and TSMC in Taiwan tend to add not only directly to market capitalization but also to the general perception of the markets they represent through brand recognition, operational excellence, and global competitiveness. Research highlights that MNCs in emerging markets also drive foreign direct investment inflows, strengthen supply chains, and increase productivity spillovers to domestic firms (Luo and Tung 2007). Furthermore, their global success creates a benchmarking effect, pushing smaller firms to improve governance and efficiency, thereby enhancing market-wide valuations. These companies are therefore economic anchors that stabilize returns and attract foreign investors to emerging markets and also provide value-added innovation with strong potential for future earnings growth. As we will see in the section on regression analysis, innovation, in particular, is a key driver of EM valuations (Fig. 5).

Ticker ▶	Name ▶	Sector ▶	Asset Class▶	Market Value▶	Weight (%)▶
2330	TAIWAN SEMICONDUCTOR MANUFACTURING	Information Technology	Equity	$1,792,754,197.87	10.50
700	TENCENT HOLDINGS LTD	Communication	Equity	$773,564,672.79	4.53
9988	ALIBABA GROUP HOLDING LTD	Consumer Discretionary	Equity	$383,182,154.16	2.24
005930	SAMSUNG ELECTRONICS LTD	Information Technology	Equity	$382,689,392.79	2.24
HDFCBANK	HDFC BANK LTD	Financials	Equity	$259,461,560.84	1.52
3690	MEITUAN	Consumer Discretionary	Equity	$214,539,317.32	1.26
RELIANCE	RELIANCE INDUSTRIES LTD	Energy	Equity	$191,703,987.47	1.12
939	CHINA CONSTRUCTION BANK CORP H	Financials	Equity	$177,821,387.21	1.04
ICICIBANK	ICICI BANK LTD	Financials	Equity	$173,299,439.39	1.01
INFY	INFOSYS LTD	Information Technology	Equity	$161,871,362.49	0.95

Fig. 5 Top 10 holding position in iShares MSCI Emerging Market ETF in 2024. *Source*: iShares, 2024

In summary, analysis from Bekaert et al. (2023) argues that "emerging markets have morphed into high-beta investments that are highly correlated with developed markets. The historical performance of emerging market investing is much improved by replacing value-weighted indices with alternative weighting schemes, including equal weights, valuation-based weights, and GDP weights".

Endogenous factors are also important. Shleifer and Wolfenzon (2002) found that improving corporate governance enhances the efficiency of markets and lowers the cost of capital for firms in such markets. For instance, Mehta (2022) states that the quality of regulation and financial literacy is a key component of institutional strength for enhancing market efficiency, investor participation in EMs, and subsequently stock returns. By and large, therefore, firms in EMs with good governance practices are likely to exhibit superior operational performance, which in turn enhances stock market performance and valuations. Indeed, a significant change witnessed within the emerging markets has been their convergence towards international accounting and reporting standards. Improved comparability and consistency in the levels of corporate transparency increase investors' trust towards performance appraisals and valuations (Dimensional Fund Advisors 2023). And yet, on the negative side of the equation, emerging market firms often issue significant quantities of new shares in their capital structures, either to raise funds for expansion, deleverage, or based on regulatory pressures for greater financial stability. While earnings growth has generally been impressive across these markets, excessive share issuance has also diluted many firms' earnings per share on several occasions; this negatively affects long-term equity returns (Northern Trust 2024).

It is a truism that fundamental factors of risk and return drive asset value in both listed and private companies. Indeed, the relationship between company fundamentals and equity returns has been a cornerstone of corporate financial research. Several such studies such as Novy-Marx 2013 looked at the effect of profitability, leverage, and growth potential in driving long-term equity performance, and, of course, Fama and French's demonstration in 1992 of how firm-specific factors, including size and book-to-market ratios, played a critical role in explaining stock returns. A fascinating study by Mosoeu and Kodongo (2022), utilizing the Fama & French framework, argued that there is a relationship between average returns and firm size (SMB), value (B/M), profitability (OP), and investment (INV) and found that "profitability is the single most important factor explaining average equity returns in emerging markets".

We can also develop our own analyses of key stock value drivers via regression analysis, a statistical method that estimates the relationship between a dependent variable and one or more independent variables. This method can be used to predict future relationships between variables or to assess the strength of the current relationship and as such, it can be extremely useful for valuation to better comprehend empirical relationships between value and value drivers for broad market pricing and bespoke firm specific analyses. We will apply an illustrative step-by-step approach to try and isolate and comprehend the key financial and performance metric which can help explain valuation multiples in EM stocks. The objective is to supplement the conceptual and theoretic discussion so far in this chapter, enabling readers to utilize broad techniques and apply them in their own valuation endeavours, particularly in relative valuation where the search for an assertive "comparative" baseline is of the utmost importance. A detailed theoretical and methodological discussion of regression in valuation is beyond the scope of this book, but readers can refer to Damodaran (2012), Greene (2018), or Lie and Lie (2002) for a deeper understanding.

A Practical Example: Regression Analysis: What Drives EM Stock Valuations?

We want to understand what drives valuation multiples in the EM equity universe. Instead of analysing individual stocks, this regression will be based on professor Damodaran's aggregated emerging market (EM) sector data which are updated annually, and which constitute key financial metrics and valuation multiples at an industry level, for example software, machining, or consumer goods. In such a way, it aims to present a broader and more stable view of the valuation drivers and structural relationships, avoiding potential company-specific noise and short-term market distortions that might take place in individual stock data. The 'average is our friend' as the old financial market adage goes. At a practical level, it may make sense to analyse specific comparable firms to better understand intra-sector specific trends and dynamics during a valuation exercise. Our example to follow is merely for illustration purposes and is not meant to be an exhaustive or detailed contribution.

Our data is based on 85 market sectors, removing financial services related segments. Using the open-source regression tools:

- Statisty App.
- SimpleR.

We will run our regression analysis with the following dependent and independent variables:

- **Forward P/E (Dependent Variable):** The Price to Earnings multiple is amongst the most widely accepted equity valuation multiples since it serves as a connection between the marketplace price of an entity and the earnings thereof—the very intuitive logical measurement for how much every investor is prepared to pay per unit of earned income. In that sense, earnings are major drivers of intrinsic value, with the P/E ratio therefore constituting a handy proxy for expectations regarding growth and risk by various investors. Because the forward P/E ratio is calculated using an estimate of future earnings rather than past earnings, it tends to be more accurate and predictive than current multiples since it can reduce the distortions caused by one-time earnings shocks and cyclicality. Standard errors are usually smaller than in trailing P/E as well. As Damodaran (2006) relates, forward multiples are generally preferred in valuation since markets price stocks based on expected future cash flows rather than historical performance.

n (Valid number of cases)	85

	Forward P/E	Expected Revenue Growth - Next 5 years (%)	D/(D+E)	R&D/Sales (%)
Mean	24.69	0.2	0.27	0.02
Std. Deviation	11.39	0.1	0.16	0.03
Minimum	9.26	-0.04	0.01	0
Maximum	66.1	0.52	0.72	0.21
Median absolute deviation	6.54	0.05	0.11	0.01
95% Confidence interval of Mean	22.23 - 27.15	0.18 - 0.22	0.23 - 0.3	0.01 - 0.03
Mean ± Standard Deviation	24.69 ± 11.39	0.2 ± 0.1	0.27 ± 0.16	0.02 ± 0.03

Fig. 6 Descriptive statistics

- **Expected Revenue Growth:** The average annualized growth in revenue that is expected over the next 5 years. Logically, the larger the expected growth, the greater the valuation multiples, since higher growth is rewarded by investors.
- **D/(D + E)—Debt to Total Capital Ratio:** This metric reflects the share of the firm's capital structure financed by debt. A higher ratio can increase valuation if leverage enhances returns due to the tax shield on interest payments, but high levels of debt raise financial risk, depressing valuations through higher required returns and default risk concerns.
- **R&D/Sales (%)—Research & Development Intensity:** This is the ratio that explains the degree of investment in innovation with respect to revenue. The share of R&D in sales will raise the valuation of companies in the technology and pharmaceuticals sectors, showing high growth and competitive advantage potential in the future (Fig. 6).

Testing Analytics at a Glance

- The Kolmogorov–Smirnov test ($p = 0.231$) suggests that the Forward P/E distribution does not significantly deviate from normality at conventional significance levels.

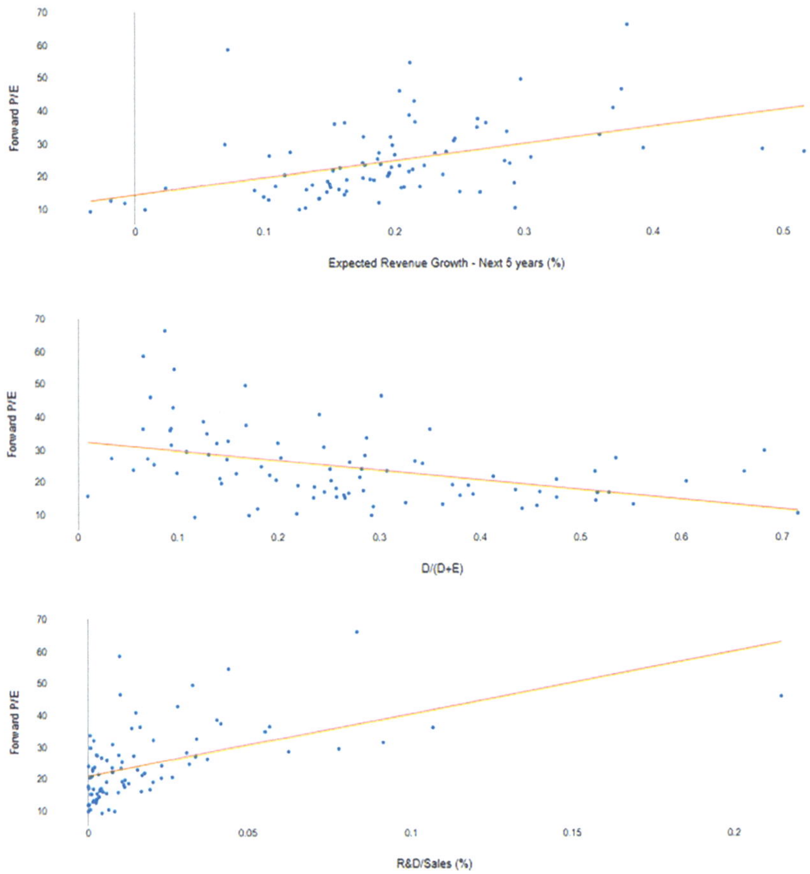

Fig. 7 Linearity of independent variables

- The ANOVA results confirm that the overall regression model is statistically significant: The F-statistic is 22.58 with a p-value of <0.001, indicating that at least one of the predictor variables has a significant relationship with Forward P/E.
- The multicollinearity sense check, based on Tolerance and VIF (Variance Inflation Factor), shows that none of the variables exhibit problematic multicollinearity, ensuring stable coefficient estimates (Figs. 7, 8, 9, 10):
  - Expected Revenue Growth—Next 5 years (%): Tolerance = 0.94, VIF = 1.07.
  - D/(D + E): Tolerance = 0.82, VIF = 1.22.
  - R&D/Sales (%): Tolerance = 0.78, VIF = 1.28.

R	R^2	Adjusted R^2	Standard error of the estimate
0.67	0.46	0.44	8.56
Model	df	F	p
Regression	3	22.58	<.001

	Unstandardized Coefficients	Standardized Coefficients				95% confidence interval for B	
Model	B	Beta	Standard error	t	p-value	lower bound	upper bound
(Constant)	19.45		2.76	7.05	<.001	13.95	24.94
Expected Revenue Growth - Next 5 years (%)	43.48	0.37	9.98	4.36	<.001	23.62	63.34
D/(D+E)	-20.64	-0.29	6.35	-3.25	.002	-33.28	-8.01
R&D/Sales (%)	119.38	0.32	34.56	3.45	.001	50.61	188.15

Fig. 8 Model summary, ANOVA, and coefficients

	Min	Q1	Median	Q3	Max	Mean	SD
Residual	-12.71	-5.94	-1.73	2.99	35.98	0	8.41
Std. Residual	-1.54	-0.7	-0.21	0.36	4.32	0	1.01

Fig. 9 Residual statistics

Regression Findings

The impact of the variables D/(D + E), R&D/Sales (%), and Expected Revenue Growth. Next 5 years (%) on the variable Forward P/E was investigated using a multiple linear regression analysis.

The following regression model is obtained:

Forward P/E = 19.45 + 43.48 Expected Revenue Growth–Next 5 years (%) – 20.64 D/(D + E) +119.38 R&D/Sales (%)

When all independent variables are 0, the value of the variable Forward P/E is 19.45.

According to the regression model, an Adjusted R^2 of 0.44 indicates that 44% of the variance in Forward P/E is explained by the model. While a higher R^2 (e.g., 0.7) is generally considered a 'good fit' lower values are common in valuation research, particularly in cross-sectional sector-based studies. This is because firm valuations are influenced by a wide range of unobservable factors. As Damodaran (2012) notes, R^2 values below 0.5 are not unusual in such models.

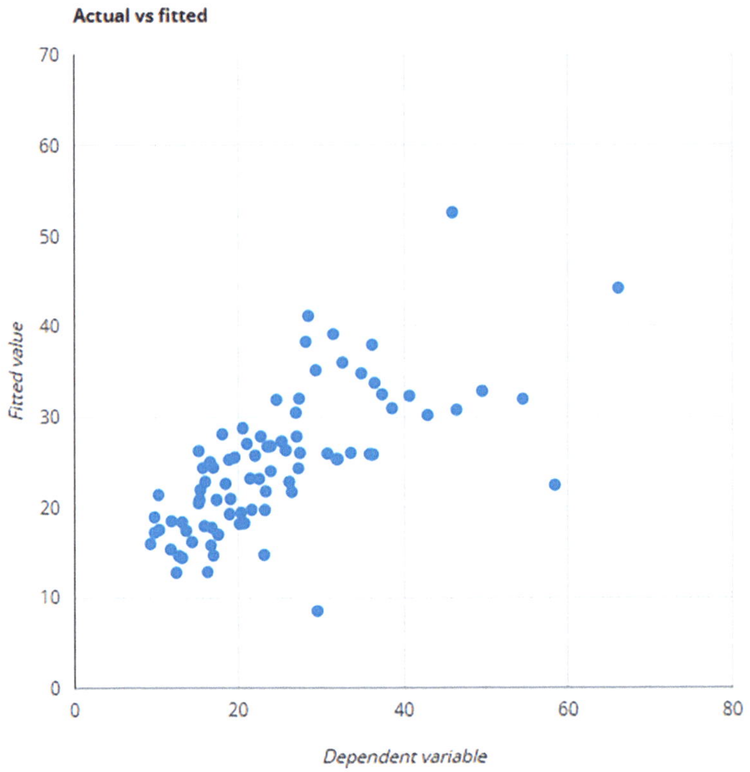

Fig. 10 Scatter plot of actual vs fitted values

Even with a moderate R^2, significant p-values for key independent variables indicate that they still have explanatory power for valuation multiples, making the model useful for relative valuation. At a practical level, analysts typically refine regression models for improved statistical fit, but best practices suggest that variables should align with fundamental valuation principles—risk, return, and asset size metrics.

To determine whether this number deviated significantly from 0, an ANOVA was employed. The effect was determined to be substantially different from 0 using the current sample ($F = 22.58$, $p = <0.001$, $R2 = 0.46$). In this model, the variable Expected Revenue Growth-Next 5 years (%) has the greatest influence on the variable Forward P/E. Based on this model and its explanation of value drivers, we could use the findings to estimate valuation multiples for specific public or private firms (with suitable additional adjustments) based on their intrinsic fundamentals.

Closing Thoughts: Maximizing EM Returns

As a professional investment advisor in EMs, the author would complement this chapter's literature review and practical regression analysis with some additional experience-based insights around how investors could potentially optimize their investment strategies in EMs, merely as a conceptual guide:

- **Diversification:** Emerging markets' complexity can be managed with a broadened and diversified portfolio. Investors can avoid idiosyncratic risks by diversifying their investments across multiple countries and sectors, positioning to capture returns wherever they occur. Research suggests that the broader the portfolio, the better the performance; this is underlined by diversified strategies' constant outperformance versus more narrow ones. Active managers with broader exposure to EM benchmarks have frequently delivered stronger results which emphasizes the positive impact of geographic, sectoral, asset type, and company specific diversification to help mitigate the risks posed by localized economic shocks, political instability, or sector-specific volatility, making it a foundational approach to reduce portfolio risk.
- **Adopt a Long-Term Investment Horizon:** A long-term 'buy-and-hold' approach can help investors across behavioural pitfalls in harnessing intrinsic growth potential throughout the EM economies. It often pays to be a patient investor as the fundamental drivers of these markets such as rising consumer demand, industrial expansion, and demographic growth play out over time. Or as Warren Buffet has said "the best moves are usually boring".
- Besides, emerging markets have proved resilient; after periods of volatility, performance bounces back strongly, and a long-term approach is important to realizing their full return potential. As a paper from Boston Partners (2020) states: "Further, increased volatility typically increases the likelihood that investors fall victim to behavioural pitfalls by selling low and/or buying high". Figure 11 shows that instead of keeping a steady EM allocation, the EM ETF investor has altogether lost out on almost 5% in annualized returns by trying to 'time' market movements by trying to sell low and buy high. Or as Warren Buffet has famously said: "The stock market is a device to transfer money from the impatient to the patient".
- **Style Investing for Alpha Generation:** Historically, style factors such as value, quality, momentum, and low-volatility factors have been known to give consistent excess and risk-adjusted returns in emerging markets. Mispricing and asymmetry of information are the base inefficiencies that combine to give positive risk-adjusted returns. Value investing can locate well-fundamentally sound companies when they are undervalued through specific strategic asset allocation management models. The on-going outperformance of style factors underlines their role as powerful tools in the navigation of volatility and heterogeneity in EM markets. By integrating the factor-based framework into their portfolios, investors can reduce risks while enhancing returns, even in the most challenging market conditions, according to Northern Trust Asset Management (2024). We can see

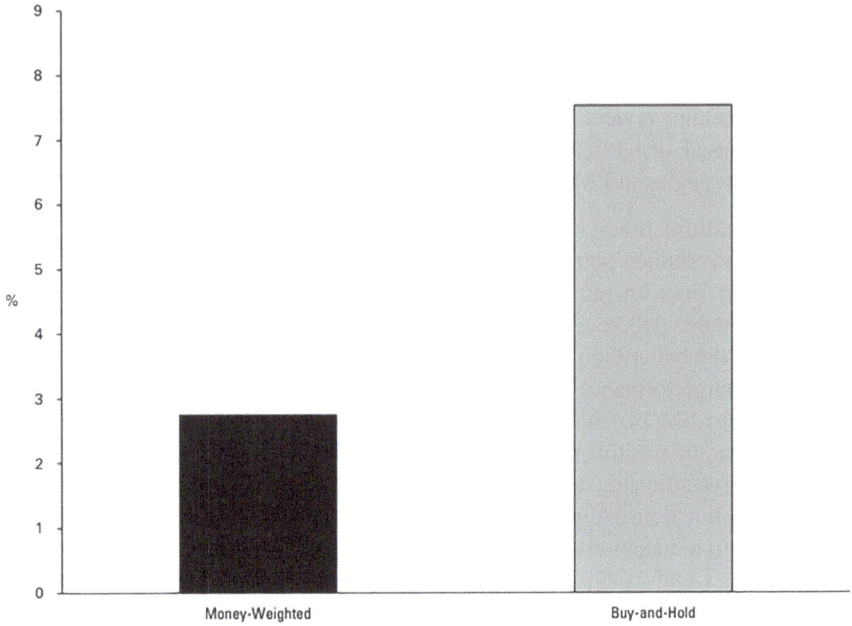

Fig. 11 Emerging Markets ETFs: Annual Money-Weighted and Buy-and-Hold Nominal Returns (2009–2020). *Source*: Boston Partners (2020)

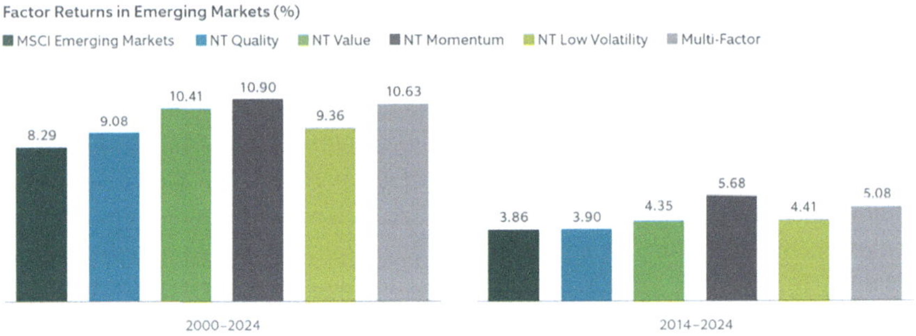

Fig. 12 The resilient performance of style factors. *Source*: Boston Partners (2020)

that such factors and investment theses generate greater returns—average of 9.7%—than the broader MSCI Index—7.51%—over a longer time frame (see for example the above return data from MSCI) (Fig. 12).

- **Capitalize on Demographic and Consumer Trends:** Broadly speaking, EMs are seeing a growing middle-class population, rising incomes, and discretionary spending that offer tremendous opportunities in consumer-driven sectors like e-commerce and the digital economy, retail, health care, and education. For

Oxford Economics (2024) "The middle-class population in emerging markets is set to double over the next decade, expanding from 354 million households in 2024 to 687 million households by 2034". This secular trend will have a positive impact on consumer demand, the backdrop for corporates, and should help drive flows to equity markets. Investment strategies that seek to gain exposure to both EM companies and global MNCs active in this space could be well positioned to take advantage of this future growth.

- **Leverage Local Expertise for Enhanced Insights:** EMs are heterogeneous, not homogeneous, with huge divergence in regulatory environments, consumer behaviours, and standards of corporate governance. Local investment managers or funds in these emerging markets can help provide local knowledge to the global investor in uncovering potentially under-researched opportunities mainly in the mid-cap and small-cap segments. In sectors such as technology in South Korea, pharmaceuticals in India, or agribusiness in Brazil, where rapid innovation and structural tailwinds are driving growth, such local expertise is even more important. What's more, new innovative investment vehicles are continuously being created: thematic and regional funds, enhanced indices, active strategies that can help global investors to tailor an approach to their preferred risk-adjusted return profile in EMs. The combination of the best local expertise and global strategies thus ensures sophistication while availing benefits accruing from both regional drivers of growth and structural inefficiencies.

Conclusion

EM equities are gaining importance in global investment portfolios, representing a double-edged sword of opportunity and risks for investors in search of growth and diversification. This chapter discussed some of the key drivers of return and valuation: exogenous factors, such as global economic performance, currencies and interest rates, commodity fluctuations, and external shocks, and endogenous factors, such as financial performance and corporate governance. We built on this theoretical discussion with our own regression analysis, which showed that fundamental factors such as revenue growth, debt dynamics, and R&D investment can explain the variation in EM equity valuations. Finally, we summarized some broad insights on how investors and corporate leaders can enhance equity returns in these markets by taking advantage of secular trends, style factor investing, diversification, and a long-term allocation thesis. As EMs continue to evolve, their stock markets will become one of the key contributors to investment returns which is why understanding their value drivers is of utmost importance.

Disclaimer Information in this chapter is provided for informational and educational purposes only and is not intended to be, and should not be understood as, an offer or recommendation of investment advice with respect to EM equities and assets.

References

Bacha E (2020) Brazil in transition: beliefs, leadership, and institutional change. Princeton University Press

Bekaert G, Harvey CR (2003) Emerging markets finance. J Empir Financ 10(1–2):3–56

Bekaert G, Harvey CR, Lundblad C (2015) Does financial liberalization spur growth? J Financ Econ 77(1):3–55

Bekaert G, Harvey CR, Mondino T (2023) Emerging equity markets in a globalized world. Emerg Mark Rev 56:101034. https://doi.org/10.1016/j.ememar.2023.101034. Accessed January 2025

Boston Partners (2020) Emerging market equity investing: a factor approach. Boston Partners Research Report

Chang K, Lin C, Ma Y (2022) The impact of political risk on emerging market investments. Emerg Mark Rev 52:101–130

Damodaran A (2006) Damodaran on valuation: security analysis for investment and corporate finance, 2nd edn. Wiley, Hoboken, NJ

Damodaran A (2012) Investment valuation: tools and techniques for determining the value of any asset, 3rd edn. John Wiley & Sons, Hoboken, NJ

Damodaran A (2025) *Country risk: determinants and implications for return expectations*. https://pages.stern.nyu.edu/~adamodar/New_Home_Page/datacurrent.html. Accessed December 2024

Dimensional Fund Advisors (2022) Are emerging markets worth the risk? Dimensional Research Report

Dimensional Fund Advisors (2023) *Ins and outs of emerging markets investing*. https://www.dimensional.com/hk-en/insights/ins-and-outs-of-emerging-markets-investing. Accessed December 2024

Efe İ (2021a) The determinants of stock market returns. Emerg Mark J 11(2) https://emaj.pitt.edu

Efe T (2021b) Institutional investors and volatility in emerging markets. Emerg Mark Financ Trade 57(3):655–678

Eichengreen B (2001a) Globalizing capital: a history of the international monetary system. Princeton University Press, Princeton, NJ

Eichengreen B (2001b) Capital account liberalization: what do the cross-country studies tell us? World Bank Econ Rev 15(3):341–365

Fama EF, French KR (1992) The cross-section of expected stock returns. J Financ 47(2):427–465

Greene WH (2018) Econometric analysis, 8th edn. Pearson, New York

Janus Henderson Investors (2024) *The case for emerging market equities in an era of transitioning secular drivers*. https://www.janushenderson.com/en-gb/investor/article/the-case-for-emerging-market-equities-in-an-era-of-transitioning-secular-drivers/. Accessed January 2025

Klement J (2014) Asset allocation and emerging markets: historical perspective and future outlook. CFA Institute Research Foundation

Kruger A (2021) Emerging markets: risks and opportunities. Financial Times Press

Kumar A, Waheed M (2020) Monetary policy and capital flows in emerging economies. Econ Model 87:312–330

Kwon D (2022) What drives emerging stock market returns? A factor-augmented VAR approach. Emerg Mark Financ Trade 58(5):1215–1232

Lesmond D (2008) Liquidity costs in emerging markets. J Financ Econ 92(1):1–32

Lie E, Lie HJ (2002) Multiples used to value corporate acquisitions. Financ Anal J 58(2):44–54

Luo Y, Tung RL (2007) International expansion of emerging market enterprises: a springboard perspective. J Int Bus Stud 38(4):481–498

Mehta P (2022) Exchange rate volatility and FDI in emerging markets. J Int Econ 135:103–127

Morgan Stanley (2024) *Emerging markets: stepping into the spotlight*. https://www.morganstanley.com/im/en-us/individual-investor/insights/articles/emerging-markets-stepping-into-the-spotlight.html

Mosoeu S, Kodongo O (2022) The Fama-French five-factor model and emerging market equity returns. Q Rev Econ Finance 85:55–76

MSCI (2022a) Emerging markets: understanding the MSCI EM index. MSCI Research Report
MSCI (2022b) The history and impact of the MSCI emerging markets index
MSCI (2024) *MSCI Index Factsheet.* https://www.msci.com/documents/10199/c0db0a48-01f2-4ba9-ad01-226fd5678111
Nguyen T, Pham H, Tran L (2020a) Corporate governance and performance in emerging markets. Emerg Mark Rev 45:101–125
Nguyen CP, Schinckus C, Su TD, Chong FHL (2020b) Liquidity and stock market development. Int J Finance Econ
Northern Trust (2024) The role of ESG in emerging markets investment decisions. Northern Trust Global Research Report
Novy-Marx R (2013) The other side of value: the gross profitability premium. J Financ Econ 108(1):1–28
Ocampo JA (2015) The retreat of neo-liberalism in Latin America? J Lat Am Stud 47(1):53–79
Oxford Economics (2024) The future of the middle class in emerging markets. https://www.oxfordeconomics.com/resource/the-future-of-the-middle-class-in-emerging-markets/. Accessed January 2025
Prasad ES (2014) The Dollar trap: how the U.S. Dollar tightened its grip on global finance. Princeton University Press, Princeton, NJ
Reinhart CM, Rogoff KS (2004) Serial default and the "paradox" of rich-to-poor capital flows. Am Econ Rev 94(2):53–58
Sharma R (2000) *Breakout nations: in pursuit of the next economic miracles.* W.W. Norton & Company, New York
Shleifer A, Wolfenzon D (2002) Investor protection and equity markets. J Financ Econ 66(1):3–27

Understanding the Unique Characteristics of Valuation in Emerging Markets

Kelvin Leong

Abstract This chapter explores the process of valuation, which involves determining the value of assets, companies, and investments. It provides an overview of the historical development of valuation, its core principles, and key methods, such as discounted cash flow and market comparisons. The chapter examines the unique challenges of valuation in emerging markets, including economic instability, currency fluctuations, and limited access to reliable financial data. It also highlights the role of modern technologies like artificial intelligence and data analysis in enhancing valuation accuracy through real-time and comprehensive insights. This chapter offers a clear and structured understanding of valuation, emphasizing its importance in supporting financial decisions and economic development in dynamic and evolving markets.

Keywords Value · Principles · Approaches · DCF · Markets · Economics

The History of Valuation

Valuation is the process of determining the worth of things, such as an asset, a company, an investment, or other entities. It is a fundamental concept in finance.

The concept of valuation could be traced back thousands of years to ancient Sumeria, where the invention of interest payments laid the groundwork for financial innovations (Rzepczynski 2017). As economies developed, the need for standardized valuation methods became essential. During the Renaissance, advancements in accounting and finance laid the foundation for modern valuation practices. A significant milestone was the introduction of double-entry bookkeeping in the fifteenth century by Luca Pacioli, which allowed businesses to systematically record their assets and liabilities (Ovunda 2015). In 1912, the formal theory of valuations

K. Leong (✉)
University of Chester, Chester, UK
e-mail: k.leong@chester.ac.uk

S. Derindere Köseoğlu, A. Patterson (eds.), *Valuation in Emerging Markets*, Contributions to Finance and Accounting,
https://doi.org/10.1007/978-3-031-93526-8_4

was established by Hungarian mathematician Josef Kürschák, who formulated the valuation axioms as we know them today (Roquette 2003).

In the twentieth century, financial theories continued to evolve, leading to more advanced valuation methods. One key development was the discounted cash flow (DCF) model, introduced by economist Irving Fisher in 1930 as per Edwards and Warman (1981). This model estimates the present value of future cash flows, making it a fundamental tool in corporate finance. Over time, additional valuation techniques have emerged to address different financial situations. Methods, such as market multiples, which compare a company's value to similar businesses, and real options analysis, which evaluates investment opportunities under uncertainty, have expanded the tools available for financial decision-making.

The Importance of Valuation in Economic Development

An increasing number of valuation methods and techniques have emerged for two main reasons. First, valuation must take the market context into account. Second, it plays a crucial role in supporting economic development. Understanding the economic implications of valuation is essential, as it directly influences financial decision-making and market stability.

In supporting economic development, valuation ensures efficient resource allocation, promotes investment confidence, and facilitates financial stability. Accurate valuation helps businesses, investors, and policymakers make informed decisions about asset pricing, capital allocation, and investment strategies (Adrian et al. 2014). When assets, companies, or investments are properly valued, financial markets function more transparently, reducing uncertainty and fostering investor trust. This, in turn, encourages domestic and foreign investment, driving economic growth.

Moreover, valuation is essential for business expansion and entrepreneurship. Startups and growing enterprises rely on valuation to attract funding, whether through venture capital, private equity, or public offerings. An accurate assessment of a company's worth helps investors assess risks and potential returns, enabling businesses to secure the capital needed for innovation and job creation. This process stimulates economic activity by enhancing productivity and fostering industry competition.

In addition, valuation supports regulatory and fiscal policies. Governments use valuation techniques to assess corporate assets, determine tax liabilities, and guide monetary policies. Proper valuation ensures fair taxation, reducing financial imbalances and improving public revenue management. It also aids in determining the fair value of public assets and infrastructure projects, facilitating effective government spending and economic planning.

Lastly, valuation contributes to financial system stability by preventing asset bubbles and reducing the risks of market crashes. Overvaluation or undervaluation of assets can lead to mispricing in financial markets, increasing systemic risk. By providing a realistic measure of asset values, valuation helps mitigate these risks, ensuring a balanced and resilient economy. As economies continue to evolve, the role of valuation will remain vital in fostering sustainable growth and long-term prosperity. A real-world example is the U.S. housing market bubble and subsequent crash in 2008, which led to a global financial crisis. In the years leading up to 2008, there was significant overvaluation in the U.S. housing market. This overvaluation was fuelled by several factors, including lax lending standards, low interest rates, and speculative buying. The ratio of house prices to rents and incomes reached historically high levels, indicating that valuations were stretched beyond fundamental values (Board of Governors of The Federal Reserve System 2021). As a result of this mispricing, a housing bubble formed. When it eventually burst, it triggered a chain reaction that severely impacted the financial system and the broader economy. Banks and financial institutions that had heavily invested in mortgage-backed securities faced substantial losses, leading to a credit crunch and a broader economic downturn (Adrian et al. 2014).

The Theoretical Foundations of Valuation: Principles, Models, and Applications

Given the importance of valuation in economic development, it has been extensively studied and analysed across various financial and economic disciplines.

The modern study of valuation is built upon core principles such as the time value of money, risk-return trade-off, market efficiency, and the cost of capital. These principles guide the methodologies used to estimate the intrinsic or relative value of assets. Different valuation models have been developed to address various financial scenarios, including intrinsic valuation approaches like discounted cash flow (DCF), relative valuation using market multiples, and contingent claim valuation through option pricing models.

Beyond theoretical constructs, valuation has practical applications across numerous domains, including corporate finance, investment analysis, risk management, and regulatory compliance. Understanding these valuation frameworks enables stakeholders to make informed decisions regarding capital allocation, investment strategies, and financial reporting. This paper explores the theoretical foundations of valuation by examining its key principles, the models used in practice, and their real-world applications.

Principles of Valuation

The theoretical foundations of valuation are built upon fundamental economic, financial, and mathematical principles that guide the assessment of an asset's worth. At its core, valuation relies on the principle of the time value of money, which asserts that a dollar today is worth more than a dollar in the future due to its potential earning capacity. This principle is central to discounted cash flow (DCF) analysis (Kruschwitz and Loeffler 2006), where expected future cash flows are discounted to their present value. Additionally, valuation incorporates the risk-return trade-off, recognizing that investors demand higher returns for taking on greater risk. This concept is often modelled using discount rates that adjust for varying levels of uncertainty and market volatility.

Another key foundation is the Efficient Market Hypothesis (EMH) (Malkiel 1989), which suggests that in a perfectly efficient market, asset prices reflect all available information. While some valuation models operate under this assumption, others acknowledge that inefficiencies and information asymmetry can lead to mispricing, creating opportunities for arbitrage. The cost of capital is also a crucial component in valuation, as it represents the required return that investors expect.

Valuation Models

The principles of valuation provide the fundamental concepts that guide how value is assessed, such as fair market value, risk and return, and the time value of money. In contrast, valuation models are the practical tools used to apply these principles, including methods like Discounted Cash Flow (DCF) and the Capital Asset Pricing Model (CAPM). While principles establish the theoretical foundation for valuation, models translate these concepts into quantitative frameworks for measuring asset worth in financial decision-making.

Valuation models can be broadly categorized into intrinsic, relative, and contingent claim valuation approaches (Thomas and Gup 2010).

Intrinsic Valuation Models

Intrinsic valuation seeks to determine an asset's value based on its underlying financial fundamentals. The discounted cash flow (DCF) model is the most widely applied, calculating an asset's worth by discounting future expected cash flows to present value. Variants such as the Free Cash Flow to Firm (FCFF) and Free Cash Flow to Equity (FCFE) models adjust cash flows based on stakeholder perspectives, while the Dividend Discount Model (DDM) values assets based on expected future dividends. Another intrinsic approach is the Residual Income Model (RIM), which measures value based on economic profit rather than traditional accounting profit.

Example: Valuing a Retail Firm Using the Discounted Cash Flow (DCF) Model
A retail firm is projected to generate the following free cash flows over the next 5 years:

Year	Free Cash Flow (FCF) ($ Million)
1	20
2	25
3	30
4	35
5	40

The firm's terminal growth rate is 3%, and the weighted average cost of capital (WACC) is 10%. We would like to know the firm's value at the end of Year 5.

Steps

1. Discount each cash flow to present value using the formula:

$$\text{Present Value (PV)} = \frac{\text{FCF}}{(1 + \text{WACC})^t}$$

where t is the year.
Example for PV of Year 1 and 2:

$$\text{PV of Year } 1 = \frac{20}{(1 + 0.1)^1} = 18.18 \text{ million}$$

$$\text{PV of Year } 2 = \frac{25}{(1 + 0.1)^2} = 20.66 \text{ million}$$

Sum of PV of FCF for Years 1 to 5:

$$18.18 + 20.66 + 22.54 + 23.90 + 24.84 = 110.12 \text{ million}$$

2. Calculate the terminal value (TV) at the end of Year 5:

$$\text{TV} = \frac{\text{FCF}_5 \times (1 + g)}{\text{WACC} - g}$$

where g = terminal growth rate of the firm.

$$\text{TV} = \frac{40 \times (1 + 0.03)}{0.1 - 0.03} = 588.57 \text{ million}$$

3. Calculate the Present Value of the terminal value at year 5:

$$\text{PV}_{\text{TV}} = \frac{\text{TV}}{(1 + \text{WACC})^5} = \frac{588.57}{(1 + 0.1)^5} = 365.45 \text{ million}$$

4. Calculate the total firm value:

$$\text{Firm Value} = \text{Sum of PV of FCF for year 1 to 5} + PV_{TV} = 110.2 + 365.45$$
$$= 475.57 \text{ million}$$

Relative Valuation Models

Relative valuation determines value by comparing an asset to similar assets in the market. This method often relies on price multiples, such as the price-to-earnings (P/E) ratio, price-to-book (P/B) ratio, and enterprise value-to-EBITDA (EV/EBITDA) ratio. These multiples provide benchmarks that allow analysts to assess whether an asset is overvalued or undervalued in relation to its peers.

Example: Valuing a Tech Company Using EV/Revenue Multiples
A tech company in India generated $10 million in revenue last year. Similar companies in the same region trade at an average EV/Revenue multiple of 6×.

Steps
1. Determine the enterprise value (EV):

$$EV = \text{Revenue} \times EV/\text{Revenue Multiple}$$

$$EV = 10 \times 6 = 60 \text{ million}$$

2. Adjust for debt and cash to calculate equity value:
   Assume $10 million in debt and $5 million in cash:

$$\text{Equity Value} = EV + \text{Cash–Debt} = 60 + 5 - 10 = 55 \text{ million}$$

Contingent Claim Valuation (Option Pricing Models)

Contingent claim valuation is used for assets with uncertain future payoffs, such as stock options or real options. Models like the Black–Scholes Model and the Binomial Model provide a framework for pricing options based on variables such as volatility, time to expiration, and risk-free rates. These models help investors and firms assess the value of financial derivatives and strategic investment opportunities under uncertainty.

Applications of Valuation

The effective use of a valuation model must take into account the context of its application. In fact, valuation is applied across various domains, including corporate finance, investment analysis, risk management, and regulatory compliance, following are some examples.

Corporate Finance

In corporate finance, valuation plays a critical role in mergers and acquisitions, capital budgeting decisions, and financial reporting. It helps firms determine fair acquisition prices, assess investment opportunities, and comply with fair value accounting standards.

Investment Analysis

In investment analysis, valuation is essential for equity research, portfolio management, and venture capital funding, to understand whether a company is overvalued, undervalued, or fairly priced. Analysts use valuation models to recommend stocks, allocate assets, and price funding rounds for startups.

Illustrative Example: Valuing a Fintech Firm in an Emerging Market
Key considerations when valuing a firm in an Emerging Market:

- Inflation adjustments should be factored in to reflect the real value of projected cash flows.
- Incorporating a country risk premium (CRP) in the discount rate ensures that risks specific to India, such as political and currency risks, are adequately accounted for.

Consider the same tech company example in "Relative Valuation Models" in Section above, which trades at an EV/Revenue multiple of 6×. Assuming risk-free rate is 3%, Equity Risk Premium (ERP) is 5 %, Country Risk Premium (CRP) is 7%, inflation is 5%.

Step 1 Calculate the adjusted discount rate:

$$r = \text{Risk} - \text{Free Rate} + \text{Equity Risk Premium} + \text{Country Risk Premium} + \text{Inflation}$$

$$r = 3\% + 5\% + 7\% + 5\% = 20\%$$

Step 2 To incorporate the new discount rate (20%), we need to adjust the multiple or use a Discounted Cash Flow (DCF) approach. There are two methods to do the valuation.

Method 1: Adjust the EV/Revenue Multiple

$$\text{New Multiple} = \frac{\text{Original multiple}}{1 + \text{Adjusted Discount Rate}}$$

$$\text{New Multiple} = \frac{6}{1 + 0.2} = 5$$

Recalculate the Enterprise Value (EV):

$$\text{EV} = \text{Revenue} \times \text{New Multiple} = 10 \text{ million} \times 5 = 50 \text{ million}$$

Method 2: Discounted Cash Flow (DCF) Approach

$$\text{EV} = \frac{\text{Cash flow}}{\text{Adjusted discount rate } (r)}$$

$$\text{EV} = \frac{10 \text{ million}}{0.2} = 50 \text{ million}$$

Step 3 Recalculate Equity Value

Using the new EV of $50 million, adjust for debt and cash to calculate the Equity Value:

$$\text{Adjusted Equity Value} = \text{EV} + \text{Cash} - \text{Debt} = (50 + 5 - 10) \text{ million} = 45 \text{ million}.$$

The adjusted EV incorporating inflation (5%) and country risk premium (7%) increased the discount rate to 20%, which reduced the EV/Revenue multiple from 6× to 5×. As a result, the Enterprise Value decreased from 60 million to 50 million, and the Equity Value decreased from 55 million to 45 million. This reflects the higher risk and lower valuation due to inflation and country-specific risks.

This example highlights how relative valuation is adapted for emerging markets, emphasizing the impact of market-specific factors like currency volatility, regulatory risks, and local growth potential.

Risk Management

Valuation is also crucial in risk management, where it is used to assess credit risk, price derivatives, and evaluate real options. Financial institutions and investors rely on valuation techniques to mitigate potential losses and optimize risk-return profiles.

Regulatory Compliance and Litigation

Beyond finance and investments, valuation has applications in litigation, bankruptcy proceedings, and tax assessments, where precise asset valuation is necessary for legal and regulatory purposes. Courts and regulatory bodies often require rigorous valuation methodologies to ensure compliance and fair treatment in financial disputes.

Emerging Markets Is an Important Topic in Valuation

As previously mentioned, the effective use of a valuation model must consider the context of its application. In this regard, emerging markets have gained increasing attention in valuation due to their strong economic growth potential and appealing investment opportunities.

There are numerous figures available to highlight the significance of emerging markets in the global economy. For example, as of Q3 2024, the MSCI Emerging Markets Value Index trades at 9.4 times P/E NTM, below its 20-year average of 11.5 times, offering investors higher profitability, free cash flow yield, and dividend yield compared to the standard MSCI EM Index (Lazard Asset Management 2024).

In fact, as global investment trends shift, emerging markets have gained increasing attention from institutional and individual investors. These markets offer substantial growth potential, driven by expanding middle-class populations, technological advancements, and industrialization. However, they also present unique challenges, including political instability, volatile exchange rates, and evolving regulatory environments. Understanding the complexities of valuation in emerging markets requires a multi-faceted approach that takes into account local economic conditions, capital market structures, and the influence of global financial trends.

In brief, emerging markets refer to economies that are in the process of rapid industrialization, modernization, and economic development but have not yet reached the stability and maturity of developed markets. From an investment perspective, these markets are characterized by high growth potential, dynamic financial systems, and evolving regulatory structures. Investors are drawn to emerging markets due to the prospect of strong returns, often driven by factors such as expanding consumer demand, abundant natural resources, and favourable demographic trends.

Unlike developed markets, where economic growth rates tend to be stable but moderate, emerging markets often experience higher levels of volatility. This volatility stems from factors such as political uncertainty, currency fluctuations, and underdeveloped financial institutions. Despite these risks, emerging markets provide investors with diversification opportunities, as their economic cycles may not always be correlated with those of advanced economies. Organizations such as the International Monetary Fund (IMF), the World Bank, and Morgan Stanley Capital

International (MSCI) classify countries as emerging markets based on criteria such as GDP per capita, market liquidity, regulatory transparency, and ease of capital movement. Some well-known emerging markets include China, India, Brazil, South Africa, Indonesia, and Mexico, each presenting unique investment landscapes shaped by local economic conditions.

The Unique Characteristics of Emerging Markets in Valuation Principles, Models, and Applications

The valuation process differs significantly between emerging markets and developed (non-emerging) markets due to variations in economic stability, financial regulations, market efficiency, and risk factors. Although the core principles of valuation remain consistent, their application requires adjustments to account for the distinct characteristics of each market. Emerging markets tend to exhibit higher volatility, limited financial transparency, and increased risk factors, which necessitate modifications in valuation models and techniques. In contrast, developed markets benefit from more efficient financial systems, robust regulatory frameworks, and better access to reliable data. Understanding these differences is essential for conducting accurate and meaningful valuations in diverse financial environments.

Differences in Valuation Principles

The foundational principles of valuation, including the time value of money, risk-return trade-off, market efficiency, and cost of capital, apply to both emerging and developed markets. However, their practical application varies due to economic and financial disparities.

The time value of money operates more predictably in developed markets, where inflation rates and interest rates remain relatively stable. Investors often rely on risk-free benchmarks, such as U.S. Treasury bonds, to discount future cash flows with greater certainty. In contrast, emerging markets often experience high and unpredictable inflation, leading to greater difficulty in forecasting the real value of future earnings. This requires adjustments in discount rates to reflect inflation risks and currency depreciation.

The risk-return trade-off is also more pronounced in emerging markets. Investors demand higher returns due to political instability, currency volatility, and weaker legal protections. Traditional models, such as the Capital Asset Pricing Model (CAPM), are widely used in developed markets to estimate the required rate of return based on systematic risk. However, in emerging markets, an additional country risk premium (CRP) is often included to account for the extra risks posed by unpredictable regulatory environments and macroeconomic uncertainties.

Market efficiency, as described by the Efficient Market Hypothesis (EMH), differs substantially between emerging and developed markets. In developed economies, financial markets tend to be more efficient, incorporating all available information into asset prices. This efficiency is supported by strong regulatory oversight, transparent financial disclosures, and widespread access to financial data. In emerging markets, however, inefficiencies are common due to limited investor participation, lower financial transparency, and occasional government interventions in markets. These inefficiencies can lead to mispriced securities and increased opportunities for arbitrage, though they also introduce greater risks for investors.

The cost of capital is another area of divergence. In developed markets, companies can access a broad range of financing options, including deep and liquid equity and debt markets. This allows for more predictable estimates of the weighted average cost of capital (WACC). In contrast, firms in emerging markets often face higher borrowing costs, limited access to capital, and fluctuating interest rates. As a result, their cost of capital is higher, making investment decisions more complex and requiring valuation models to account for higher discount rates and greater financing risks.

Differences in Valuation Models

Valuation models, including intrinsic valuation, relative valuation, and contingent claim valuation, are used in both emerging and developed markets. However, their effectiveness and implementation differ due to data availability, market structure, and economic volatility.

The Discounted Cash Flow (DCF) Model is a fundamental approach to valuation in both market types, yet its application in emerging markets requires additional considerations. In developed economies, where companies operate in stable environments, cash flow projections are more reliable, and discount rates can be estimated with greater confidence. In emerging markets, economic fluctuations, political risks, and currency depreciation make future cash flows harder to predict. As a result, analysts often employ scenario analysis, stress testing, and higher discount rates to account for the added uncertainty. Additionally, inflation-adjusted cash flow projections are necessary to ensure that valuation reflects real purchasing power.

Relative valuation models, such as price-to-earnings (P/E) and enterprise value-to-EBITDA (EV/EBITDA) multiples, are widely used in both emerging and developed markets. However, developed markets benefit from a larger number of comparable companies with standardized financial reporting, making relative valuation more reliable. In emerging markets, financial disclosures are often inconsistent, and fewer publicly traded firms exist within specific industries, making direct comparisons difficult. To address this, analysts sometimes use international comparables, adjusting for macroeconomic and industry-specific factors to ensure meaningful valuations.

Practical Example: Fintech Valuation Multiples in Developed and Emerging Markets

Fintech firms demonstrate distinct valuation multiples in developed and emerging markets due to variations in market maturity, risk levels, and growth potential.

Below is a comparative example illustrating these differences:

Metric	Developed markets (DMs)	Emerging markets (EMs)
EV/Revenue Multiple	8–12×	4–7×
P/E Ratio	25–30×	15–20×
EV/EBITDA Multiple	15–20×	8–12×

For instance, a US-based fintech firm with robust cash flows and established operations might trade at an EV/Revenue multiple of 10×, reflecting its stable business model and transparent financial reporting. By contrast, an Indonesian fintech firm in its growth phase might trade at an EV/Revenue multiple of 5× due to higher political risks, regulatory challenges, and currency volatility despite a higher growth trajectory.

These valuation differences emphasize the need to adjust relative valuation models to account for country-specific factors, such as macroeconomic stability, legal frameworks, and market dynamics.

Contingent claim valuation, which includes option pricing models such as the Black–Scholes Model and the Binomial Model, is more commonly applied in developed markets due to well-established derivatives markets and greater liquidity. In emerging markets, where financial derivatives are less prevalent, these models have limited applicability. However, real options valuation is frequently used in emerging markets, where investment decisions often involve strategic flexibility. Given the uncertainty in regulatory policies and economic growth, companies in emerging markets frequently defer investment decisions or expand operations in phases, making real options an essential tool for valuation in these environments.

Differences in Valuation Applications

Valuation can be used in corporate finance, investment analysis, risk management, and regulatory compliance in both emerging and developed markets, but with key distinctions in execution and reliability.

In corporate finance and mergers & acquisitions (M&A), developed markets provide a well-regulated environment with clear financial disclosures and legal protections, facilitating accurate valuation of target companies. In contrast, M&A transactions in emerging markets involve additional risks, including uncertain legal protections, opaque financial reporting, and political interference. Due diligence is more complex and costly, and valuation models must incorporate substantial adjustments for legal, economic, and political uncertainties.

For investment analysis and equity research, developed markets offer extensive financial data, standardized accounting rules, and stable economic conditions, making valuation methodologies more predictable. In emerging markets, financial statements may be less reliable due to weaker regulatory enforcement and potential manipulation. Investors also face liquidity risks, as stock markets in these regions often have lower trading volumes. Additionally, currency risk is a major factor, as exchange rate fluctuations can significantly impact foreign investors' returns. Analysts must integrate currency-adjusted valuation models and apply risk premiums to account for these challenges.

In risk management and credit analysis, the unpredictability of macroeconomic conditions in emerging markets necessitates more comprehensive risk assessment methodologies. Stress testing, scenario planning, and the use of credit default swap (CDS) spreads as indicators of sovereign risk are common risk mitigation techniques. Developed markets, with their stable financial institutions and credit rating systems, allow for more standardized risk assessment approaches.

From a regulatory and legal perspective, valuation methodologies in developed markets follow international accounting standards such as IFRS and GAAP, ensuring consistency and transparency. In emerging markets, weak regulatory oversight and inconsistent enforcement often lead to variations in financial reporting quality. This can create challenges in valuation for tax purposes, litigation, and financial reporting, requiring adjustments to standard valuation models to reflect local regulatory realities.

Summary of Unique and Specific Factors to Consider When Applying Valuation Models in Emerging Markets

The effectiveness of valuation models depends on considering various market factors to ensure accuracy and relevance. In practice, various factors would influence cash flow projections, discount rates, market multiples, and risk assessment. Below are some key considerations in these markets:

Macroeconomic Stability and Inflation Adjustments

In emerging markets, inflation tends to be more volatile and unpredictable than in developed markets. This affects the discounting of future cash flows, requiring analysts to adjust valuation models for inflationary risks. High inflation can erode real cash flows, making it essential to apply inflation-adjusted discount rates or use real cash flow estimates rather than nominal figures.

Currency Risk and Exchange Rate Volatility

Emerging markets often experience significant fluctuations in exchange rates, affecting foreign investment valuations. Analysts must incorporate exchange rate risk into valuation models, either by using risk-adjusted discount rates or scenario analysis to capture the potential impact of currency depreciation on future earnings. In contrast, developed markets typically offer more stable currencies, reducing the need for such adjustments.

Country Risk Premium (CRP) and Political Stability

Political and regulatory risks are more pronounced in emerging markets, where government interventions, policy changes, and geopolitical instability can impact business operations. When applying valuation models such as the Discounted Cash Flow (DCF) Model or Capital Asset Pricing Model (CAPM), an additional Country Risk Premium (CRP) must be included in the discount rate to reflect these uncertainties. Developed markets, with more predictable policies and stronger legal protections, require lower or no CRP adjustments.

Market Efficiency and Data Availability

Emerging markets tend to be less efficient due to limited financial transparency, weak regulatory frameworks, and lower investor participation. These inefficiencies result in mispriced securities and unreliable financial data. Analysts must account for potential financial statement distortions and use conservative assumptions when projecting cash flows and growth rates. Developed markets, with higher transparency and standardized financial reporting, allow for more straightforward application of valuation models.

Liquidity Constraints and Trading Volumes

Stock markets in emerging economies often suffer from lower liquidity and thin trading volumes, which can lead to price distortions and increased bid-ask spreads. This affects relative valuation models, such as Price-to-Earnings (P/E) or EV/EBITDA multiples, as market-based comparisons may not accurately reflect fair value. Analysts may need to apply liquidity discounts or use international comparable with appropriate adjustments. Developed markets benefit from deep and liquid capital markets, making relative valuation more reliable.

Cost of Capital and Access to Financing

Firms in emerging markets generally face higher costs of capital due to limited access to debt and equity financing, high-interest rates, and weaker investor confidence. As a result, Weighted Average Cost of Capital (WACC) calculations require higher risk premiums, and analysts must consider financing constraints when estimating growth projections. Developed markets provide greater financial stability, leading to lower borrowing costs and more predictable capital structures.

Accounting Standards and Financial Reporting Quality

Financial statements in emerging markets may be subject to inconsistencies, weaker auditing standards, or even manipulation. This affects valuation models relying on financial data, such as Residual Income Models (RIM) and Discounted Cash Flow (DCF) Models. Analysts must carefully adjust financial statements, apply forensic accounting techniques, and consider the reliability of reported earnings when conducting valuations. Developed markets, following standardized accounting rules, such as IFRS and GAAP, provide greater confidence in financial reporting.

Use of Multiples in Relative Valuation

When using market multiples for relative valuation in emerging markets, industry-specific and regional adjustments are necessary. Multiples tend to be lower due to higher risk and lower investor confidence, making direct comparisons with developed market firms misleading. Adjustments should be made for economic conditions, taxation, regulatory environment, and capital market depth. In developed markets, where multiples are more stable and comparable across industries, relative valuation is easier to implement with minimal adjustments.

Impact of Corporate Governance and Ownership Structures

Corporate governance practices vary significantly between emerging and developed markets. Many emerging market firms have concentrated ownership structures, often with significant government or family control, leading to agency conflicts and reduced transparency. Analysts must incorporate governance risks into their valuation models by applying control premiums or minority shareholder discounts. In developed markets, better governance structures enhance investor protections, reducing the need for such adjustments.

Variations in Valuation Factors Across Different Groups of Emerging Markets

It is worth noting that emerging markets are not homogenous; they vary significantly based on economic structure, political stability, financial development, and market openness. The key factors influencing valuation—such as inflation, currency risks, market efficiency, and governance—differ across different groups of emerging markets.

Broadly, emerging markets can be categorized into commodity-driven economies, industrializing economies, frontier markets, and transitioning economies. Each group presents unique valuation challenges and considerations.

Commodity-Driven Economies (e.g., Brazil, Russia, Saudi Arabia, Nigeria)

Commodity-driven economies rely heavily on exports of natural resources such as oil, gas, and minerals. Their valuation dynamics are influenced by commodity price fluctuations, government policies, and geopolitical factors.

Macroeconomic Stability and Inflation Adjustments

Inflation rates in commodity-driven economies tend to be highly volatile, driven by fluctuations in global commodity prices. During commodity booms, these countries experience rapid economic growth and currency appreciation, while downturns result in recessions, inflation spikes, and currency devaluations. Valuation models must incorporate commodity price sensitivity analysis and adjust cash flow projections based on global demand and supply trends.

Currency Risk and Exchange Rate Volatility

Commodity price swings directly impact currency values in these economies. For example, oil-exporting nations like Russia and Saudi Arabia see their currencies strengthen when oil prices rise but weaken during downturns. Analysts must adjust valuation models for commodity-linked currency risk, using hedging strategies or alternative discount rates that account for currency fluctuations.

Cost of Capital and Access to Financing

While some commodity-driven economies, like Saudi Arabia and Russia, have strong sovereign wealth funds and access to global financing, others, like Nigeria and Venezuela, struggle with capital flight and credit risk. The cost of capital varies widely, with higher risk premiums required in politically unstable countries. WACC calculations must include sovereign risk adjustments to reflect these uncertainties.

Corporate Governance and Ownership Structures

Many commodity-driven economies have a high degree of state ownership in major industries, particularly energy and mining. This introduces political risks and government intervention concerns, requiring control premiums or discounts in valuation models. Minority shareholder protections may be weaker, necessitating governance risk adjustments.

Industrializing Economies (e.g., China, India, Mexico, Indonesia, Turkey)

Industrializing emerging markets are characterized by large populations, rapid urbanization, and expanding manufacturing sectors. Their valuation considerations differ from commodity-driven economies due to a greater focus on domestic consumption, trade, and technological advancements.

Inflation and Monetary Policy Adjustments

Inflation in industrializing economies is typically moderate but varies by country. For instance, India and Turkey have historically faced higher inflation, while China and Mexico have maintained more stable monetary policies. Valuation models must integrate country-specific inflation risk adjustments when discounting future cash flows.

Market Efficiency and Financial Transparency

Market efficiency varies widely within this group. China's markets, despite being large, remain subject to government intervention and lack full transparency, whereas Mexico and Indonesia have more open and efficient markets. When using relative valuation models, analysts must adjust for financial disclosure quality and government influence in capital markets.

Currency Risks and Capital Flows

Industrializing economies experience moderate currency risks, often tied to trade balances and foreign direct investment inflows. Countries like India and Indonesia are vulnerable to capital flight, which can cause sudden currency devaluations. Valuation models must incorporate foreign exchange risk hedging and scenario testing for capital flow volatility.

Corporate Governance and Market Access

Corporate governance standards vary. China has state-controlled enterprises with opaque financial reporting, requiring governance-related valuation discounts. India, by contrast, has a relatively strong legal framework protecting investors. Analysts must assess governance risks differently across countries within this category.

Frontier Markets (e.g., Bangladesh, Vietnam, Kenya, Pakistan, Argentina)

Frontier markets are the least developed emerging economies, characterized by high growth potential but extreme economic volatility, weak institutions, and underdeveloped financial systems.

Macroeconomic Stability and Inflation Adjustments

Frontier markets often experience high and unpredictable inflation, sometimes exceeding 20% annually, as seen in Argentina and Zimbabwe. Hyperinflation necessitates adjusted valuation models, using inflation-indexed discount rates and real cash flows instead of nominal ones.

Liquidity Constraints and Trading Volumes

These markets have low liquidity and small capital markets, making relative valuation models challenging due to the lack of comparable firms. Analysts must use international peer comparisons with size and risk adjustments when applying valuation multiples.

Currency Risks and Sovereign Creditworthiness

Currency risk is one of the most significant challenges in frontier markets. Many of these countries rely on external borrowing, making them vulnerable to currency devaluations and default risks. Discount rates must reflect sovereign credit risks, with risk-adjusted discount rate premiums to account for extreme exchange rate volatility.

Market Efficiency and Financial Transparency

Frontier markets often suffer from poor financial reporting standards and limited investor protections. Analysts must conduct extensive due diligence and apply higher information risk discounts when using intrinsic valuation models like DCF.

Corporate Governance and Political Risks

Frontier markets frequently exhibit weak governance, corruption, and unstable regulatory environments, increasing the risk of expropriation and business disruptions. These risks necessitate higher discount rates, legal risk premiums, and sensitivity analysis in valuation models.

Transitioning Economies (e.g., Eastern European Countries Like Poland, Hungary, and Romania; Gulf States Like UAE and Qatar; Latin American Economies Like Chile and Colombia)

Transitioning economies are emerging markets that have relatively stable institutions and growing financial markets, often aspiring to become developed markets.

Inflation and Interest Rate Stability

Inflation in transitioning economies is generally lower than in other emerging markets but can still be volatile. Poland and Chile have adopted strong monetary policies, while others, like Hungary, have experienced inflation fluctuations. Valuation models must assess monetary policy credibility when selecting discount rates.

Market Efficiency and Financial Depth

Transitioning economies have moderately efficient financial markets, making relative valuation models more applicable. However, financial transparency varies, requiring data quality adjustments when estimating earnings multiples.

Foreign Exchange Risks and Capital Market Integration

Many transitioning economies peg their currencies to major global currencies or have strong foreign exchange reserves, reducing currency risk. However, valuation models should still incorporate sovereign credit spreads and external debt risks, particularly for countries exposed to global capital flows.

Corporate Governance and Institutional Quality

Transitioning economies generally have stronger legal protections and better corporate governance than frontier or industrializing markets. Valuation models can be applied with fewer governance-related discounts, making them more comparable to developed markets.

Data Mining as Advanced Valuation Approaches in the Big Data Age

With the rapid expansion of data availability and computational power, a promising direction of valuation approach is evolving to incorporate data mining techniques for more insightful analysis. Unlike traditional valuation models that primarily rely on historical financial statements and market benchmarks, data mining integrates real-time information, alternative data sources, and machine-learning algorithms to enhance decision-making in valuation.

Data-mining approaches and traditional valuation models such as the Capital Asset Pricing Model (CAPM), Discounted Cash Flow (DCF), and Price-to-Earnings (P/E) ratios differ significantly in methodology, data sources, analytical techniques, and application.

In brief, traditional valuation approaches rely on established financial theories and structured formulas to determine asset values. These methods are built on fundamental economic principles, assuming that financial statements and historical market prices can provide accurate indicators of future performance.

In contrast, data-mining approaches take a more dynamic, data-driven approach by utilizing statistical algorithms, machine learning (ML), and artificial intelligence (AI) to uncover patterns and relationships within vast data sets. Unlike traditional models, which operate on predefined assumptions, data-mining techniques are more exploratory, allowing for the identification of trends and anomalies that might not be captured through conventional valuation models.

In terms of data sources and inputs, traditional valuation models primarily depend on structured financial data, including earnings reports, balance sheets, and historical price movements. These models assume that financial fundamentals and past performance serve as reliable predictors of an asset's future value. However, data mining expands the scope of valuation by incorporating both structured and unstructured data from various alternative sources. These may include social media sentiment analysis, consumer transaction data, macroeconomic indicators, satellite imagery, and even geolocation data. By leveraging a broader data set, data-mining techniques provide a more holistic and real-time assessment of asset valuation, making them particularly useful in rapidly evolving markets.

From risk assessment perspective, traditional valuation models are often based on systematic market risk and beta coefficients, as seen in CAPM. These models assume a linear relationship between risk and expected return, which may not always hold true in volatile or uncertain market conditions. On the other hand, data-mining approaches employ advanced analytical techniques, such as neural networks, regression trees, and deep learning, to detect non-linear relationships and hidden risk factors. These methods allow for a more dynamic understanding of risk, incorporating market sentiment, external shocks, and behavioural factors that traditional models may overlook. By identifying previously unseen correlations, data mining can enhance predictive accuracy and provide a more comprehensive view of an asset's risk profile.

One of the key limitations of traditional valuation models is their rigidity. They often operate under strict assumptions, such as market efficiency, rational investor behaviour, and a stable economic environment. As a result, they may struggle to adapt to rapid market fluctuations, unexpected economic crises, or behavioural biases in investor decision-making. In contrast, data-mining approaches are inherently flexible and adaptive, continuously updating as new data becomes available. Machine-learning algorithms improve over time, refining their predictive capabilities based on real-time information. This adaptability makes data mining particularly valuable in fast-moving financial markets, where timely insights can provide a competitive advantage.

Enhancing Valuation in Emerging Markets Through Data Mining

Emerging markets have distinct economic, technological, and financial characteristics that make traditional valuation methods less effective in capturing the full scope of investment opportunities and risks. On the other hand, data-mining approaches, which leverage advanced analytics, machine learning, and alternative data sources, offer a more adaptable and comprehensive valuation framework suited to the dynamic nature of these markets. By analysing large volumes of both structured and unstructured data, data mining can provide deeper insights into valuation in these fast-growing economies.

In fact, data-mining approaches are better suited for valuation in emerging markets because they can be more effectively to address the unique challenges and opportunities presented by these economies.

The following are some key reasons:

- High market volatility and unstable economic conditions

  Emerging markets are often characterized by greater economic volatility due to fluctuating currency values, political instability, and inconsistent regulatory environments. Traditional valuation models like CAPM and Discounted Cash Flow (DCF) assume relatively stable market conditions and rely on historical financial data, which may not accurately reflect the rapidly changing nature of these economies. In contrast, data-mining approaches are more dynamic, allowing real-time data analysis to adjust valuations based on current market conditions. By incorporating macroeconomic indicators, sentiment analysis from news and social media, and geopolitical risk assessments, data mining can provide more adaptive and reliable valuations in uncertain environments.
- Limited financial data availability and transparency issues

  A major challenge in emerging markets is the lack of comprehensive financial records and lower levels of corporate transparency. Many companies, especially smaller or family-owned businesses, may not have long histories of audited financial statements, making it difficult to apply traditional valuation models that rely on such data. Data mining helps overcome this limitation by using alternative data sources, such as mobile transaction records, satellite imagery, e-commerce activity, and social media engagement metrics. These data points offer valuable insights into company performance, consumer behaviour, and market trends, providing a more complete picture of valuation even when traditional financial reports are unavailable.
- High mobile and digital penetration

  Unlike developed markets, where financial services have evolved over decades through traditional banking, emerging markets have often leapfrogged traditional financial infrastructure, moving directly to mobile banking, digital payments, and fintech-driven financial services. This creates an abundance of real-time transaction data that traditional valuation methods struggle to incorporate effectively. Data-mining techniques, however, can analyse vast amounts of mobile payment data, peer-to-peer lending trends, and digital financial activity to assess the economic health of businesses and consumers in a way that conventional models cannot. By leveraging real-time transactional data, data mining can offer more timely and relevant valuation insights for investors operating in these markets.

- Diverse and fragmented markets

  Emerging markets are often highly fragmented, with significant differences in economic development, consumer behaviour, and regulatory environments across regions and industries. Traditional valuation models, which assume homogeneous market conditions, may not be able to capture these local nuances. Data-mining approaches, on the other hand, can segment markets based on demographic, behavioural, and economic factors, allowing for more granular and customized valuations. Machine-learning algorithms can detect patterns within these fragmented datasets, identifying regional investment opportunities and hidden risks that traditional models might overlook.
- Challenges in credit and risk assessment

  Access to credit is often a challenge in emerging markets, where large segments of the population remain unbanked or underbanked. Traditional credit rating systems may not exist or may be underdeveloped, making it difficult to assess the creditworthiness of individuals and businesses using standard financial models. Data mining can fill this gap by analysing alternative credit indicators, such as mobile payment history, utility bill payments, online purchasing behaviour, and social network interactions. By leveraging these non-traditional data sources, financial institutions can better assess risk, improve lending decisions, and enhance valuation models for companies operating in emerging economies.
- Regulatory evolution and adaptability

  Regulatory frameworks in emerging markets are often in flux, with frequent changes in financial policies, investment laws, and taxation rules. Traditional valuation models assume relatively stable regulatory environments, which may not be the case in these rapidly evolving economies. Data mining enables real-time tracking of regulatory changes, allowing businesses and investors to adapt valuation models accordingly. For instance, AI-driven compliance monitoring tools can assess the potential impact of new tax laws or trade policies on company earnings, providing a more forward-looking approach to valuation.

Summary

Valuation has a long and dynamic history, evolving from early financial practices in ancient civilizations to modern-day methodologies that shape economic decision-making. Over centuries, developments such as double-entry bookkeeping, financial theories like discounted cash flow (DCF), and innovations in risk assessment have refined how assets, companies, and investments are valued. Today, valuation remains essential for efficient resource allocation, investment confidence, and financial stability across global markets.

This chapter explores the history, principles, models, and applications of valuation, emphasizing its crucial role in financial decision-making and economic development. Valuation has evolved from ancient financial practices to modern methodologies, such as discounted cash flow (DCF), relative valuation, and option pricing models. It is widely applied in corporate finance, investment analysis, risk management, and regulatory compliance. The chapter also examines the unique challenges of valuing assets in emerging markets, where factors such as inflation, currency risk, market efficiency, and corporate governance significantly impact valuation approaches. Furthermore, advancements in data mining and artificial intelligence are transforming valuation techniques, allowing for more real-time and adaptive assessments.

Traditionally, developed markets have been considered stable due to their efficient financial systems, transparent regulatory environments, and reliable access to data. However, recent geopolitical and economic disruptions, such as Brexit, the policies of Donald Trump, and increasing geopolitical tensions, have introduced higher levels of uncertainty even in these mature economies. Inflation spikes, supply chain disruptions, financial crises, and policy shifts have caused volatility, narrowing the historical stability gap between developed and emerging markets.

Emerging markets, once categorized based on economic growth potential, financial infrastructure, and political risk, are also undergoing rapid transformation. The classification of emerging markets into groups—commodity-driven economies, industrializing nations, frontier markets, and transitioning economies—is increasingly fluid. The rise of digital finance, geopolitical realignments, and the shifting role of major economies like China, India, and Brazil in global markets suggest that these classifications must be continuously reassessed.

Furthermore, the rapid advancement of technology, particularly artificial intelligence (AI), machine learning, and quantum computing, is revolutionizing valuation methodologies. In the big data era, these innovations have profound implications for valuation applications, particularly in emerging markets where traditional data sources may be unreliable, incomplete, or difficult to access. Generative AI models, such as large language models and deep learning systems, have the potential to transform financial forecasting and risk assessment by processing vast amounts of unstructured data, including financial reports, news sentiment, and market trends. AI-powered valuation systems can automate financial modelling, detect anomalies in corporate financial statements, and provide more accurate projections by analysing historical patterns and external economic variables. As technology continues to evolve, the combination of AI and big data analytics will redefine how valuations are conducted across global markets. These technologies will enable faster, more accurate, and more adaptive valuation models that integrate diverse data sources, real-time economic signals, and advanced risk analysis. For emerging markets, this technological leap will bridge existing gaps in financial transparency, reduce valuation uncertainties, and attract greater investment by providing deeper insights into economic potential. However, it also presents challenges, including data privacy concerns, algorithmic biases, and regulatory adaptation to new valuation methodologies.

In summary, as the world becomes more interconnected and unpredictable, valuation methodologies must adapt to reflect a fast-changing global environment. With both developed and emerging markets facing new economic, political, and technological disruptions, the ability to incorporate dynamic, data-driven insights into valuation models will be critical for investors, businesses, and policymakers navigating an increasingly uncertain financial landscape.

References

Adrian T, Covitz D, Liang N (2014) Financial stability monitoring (601; Federal Reserve Bank of New York Staff Reports)

Board of Governors of the Federal Reserve System (2021) Financial stability report. Board of Governors of the Federal Reserve System. https://www.federalreserve.gov/publications/2021-november-financial-stability-report-purpose.htm

Edwards JR, Warman A (1981) Discounted cash flow and business valuation in a nineteenth century merger a note. Account Hist J 8(2):37–50. https://doi.org/10.2308/0148-4184.8.2.37

Kruschwitz L, Loeffler A (2006) Discounted cash flow: a theory of the valuation of firms. Wiley

Lazard Asset Management (2024) Why emerging markets value. Lazard Asset Management. https://www.lazardassetmanagement.com/docs/-m0-/133581/WhyEmergingMarketsValue.pdf

Malkiel BG (1989) Efficient market hypothesis. In: Eatwell J, Milgate M, Newman P (eds) Finance. Palgrave Macmillan UK, pp 127–134. https://doi.org/10.1007/978-1-349-20213-3_13

Ovunda AS (2015) Luca Pacioli's double-entry system of accounting: a critique. Res J Financ Account 6(18):132–139

Roquette P (2003) History of valuation theory Part I. In: Kuhlmann F-V, Kuhlmann S, Marshall M (eds) Valuation theory and its applications, vol 1. American Mathematical Society. https://doi.org/10.1090/fic/032

Rzepczynski MS (2017) The origins of value: the financial innovations that created modern capital markets (a review). Financ Anal J 2(1). https://doi.org/10.2469/br.v2.n1.5

Thomas R, Gup BE (2010) The valuation handbook: valuation techniques from today's top practitioners. Wiley

Valuation Methods and Techniques: Fundamental Principles of Valuation Theory in Emerging Markets

Sinem Derindere Köseoğlu

"Emerging markets are not for the faint of heart. Volatility is a feature, not a bug, but that's where the best opportunities lie."
—Ruchir Sharma, Head of Emerging Markets at Morgan Stanley
"Don't overthink your approach to valuation in emerging markets. The risks of investing in emerging markets are real, but…standard valuation principles still apply"
—McKinsey & Company

Abstract Enterprise valuation techniques in emerging markets require a practical approach that considers the unique challenges and characteristics of these markets. Traditional valuation methods often need to be modified to account for the specific risks and opportunities present in emerging economies. This chapter provides a comprehensive overview of valuation methods, highlighting the key differences between emerging and developed markets. The chapter presents a case study focused on Turkey, illustrating the practical application of valuation techniques in an emerging market context. The case study highlights the challenges of valuing enterprises in a dynamic and unpredictable environment, offering insights into how analysts can navigate these complexities to arrive at more accurate and reliable valuations. By addressing these critical issues, the chapter aims to equip readers with the tools and knowledge necessary to effectively value enterprises in emerging markets while acknowledging the inherent uncertainties and risks involved.

Keywords Valuation methods · Emerging markets · Equity risk premium · Risk adjustment

S. Derindere Köseoğlu (✉)
Istanbul University, Istanbul, Turkey
e-mail: sderin@istanbul.edu.tr

S. Derindere Köseoğlu, A. Patterson (eds.), *Valuation in Emerging Markets*, Contributions to Finance and Accounting,
https://doi.org/10.1007/978-3-031-93526-8_5

Overview of Valuation Methods

The **International Valuation Standards (IVS) 2022** outline core valuation approaches that professionals should use to estimate the value of assets, liabilities, or businesses. These approaches are broadly categorized into three main categories: Market-Based, Income-Based, and Cost-Based Approaches (IVS 105 Valuation Approaches and Methods). In addition to the three basic approaches to valuation in the literature, some other methods such as real options and simulations are also mentioned (Newton et al. 2004; Jägle 1999). The choice of valuation method often depends on the specific context, industry, and the analyst's expertise, with many practitioners using a combination of approaches to arrive at a comprehensive valuation (Allee et al. 2020; Green et al. 2016). Care should be taken to ensure that valuation approaches are appropriate and relevant to the context of the assets being valued. The three approaches identified and explained below are the basic approaches used in valuation. All of these are based on the principles of price equilibrium, benefit expectation, or substitution economics (IVS para 10.1) (Fig. 1).

Market-Based Approach (Relative Valuation)

This method aims to make a value estimate by comparing the target company with other companies with similar characteristics (Damodaran 2007). The IVS describes the approach as "*The market approach provides an indication of value by comparing the asset with identical or comparable (that is similar) assets for which price information is available*" (IVS para 20.1). The basic approach of market-based valuation is the belief that similar assets will trade at similar prices under efficient market conditions (Esty 2000). The foundations of this method are based on the efficient market hypothesis. Since business valuations in an efficient market reflect all available information, market valuations of similar companies reflect all available information (Fama 1970). This situation leads to the convergence of valuations of similar companies over time (Schreiner and Spremann 2007).

Comparable Transaction Method (CTM, or Precedent Transactions Analysis PTA) (IVS para 30.1) and Publicly Comparable Companies Methods (CCM) (IVS para 30.9) are main methods under the Market-Based Valuation Approach. CTM looks at venture capitalist investments, acquisition prices of similar companies, or assets. CCM compares the valuation multiples of the target company with similar companies in the same industry. The **main difference** between the **CTM** and **CCM** lies in their data sources. CTM uses **M&A transaction, Venture Capitalists Investments data**, reflecting valuations at the time of acquisitions, including control premiums and market sentiment during deal negotiations. **CCM** uses **stock market data**, which reflects real-time investor sentiment, trading dynamics, and current market conditions.

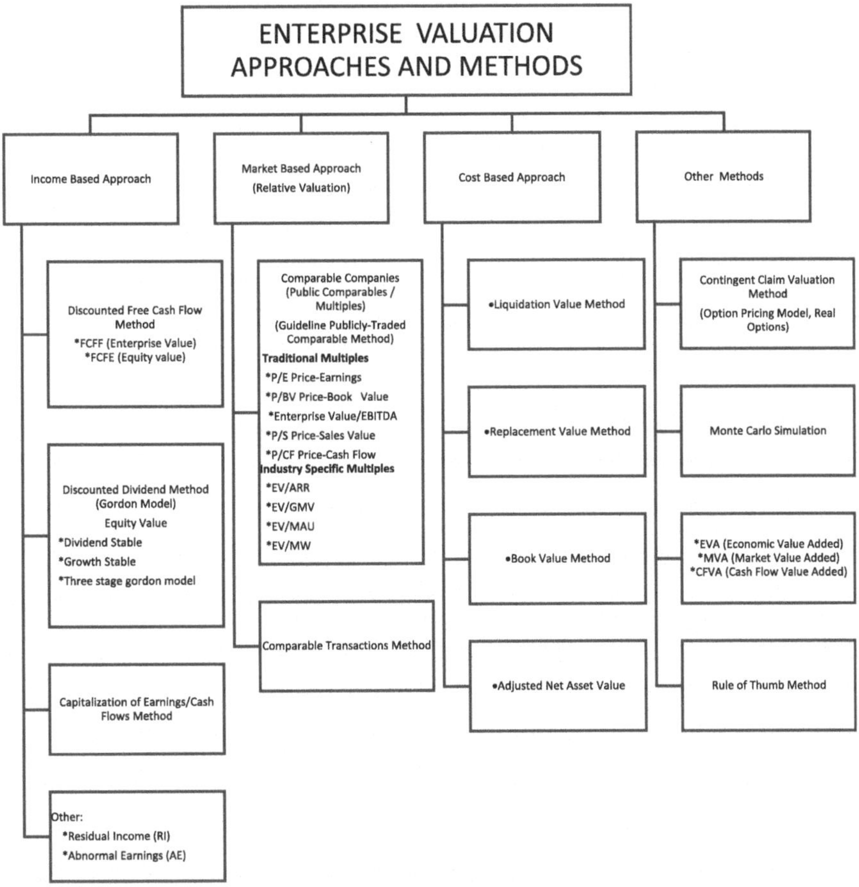

Fig. 1 Enterprise valuation methods. Source: Author's Creation

Process of Relative Valuation

Relative valuation involves estimating the value of a company by comparing it to similar companies based on financial multiples. Schreiner (2007) succinctly summarized the valuation process in four steps: choosing the appropriate measures, selecting comparison groups, estimating multiples of comparable companies, and carrying out the valuation process. The figure below outlines the six key steps involved in the relative valuation process, incorporating essential adjustments.

The first step is to identify a set of comparable companies that operate in the same industry, have similar business models, and share comparable risk profiles. The second step involves choosing the appropriate valuation multiples based on the company type, industry, and data availability. The next step is computing the valuation multiples for each comparable company using their financial data. Then the next step is making the adjustment the multiples, like size, liquidity, accounting,

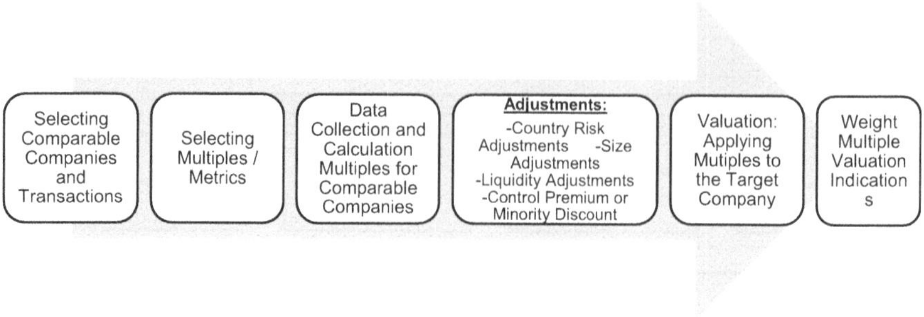

Fig. 2 Steps of relative valuation. Source: Authors Creation

and growth adjustments, to account for differences between the target company and the selected comparable (Fig. 2).

Peer Company Multiple

According to Pereiro (2002), multiples offer several advantages, including ease of application, ease of understanding, and accessibility. These advantages make multiples a popular and practical tool in valuation.

Traditional Multiple Using in Valuation

According to this method, while determining the Market Value of a company, certain elements are examined on the financial statements of the company and a price is reached by comparing these elements with similar companies. This is the logic on which the Guideline Publicly Traded Comparable Method is based and the main elements used here are defined as "multiples" in the valuation process. The main multiplies used in the Guide Comparatives Method on the Stock Exchange are as follows:

- **Price-to-Earnings** (Market Cap/Net Profit or Stock Price/Earnings per Share) ("*P/E*")
- **Enterprise Value to EBITDA** ("EV/EBITDA")
- **Enterprise Value to Sales** ("EV/Sales")
- **Price-to-Book Value** ("Market Value/Book Value")

The terms used here and their explanations are as follows:

Market Value (MV) = **Market Cap** = Capital * Latest Closing Price (Capital here refers to the Number of outstanding shares)
Enterprise Value (EV) = Market Value + Net Debt
Net Debt = Total Financial Debts – Cash and Cash Equivalents

Cash and Cash Equivalents = Cash, Bank, Other Liquid Assets
EBITDA = Earnings before Interest, Tax, Depreciation, and Amortization
Sales = Net Sales

In order to determine the indicative value in the guide comparable method on the stock exchange, information regarding comparables traded on the stock exchange that are the same or similar to the asset in question is used. The latest data of the comparable companies during the period when the valuation study is conducted are taken into account. The data belong to the last one year/last twelve month. **Retrospective 12-month data are taken**. For example, for the valuation of March 31, 2023, 1 year of data for the period March 31, 2023–March 31, 2022, is taken.

EV/Sales = Enterprise/LTM Net Sales (The Last Twelve Months net sales of all companies as of the valuation date are taken into account.)

FV/EBITDA = Enterprise/EBITDA (The last one-year EBITDA of all companies as of the valuation date are taken into account.)

MV/BV = Market Value/Book Value Ratio (Market Value/Equity, the last equity amount of all companies as of the valuation date is taken into account.)

P/E = Market Value/Total Net Profit (Market Value/Yearly Net Profit, the last yearly net profit of all companies announced as of the valuation date is taken into account.)

- Each traditional multiple has specific **advantages and disadvantages** based on different criteria.

For example, the Price-to-Earnings (P/E) ratio is easy to calculate and widely used and more understood by investors, however; it cannot be applied to companies with negative earnings (Hitchner 2017). In addition, it is susceptible to short-term earnings fluctuations and accounting choices.

Enterprise Value to EBITDA (EV/EBITDA) is useful for capital-intensive industries by considering both debt and equity and focuses on operating performance, but it does not account for changes in working capital. In addition, it can be affected by depreciation policies of companies.

The Price-to-Book (P/B) ratio is useful for valuing asset-heavy industries such as manufacturing and it is less affected by temporary earnings volatility, however; it fails to capture the value of intangible assets in modern companies. Therefore, it is not suitable for high-tech and service sectors which have significant intangible assets.

The Enterprise Value-to-Sales (P/S) ratio can be useful for valuing companies without positive earnings or cash flows, and can be applied across various industries but it fails to differentiate companies with varying cost structures and profit margins (Fernández 2007).

Therefore, multiple selection is a critical step and affects the value significantly.

Industry-Specific Multiples Using in Valuation

Industry-specific multiples are valuation metrics tailored to particular sectors to reflect their unique operating and financial characteristics. These multiples help provide more accurate valuations by focusing on the specific factors that drive value in an industry. Below is an overview of some common industry-specific multiples and their applications:

Energy Sector

- Enterprise Value per Megawatt (EV/MW ratio)

Technology and SaaS Industry

- EV to Annual Recurring Revenue
- EV to Customer:

Social Media Platforms

- EV to Monthly Active Users

E-Commerce

- EV to Gross Merchandise Value

Game Applications

- EV to Monthly Active Users
- EV to Total Installs

EV/Number of subscribers for telecom companies or EV/Reserves for oil and gas firms

Adjustments of Multiplies

Relative valuation methods using multiples are widely employed in financial analysis, but their accuracy can be improved through various adjustments and considerations. The accuracy of these methods depends on the fundamentals used, adjustments made, conditioning variables, and the selection of comparable (Nissim 2012). If the method is not used correctly, it may lead to incorrect results (Pereiro 2002). These adjustments are made based on the analyst's experience and industry knowledge.

$$M_{\text{adj}} = M_{\text{org}} * (1 + \text{Positive Adjustments Factors}) * (1 - \text{Negative Adjustments Factors})$$

$$M_{\text{adj}} = \text{Adjusted Multiple}$$

$$M_{\text{org}} = \text{Original Multiple}$$

Factors	Factors that need positive adjustments	Factors that need negative adjustments
Company size (small vs large)	Large companies with economies of scale	Small companies with higher volatility
Market liquidity	Easily tradable shares/assets, high trading volume in public markets	Illiquid shares or difficult asset sales, illiquid markets or low trading volume or private companies
Company type (Public vs private)	Public companies, with easier access to capital, liquidity, and regulatory oversight	Private companies with higher risk, limited access to capital and liquidity
Leverage (D/E) and equity ratio	High equity ratio and low financial risk, strong balance sheet	High leverage, increasing financial distress risk
Sector leadership	Market leader with competitive advantage	Weak market position or declining market share
Country risk	Operations in developed or politically stable markets	Emerging markets with high political and economic risks
Industry dynamics	Stable or high-growth industry sectors	Volatile or declining industries
Revenue composition	Export-oriented, diversified markets	High local market or single-customer dependence
Growth potential	Strong revenue and market expansion	Declining growth rates
Corporate governance	High transparency and investor confidence	Poor governance, shareholder disputes
Control premium or minority discount	Control premium for larger shares with decision-making power	Minority discount for minority shareholders without decision-making power
Currency risk exposure	Hedged or minimal currency risk	High exposure to currency fluctuations

Example

***Positive Adjustments**: Strong growth potential, Highly liquid market*

***Negative Adjustments** High Debt, Emerging Market*

***Original EV/EBITDA Multiple**: 10×*

$$\text{EV/EBITDA Modified} = \text{EV/EBITDA Original} \times (1 + \text{strong growth adjustment}) \times (1 + \text{high liquidity adjustment}) \times (1 - \text{high leverage adjustment}) \times (1 - \text{emerging market risk adjustment})$$

$$\text{EV/EBITDA Modified} = 10 \times [(1 + 0.10) \times (1 + 0.08) \times (1 - 0.10) \times (1 - 0.15)]$$

$$\text{EV/EBITDA Modified} = 9.085$$

Calculation Multiples and Weighting

- **Valuation with Price-to-Earnings Multiple**
  The Market Value for the Annual Net profit multiple indicates the relationship between a company's market value and its annual net profit. It represents the ratio of market value to total net profit.

$$P/E = \text{Market Value}/\text{Total Annual Net Profit}$$

In this context, according to the P/E ratio method, the Company's Market Value is calculated as follows:

$$\text{Market Value} = \text{Industry Average } P/E^{*} \text{ Company Total Annual Net Profit}$$

- **Valuation with Market Value/Book Value Multiple**
  The Market Value/Book Value Multiple is the ratio of the Market Value of a company's shares to the company's book value (equity). In this method, to compute the market value, the company's current period equity total is multiplied by the Market Value/Book Value ratio of similar companies operating in the same industry as the company, and the company value is reached.

$$\text{Market Value}/\text{Book Value} = \text{Share Price}/\text{Book Value per Share}$$

In this context, according to the MV/BV ratio method, the Company's Market Value is calculated as follows:

$$\text{Market Value} = \text{Industry } MV/BV^{*} \text{ Company BV}$$

- **Valuation with Firm Value/Total Net Sales Multiple**
  Enterprise Value/Total Net Sales Multiple shows how many times the company's Enterprise Value is equal to the total of one-year net sales. It is the ratio of the company value to the total of net sales.

$$EV/\text{Sales} = \text{Enterprise Value}/\text{Total Net Sales}$$

In this context, the Company's Market Value is calculated as follows according to the EV/Sales ratio method:

$$\text{Enterprise Value} = (\text{Sector FV/Sales}^{*}\ \text{Company Total Net Sales})$$

$$\text{Market Value} = \text{Enterprise Value} - \text{Company Net Debt}$$

- **Valuation with Enterprise Value/Total EBITDA Multiple**
  The Enterprise Value/Total EBITDA Multiple shows how many times the company's Enterprise Value exceeds total annual EBITDA. It is the ratio of the company value to the total EBITDA.

$$\text{EV/EBITDA} = \text{Enterprise Value/Total EBITDA}$$

In this context, the Company's Market Value is calculated as follows according to the FV/EBITDA ratio method:

$$\text{Market Value} = \text{Industry FEV/EBITDA}^{*}\ \text{Company Total EBITDA} - \text{Company Net Debt}$$

A key point: Multiples are generally based on past data. However, the company's operations usually continue into the future. For example, the company we are evaluating is making a new investment and this investment has a positive perspective in the future. It will provide a cost advantage, increase sales, etc. Therefore, we calculate this, but we usually take the coefficient as zero. For example, if we reduce the sales of 2027 to today with a new investment in a company and use the EV/sales multiple, we see that the value is closer to the DCF. If it were assumed that it did not make any investments and maintained its current status, the results of the comparable valuation could be a little closer to the DCF results and be more reasonable.

Income-Based Approach

Fundamental equity valuation models rely on income-based approaches that use **dividends**, (free) **cash flows**, or **(abnormal) earnings** to estimate a company's value. These models involve computing the present value of expected future payoffs, as demonstrated in methods such as the Dividend Discount Model (DDM), Discounted Cash Flow (DCF), Residual Income Valuation (RIV), and Abnormal Earnings Growth (AEG) (Schreiner 2007). According to the IVS: "*The income* *approach provides an indication of value by converting future cash flow to a single current value. Under the income approach, the value of an asset is determined by reference to the value of income, cash flow or cost savings generated by the asset"* (IVS para 40.1)

Intrinsic value, as defined by Benjamin Graham in *The Intelligent Investor* and *Security Analysis*, represents the true value of an asset, independent of its market price (Graham 2006; Graham and Dodd 2009). Warren Buffett further elaborates this concept by describing intrinsic value as "the present value of future cash flows." This perspective emphasizes that intrinsic value is determined by the underlying financial performance and potential of a company, rather than the fluctuations of its market price, aligning with the principles of value investing. Kennedy and Sinaga (2022) discuss intrinsic value as the actual value of stocks, which may not align with market prices. It employs the Discounted Cash Flow (DCF) method, specifically the Free Cash Flow to Equity (FCFE) approach, to estimate intrinsic value based on future cash flows. This aligns with Benjamin Graham's and Warren Buffett's definitions, emphasizing that intrinsic value reflects the underlying worth of an asset, independent of market fluctuations, guiding investment decisions effectively.

Discounted Free Cash Flow Analysis

The **Discounted Cash Flow (DCF) Method** is a fundamental approach in business valuation, where projected future cash flows are discounted to the present value at the valuation date. This method is widely used for valuing assets, companies, or projects by estimating the value of expected future economic benefits, adjusted for time value of money.

The steps involved in the DCF method are as follows (Fig. 3):

1. **Selection of Appropriate Cash Flow Type**: The first step is to determine the most suitable type of cash flows that align with the nature of the asset and the specific purpose of the valuation. This includes deciding between pre-tax or post-tax cash flows, total or equity cash flows, and real versus nominal cash flows, depending on the particular circumstances of the valuation task.

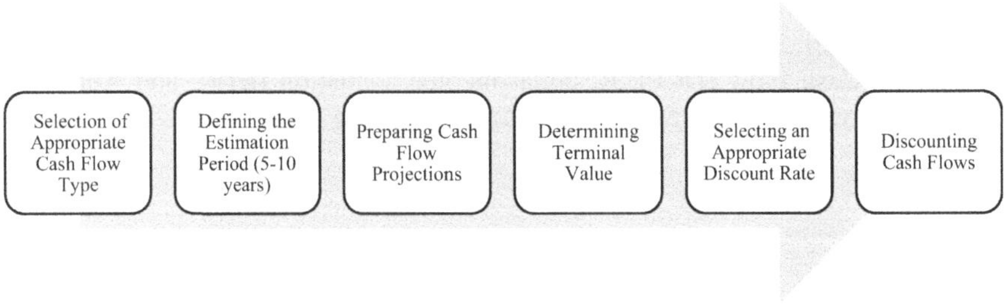

Fig. 3 Steps of DCF method. Source: Authors Creation

2. **Defining the Forecast Period**: The second step involves identifying the appropriate time horizon for the cash flow estimates. This may vary depending on the asset's characteristics and the specific nature of the valuation. In some cases, a finite period is used for estimation, while in others, the period might extend indefinitely.
3. **Preparing Cash Flow Projections**: In this step, the projected cash flows for the specified period are estimated, often based on historical financial performance, industry trends, and forecasts. These projections should be as realistic and detailed as possible to ensure the accuracy of the valuation.
4. **Determining Ongoing Value**: Once the finite period for cash flow estimation has been established, it is crucial to assess whether an ongoing value (terminal value) at the end of this period is relevant and justifiable. The ongoing value should reflect the long-term sustainability of the asset and may be calculated using methods such as perpetuity or exit multiples, depending on the nature of the asset.
5. **Selecting an Appropriate Discount Rate**: The next step is to determine the discount rate that reflects the asset's risk profile and the opportunity cost of capital. This rate is crucial in adjusting the future cash flows to their present value. The discount rate may vary based on factors such as the asset's risk, the cost of capital, and market conditions.
6. **Discounting Cash Flows**: Finally, the estimated future cash flows, including any ongoing value, are discounted back to their present value using the selected discount rate. This step combines the time value of money with the estimated cash flows to determine the asset's intrinsic value at the valuation date.

DCF is a valuation method based on a company's ability to generate cash flows, and accepts the value created by discounting these cash flows to the present and offsetting the current cash and some other elements (some assets and liabilities not used in the projection) as the company's Market Value.

The following main categories are used as a basis in calculating the company's cash flows:

- Cash flows from operations
- Cash flows from asset acquisition and investment activities
- Cash flows from financing expenses
- Changes in working capital
- Tax
- Cash flows from capital
- Current net cash and other assets and liabilities not used in the projection

A cash inflow or cash outflow occurs for each of the above elements. After offsetting these cash inflows and outflows, the cash flow amounts obtained are discounted to the present at an adequate rate (Weighted Average Cost of Capital), and the company's Market Value is computed.

In the Discounted Cash Flow Method, after estimating the cash flows in the foreseeable future of the company, it is assumed that the company, which is assumed to live forever, will generate cash flows forever at a certain rate (called the "Terminal

Value Growth Rate") in the following years. After all these cash flows are discounted to the present, the current net cash (or net debt) and some other non-core activity elements are offset and the company's Market Value is reached.

The discount rate used in valuation, the "Weighted Average Cost of Capital (WACC)," is a combination of the companies' financial debt ratio and the cost of equity ratio. As the name suggests, it reflects the weighted average of these two primary sources. The formula is as follows:

$$\text{WACC} = k_e \times \frac{E}{E+D} + k_d \times (1 - \text{Tax}) \times \frac{D}{E+D}$$

$$E : \text{Equity}$$

$$D : \text{Debt}$$

$$k_d : \text{Cost of Debt}$$

$$k_e : \text{Cost of Equity}$$

Equity costs and borrowing costs are calculated as follows:

$$k_e = R_f + \beta * (R_m - R_f) + \text{Company or Liqudity Risk Premium}$$

R_f: Risk-Free Rate of Return
R_m: Capital Market Return Expectation
$(R_m - R_f)$: Market Risk Premium (Implied Equity Risk Premium)
Tax: Corporate Tax Rate in the Country

Beta It is the coefficient representing the historical change in the price fluctuations of a particular stock according to the general fluctuations in the stock market.

The formulas shown above are valid for companies that have achieved a certain working order and are making sustainable progress.

Unlevered beta is calculated with the following formula:

$$\text{Unlevered Beta} = \frac{\text{Levered Beta}}{1 + (1 - \text{Corporate Tax Rate}) * \frac{\text{Debt}}{\text{Equity}}}$$

$$\text{Terminal Value} = \text{Free Cash Flow}_t * \frac{1+g}{i-g}$$

FCF: Free Cash Flow (t: forecast period)
g: Perpetuity Growth Rate
i: Discount Rate (Weighted Average Cost of Capital)

Cost-Based Approach

"The cost approach provides an indication of value using the economic principle that a buyer will pay no more for an asset than the cost to obtain an asset of equal utility, whether by purchase or by construction, unless undue time, inconvenience, risk or other factors are involved. The approach provides an indication of value by calculating the current replacement or reproduction cost of an asset and making deductions for physical deterioration and all other relevant forms of obsolescence." (IVS para 60.1). In the cost approach, it is assumed that the party that will purchase the company in question will not pay a price higher than the cost of purchasing the company's assets and liabilities individually. In this approach, all assets and liabilities of the company are adjusted one by one to reflect their current market values. The most frequently used valuation method in the cost approach is the adjusted net asset valuation method (Summation Method, IVS paras 70.8-70.9). In the adjusted net asset valuation method, it is assumed that the assets have to be sold individually as of the valuation date. Therefore, all assets on or off the balance sheet are adjusted individually to reflect their current sales prices. In addition to all assets, liabilities are also adjusted to reflect their values on the valuation date. After the necessary adjustments, the difference between the adjusted assets and adjusted liabilities is the equity value of a company. However, the cost approach and the adjusted net asset value method are criticized for not reflecting the future potential of a company.

The "Information Gap" in Emerging Markets

The "information gap" is a critical factor, as emerging markets often lack reliable data and suffer from information asymmetry (Sanders and Boivie 2003), and this creates challenges for investors and analysts. The information gap in emerging market valuation arises from several factors. Many firms in these markets lack historical financial data and standardized reporting practices, making it difficult for investors to assess their true value. In addition, weak regulatory frameworks and inconsistent enforcement of financial disclosure laws contribute to unreliable or incomplete information. Limited access to credit and capital markets restricts firms from developing transparent financial histories exacerbating these valuation challenges. Additionally, high levels of family-owned enterprises often result in opaque corporate governance structures. Moreover, macroeconomic and political instability increases uncertainty, reducing the availability of comparable market data and making risk assessment more complex for investors.

The information gap in emerging market firm valuation presents significant challenges, but several solutions have been proposed. The role of accounting is shifting back toward its stewardship roots to control conflicts of interest, particularly in private equity markets that are increasingly important for emerging market firms. This focus on mitigating conflicts through accounting information can improve the quality of information available for valuation (Zimmerman 2015). Developing stronger institutional environments can also help mitigate information gaps. Better institutions reduce the negative impact of limited credit access on innovation, which is crucial for accurate firm valuation (Qi and Ongena 2019). Additionally, firms can implement internal linkage strategies, such as cross-unit R&D teams, to protect knowledge assets in weak intellectual property rights environments, potentially improving valuation accuracy (Belderbos et al. 2021). The adoption of International Financial Reporting Standards (IFRS) in emerging markets like Saudi Arabia has shown mixed but generally positive effects on the value relevance of accounting information. This standardization can help bridge information gaps by increasing the explanatory power of earnings and improving the relevance of equity information for valuation purposes (Chehade and Procházka 2023).

Comparison with Valuation Methods in Developed Markets

Valuing firms in emerging markets requires a nuanced approach due to the unique challenges and opportunities these markets present. Unlike developed markets, emerging markets are characterized by higher volatility, diverse economic conditions, and varying institutional frameworks. These factors necessitate additional layers of analysis and risk adjustment to accurately assess firm value. The following sections outline key considerations for valuing firms in emerging markets.

Risk Factors
Emerging markets are subject to significant risk factors such as currency fluctuations, economic instability, inflation, and liquidity issues. These risks must be carefully evaluated and incorporated into valuation models to ensure accurate assessments (Godi 2024). Political stability and regulatory frameworks also play a crucial role in determining firm value, as they can impact operational efficiency and profitability (Angelov 2024).

Institutional Distance and Stigma
Emerging market firms often encounter bias when acquiring or merging with companies in developed markets, which can result in higher acquisition premiums. This bias is linked to the perceived institutional weaknesses of their home countries (Osuji et al. 2024). Institutional distance, or the difference in institutional frameworks between countries, affects foreign equity valuations. A curvilinear relationship exists, where moderate institutional distance can be beneficial, but extreme distances pose challenges (Purkayastha and Filatotchev 2023).

Diversification and Growth Potential
Emerging markets offer significant growth potential due to demographic trends and economic transitions from manufacturing to services. This potential can enhance firm valuations if effectively leveraged (Angelov 2024). Geographic diversification through investments in emerging markets can provide benefits to global investors,

mitigating some risks associated with these markets (Purkayastha and Filatotchev 2023).

Systemic Risk and Market Connectedness

In sectors like energy, systemic risk and market connectedness are critical factors. Understanding the idiosyncratic components of stock returns in emerging markets can offer diversification opportunities and identify systemically important firms (Chuliá et al. 2023).

In summary, while core valuation methodologies remain consistent, the inputs and assumptions must be carefully adapted to reflect the heightened risks and uncertainties inherent in these economies. While emerging markets present unique challenges, they also offer substantial opportunities for growth and diversification. Investors must balance these factors, considering both the risks and potential rewards, to make informed valuation decisions. Understanding the interplay between institutional frameworks, market dynamics, and firm-specific factors is essential for accurate firm valuation in these markets.

EM Risks and Premiums

Emerging markets face unique risks and require specific premiums to account for these challenges. The traditional Capital Asset Pricing Model (CAPM) is often modified to include country-specific risk when applied to emerging markets (Pereiro 2005). Factors such as size, liquidity, and currency fluctuations play a crucial role in valuation (Pereiro 2001, 2005). Furthermore, Environmental, Social, and Governance (ESG) factors are increasingly important in emerging markets, with ESG scores positively impacting firm valuation and ESG controversies negatively affecting it (Rahat and Nguyen 2024).

Research indicates that the majority of errors in estimating the cost of equity capital stem from risk premium estimates rather than beta calculations, suggesting that analysts should focus on improving risk premium estimation methods (Ferson and Locke 1998), which are especially important in "riskier" emerging markets.

The premiums are based on a study by Aswath Damodaran. All data are as of January 9, 2025. Here are the steps Damodaran took to determine a country's equity risk premium:

Step	Example—Turkey
1. Search for a country's credit (bond) risk rating.	Credit risk rating: B1
2. Depending on that rating, find the credit spread, which is the additional yield over a risk-free rate	Credit spread for B1 rating = 3.21%
3. To account for the additional risk shares carry over bonds, multiply the credit spread by the relative equity market volatility	3.21% credit spread × 1.347 relative equity market volatility
The result is the country risk premium	= 4.325% country risk premium

(continued)

Step	Example—Turkey
4. Add the country risk premium to the mature market risk premium (Implied ERP for S&P 500)	4.325% country risk premium + 4.33% mature market risk premium
5. The resulting value is the country equity risk premium	8.66% country equity risk premium

Below, the equity risk premium data for some key emerging markets as of January 2025 are presented.

Country	Country risk premium	10-year CDS spread	Total equity risk premium	Country risk premium
Brazil	3.34%	2.82%	8.13%	3.80%
China	0.94%	0.56%	5.08%	0.75%
Egypt	10.01%	5.94%	12.33%	8.00%
India	2.93%	0.54%	5.06%	0.73%
South Africa	4.02%	2.59%	7.82%	3.49%
Turkey	6.01%	3.21%	8.66%	4.33%

Frontier Markets (no sovereign ratings)

Country	PRS composite risk score	ERP	CRP	Default spread
Russia	69.25	8.35%	4.02%	2.98%

Source: Aswath Damodaran, Country Default Spreads and Risk Premiums, https://pages.stern.nyu.edu/~adamodar/New_Home_Page/datafile/ctryprem.html

Equity risk premiums shift over time as a country's credit rating, credit spread, and equity market volatility change.

Company Case Study in Turkey

CornStar Global is a company operating in Turkey, a country with emerging market status, which produces starch and rice flour. The company's past IFRS-based financial position statement and income statement for the years 2021, 2022, and 2023 are as follows. A valuation is requested for the company in order to bring in a new partner.[1]

	December 31, 2022	December 31, 2023	December 31, 2024
Current assets	**71,646**	**4,373,898**	**10,306,758**
Cash and cash equivalents	1061	120,205	204,720
Trade receivables	31,662	1,476,762	5,598,872

(continued)

[1] This example has been developed by the author and has no relation to real company data.

	December 31, 2022	December 31, 2023	December 31, 2024
Other receivables	–	75,865	567,849
Inventories	741	2,196,700	3,490,260
Prepaid expenses	530	430,339	210,080
Other current assets	37,652	74,027	234,977
Non-current assets	**452,081**	**2,369,125**	**5,747,835**
Other receivables	2.6	2.6	2.6
Investment properties	45,000	55,000	150,000
Fixed assets	407,078	2,290,704	5,593,043
Right of use assets	–	18,706	–
Intangible assets	–	4713	4790
Total assets	**523,727**	**6,743,023**	**16,054,593**
Current liabilities	**480,300**	**3,779,466**	**9,021,910**
Short-term financial borrowings	–	1,530,078	3,983,652
Current portion of long-term borrowings	–	462,731	1,263,564
Trade payables	479,222	1,116,632	2,179,252
Employee benefit obligation	–	12,943	14,533
Other payables	14	5268	7259
Obligations arising from customer contracts	1064	597,216	1,344,119
Current income tax liabilities	–	53,081	223,678
Short-term provisions	–	1517	5853
Non-current liabilities	**6005**	**730,310**	**888,140**
Long-term financial borrowings	–	506,890	344,063
– Bank Loan	–	506,890	344,063
Other borrowings	1950	–	–
Non-current provisions for employee benefits	–	3991	18,122
Deferred tax liabilities	4055	219,430	525,955
EQUITY	**37,421**	**2,233,247**	**6,144,543**
Paid-in capital	1000	600,000	600,000
Capital adjustment differences	–	1,580,403	4,303,506
Restricted reserves allocated from profit	2	2	2
Retained earnings/(losses)	33,367	36,419	52,842
Net income/(loss) for the period	3052	16,424	1,194,682
Total liabilities and equity	**523,727**	**6,743,023**	**16,054,593**

	January 1–December 31 2022	January 1–December 31 2023	January 1–December 31 2024
Revenues	70,212	9,270,819	38,899,644
Cost of goods sold (–)	(69,816)	(8,104,976)	(31,684,205)

(continued)

	January 1–December 31 2022	January 1–December 31 2023	January 1–December 31 2024
Gross profit/(loss)	**396**	**1,165,843**	**7,215,439**
General and administrative expenses (–)	(2441)	(111,256)	(229,468)
Marketing, sales, and distribution expenses (–)	(33)	(660,547)	(4,444,031)
Other income from main operations	750	498,697	1,196,374
Other expenses from main operations (–)	(501)	(311,623)	(924,142)
Operating profit/(loss)	**(1829)**	**581,113**	**2,814,171**
Income from investment activities	5000	10,000	106,239
Operating income before financial income/(expense)	**3171**	**591,113**	**2,920,410**
Financial income	–	1214	98,898
Financial expenses (–)	(31)	(547,249)	(1,283,418)
Profit before tax	**3139**	**45,078**	**1,735,890**
Tax expense	(87)	(28,654)	(541,208)
Taxes on income	–	(63,685)	(472,555)
Deferred tax income	(87)	35,032	(68,653)
Net profit for the period	**3052**	**16,424**	**1,194,682**

Valuation of CornStar Global Using the Discounted Cash Flow (DCF) Method

In the valuation process of CornStar Global using the Discounted Cash Flow (DCF) Method, the company's independent audit report was utilized. After analyzing this data, future projections were created by combining the company's potential, capacity, and market conditions, resulting in the following assumptions and estimates.

The company's revenue sources related to its core operations have been categorized as follows:

i. **Net Sales**
ii. **Other Income from Core Operations**

These revenue categories have been structured in accordance with the classifications presented in the independent audit report.

Net sales represent the primary revenue source derived from the company's domestic and international sales. Additionally, foreign exchange gains from commercial activities, incentives, and other income directly related to core operations have been classified under **"Other Income from Core Operations."** These income sources are continuous and have been included accordingly.

The company's past expenses primarily consisted of **cost of goods sold (COGS)**, including raw material and supplies expenses, labor expenses, general production expenses, provision for severance pay expenses, provision for leave pay expenses, and depreciation expenses. Additionally, the company incurred costs related to the sale of commercial goods and cash outflows from **operating expenses**, which were categorized as general administrative expenses and marketing expenses, reflecting the company's ongoing operational activities.

Expenses have been identified based on cash outflows. Depreciation and inventory changes are not included in these expenses. Depreciation is excluded as it does not represent a cash outflow, while inventory changes are omitted from this section since they are considered in the working capital calculation.

The company's **operating profit before depreciation (like EBITDA)** has been calculated as the difference between its revenues and expenses. The **operating profit margin**, determined as the ratio of operating profit to sales, reflects the company's operational profitability and has been used as a basis for future projections. Corporate tax has been calculated based on this operating profit, with a **corporate tax rate of 25%** assumed for future periods.

While calculating **net working capital**, certain adjustments were made to the company's trade receivables, inventories, and trade payables. The following steps were taken:

1. **Trade receivables from related and non-related parties** were fully considered as trade receivables, but adjustments were made to specific items within these categories. In this context, **Receivables Discount** and **Receivables Discount from Related Parties** were excluded.
2. **Work Advances** under **Other Receivables from Non-Related Parties** were classified as trade receivables.
3. **All Prepaid Expenses** were considered as trade receivables.
4. **No adjustments** were deemed necessary for inventories.
5. While calculating **trade payables**, the balances of **Trade Payables to Related and Non-Related Parties** were adjusted by eliminating **Trade Payables Discount from Related Parties** and **Trade Payables Discount**, with the remaining amounts considered as trade payables.
6. **Liabilities from Customer Contracts** were entirely classified as **order advances** and considered trade payables.

Over this period, the company's **average trade receivables turnover period** was **32.0 days**, the **average inventory turnover period** was **32.3 days**, and the **average trade payables turnover period** was **24.3 days**. It has been assumed that these periods will remain at the same levels in future periods. The company's **net working capital requirement** was determined by subtracting the average trade payables amount from the sum of the average trade receivables and average inventory amounts. The difference in net working capital requirements between two periods was offset against free cash flows under the item **"Net Working Capital Change."**

The **operating cycle** is calculated as the sum of the trade receivables turnover period (32 days) and the inventories turnover period (32 days), resulting in a total of 64 days.

The **cash conversion cycle (CCC)** is then determined by subtracting the trade payables turnover period (24.3 days) from the operating cycle. This calculation results in a CCC of 40 days, indicating the average number of days it takes for the company to convert its investments in inventory and receivables into cash, after accounting for its trade payables.

Net Working Capital Estimates	2023/12	2024/12
Trade Receivables Turnover Period (days)	32.0	32.0
Inventories Turnover Periods (days)	32.3	32.3
Trade Payables Turnover Period (days)	37.7	24.3
Operating Cycle	**64**	**64**
Cash Conversion Cycle	**27**	**40**

In 2023, the ratio of **VAT receivables** to **revenues** was **0.8%**, and it is assumed that this ratio will remain at the same level in future periods.

	2023/12	2024/12
Revenues	**9,769,515 TL**	**40,096,018 TL**
Net Sales	**9,270,819 TL**	**38,899,644 TL**
Revenues from Main Activities	**498,697 TL**	**1,196,374 TL**
Revenues Change (Yearly)		*310.42%*
Expenses	**9,678,540 TL**	**35,877,736 TL**
Cash Outflows from COGS	**9,218,359 TL**	**32,128,379 TL**
Cash Outflows from Operating Expenses	**771,804 TL**	**4,673,500 TL**
Expenses from Main Activities	**311,623 TL**	**924,142 TL**
Expenses/Revenues	*99.07%*	*89.48%*
Main Operating Profit (Excluding Depreciation)	**90,975 TL**	**4,218,281 TL**
Depreciation Expenses	**11,574 TL**	**139,033 TL**
COGS Depreciation	10,554 TL	138,013 TL
Operating Expense Depreciation (General Administrative Expenses)	1020 TL	1020 TL
Net Working Capital Need	**981,078 TL**	**3,963,944 TL**
Average Trade Receivables (Excluding VAT)	882,314 TL	3,511,779 TL
Average Inventories	1,098,721 TL	2,843,480 TL
Average Trade Payables (Excluding VAT)	999,956 TL	2,391,315 TL
Average Trade Receivables Turnover Period	*33.0 day*	*32.0 day*
Average Inventories Turnover Period	*43.5 day*	*32.3 day*
Average Trade Payables Turnover Period	*37.7 day*	*24.3 day*
Net Working Capital Change	**981,078 TL**	**2,982,866 TL**
Total VAT Receivables	**128,678 TL**	**306,643 TL**
Total VAT Receivables/Revenues	*1.3%*	*0.8%*
Total VAT Receivables Change		
Routine CAPEX	**95,093 TL**	**488,073 TL**

Investment expenditures (CAPEX) also represent cash outflows. When estimating the company's future routine CAPEX, the ratio of total investments made in **2022 and 2023** to total revenues was calculated. This ratio is **1.2%**, and based on this, investment expenditures for the upcoming years were estimated. The valuation was carried out **excluding depreciation**, and the tax benefits from these investments were added back to the cash flows. When calculating the tax advantage of the investment expenditures, it was assumed that the depreciation period would be **5 years**, and the amount was **discounted** over an average period of **2.5 years**. In this context, the **25% tax advantage** of the investments for the relevant year was discounted over an average of **2.5 years**.

After offsetting the company's cash inflows and outflows, the resulting **free cash flow** is discounted to the present using the **Weighted Average Cost of Capital (WACC)**, which leads to the determination of the company's **market value**.

In the **Discounted Cash Flow (DCF)** method, after forecasting the company's cash flows for the foreseeable future, it is assumed that the company will continue to operate indefinitely and will generate cash flows at a certain rate in the following years, referred to as the **"Terminal Value Growth Rate."** After discounting all these cash flows to the present, the company's **current net cash (or net debt)** and other non-operating items are also offset, resulting in the company's **market value.**

In the DCF method applied to **CornStar Global**, the company's cash inflows and outflows were grouped based on their sources, and the cash flows from each group were identified. The amounts for each year's cash flow were calculated and then discounted to the present. The final value was adjusted by offsetting some of the company's existing assets and liabilities to determine the **market value**.

It was assumed in the valuation that CornStar Global will operate indefinitely.

Since the valuation is conducted in **TRY (Turkish Lira)**, the **Risk-Free Interest Rate** used is the **10-year government bond yield** as of the valuation date (**December 31, 2024**). This rate was **28%** on December 31, 2024.

In calculating the **beta coefficient**, since CornStar Global is not listed on the stock exchange, the **beta values of food industry companies** listed on **Borsa İstanbul** were used. The beta values of food sector companies were calculated based on daily data for the past three years from the valuation date. In this context, the **industry beta** was calculated to be **0.75**.

In calculating the **unlevered beta**, the **equity and financial debt amounts** reported by food industry companies in Borsa Istanbul for the last three years, broken down into quarterly periods, were taken into account.

Company	Beta	Financial debt/equity	Unlevered beta
AVOD	0.80	54.2%	0.57
AEFES	0.85	122.2%	0.44
BANVT	0.30	86.8%	0.18
CCOLA	0.79	90.9%	0.47
DARDL	0.80	93.3%	0.47
ELITE	0.31	36.1%	0.24

(continued)

Company	Beta	Financial debt/equity	Unlevered beta
ERSU	0.51	0.0%	0.51
FADE	0.55	14.0%	0.50
FRIGO	0.66	11.9%	0.61
KERVT	0.75	65.6%	0.51
KRVGD	0.66	82.2%	0.41
KNFRT	0.62	51.8%	0.45
KRSTL	0.83	2.9%	0.82
KTSKR	0.62	5.7%	0.60
MERKO	0.74	14.5%	0.67
ORCAY	0.20	77.4%	0.13
OYLUM	0.68	51.9%	0.49
PENGD	0.72	28.5%	0.59
PETUN	0.55	14.5%	0.49
PINSU	0.53	197.1%	0.21
PNSUT	0.72	34.1%	0.57
SELGD	0.55	0.9%	0.54
SELVA	0.12	134.1%	0.06
TATGD	0.65	76.4%	0.41
TETMT	0.44	71.7%	0.29
TUKAS	0.64	68.8%	0.42
ULUUN	0.56	176.7%	0.24
ULKER	0.75	333.0%	0.21
VANGD	0.57	0.0%	0.57
YYLGD	0.51	154.3%	0.24
Industry (food)	**0.75**	**118.9%**	**0.397**

As shown in the table, the **unlevered beta** of the food industry has been determined to be **0.385**.

The leveraged beta for **CornStar Global** has been calculated as **0.665**, as shown in the table below.

Unleveraged beta	**0.397**
Company financial debt	5,591,278
Adjusted equity	6,144,543
Company debt/equity	91.00%
Leveraged beta	**0.668**

The **leveraged beta** has been used as the company's beta.

The **company risk premium** has been set at **3%**. Since the company in question is not publicly traded, its shares are **illiquid**, meaning they cannot be easily bought or sold on the stock market. This **lack of liquidity** increases risk for investors. Thus, a **liquidity risk premium** is added to account for this additional risk.

The **financial leverage ratio** of the company has been calculated to be an average of **35%** based on the data in the independent audit report.

As shown in the table below, the **Weighted Average Cost of Capital (WACC)** for **CornStar Global** has been calculated to be **30.48%** for 2025 and beyond. The data prepared by the company has been utilized in the discounted cash flow method. In this context, the information provided by **CornStar Global** has been interpreted and restructured based on market conditions.

Weighted average cost of capital	
Cost of equity	
Risk-free rate of return	28.00%
Beta	0.668
Market risk premium (for mature market)	5.00%
Company risk premium	3.00%
k_e (Cost of equity)	**34.34%**
Cost of debt	
Cost of debt	35.00%
Tax rate	25.00%
k_d (Cost of debt)	**26.25%**
Debt/(Debt + equity)	47.64%
WACC	**30.48%**

The valuation assumes that CornStar Global will generate cash flows up until 2031. For subsequent periods, it is assumed that CornStar Global will continue to generate cash flows indefinitely at a fixed return rate.

The valuation date is December 31, 2024, and cash flows after this date have been projected and added to the forecast.

In the valuation, it has been assumed that the company will continue its operations indefinitely from 2030 onward, with a growth rate applied each year. The Perpetuity Growth Rate has been assumed to be 5%. This growth rate has been used to calculate the company's Terminal Value.

The Perpetuity Growth Rate (for 2030 and subsequent years) assumes a **5%** inflation rate, in line with the Central Bank of the Republic of Turkey's target inflation rate.

After calculating the present value of the cash flows and the continuing value, **CornStar Global's** other assets and liabilities were offset against the market value.

In this context:

1. **Cash and cash equivalents** of CornStar Global's were added to the market value.
2. **Financial debts** were deducted from CornStar Global's market value.
3. **Other short-term receivables** were added to the company's market value.
4. **Investment properties** were added to the market value in case of sale.
5. **Employee benefits-related liabilities** were deducted from the market value.
6. **Other liabilities** were deducted from the market value.
7. **Income tax liabilities** were deducted from the market value.
8. **Short-term provisions** were deducted from the market value.
9. **Long-term provisions related to employee benefits** were deducted from the market value.

As shown below, according to the **Discounted Cash Flow (DCF) method** based on **December 31, 2024**, the market value of **CornStar Global** has been calculated as **879,475 USD**.

Discounted cash flow method	2023/12	2024/12	2025/12F	2026/12F	2027/12F	2028/12F	2029/12F	2030/12F	2031/12F
Revenues	**9,769,515 TL**	**40,096,018 TL**	**70,168,031 TL**	**119,285,652 TL**	**178,928,478 TL**	**232,607,022 TL**	**279,128,426 TL**	**304,333,723 TL**	**313,463,734 TL**
Net Sales	**9,270,819 TL**	**38,899,644 TL**							
Revenues from Main Activities	**498,697 TL**	**1,196,374 TL**							
Revenues Change (Yearly)		*310.42%*	*75.00%*	*70.00%*	*50.00%*	*30.00%*	*20.00%*	*9.03%*	*3.00%*
Expenses	**9,678,540 TL**	**35,877,736 TL**	**62,786,038 TL**	**106,736,265 TL**	**160,104,398 TL**	**208,135,717 TL**	**249,762,861 TL**	**272,316,447 TL**	**280,485,940 TL**
Cash Outflows from COGS	**9,218,359 TL**	**32,128,379 TL**	**56,224,663 TL**	**95,581,927 TL**	**143,372,890 TL**	**186,384,757 TL**	**223,661,708 TL**	**243,858,360 TL**	**251,174,111 TL**
Cash Outflows from Operating Expenses	**771,804 TL**	**4,673,500 TL**	**6,561,376 TL**	**11,154,339 TL**	**16,731,508 TL**	**21,750,961 TL**	**26,101,153 TL**	**28,458,087 TL**	**29,311,829 TL**
Expenses from Main Activities	**311,623 TL**	**924,142 TL**							
Expenses/Revenues	*99.07%*	*89.48%*	*89.48%*	*89.48%*	*89.48%*	*89.48%*	*89.48%*	*89.48%*	*89.48%*
Main Operating Profit (Excluding Depreciation)	**90,975 TL**	**4,218,281 TL**	**7,381,992 TL**	**12,549,387 TL**	**18,824,080 TL**	**24,471,304 TL**	**29,365,565 TL**	**32,017,276 TL**	**32,977,794 TL**
Depreciation Expenses	**11,574 TL**	**139,033 TL**	**139,033 TL**	**139,033 TL**	**139,033 TL**	**139,033 TL**	**139,033 TL**	**139,033 TL**	**139,033 TL**
COGS Depreciation	10,554 TL	138,013 TL	138,013 TL	138,013 TL	138,013 TL	138,013 TL	138,013 TL	138,013 TL	138,013 TL
Operating Expense Depreciation	1,020 TL	1,020 TL	1,020 TL	1,020 TL	1,020 TL	1,020 TL	1,020 TL	1,020 TL	1,020 TL
Net Working Capital Need	**981,078 TL**	**3,963,944 TL**	**6,936,902 TL**	**11,792,734 TL**	**17,689,101 TL**	**22,995,831 TL**	**27,594,997 TL**	**30,086,826 TL**	**30,989,430 TL**
Average Trade Receivables (Excluding VAT)	882,314 TL	3,511,779 TL	6,145,613 TL	10,447,543 TL	15,671,314 TL	20,372,708 TL	24,447,250 TL	26,654,837 TL	27,454,482 TL
Average Inventories	1,098,721 TL	2,843,480 TL	4,976,090 TL	8,459,353 TL	12,689,029 TL	16,495,738 TL	19,794,886 TL	21,582,364 TL	22,229,835 TL
Average Trade Payables (Excluding VAT)	999,956 TL	2,391,315 TL	4,184,801 TL	7,114,162 TL	10,671,243 TL	13,872,616 TL	16,647,139 TL	18,150,375 TL	18,694,887 TL
Average Trade Receivables Turnover Period	*33.0 gün*	*32.0 gün*	*32.0 gün*	*32.0 gün*	*32.0 gün*	*32.0 gün*	*32.0 gün*	*32.0 gün*	*32.0 gün*
Average Inventories Turnover Period	*43.5 gün*	*32.3 gün*	*32.3 gün*	*32.3 gün*	*32.3 gün*	*32.3 gün*	*32.3 gün*	*32.3 gün*	*32.3 gün*
Average Trade Payables Turnover Period	*37.7 gün*	*24.3 gün*	*24.3 gün*	*24.3 gün*	*24.3 gün*	*24.3 gün*	*24.3 gün*	*24.3 gün*	*24.3 gün*
Net Working Capital Change	**981,078 TL**	**2,982,866 TL**	**2,972,958 TL**	**4,855,832 TL**	**5,896,367 TL**	**5,306,730 TL**	**4,599,166 TL**	**2,491,828 TL**	**902,605 TL**
Total VAT Receivables	**128,678 TL**	**306,643 TL**	**536,625 TL**	**912,262 TL**	**1,368,393 TL**	**1,778,911 TL**	**2,134,693 TL**	**2,327,455 TL**	**2,397,279 TL**
Total VAT Receivables/Revenues	*1.3%*	*0.8%*	*0.8%*	*0.8%*	*0.8%*	*0.8%*	*0.8%*	*0.8%*	*0.8%*
Total VAT Receivables Change			**229,982 TL**	**375,637 TL**	**456,131 TL**	**410,518 TL**	**355,782 TL**	**192,763 TL**	**69,824 TL**
Routine CAPEX	**95,093 TL**	**488,073 TL**	**820,599 TL**	**1,395,018 TL**	**2,092,527 TL**	**2,720,285 TL**	**3,264,342 TL**	**3,559,113 TL**	**3,665,886 TL**
Routine CAPEX Tax Advantage			**105,480 TL**	**179,316 TL**	**268,974 TL**	**349,666 TL**	**419,599 TL**	**457,489 TL**	**471,214 TL**
Free Cash Flows (FCFF)			**2,015,341 TL**	**3,620,145 TL**	**6,911,020 TL**	**11,516,983 TL**	**15,720,567 TL**	**19,855,413 TL**	**22,242,941 TL**
WACC			*30.48%*	*30.48%*	*30.48%*	*30.48%*	*30.48%*	*30.48%*	*30.48%*
Discount Coefficient		**1.00**	**0.77**	**0.59**	**0.45**	**0.34**	**0.26**	**0.20**	**0.16**
Discounted Free Cash Flow			**1,544,501 TL**	**2,126,205 TL**	**3,110,720 TL**	**3,972,804 TL**	**4,155,911 TL**	**4,022,689 TL**	**3,453,579 TL**
Present Value of Free Cash Flows	**22,386,409 TL**								
Terminal Value	**14,229,020 TL**								
Cash and Cash Equivalents	**204,720 TL**								
Financial Debts	**−5,591,278 TL**								
Other Short-Term Receivables	**21,274 TL**								
Investment Properties	**150,000 TL**								
Employee Benefits Payables	**−14,533 TL**								

(contined)

Discounted cash flow method	2023/12	2024/12	2025/12F	2026/12F	2027/12F	2028/12F	2029/12F	2030/12F	2031/12F
Other Payables	**−7259 TL**								
Taxes on Current Period Profit Liability	**−223,678 TL**								
Short-Term Provisions	**−5853 TL**								
Long-Term Provisions for Employee Benefits	**−18,122 TL**								
Market Value TL	**31,130,699 TL**								
Exchange Rate TL/USD	**35.3969**								
Market Value USD	**879,475 USD**								

Valuation of CornStar Global Using the Relative Valuation Method

In the valuation of CornStar Global, data from food industry companies operating in Turkey and listed on Borsa Istanbul have been utilized. The food industry companies used as a basis for the valuation are as follows:

- A.V.O.D. Dried Food and Agricultural Products Industry and Trade Inc. ("AVOD")
- Banvit Bandırma Vitamin Feed Industry Inc. ("BANVT")
- Dardanel Önentaş Food Industry Inc. ("DARDL")
- Elite Naturel Organic Food Industry and Trade Inc. ("ELITE")
- Fade Food Investment Industry and Trade Inc. ("FADE")
- Frigo-Pak Food Products Industry and Trade Inc. ("FRIGO")
- Kerevitaş Food Industry and Trade Inc. ("KERVT")
- Kervan Food Industry and Trade Inc. ("KRVGD")
- Konfrut Food Industry and Trade Inc. ("KNFRT")
- Kütahya Sugar Factory Inc. ("KTSKR")
- Orçay Ortaköy Tea Industry and Trade Inc. ("ORCAY")
- Oylum Industrial Investments Inc. ("OYLUM")
- Penguen Food Industry Inc. ("PENGD")
- Pınar Integrated Meat and Flour Industry Inc. ("PETUN")
- Selva Food Industry Inc. ("SELVA")
- Tat Food Industry Inc. ("TATGD")
- Tukaş Food Industry and Trade Inc. ("TUKAS")
- Ulusoy Flour Industry and Trade Inc. ("ULUUN")
- Yayla Agro Food Industry and Trade Inc. ("YYLGD")

In the valuation of CornStar Global, the most recent data disclosed on the Public Disclosure Platform at the time of the valuation study were taken into account for the peer companies.

The data used include:

- Company
- Market value
- Enterprise value
- Net debt
- Equity
- Net sales

From these figures, totals were calculated, and weighted average industry multiples were derived from the total values. Industry peers are as follows:

Industry	Multiple
P/E	14.11
EV/EBITDA	11.55

(continued)

Industry	Multiple
EV/Sales	1.31
MV/BV	3.38

Source: Public Disclosure Platform (https://www.kap.org.tr/), Finnet

Financials of CornStar Global	
Net financial debt	5,386,558
Equity	6,144,543
Net sales	38,899,644
EBITDA	4,218,281
Net profit	1,194,682

The market value of CornStar Global has been calculated as 31,633,020 TL based on the average of the values determined using multiples under the Guideline Public Company Method.

Guideline Public Company Method	Calculated market value	Weight	Weighted market value
Industry Average P/E	16,856,959	25.00%	4,214,240
Industry Average EV/EBITDA	43,334,590	25.00%	10,833,648
Industry Average EV/Sales	45,571,975	25.00%	11,392,994
Industry Average BV/MV	20,768,556	25.00%	5,192,139
Market value			**31,633,020 TL**
Exchange rate TL/USD			**35.3969**
Market value (USD)			**893,666 USD**

Cost-Based Valuation

In the Summation Method table prepared for CornStar Global, its market value according to the Summation Method is determined as the company's equity value, which is 6,144,543 TL.

This is based on the fact that CornStar Global's financial statements are prepared in accordance with IFRS, its receivables and liabilities have been adjusted to reflect their fair value, its real estate assets have been recorded according to the values stated in valuation reports, and all other necessary adjustments have been made.

Result

Three methods were used in the valuation study for CornStar. The values and weights obtained from each of the three methods are shown in the table below.

Method	Calculated market value	Weight	Weighted market value
Discounted Cash Flow (DCF) Method	31,130,699	50%	15,565,349
Guideline Public Company Method	31,633,020	50%	15,816,510
Summation Method	6,144,543	0%	0
Market value (Turkish Lira)			**31,381,859 TL**
Exchange rate TL/USD			**35.3969**
Market value (USD)			**886,571 USD**

As seen in the table, the Discounted Cash Flow Method is weighted at 50%, the Guide Comparables Method at the Stock Exchange is weighted at 50%, and the Net Asset Value Method is weighted at 0%. The Net Asset Value Method is a method created with the assumption that the company will cease its activities, and since the company is still in operation and the Market Value obtained from the cash flows generated from these activities is higher, its weighting is taken into account as 0%. Other methods are weighted equally. As a result of the valuation study, CornStar's Market Value was determined as 886,571 USD.

References

Allee KD, Erickson D, Esplin AM, Yohn TL (2020) The characteristics, valuation methods, and information use of valuation specialists. Account Horiz 34(3):23–38. https://doi.org/10.2308/horizons-19-057

Angelov S (2024) Emerging markets and investment opportunities. 1:129–139. https://doi.org/10.58861/tae.grdier.2024.13

Belderbos R, Carree M, Park J (2021) Do R&D investments in weak IPR countries destroy market value? The role of internal linkages. Strateg Manag J 42(8):1401–1431. https://doi.org/10.1002/smj.3268

Chehade S, Procházka D (2023) Value relevance of accounting information in an emerging market: the case of IFRS adoption by non-financial listed firms in Saudi Arabia. J Account Emerg Econ 14(1):220–246. March.

Chuliá H, Muñoz Mendoza JA, Uribe JM (2023) Energy firms in emerging markets: systemic risk and diversification opportunities. Emerg Mark Rev 56:101053. https://doi.org/10.1016/j.ememar.2023.101053

Damodaran A (2007) Valuation approaches and metrics: a survey of the theory and evidence. Found Trends Finance 1(8):693–784

Esty BC (2000) What determines comparability when valuing firms with multiples? J Financ Educ 2000:24–33

Fama EF (1970) Efficient capital markets. J Financ 25(2):383–417

Fernández P (2007) Company valuation methods. The most common errors in valuations. IESE Bus School 449:1–27

Ferson WE, Locke DH (1998) Estimating the cost of capital through time: an analysis of the sources of error. Manag Sci 44(4):485–500. https://doi.org/10.1287/mnsc.44.4.485

Godi J (2024) Analysis of risk factors for investors in emerging markets. J Risk Anal Crisis Response 14(2). https://doi.org/10.54560/jracr.v14i2.469

Graham B (2006) The intelligent investor: The definitive book on value investing, Rev. edn. HarperBusiness

Graham B, Dodd DL (2009) Security analysis, 6th edn. McGraw-Hill Education

Green J, Zhang XF, Hand JRM (2016) Errors and questionable judgments in analysts' DCF models. Rev Account Stud 21(2):596–632. https://doi.org/10.1007/s11142-016-9352-4

Hitchner JR (2017) Financial valuation: applications and models, 4th edn. Wiley

Jägle AJ (1999) Shareholder value, real options, and innovation in technology-intensive companies. R&D Manag 29(3):271–288. https://doi.org/10.1111/1467-9310.00136

Kennedy PSJ, Sinaga MK (2022) The influence of the intrinsic value of stocks on its market price. Image 11(2):83–93. https://doi.org/10.17509/image.v11i2.45928

Newton DP, Widdicks M, Paxson DA (2004) Real R&D options. Int J Manag Rev 5–6(2):113–130. https://doi.org/10.1111/j.1460-8545.2004.00099

Nissim D (2012) Relative valuation of U.S. insurance companies. Rev Account Stud 18(2): 324–359. https://doi.org/10.1007/s11142-012-9213-8

Osuji J, Torres de Oliveira R, Tupper C (2024) Escaping the stigma of firm operations in emerging markets: are you willing to pay the price? J Bus Res. https://doi.org/10.1016/j.jbusres.2024.114714

Pereiro LE (2001) The valuation of closely-held companies in Latin America. Emerg Mark Rev 2(4):330–370. https://doi.org/10.1016/s1566-0141(01)00024-3

Pereiro LE (2002) Valuation of companies in emerging markets – a practical approach. Wiley, New York

Pereiro LE (2005) The practice of investment valuation in emerging markets: evidence from Argentina. J Multinatl Financ Manag 16(2):160–183. https://doi.org/10.1016/j.mulfin.2005.06.001

Purkayastha A, Filatotchev I (2023) Foreign equity valuations of emerging market firms: the effects of institutional distance and information spillovers. Manag Int Rev 63:1021–1062. https://doi.org/10.1007/s11575-023-00516-2

Qi S, Ongena S (2019) Fuel the engine: bank credit and firm innovation. J Financ Serv Res 57(2): 115–147. https://doi.org/10.1007/s10693-019-00316-6

Rahat B, Nguyen P (2024) The impact of ESG profile on firm's valuation in emerging markets. Int Rev Financ Anal 95:103361. https://doi.org/10.1016/j.irfa.2024.103361

Sanders WG, Boivie S (2003) Sorting things out: valuation of new firms in uncertain markets. Strateg Manag J 25(2):167–186. https://doi.org/10.1002/smj.370

Schreiner A (2007) Equity valuation using multiples: an empirical investigation. Deutscher Universitäts-Verlag, Wiesbaden. https://doi.org/10.1007/978-3-8350-9531-1

Schreiner A, Spremann K (2007) Multiples and their valuation accuracy in European equity markets. Available at SSRN 957352

Zimmerman JL (2015) The role of accounting in the twenty-first century firm. Account Bus Res 45(4):485–509. https://doi.org/10.1080/00014788.2015.1035549

Public Company Valuation in Emerging Markets: A Simplified and Practical Step-by-Step Approach via DCF

Adam Patterson

"The stock market is filled with individuals who know the price of everything, but the value of nothing."
—*Philip Fisher*
"Go where it is darkest: *[the]* biggest payoff is in valuing companies where there is uncertainty about the future."
—*Aswath Damodaran*
"In emerging markets, the complexity of valuations stems from their volatile environments, making it essential to ground analysis in both macroeconomic trends and company fundamentals."
—*Elroy Dimson, Professor of Finance, University of Cambridge*

Abstract This chapter offers a compendious and holistic guide to listed emerging market company valuation, seeking to integrate corporate finance theory and real-world examples in a common-sense approach. It outlines the key valuation issues and theory-based solutions to market-specific risk and opportunities, offering step-by-step procedures to estimate fundamental company value. Through a straightforward framework-based approach based on the work of multiple authors in the space, readers can gain practical knowledge of financial forecasting, cost of capital, and best practices in valuation, enhancing their abilities in analysing and interpreting stock value in these fascinating and increasingly important markets but which nonetheless provide challenges to the valuation professional.

Keywords Discounted cash flow · FCFF · FCFE · Forecasts · Cost of capital · Country risk · Perpetuity · Enterprise value · Equity value · Stocks

A. Patterson (✉)
Redirection Corporate Advisory, London, UK
e-mail: adam@redirection.com.br

S. Derindere Köseoğlu, A. Patterson (eds.), *Valuation in Emerging Markets*, Contributions to Finance and Accounting,
https://doi.org/10.1007/978-3-031-93526-8_6

Introduction

The objective of this book is to provide a comprehensive and insightful overview of company valuation and the key market factors in the emerging economy nexus and aims to do this by blending theoretical and practical foundations, covering both advanced topics in the literature and step-by-step examples. The focus of this chapter is to lay out a simplified model for valuing publicly listed emerging market firms. We will consider some of the key technical challenges and provide solutions based on valuation best practices. If the reader has read through all previous chapters of this volume before getting here, you will be well placed to quickly understand and follow through the main steps we will map out. However, the chapter also works as a standalone guide for emerging market stock market valuations even for those with only basic knowledge of corporate finance and valuation approaches, or those who would like to learn more about the subject matter. We will not seek to reinvent the valuation wheel here but try to holistically bring together the most important concepts and choices we face when valuing EM equities so readers can either conduct their own valuations or at the very least better understand the key value drivers. After all, as the philosopher Immanuel Kant once said, "it is beyond a doubt that all our knowledge begins with experience". With that being said then, let us jump into a practical EM valuation example.

Valuation Standards

We will value a listed emerging market firm to estimate if the stock currently provides an interesting investment opportunity. We will purposely generalize its location and certain characteristics to focus on the core value drivers and methods whilst maintaining consistency with key valuation principles. As always, valuation professionals should endeavour where possible to abide by International Valuation Standards (IVS 2021) as formalized by the International Valuation Standards Council (IVSC), including the purpose, basis and participants of the valuation assignment.

As such, in this chapter, the valuation is conducted to estimate the potential Investment Value of a stock. According to IVS 104, Investment Value is defined as: "The value of an asset to a particular owner or prospective owner for individual investment or operational objectives". While Market Value is often used for public stock analysis, Investment Value is often more appropriate for guiding individual investment decisions. It involves specific assumptions about cash flows, growth rates and risk factors, tailored to the investor's expectations, rather than relying on prevailing market consensus—particularly in the case of private firm investments. The exercise in this chapter is intended to support investment decision-making and provide insights into the intrinsic value of the company, which may differ from its market value due to specific market inefficiencies or external factors. Our valuation employs the Income Approach, specifically the Discounted Cash Flow (DCF) method, focusing on the company's ability to generate future economic benefits. We will also expand upon this and delve deeper into the differing types of free cash flow, such as cash flow to the firm (FCFF) or to equity (FCFE). Nonetheless, as the focus is predominantly pedagogical, we will streamline some elements here in order to illustrate a conceptual and technical approach to equity valuation which can be utilized for personal understanding and as a foundation to build in more advanced techniques and robust assumptions. As Damodaran (2012a, b) has argued, we should elect to build simpler models wherever possible, borrowing from the parsimony principle in natural sciences. In other words, if we can effectively value firms with less inputs and assumptions whilst sustaining consistency, rationality and building a solid narrative, then we should endeavour to do so. Thus, the example to follow is not meant to be exhaustive or a "perfect" valuation because in the author's opinion, such a perception at the practical level does not really exist, all valuations can be imprecise, subjective and certainly open to critiques and improvements. The objective here is to provide a working example model from scratch as a learning tool. With that caveat given, we do nevertheless have to "start somewhere to get somewhere" as the popular saying goes, so let us begin.

Setting the Scene: About the Company

We are valuing a hypothetical company headquartered and listed in a generic emerging market country in Latin America. The company is a conglomerate specializing in delivering innovative solutions across the Advertising, Entertainment and Information Services sectors. It operates in three key regions: Latin America, the United States and Asia, with limited sales and production facilities in its home country. As a company with global operations, its risk and return profile should therefore be a function of this international exposure. The world is after all increasingly globalized and connected.

We choose to value the company in US dollars as most of the markets the company operates in are dollar-based, as we will see, and it also reports its financial statements in both the local currency and US dollars. Demonstrating our example in dollars also broadens the method applicability for other markets as analysts often conduct EM valuations in the American currency. However, such an approach requires that our cash flow projections will be in dollars in both the explicit forecast period and in perpetuity and equally our costs of capital will also need to be currency and market consistent.

The company has been growing over the last few years and is profitable. It boasts revenues of $2.25 billion and operating earnings of $450 million. For developed markets this revenue level could be considered as within a broad "Mid-Cap" range but for emerging markets its relative size could indeed be larger due to the smaller size of local indexes and the impact on converting from dollars to the local currency. For instance, based on data from the Stock Analysis website (2024) the median company revenue in the S&P500 index is estimated at around $13 billion with only

Fig. 1 EM company financials. Source: Author's own creation

Headline Numbers	
Revenue LTM	$2.250
5yr Revenue CAGR	8,50%
EBIT LTM	$450,0
EBIT Margin %	20,0%
Market value of debt	$600,9
Debt Ratio	25%

around 18% of firms having revenue below $5 billion. In Mexico, the second largest stock exchange in the region after Brazil, the top 30 listed companies by revenue have a median turnover of $3.2 billion (according to data from *CompaniesMarketCap* 2024). Of course, generally speaking, different sectors (e.g., tech vs. utilities) and company lifecycles exhibit different revenue-to-market-cap ratios and opinions do vary on relative capitalization size.

We summarize below the company's most recent financial performance which will serve as the risk and return building blocks for our valuation. For listed firms, financial information is easier to gather through publicly available data sites or even paid options (Fig. 1).

For our valuation starting point we will use the LTM (Last Twelve Months) performance (Fig. 1), also sometimes known as the trailing or rolling twelve months. LTM figures are by definition more current than annual or fiscal financial statements. LTM data consequently reflect the latest performance of the business, capturing seasonality and current business conditions. In a dynamic environment, like a high-growth emerging market, where macroeconomic and/or industry conditions can shift rapidly, LTM financials are a good starting point.

We highlight that using non-annual data as the base period requires pro-forma financials as a bridge alongside the standard 5-year projection map, thus avoiding gaps between LTM and the explicit forecast period. This "stub period" is a time interval between a transaction or valuation date and the start of a financial year. It's usually a fraction of a year or quarter. Stub periods can arise for a number of reasons, such as valuation exercises conducted throughout the year and when the transaction date and valuation date are different. This means that if our LTM period is to the second quarter, we would build out a 6-month cash flow outlook on top of our five-year model and also adjust our discount periods if necessary. Or alternatively our projected periods could also be in the 12-month view, whereby the first "year" would be the next twelve months ("NTM") and so on. Here, to simplify we will skip this step and thus implicitly assume that the full base-year results will be equal to LTM performance. We also use the end of year convention for discounting cash flows. The end of year approach is often used because it is more conservative, more well-known and may work better for companies with seasonal sales patterns.

In our example, the firm was founded around ten years ago and has been listed for five years. Based on its growth prospects, product offering and the life cycle of competitor firms we estimate that the firm is still in growth mode. The length of the growth period utilized in valuation—until maturity is reached—is a function of the strength and sustainability of the company's competitive advantages. We therefore adopt a two-stage growth model with a five-year forecast period and terminal value to calculate the company's intrinsic value. As such, we assume that the firm will be in a maturity phase by year five, in line with sector averages.

Building the Growth Narrative

Arguably the most important assumptions in valuation are the growth rates in revenue and earnings which are adopted. Our estimates for revenue are of particular importance as the potential starting point for cash flow modelling. A lot of the broader assumptions, such as reinvestment and even risk, are essentially a function of this top-line number. A company with high and consistent revenue growth, which indicates a solid market position and the potential for future profitability and cash flow generation, would generally present a valuation premium.

So, what are our options to forecast this cornerstone of financial models? Methods vary based on the complexity of the core business, stage and data availability. Damodaran (2012a, b) emphasizes a bottom-up approach, where revenue is projected by analysing individual market segments and scaling them based on fundamental growth assumptions (more on this author's approach shortly). Penman (2013) suggests anchoring projections in historical performance, adjusted for macroeconomic trends and competitive dynamics. Koller et al. (2020) argue for integrating strategic insights, such as market share expectations and pricing power, into top-down or bottom-up forecasting frameworks to enhance accuracy. Taken as a whole, across the literature, there is a consensus on aligning projections with industry life cycles, cyclicality, the company's performance trends and validating them against comparable firms. Best practices also include stress-testing assumptions and reconciling revenue growth rates with reinvestment and the broader market outlook to ensure internal consistency.

Let us borrow again from Damodaran (2012a, b), who argues that there are three main ways for estimating a firm's revenue, which we will quote in full:

(a) **Historical view:** "When estimating the expected growth for a firm, we generally begin by looking at the firm's history. How rapidly have the firm's operations as measured by revenues or earnings grown in the recent past? While past growth is not always a good indicator of future growth, it does convey information that can be valuable while making estimates for the future. While this can be a useful input when valuing stable firms, there are both dangers and limitations in using this growth rate for high growth firms. The historical growth rate can often not be estimated, and even if it can, it cannot be relied on as an estimate of expected future growth".

(b) **Equity research analyst forecasts:** "The second [basic way of estimating growth] is to trust the equity research analysts that follow the firm to come up with the right estimate of growth for the firm and to use that growth rate in valuation. While many firms are widely followed by analysts, the quality of growth estimates, especially over longer periods, is poor. Relying on these growth estimates in a valuation can lead to erroneous and inconsistent estimates of value".

(c) **Looking at company fundamentals:** "The third way is to estimate the growth from a firm's fundamentals. A firm's growth ultimately is determined by how much is reinvested into new assets and the quality of these investments, with investments widely defined to include acquisitions, building up distribution channels or even expanding marketing capabilities. By estimating these inputs, you are, in a sense, estimating a firm's fundamental growth rate".

In addition, your author would suggest that we have a few other options in our forecast toolkit, which one will summarize below:

(d) **Sector-based forecasting for stable firms:** For stable or established firms, revenue forecasting can be based on sector-wide growth estimates. Using data from industry reports, top-down market share estimates and historical sector trends, this approach provides a macroeconomic and sectorial context to the performance of individual companies. This approach best applies to firms with stable revenue trends and ensures that forecasts are aligned with external benchmarks and does not over-depend on firm-specific factors. It is generally regarded as effective for consumer staples, utilities and other low-volatility industry companies (Porter 2008). Also, for stable businesses with exposure in multiple segments, a bottom-up approach can be employed with sector projections scaled by division sales, for instance.

(e) **Regression modelling on exogenous and endogenous factors:** Regression-based models offer a quantitative approach to forecasting by correlating revenue with both exogenous variables (e.g., GDP growth, interest rates and commodity prices) and endogenous factors (e.g., marketing expenditure, R&D investment). These models identify statistical relationships and correlations, which also help with dynamic scenario analysis and sensitivity testing. Regression methods are particularly valuable in emerging markets, where macroeconomic volatility requires flexible models capable of adjusting to external shocks and underlying trends. By incorporating multiple independent variables, these models enhance the robustness and credibility of revenue forecasts (Gujarati and Porter 2020; Koller et al. 2020).

(f) **Pipeline and opportunity stage forecasting:** For valuation assignments with private firms where we have the opportunity to directly engage with management, we can use pipeline forecasting by leveraging data from a company's commercial pipeline, including input from sales teams, specific leads or geographical locations, to estimate revenue. By incorporating metrics such as contract size, sales cycle length and win rates this method allows for micro level and company-specific forecasts based on their commercial and business development processes. Unit economics analytics can be used here by helping to accurately predict demand for products looking at a business's direct costs, revenues per unit and churn rates. Opportunity stage forecasting complements this approach by evaluating the likelihood of closing deals at various stages of the sales funnel or in other words, builds out probability-weighted revenue estimates aligned with company's budgets and management planning. These methods are particularly useful for firms in high-growth or project-based sectors, where deal pipelines are directly tied to revenue generation (Cohen et al. 2019).

Regardless of the chosen method, the key to robust revenue forecasting lies in aligning internal performance and capacity metrics and management outlook with external market conditions. A successful valuation narrative goes beyond simple quantitative inputs, which a spreadsheet easily accepts, and thus from answering "how much will the company grow" to addressing the "why" and "how" of growth. In a nutshell, this is the concept behind Damodaran's (2014) "possible, plausible and probable" framework. At the practical level, this involves evaluating strategic goals, consistency with cost structures, reinvestment needs and the feasibility of executing planned initiatives within the broader market demand milieu. As valuators, we of course also need to use a good dose of common sense and our own intuition to add value to our forward-looking number crunching. It is crucial to balance optimism with realism, ensuring that projected growth is grounded in achievable goals while remaining mindful of potential constraints in execution. We recall Mike Tyson's famous paraphrasing of Helmuth von Moltke: "everyone has a plan until they get punched in the mouth". The conceptual 'puncher' in this case being the market and operational realities. Once again, scenario, sensibility and Monte Carlo advanced analyses can help in this regard. This integrated approach strengthens the credibility and utility of the valuation.

Projecting Company Performance

To forecast revenue, we analyse the company's historic growth rate and recent investor relations reports, study equity analyst papers, research sector trend outlooks, and build a regression model based on economic variables. Based on this analysis, we arrive at the following range of estimates and opt to use a simple average as our headline revenue growth rate (we could of course also use a specific probabilistic weighted approach). We note two additional points at this stage. Firstly, for private firm valuations we could substitute analyst expectations for management's own forecasts—after sense checking—and secondly, here we are using a fixed revenue projection over the explicit forecast period. In a real setting, growth rates—especially when utilizing regression analysis and multiple growth phases—can, and probably should, also be presented in an annual view.

We project the company's revenue to grow at 8% each year, slightly below its 5-year average but broadly in line with the wider sector which makes sense as the company starts to reach maturity, and its product offering is expected to remain essentially stable moving forward. For companies that are active with M&A we

Fig. 2 Revenue growth estimates. Source: Author's own creation

Revenue Forecast	Expected growth %	Weighting
Historic performance	7,80%	25%
Analyst expectations	8,50%	25%
Sector forecast	8,00%	25%
Regression analysis (annual average)	7,70%	25%
Average	8,00%	100%

would also need to contemplate the potential impact of nonorganic growth on our forecasts and the accompanying cost and investment impacts (Fig. 2).

Revenue growth and profitability are the primary drivers that determine free cash flows, which are the foundation of DCF valuation models. As such, in our simplified example, we will jump straight from forecasting revenue to operating profit for the sake of brevity whilst still capturing the essence of value generation. Readers can project costs and expenses using similar methods to revenue estimates, such as analysing historical cost patterns as a percentage of revenue, analysts' expectations, sector averages or regression analysis. It is important though to really understand what you are projecting by using current cost structures. Analysts should really drill down into the financial statements and check for any potential adjustments or normalizations that can be applied. Moreover, we note that some P&L costs may behave more like fixed expenses and vice versa. This can often be the case in EMs where direct and indirect costs may have different accounting treatments, for example.

As a side note on tax, not only are effective tax rates on business profits in most Latin American countries amongst the highest in the world (CIAT 2021), but in many countries in the region, corporates are subject to additional taxes directly on revenue. These taxes, often seen in countries like Brazil (e.g., PIS/COFINS federal social taxes) and Argentina (e.g., the Gross Income Tax or *Impuesto sobre los Ingresos Brutos*), can significantly impact a company's cost structure and must be carefully accounted for in financial forecasts and valuation models. This means that international financial averages often need adjusting if applied directly, especially the difference in profit margins if measured against gross revenue or net revenue. In Brazil, for instance, it is common for financial performance ratios to be applied on net revenue.

In our example, the company currently has an operating margin of 20% (of total revenue) which has been stable but with a slight upside trend. However, with the company growing over the last few years, benefiting from past investment and starting to scale we project that the company will be able to grow its profitability over the forecast period. On analysing their recent investor relations reports and public interviews with key C-suite executives we also observe the company's strategy to improve their bottom line in the coming years in a few key areas. We estimate the impact of these efficiency gains and forecast an annual improvement over the explicit model period. Based on these potential gains, we assume that the company's profitability will eventually reach the average of the sector (we could also benchmark against specific similar companies). We do this via simple linear extrapolation between two points: the current margin, which represents point A, and the desirable or expected margin, considered point B whereby we essentially "split the difference" between the two points each year. We thus assume a smooth convergence towards industry norms through competitive forces, operations management or strategic policies that align the firm with its peer group using the conceptual basis of industrial reversion, where variances from the sector norm can self-correct over time through competitive pressures and market efficiency. Penman (2013) and Koller et al. (2020) have stated that extrapolation works particularly well when underpinned by a reasoned assessment of management's intent and capability to implement necessary changes. In our example the average operating margin of the sector is 22% and we subsequently extrapolate each year's margin as follows (Fig. 3):

For the perpetuity period we will assume a long-term growth rate of 4% in both revenues, and indirectly income, by maintaining the margin at 22%. We estimate that the current sector average margin of 22%, which has been stable, is a good indication of long-term profitability for both the sector and the company. We also set our long-term risk-free rate at 4% which is our estimate for the long-term real growth rate in the local economy. This assumption is implicitly self-correcting, as if we have under or overestimated growth, we should see a similar impact on reinvestment and discount rates. In valuation, all assumptions are connected.

Putting all this together gives us the following financial projections (Fig. 4):

Fig. 3 Estimating EBIT. Source: Author's own creation

Margin Forecast (%)	
Current LTM margin	20,0%
Expected EBIT margin year 1	20,4%
Expected EBIT margin year 2	20,8%
Expected EBIT margin year 3	21,2%
Expected EBIT margin year 4	21,6%
Expected EBIT margin year 5	22,0%

P&L	**LTM**	**Year 1**	**Year 2**	**Year 3**	**Year 4**	**Year 5**	**Perpetuity**
Revenue	2.250,0	2.430,0	2.624,4	2.834,4	3.061,1	3.306,0	3.438
Revenue Growth		8,0%	8,0%	8,0%	8,0%	8,0%	4,0%
Operating Income (EBIT)	450,0	495,7	545,9	600,9	661,2	727,3	756,4
EBIT Margin %	20,0%	20,4%	20,8%	21,2%	21,6%	22,0%	22,0%
Projected EBIT Growth %		10,2%	10,1%	10,1%	10,0%	10,0%	4,0%

Fig. 4 Revenue and profit estimates. Source: Author's own creation

Going with the (Cash) Flow: From Dividends to Free Cash Flow

Early DCF models focused primarily on dividends as the basis for firm valuation, exemplified by the dividend discount model (DDM), formalized by Gordon and Shapiro (1956). The constant-growth form of the DDM, also known as the Gordon growth model, is considered the most common and straightforward calculation of a dividend valuation model. These approaches were well-suited for firms with stable dividend policies but became less applicable as the financial landscape evolved, particularly with the rise of growth companies that retained earnings to finance expansion or used share buybacks. Moreover, dividends are paid at the discretion of the company's management and therefore may not indicate the company's long-run ability to generate cash returns, especially from a majority shareholder point of view. Such limitations of the DDM led to a search for broader valuation frameworks. Authors such as Miller and Modigliani (1961) started to shift the valuation focus to earnings and cash flows, laying the groundwork for Free Cash Flow (FCF) methodologies, which started to gain traction from the 1980s.

Stewart (1991) was amongst the first to popularize "free cash flow" as a valuation tool in corporate finance, while Copeland et al. (1990) helped develop the specific use of the two distinct but related concepts of free cash flow to the firm (FCFF) and equity (FCFE) which could be used in mergers and acquisitions and financial analysis. These frameworks addressed the need to evaluate firm value independently of payout policies, thus making them adaptable for both equity and enterprise-level assessments. FCFF considers cash flow returns available to all providers of capital which are discounted by the cost of capital, whereas FCFE narrows the focus to equity holders after taking into account debt obligations and are discounted based on the cost of equity. Both approaches are now central to company valuation. Data from the CFA Institute (2024) states that 86.9% of market analysts use discounted free cash flow models for value estimates.

Free cash flow approaches have been well discussed by multiple modern authors in the literature. Writers such as Damodaran (2002), Penman (2013) and Pablo Fernándezndez (2019) et al all emphasize their adaptability, complementarity and solid financial foundations. Of course, the challenge is in having to estimate these hypothetic cash flows. Information on dividend payments and policies is readily available, free cash flow not so much. Nevertheless, this is the key point: we are interested in understanding the firm's effective capacity to remunerate capital owners and not only what they effectively pay out.

We quickly summarize both formulas:

$$\begin{aligned} \text{FCFF} = \text{EBIT}(1 - \text{Tax Rate}) &+ \text{Depreciation and Amortization} \\ &- \text{Capital Expenditures} - \Delta \text{ Working Capital} \end{aligned}$$

$$\text{FCFE} = \text{Net Income} + \text{Depreciation and Amortization} - \text{Capital Expenditures} - \Delta\ \text{Working Capital} + \text{Net Borrowings}$$

Both approaches estimate equity value, be it directly (via FCFE) or indirectly (via FCFF). In the FCFF view, the value of equity can be derived from the firm's value by subtracting the market value of debt. This can simplify the valuation process by avoiding direct consideration of debt-related cash flows. The firm approach is recommended when the firm has shifting leverage (and thus simplifying estimating debt-related cash flow assumptions) about and most commonly used in M&A valuation and deal structuring processes, private equity and leveraged buy outs and for debt restructuring or credit analysis. The equity approach is usually the method of choice for stock valuations, venture capital and dividend or stock buy-back analysis. The author would suggest that FCFE is potentially the optimal approach from a purely theoretical viewpoint as it can be understood as more of a "real" cash flow, debt payments are a reality for most firms after all. The use of FCFE also helps us simplify sometimes complex assumptions of debt ratios we need arrive at the WACC over the forecast period. However, according to the CFA Institute (2024), FCFF models are used approximately twice as frequently as FCFE variants. And yet, for all this underlying academic deliberation, in our example we will illustrate that the value for equity estimated from the FCFF and FCFE approaches should yield the same results if consistent assumptions are made about growth and debt.

We will now continue our company valuation example jumping from the P&L to cash flow forecasts. Before we do however, let us cover one more key assumption—that of reinvestment. In valuation, reinvestment generally means the sum of capital investment and net working capital that the firm needs to make to maintain its operations and support growth investments. Depreciation and amortization, non-cash adjustments from the P&L should also be added back into our free cash flow. In general terms, we adopt a similar toolkit from the same options used to project revenue, such as historical ratios (capex and NWC as a percentage of sales or the sales/capital ratio), industry specific averages or analyst or management expectations.

We can also utilize one of the methods which we previously cited but purposely didn't compute in our weighted revenue approach, that of fundamental growth projections. We pick up the concept at this point. Penman (2013) highlights that the reinvestment rate should align with the return on invested capital (ROIC) to ensure sustainable growth. In this view, reinvestment is tied to the efficiency of capital utilization, with firms requiring lower reinvestment if their ROIC significantly exceeds the cost of capital. Damodaran (2003) states that "With both historical and analyst estimates, growth is an exogenous variable that affects value but is divorced from the operating details of the firm. The soundest way of incorporating growth into value is to make it endogenous, i.e., to make it a function of how much a firm reinvests for future growth and the quality of its reinvestment. The reinvestment rate measures how much a firm is ploughing back to generate future growth". He goes on to provide a quantitative framework which we will cite below for the FCFF model:

$$\text{Reinvestment Rate} = \frac{\text{NOPAT}}{\text{Net Capital Expenditures} + \text{Change in Non Cash Working Capital}}$$

$$\text{Fundamental Growth Rate (g)} = \text{Reinvestment Rate} \times \text{Return on Invested Capital (ROIC)}$$

Please note that for FCFE we adjust our formula by basing it around net income and new debt and adopting the return on equity as our return metric. Ultimately, accurate reinvestment estimation involves a nuanced understanding of a firm's operational dynamics, and where it is in its growth cycle, and broader industry context. What should be clear is that this approach links growth to reinvestment and that we can estimate either growth or reinvestment by altering the formulas. In our example, as we already have our revenue growth rate, we will utilize the fundamental model to quantify reinvestment and compute a marginal tax rate for the company of 40%. Based on the firm's previous investments and current metrics, we estimate a return on capital of 18% over the forecast period (Fig. 5).

To exemplify, we arrive the reinvestment rate percent of 56.4% in the first forecast year by dividing the expected growth in EBIT by our return on capital, or:

$$\text{Reinvestment rate } \% \text{ in year } 1 = 10.2\% \times 18.0\% = 56.4\%$$

$$\text{Reinvestment in year } 1 = \text{NOPAT of } 297.4 \times 56.4\% = 167.9$$

We can sense check the projected reinvestment by also calculating the implied sales/capital ratio over each year and compare it to the broader sector or specific comparable firms. We do this and confirm that our reinvestment is in line with market performance. The ratio is computed here by calculating the delta in sales

Free Cash Flow	**Year 1**	**Year 2**	**Year 3**	**Year 4**	**Year 5**	**Perpetuity**
Operating Income (EBIT)	495,7	545,9	600,9	661,2	727,3	756,4
Taxes	198,3	218,4	240,4	264,5	290,9	302,6
NOPAT	297,4	327,5	360,5	396,7	436,4	453,8
Reinvestment Rate (% NOPAT)	56,4%	56,2%	56,0%	55,8%	55,6%	30,8%
Implied Sales/Capital	*1,07*	*1,06*	*1,04*	*1,02*	*1,01*	
- Reinvestment	167,9	184,1	201,8	221,2	242,4	139,6
FCFF	129,5	143,4	158,7	175,5	194,0	314,2

Fig. 5 Cash flow projections. Source: Author's own creation

Fig. 6 Sales/capital sense check. Source: Author's own creation

Benchmarking	Sales/Capital
Company 1	0.94
Company 2	1.01
Company 3	1.08
Company 4	1.15
Setor average	**1.05**
Valuation average	**1,04**

between two periods and dividing by the projected reinvestment of the latter period. We could also integrate a "lag" into the formula and assume that the reinvestment in one period will generate returns in future periods. Moreover, we could directly employ sector specific or company target sales/capital ratios to calculate reinvestment needs, and thus invert the fundamental formula. The formula for year one in our simple approach is as follows (Fig. 6):

$$\text{Sales/Capital ratio in year 1} = \frac{(\text{Revenue } \Delta \text{ year 1} - \text{Revenue } \Delta \text{ LTM})}{\text{Reinvestment in year 1}}$$

$$\text{Sales/Capital ratio in year 1} = \frac{(2430 - 2250)}{169.9} = 1.07$$

Calculating WACC

With our financial projections in place, we now calculate our cost of capital. Your author covers this theme comprehensively in chapter seven of this book so we will streamline here.

In order to estimate the WACC for a listed company, we rely on bottom-up betas derived from the global market segments the firm operates in. These provide more accurate and assertive unlevered betas with this approach, as these reflect the risks of the specific industries the company operates in rather than relying on a single potentially noisy historical beta for the company itself. In our analysis, the firm operates across three distinct divisions: Advertising, Entertainment and Information Services, and we calculate a simple average beta weighted proportionally by the sales contribution of each division.

For country risk, we incorporate a weighted country risk premium based on the firm's sales distribution across multiple regions. This approach recognizes that the company's exposure to regional risks varies with its geographic operations. The total ERP—a function of the regional marginal CDS plus country relative stock market/bond volatility inputs—is then added for each region by adding the default spread for sovereign risk to the mature market premium. This balances regional exposure while enhancing the accuracy of the overall cost of equity estimate. Combining segment-specific unlevered betas with regional risk premiums results in a WACC that reflects

Sector	Unlevered beta	% Revenue
Advertising	1,09	20,0%
Entertainment	0,95	40,0%
Information Services	0,96	40,0%
Weighted Beta	0,98	100%

Fig. 7 Bottom-up betas and weighted CRPs. Source: Author's own creation

Global Sales breakdown	Proportion of Sales	Total ERP	Marginal CRP
Latin America	50%	12,50%	7,80%
Asia	25%	10,20%	5,50%
United States	25%	4,70%	0,00%
Weighted Total ERP		9,98%	5,28%

Fig. 8 Weighted CRPs. Source: Author's own creation

both operational diversification and geographic exposure, two key characteristic of implied company risk (Figs. 7 and 8).

With these assumptions we now calculate our WACC. To simplify the iteration, we will estimate a single cost of capital for the forecast period and perpetuity. We remind the readers that our financial projections are in US dollars and as such so will our WACC. Our CAPM model assumes that the company's exposure to country risk is similar to its exposure to other market risk and adjusts the beta formula accordingly. As a last sense check we would analyse against cost of equity computations for similar listed firms.

We calculate the cost of debt using the risk-free rate as the base and add a firm-specific synthetic spread based on its interest rate coverage derived from global metrics as well as a weighted country risk spread based on its operations in different regions (we do however need to be mindful of potential double counting and overestimated debt costs). Our pre-tax cost of debt is therefore 10%. We use the corporate tax rate of 40% as our tax shield to arrive at the after-tax cost of debt of 6% which we consider to be in line with the company's debt payments and local market realities. Please note that we compute the debt/equity ratio based on our debt ratio of 25% through the following formula (Fig. 9):

$$\mathrm{D/E\ ratio} = \frac{0.25}{1-0.25} = \frac{0.25}{0.75} = 0.33$$

CAPM	
Risk Free Rate (Rfr)	4,00%
Total Equity Risk Premium (ERP)	9,98%
Beta	1,18
CAPM	**15,77%**
Beta	
Unlevered Beta (βu)	0,98
Marginal Tax Rate	40,00%
D/E	33,33%
Total Levered Beta	**1,18**
Cost of Debt	
Risk Free Rate (Rfr)	4,00%
Company Synthetic Default Spread	2,00%
Weighted Countries Default Spread	4,00%
Pre-Tax Cost of Debt	10,00%
CorporateTax Rate	40,00%
Net Cost of Debt %	**6,00%**
Summary: WACC Computation	
Equity %	75,00%
Cost of Equity %	15,77%
Debt %	25,00%
Net Cost of Debt %	6,00%
WACC	**13,3%**

Fig. 9 Company weighted average cost of capital. Source: Author's own creation

Putting It All Together: Firm Value

For the terminal value calculations, we assume long-term growth in revenue of 4% and the operating margin stable at 22%. We adjust our long-term return on capital to 14%, our estimate of the long-term return metric for well-established firms in the sector. This is slightly more than our WACC of 13.3% which implies a conservative and sustainable level of value creation above capital costs and thus avoids unrealistic growth assumptions or excessive ROC in perpetuity. Our growth narrative assumes that the company will eventually reach industry averages for profitability and reinvestment.

The company has a current debt of $600.9 which is equivalent to a debt ratio of 25%. This debt ratio implies a capital structure where debt accounts for 25% of total financing and equity accounts for 75%. In our pedagogical example to simplify we will allocate the debt and equity components as percentages directly to enterprise value. Under this assumption, the firm's value (EV) is allocated proportionally to debt and equity holders. By subtracting the debt portion (25%), we isolate the equity value (75%) which also includes cash and cash equivalents. This proportional approach simplifies the process while maintaining consistency with our capital structure assumptions. At the practical level we would directly subtract net debt to arrive at the equity value. Moreover, we would also need to carefully analyse any leasing commitments, contingent liabilities, crossholdings and minority interests for other adjustments.

These "final adjustments" to firm value are especially important for EM companies to ensure compliance with the International Valuation Standards. These adjustments account for unique risk factors and structural complexities which can be more prevalent in these markets. For instance, contingent liabilities—such as unresolved labour disputes, environmental remediation obligations, off-balance-sheet obligations or tax penalties—are more commonly encountered in emerging markets, where regulatory environments are often less predictable and more litigious (IVSC 2021).

Emerging market firms also tend to exhibit a higher incidence of crossholdings. This is largely a legacy of family-owned businesses and economic conglomerates that utilize cross-shareholding arrangements to maintain control over key assets. For example, in regions like Latin America and Asia, public companies often retain intricate ownership webs as a by-product of historical corporate governance practices (Khanna and Yafeh 2007). These are holdings that need to be carefully unravelled during valuation so as not to double-count value, misallocate liabilities or under or overestimate firm values. Moreover, minority interests are also common. We also need to account for less rigid reporting requirements than those prevailing in more developed economies (Damodaran 2012a, b) which can be adjusted for in adjusted earnings—especially for private firms—or as final adjustments to value.

Our base case valuation yields an estimated value for the firm of $2403.5 and an equity value of $1802.6. We divide the equity value by the company's 173.5 thousand fully diluted shares to arrive at a value per share of $10.4, significantly above the current market price of $7. This looks like the stock is undervalued with an upside potential of close to 50%. We could run scenario analysis, sensitivity and Monte Carlo modelling (or even simple error margins) to confirm that the stock is an attractive investment (Fig. 10).

Before we move on to our reconciliation of the FCFF and FCFE models we will illustrate how we can include Monte Carlo methods into our valuation.

Monte Carlo analysis is a powerful tool that can enhance valuations by simulating a wide range of possible outcomes based on uncertain variables, both endogenous and exogenous. This method uses probability distributions for key inputs—such as revenue growth, cost of capital or reinvestment rates-generating thousands of possible scenarios to create a distribution of valuation outcomes (Mun 2006).

Fig. 10 Valuation results (1/2). Source: Author's own creation

Firm value via FCFF	
Operating Cash Flow Present Value	545,1
Perpetuity	3.474,3
Present Value Perpetuity	1.858,4
Enterpise Value	2.403,5
Minus Debt	600,9
Total Equity Value	1.802,6
Number of shares	173,5
Projected value per share	10,39
Current share price	7,00
Current price as % of Estimated Value	67,4%
Potential upside	48,4%

In the context of emerging markets, such analysis can be of particular value. As we have seen EMs present increased volatility in factors such as exchange rates, political instability and economic growth and we can employ this statistical approach to model stochastic processes, to capture a range of possible outcomes and their impact on cash flows. Doing so not only refines valuation precision but also helps investors better understand tail risks associated with EM investments (Copeland et al. 2000). As always, valuation should be understood as a dynamic process and narrative rather than a single fixed—and "correct"—number.

We would add that in asset valuation, the concept of assigning a single point estimate of value is mathematically implausible, as the probability of any precise number occurring is effectively zero in a continuous probability distribution (Mun 2006). This stems from the inherent nature of valuation as a probabilistic process, influenced by numerous inputs—such as revenue growth, discount rates and reinvestment needs—that are subject to variability and uncertainty. Not to mention, a reasonable amount of valuator opinions, which may change during or after the analysis.

Thus, valuation is not just a purely mechanical exercise but rather driven by a series of storytelling processes, with assumptions around growth, risk and reinvestment driving a spectrum of firm value (Damodaran 2012a, b). Therefore, the final valuation can be best expressed as a range of values, reflecting the sensitivities of key drivers and the uncertainty inherent in forecasting future cash flows.

Ultimately, the integration of Monte Carlo methods into valuation models reflects the dynamic realities of EM environments and provides stakeholders with more robust, risk-adjusted insights. A full step-by-step approach to Monte Carlo is beyond the scope of this chapter—for more information please see, for instance, Copeland and Antikarov (2003) and Mun (2006)—but we will quickly run a Monte Carlo analysis, purely for illustration purposes, to close out our FCFF valuation.

We create probability distributions, both upside and downside, for several key value drivers from our example, such as revenue growth, expected margins, return on capital and reinvestment rates over the forecast and perpetuity periods and run 10,000 simulations. Our variable ranges can be based on historical volatility in

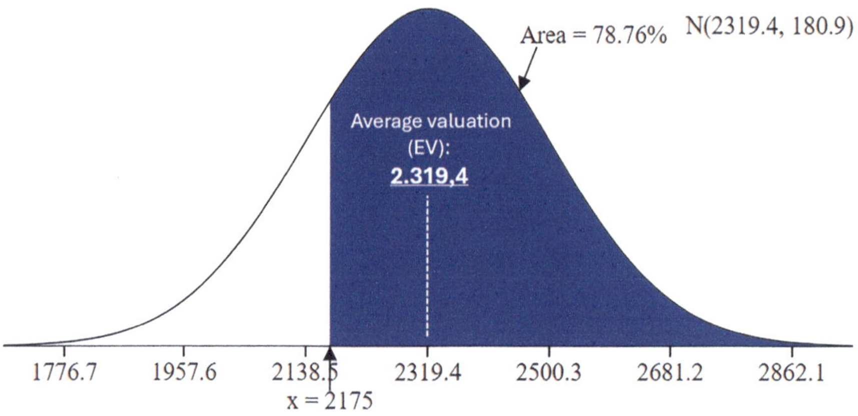

Fig. 11 FCFF Monte Carlo simulations. Source: Author's own creation

company performance, sector inputs or forward-looking estimates. We arrive at an average Enterprise Value of $2319.4 with a standard deviation of results of $180.9. This is slightly less—by 3.5%—than our base case valuation of $2403.5 but still broadly in line with our value narrative. Based on the distribution of results and subtracting company debt, we estimate a probability of ~79% that the potential upside in the stock could be at least 30% (Fig. 11).

Valuing Equity Directly via FCFE

Without much further ado, we will now run our valuation through the FCFE approach to directly estimate the company's equity value with the main objective to show how with consistent inputs the FCFF and FCFE approaches should yield the same results. In this exercise we seek to streamline for demonstration purposes and will therefore overtly simplify a few steps in the analysis.

We summarize our key assumptions below:

- We calculate the accumulated debt position using our 25% debt ratio based on the projected EV firm value each year. For interest expenses we use our pre-tax cost of debt of 10% and calculate based on the debt position of the previous year (see Fig. 12 below). We maintain the debt and equity proportions constant throughout the analysis.
- Net income is a function of EBIT less interest expense and tax payments based on our corporate tax rate of 40%.
- In this example, we will utilize the same reinvestment rate and subsequently the annual dollar amounts from the FCFF model to maintain alignment with the firm's overall growth trajectory and capital allocation strategy. Nonetheless, whilst we will use the same reinvestment figures to illustrate, in the interests of

Debt Position	LTM	Year 1	Year 2	Year 3	Year 4	Year 5	Perpetuity
Debt at end of period	600,9	648,6	699,2	752,7	809,2	868,6	903,3
+ Net Debt Issued		47,7	50,6	53,5	56,5	59,4	

Fig. 12 Capital structure projections. Source: Author's own creation

P&L	LTM	Year 1	Year 2	Year 3	Year 4	Year 5	Perpetuity
Operating Income (EBIT)	450,0	495,7	545,9	600,9	661,2	727,3	756,4
Interest Expense		60,1	64,9	69,9	75,3	80,9	86,9
Earnings Before Tax (EBT)		435,6	481,0	531,0	585,9	646,4	669,6
Taxes		174,3	192,4	212,4	234,4	258,6	267,8
Net Income		261,4	288,6	318,6	351,6	387,8	401,7
Net margin %		10,8%	11,0%	11,2%	11,5%	11,7%	
Free Cash Flow	**LTM**	**Year 1**	**Year 2**	**Year 3**	**Year 4**	**Year 5**	**Perpetuity**
Net Income		261,4	288,6	318,6	351,6	387,8	401,7
- Reinvestment		167,9	184,1	201,8	221,2	242,4	129,7
+ Net Debt Issued		47,7	50,6	53,5	56,5	59,4	34,7
FCFE		141,2	155,1	170,3	186,8	204,8	306,8

Fig. 13 Consolidated P&L and cash flow forecasts. Source: Author's own creation

Fig. 14 Valuation results (2/2). Source: Author's own creation

Equity value via FCFE	
Present Value of Equity Cash Flows	549,8
Perpetuity Value	2.605,7
Present Value Perpetuity	1.252,8
Total Equity Value	1.802,6
Number of shares	173,5
Projected value per share	10,39

brevity, that at a theoretical and practical level, reinvestment for FCFE would typically need to be calculated based on the growth rate in net income and the return on equity, rather than EBIT and the cost of capital, which underpins our FCFF. Nevertheless, with consistent assumptions, the reinvestment amounts in both the Free Cash Flow to Firm (FCFF) and Free Cash Flow to Equity (FCFE) models should be the same as the inputs are intrinsically linked.

- We will discount FCFE at the same cost of equity at the same value of 15.77% as obtained from our above WACC estimate.
- We will maintain the long-term assumptions for terminal value as used in our FCFF model, in a ceteris paribus view (Fig. 13).

Based on these simplified assumptions and model inputs we arrive at the same equity value as per the FCFF model at $1802.6 and estimated value per share of $10.4. We note that in the context of FCFE, cash is not added back to the final result, only surplus cash should be considered. The underlying reasoning is that operating cash that is not surplus is already considered in the capital structure of the firm (Fig. 14).

Closing Thoughts

In this chapter we have provided a comprehensive step-by-step approach to estimate value for a hypothetical listed emerging market firm and better understand the key valuation drivers and valuator thought processes. The objective was to discuss key concepts and techniques throughout the process, get a handle on the fundamental components of free cash flow and reconcile the FCFF and FCFE models. We have covered revenue and income projections, reinvestment methods and cost of capital calculations and in doing so provided a simplified toolkit for readers to conduct their own valuations. I hope we have shown that on the whole, the EM valuation game adopts the same principles as for developed firms but with enhanced nuances and methods to better quantify risks and returns.

Valuing businesses in emerging markets requires not just employing numbers and spreadsheet inputs but a deep understanding of macrolevel trends such as local market behaviours, from market uncertainties and opportunities, supply chain inefficiencies and consumer demand shifts in addition to specific firm-level planning, operational and execution factors. In doing so, the author hopes readers will gain heightened cognizance of not only stock prices but most importantly stock value in emerging markets.

References

CFA Institute (2024) "Free Cash flow valuation", 2024 curriculum. https://www.cfainstitute.org/insights/professional-learning/refresher-readings/2024/free-cash-flow-valuation#:~:text=Of%20those%20using%20discounted%20free,is%20in%20near%20universal%20use. Accessed 16 December 2024

CIAT (2021) Should Latin America and the Caribbean Countries cut taxes on corporate profits to stimulate investment and growth? https://www.ciat.org/ciatblog-should-latin-america-and-the-caribbean-countries-cut-taxes-on-corporate-profits-to-stimulate-investment-and-growth/?lang=en. Accessed 16 December 2024

Cohen WA, et al (2019) The art of strategic forecasting

CompaniesMarketCap (2024) Company rankings by market capitalization. Available at: https://companiesmarketcap.com (Accessed: December 2024).

Copeland T, Antikarov V (2003) Real options: a practitioner's guide. Texere

Copeland T, Koller T, Murrin J (1990) Valuation: measuring and managing the value of companies. Wiley

Copeland T, Koller T, Murrin J (2000) Valuation: measuring and managing the value of companies. 3rd edn. New York: John Wiley & Sons.

Damodaran A (2002) Investment valuation: tools and techniques for determining the value of any asset. Wiley

Damodaran A (2003) Growth and valuation. https://pages.stern.nyu.edu/~adamodar/New_Home_Page/valquestions/growth.htm. Accessed 16 December 2024

Damodaran A (2012a) Investment valuation. Wiley

Damodaran A (2012b) Damodaran on valuation: security analysis for investment and corporate finance. Wiley. https://pages.stern.nyu.edu/~adamodar/pdfiles/valn2ed/ch11.pdf. Accessed 16 December 2024

Damodaran A (2014) Applied Corporate Finance. 4th edn. Hoboken, NJ: John Wiley & Sons.
Fernández P (2019) Company valuation methods: the most common valuation methods. IESE Business School. Available at: https://papers.ssrn.com/sol3/papers.cfm?abstract_id=2749721 (Accessed: December 2024).
Gordon MJ, Shapiro E (1956) Capital equipment analysis: the required rate of profit. Manag Sci 3(1):102–110
Gujarati DN, Porter DC (2020) Basic econometrics. McGraw-Hill
International Valuation Standards (2021) International Valuation Standards Council. https://www.ivsc.org/standards. Accessed 16 December 2024
Khanna T, Yafeh Y (2007) Business groups in emerging markets: paragons or parasites?, J Econ Literature 45(2):331–372. https://doi.org/10.1257/jel.45.2.331.
Koller T, Goedhart M, Wessels D (2020) Valuation: measuring and managing the value of companies. McKinsey & Company, Wiley
Miller MH, Modigliani F (1961) Dividend policy, growth, and the valuation of shares. J Bus 34(4): 411–433
Mun J (2006) Modeling risk: applying Monte Carlo simulation, real options analysis, forecasting, and optimization techniques. Wiley
Penman SH (2013) Financial statement analysis and security valuation. McGraw-Hill Education
Porter ME (2008) Competitive strategy: techniques for analyzing industries and competitors. Free Press
Stewart GB (1991) The quest for value: a guide for senior managers. HarperBusiness
Stock Analysis (2024) Website, "S&P 500 Stocks". https://stockanalysis.com/list/sp-500-stocks/. Accessed 16 December 2024

Emerging Market Valuation Multiples

"It's All Relative"

Alexandre M. Scherer Borborema

Abstract Relative valuation is one of the most popular methods for valuing assets and companies for a range of purposes, due to its reliance on readily available market data and the simplicity of applying valuation multiples. While this intuitive method is used globally, its application in emerging markets requires specific adjustments to account for increased risks and volatility. This chapter begins by covering the basics of multiples-based valuations, followed by an examination of the unique challenges in using this method in emerging economies. Currency and inflation volatility, accounting inconsistencies, lack of comparable companies, and potential market inefficiencies make it much more difficult to apply this approach in those regions. It also evaluates solutions proposed by a number of authors to address such challenges, from normalizing financial data to adjusting multiples to account for differences between the benchmarks and the target firm. One of these adjustments involves cross-border corrections, which are recommended when multiples are imported from the developed world to be applied in emerging markets. The chapter then provides a detailed step-by-step guide to help practitioners apply the method efficiently, by using both comparable companies and precedent transactions. These concepts are illustrated with a practical example of valuing a fictitious Brazilian company, highlighting the limitations of some adjustments and the importance of professional judgment in interpreting relative-value analysis in these dynamic regions.

Keywords Relative valuation · Market approach · Valuation multiples · Comparable companies · Precedent transactions · Emerging markets · Country risk · Discount for lack of marketability · Cross-border adjustments · Regression analysis · Benchmark selection · Normalization adjustments · Market volatility · Value drivers · Private companies valuation

---

A. M. Scherer Borborema (✉)
Investment Banking, Apex Partners, Vitoria, Brazil

S. Derindere Köseoğlu, A. Patterson (eds.), *Valuation in Emerging Markets*, Contributions to Finance and Accounting,
https://doi.org/10.1007/978-3-031-93526-8_7

Relative Valuation Overview

When buying or selling goods or services, market prices are often used to establish a reference point. Valuing equity follows the same basic logic. In relative valuation, the market price of similar companies is used as a reference to value a business, based on multiples of its sales or earnings, for example. Given its simplicity and reliance on observable prices, it is one of the most popular valuation methods among decision-makers and practitioners.

Imagine the owner of a food distribution company from Colombia, seeking a valuation estimate to decide whether to open negotiations with a potential buyer or not. As information about local players was not available, he searched for US data and found that distributors there are trading at an average of 0.6x Revenues. Based on last year's revenues of $100 million, already adjusted for tax recovery, he could then estimate his company's value at around $60 million.

Of course, applying the method in practice is never that easy. His approach overlooked several important factors:

- Can US multiples be used as a reference for valuing companies in Colombia? If yes, how can multiples be applied across countries?
- Was a revenue multiple the best choice or would another metric be more suitable?
- Are multiples of publicly traded securities appropriate for valuing a controlling interest in a private company?
- How does the Colombian distributor's performance compare to the American peers, and how should differences be addressed in the valuation?
- Beyond the tax recovery adjustment, were other adjustments needed?
- Do the accounting practices align with the criteria used to calculate the US comparable financials?

If not used correctly, this case shows how misleading relative valuations can be.

This chapter provides an overview of relative valuation, its key principles, applications, strengths, and limitations. It then examines why applying this method in emerging markets is more challenging and discusses solutions. Following a step-by-step guide, the chapter concludes with a practical example, by valuing a Brazilian company in the apparel and textile sector. The case was designed to demonstrate the real-world challenges and solutions of applying this approach in an emerging market.

Conceptual Background of Relative Valuation

While discounted cash flow (DCF) models estimate intrinsic value based on expected cash flows, relative valuation derives value estimates from what the market is paying for similar assets. Therefore, it is classified as a market approach.

As defined in IFRS 13: "The market approach uses prices and other relevant information generated by market transactions involving identical or comparable (i.e., similar) assets, liabilities or a group of assets and liabilities, such as a business" (International Accounting Standards Board 2011, p. 713).

Valuation multiples, or ratios, are calculated from comparable companies using observed market prices and relevant financial metrics. If necessary, these multiples are adjusted and applied to the target company—the firm being valued.

An obvious parallel can be drawn from real estate markets. Just as property values are determined by analyzing the prices of similar assets recently sold in the area—considering factors such as size, location, and amenities—relative valuation compares companies to their peers. While a house is often valued as a multiple of its size (e.g., USD/square meter), companies can be valued as a multiple of a value indicator, such as revenues or earnings.

For the purpose of relative valuation, similar companies are referred to as benchmark companies, comparables, or guideline companies.

The general formula for calculating multiples is as follows:

$$\textbf{Multiple} = \frac{\textbf{Market Value of Benchmark Company}}{\textbf{Value Indicator}}$$

Where:

- **Market Value of Benchmark Company**: The numerator represents the benchmark company's market price as of the valuation date, expressed either as Enterprise Value (EV) or Equity Value. Equity Value commonly includes all classes of stock. Enterprise Value equals equity value plus all interest-bearing debt, net of surplus cash.
- **Value Indicator**: The denominator can be a financial or a non-financial metric, such as revenue, earnings, or even industry-specific measures like number of subscribers or units sold. The value indicator should match the returns available to the capital classes used in the numerator.

Benchmark Companies: Types and Definition

Benchmark companies provide an observable reference for the market value of a wide range of businesses, which can be used to value firms with similar characteristics. Benchmarks can be drawn either from public or private markets, using the two approaches below:

Comparable Companies Approach (CCA)

This method involves compiling the trading prices of public companies with similar characteristics and deriving their market multiples. As market data is readily available for many different sectors, this is an approach commonly used in the market.

The challenge is finding CCA benchmarks similar to the company being valued, especially if the target company is privately owned.

Precedent Transaction Approach (PTA)

Also referred to as comparable transactions, this technique analyzes the resulting multiples of mergers and acquisitions (M&A) transactions. Unlike CCA, which relies on public market data and theoretical models, PTA reflects real-world deal dynamics, whether the acquisition involves 100% ownership, a controlling or a non-controlling stake. This makes it a particularly good tool for valuing private businesses, as prices are grounded in actual M&A deals.

The problem with PTA is sourcing reliable information, as private markets are far less transparent and data sets are often unreliable, as the metrics used to calculate multiples are often not disclosed. Another challenge is that many of these M&A deals include stock swaps, non-competes, and earnouts, which complicate even more direct comparisons of multiples. In addition, PTA captures the synergies and premiums paid by the acquiring company, which are deal-specific and hinder comparability.

Defining Similar Companies

Identifying firms identical to the target company is obviously not possible, so the goal is to find benchmarks with reasonable similarities.

A common approach is to pick benchmarks from the same industry, as they are exposed to the same market forces and have similar cost structures, business models, and investment cycles.

Damodaran (2012) and Pratt et al. (2000) caution against over-relying on same-industry and same-country benchmarks, which is a strategy commonly used by analysts, as it is an intuitive and convenient way to group peers. Instead, these authors suggest that clustering firms by value drivers, such as growth, risk, and cash flow characteristics, may improve the accuracy of the method. This is supported by Serra and Fávero (2018), who find that clustering provides more precise estimates in the valuation of firms in Brazil than the industry-based grouping.

Conversely, Koller et al. (2020) acknowledge the utility of same industry comparables, but they argue that such definitions are too broad. They suggest that selecting a smaller group of peers that compete in the same markets or subsectors is more effective.

Despite these authors' slightly different views, they all agree that adjusting for differences in economic fundamentals enhances the accuracy of relative valuations.

Choosing benchmark companies depends on the quality and quantity of available market data, as will be reviewed in more detail later in this chapter.

Assumptions and Relationship with DCF Valuations

Relative valuation is based on two key assumptions:

- **Efficient Market Hypothesis (EMH):** The market is efficient and, on average, correctly prices stocks.
- **Going-Concern Assumption:** The target company will continue to operate and generate profits indefinitely.

Under these assumptions, market prices should reflect the factors that drive value in discounted cash flow models: growth, risk, and cash flow generation (Damodaran 2012). Therefore, in an efficient market, it is possible to infer that prices of a going concern firm provide the best available estimate of value, as they reflect the intrinsic value of assets.

This implies that valuation multiples are linked to the fundamental determinants of value, which can be mathematically demonstrated. Assuming a stable-growth model, where firms are treated as perpetuities, a widely known framework proposes that Enterprise Value (EV) can be expressed by the following simplified formula:

$$\mathbf{EV = FCF/(WACC - g)}$$

where

- **FCF:** Free Cash Flow to Firm.
- **WACC:** Weighted Average Cost of Capital.
- **g:** Perpetual Growth Rate.

As FCF can be expressed as a function of an earnings metric, Koller et al. (2020) derive the following Value Driver Formula, also widely discussed in the literature:

$$\mathbf{EV = \frac{NOPAT \times (1 - Reinvestment\ Rate)}{WACC - g}}$$

Where:

- **NOPAT (Net operating profit after taxes)** = EBIT × (1 – T), with T being the corporate tax rate.
- **Reinvestment Rate** = g/ROIC, which represents the fraction of NOPAT reinvested to sustain growth, where ROIC is Return on Invested Capital.

As NOPAT can be translated into different earning metrics, the Value Driver Formula can be expressed as a valuation multiple. For example, if we express EBIT as a function of NOPAT and divide the formula by EBIT, the Value Driver Formula can be represented as an EV/EBIT multiple as follows:

$$\mathbf{EV/EBIT = \frac{(1 - T) \times \left(1 - \frac{g}{ROIC}\right)}{WACC - g}}$$

This equation shows the connection between the DCF and relative valuation methods, illustrating how multiples are influenced by fundamental drivers of value.

While these mathematical developments are useful in showing the link between multiples and value drivers, they have little practical application. This is because these formulas are based on a theoretical stable-growth model and simplistic assumptions that do not reflect real-world conditions.

Advantages and Applications

The popularity of relative valuation arises from some significant advantages:

1. **Intuitive:** It is intuitive to look at the prices of similar companies in the market to substantiate valuation, hence easier for investors and clients to understand.
2. **Simple and Accessible:** Compared with DCF valuation, using market multiples is far simpler and more accessible.
3. **Speed**: Relative valuation allows for much quicker company value estimates than DCF, which requires detailed forecasting, a great deal of assumptions, and calculations of discount rates.
4. **Market Relevance**: It is empirical proof of value based on actual market quotations or transactions and, therefore, reflects current sentiment in the market better than DCF. Furthermore, this approach agrees with the belief that a business is worth what someone will pay for it.

Because of these advantages, relative-value analysis has a wide range of practical applications.

Together with the income and cost approaches, the market approach is one of the techniques recommended by IFRS 13 for measuring the fair value of assets and liabilities. Therefore, it is used globally to support valuations for accounting, tax, and legal purposes.

They also play a pivotal role in mergers and acquisitions, equity research, capital markets transactions, restructuring, private equity, and venture capital. Furthermore, they are used as a benchmarking tool, as they help identify if a stock is under or overvalued, supporting investment decisions and corporate strategies.

Relative valuation is also used in the Exit Multiple Method for calculating the terminal value in DCF valuations, as an alternative to the Gordon Growth Model.

Finally, it enables cross-checking the results of DCF valuations. If the implied multiples differ significantly from comparables, this may indicate issues with the DCF assumptions or model.

Drawbacks and Limitations

Despite the advantages outlined in the previous section, a multiples-based valuation has some severe limitations:

1. **Not Suitable in Some Cases:** The method cannot be appropriately applied for valuing distressed firms. It also has limited application for companies that report negative earnings or show very low revenues.
2. **Difficulty of Finding Truly Comparable Firms**: This approach is effective only if benchmarks share truly similar characteristics in comparison to the company being valued. As discussed earlier, this is somewhat challenging. In this scenario, analysts commonly pick same-industry companies as peers. Most of the time, selected peers differ widely from the target company, which diminishes the reliability of the analysis.
3. **Market Inefficiencies**: If the market is inefficient, for any reason, and companies are therefore under or overvalued, using multiples under these circumstances can lead to flawed conclusions.
4. **Lack of Firm-Specific Information**: DCF valuations inherently incorporate critical value drivers, including risk, growth rate, and cash flow profiles. Relative valuation, however, is based on market multiples, which do not consider such company-specific fundamentals, unless specific techniques and adjustments are adopted.
5. **Risk of Overvaluation:** In bullish markets, focusing on multiples can easily lead to overvaluation of the target company. In 2021, low interest rates and excess venture capital propelled most startup valuations to stratospheric levels. This is a great example of the danger of following market sentiment instead of the economic fundamentals.
6. **Limited Forward-Looking Perspective**: Unlike DCF models, which are inherently forward-looking, relative valuation typically uses this year's or next year's earnings as a value indicator. This creates the risk of overlooking the target company's long-term potential or the capital required to sustain its growth.
7. **High Potential for Errors**. Relative valuation is very easy to misuse. Many factors can lead to inaccuracies in the valuation analysis.

Commonly Used Multiples

As per the general formula shown earlier, multiples can be calculated either from equity value or Enterprise Value (EV). The most common valuation multiples used by practitioners are shown in Table 1.

By choosing appropriate multiples, the valuation process can be tailored to the characteristics of the company being valued.

Table 1 Valuation Multiples Definitions and Utilizations

EV/Sales or EV/Revenue (Enterprise Value-to-Sales)	Particularly useful for valuing companies with low or negative earnings, such as early-stage startups or firms in cyclical downturns. It provides insight into how much value the market assigns per dollar of revenue. When the margins of the benchmarks and the target company differ significantly, EV/Revenue may not be a good choice
EV/EBITDA (Enterprise Value-to-EBITDA)	One of the most popular ratios. EV/EBITDA neutralizes the effects of differing capital structures and tax regimes and excludes non-cash charges like depreciation and amortization, making it a good option for cross-border and cross-sector comparisons. However, it may not capture cash flow needs in capital-intensive industries, as it ignores CAPEX
EV/EBIT (Enterprise Value-to-EBIT)	EV/EBIT is particularly useful in asset-intensive industries, where depreciation acts as a proxy for future CAPEX required to replace assets. By deducting depreciation, EBIT provides a closer approximation of future cash flows, making it more suitable than EV/EBITDA in these situations
P/E (Price-to-Earnings)	This equity multiple is commonly used for valuing mature, profitable companies but is less reliable across different tax regimes. Some authors, like Koller et al. (2020), caution against its use as a valuation tool, as it combines the effects of capital structure and non-operating items with operating earnings
P/B (Price-to-Book)	This ratio compares the market value of a company's equity to its book value. P/B is particularly useful for valuing financial institutions and asset-heavy businesses, where book value approximates the value of underlying assets. Analysts also use this multiple to identify potentially undervalued stocks, focusing on companies trading at a discount to peers
EV/Operating Metrics	These multiples are calculated relative to non-financial, industry-specific operating metrics. Examples include number of subscribers or users (telecoms, video streaming, SaaS, social media), tons of production or reserves (steel manufacturing, mining, paper & pulp), and number of students (education). Particularly valuable in industries where operating metrics are key drivers of value. It is also useful for valuing early-stage companies, where financial metrics may not yet indicate true future potential

Source: Author

Using Relative Valuation in Emerging Markets

With a population over 4.3 billion, emerging markets contributed 66.7% of global GDP growth between 2013 and 2023 (World Economics 2025). The rise of emerging markets in the global scenario is seen through an increase in publicly listed companies, cross-border acquisitions, and the expansion into developed markets of firms such as Brazil's Vale, Mexico's América Móvil, and India's Tata Group.

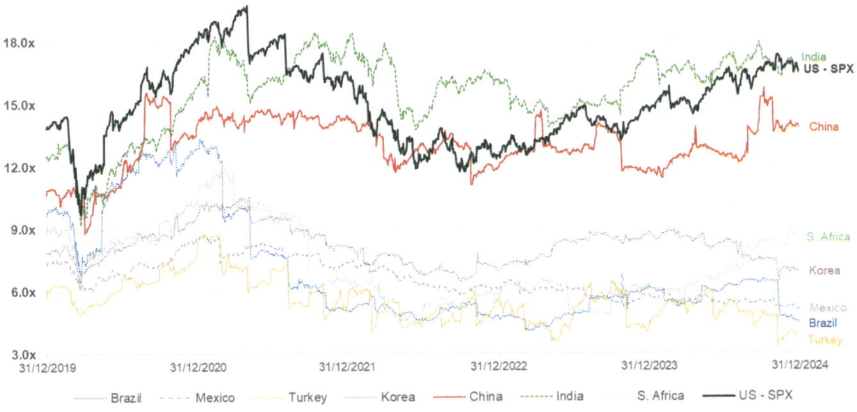

Fig. 1 EV/EBITDA Evolution 2019–2024: US vs Selected Emerging Markets. Source: Bloomberg (*Note*: All data extracted from Bloomberg were not verified for potential inconsistencies)

Robust demographics, higher growth rates, and appealing entry valuations are increasingly attracting investors to these regions, which can deliver attractive returns. This is demonstrated by the International Finance Corporation's 2500 minority equity investments in emerging economies between 1961 and 2019, which delivered an average return that was 15% higher than the S&P 500 (Cole et al. 2020).

While their potential is undeniable, the path is not without hurdles. Many emerging economies experience increased country risk. As a result, stocks in most of these markets trade at a discount to those in the United States, except for India and China, where multiples have generally remained more level with the SPX, as illustrated by Fig. 1.

Despite growing interest, literature on relative valuation in emerging markets remains limited. Most of the works are centered on DCF, which leaves relative valuation less explored. Damodaran (2009) and Pereiro (2002) are some of the few renowned authors who have examined the challenges of relative valuation in emerging economies and proposed solutions to them.

This section examines how country-specific factors influence multiples, the challenges of using multiples in emerging markets, as well as common adjustments and solutions to overcome these challenges. It integrates insights from key literature and the author's own perspectives to balance theory with actionable strategies.

Challenges of Using Multiples in Emerging Economies

The unique characteristics of emerging markets not only affect valuation multiples but also introduce challenges and uncertainty into the relative valuation process.

This section examines these issues, which have been highly debated by authors like Pereiro (2002), Damodaran (2009), Guimaraes and Koller (2021), and Koller et al. (2020).

1. **Volatility**

   Currency and inflation volatility are defining characteristics of many emerging markets. While inflation erodes purchasing power, currency depreciation can significantly reduce returns in US dollars. A notable example is Turkey, which experienced an accumulated currency depreciation of over 1400% against the US dollar between 2015 and 2025.
2. **Lack of Comparable Companies**

   The small number of publicly listed firms in emerging markets makes it very difficult to identify comparables within most industries (Pereiro 2002). At the end of 2023, while there were over 5700 companies listed on the NYSE and Nasdaq combined, Brazil, South Africa, and Mexico had only 344, 284, and 131 listed companies, respectively (Statista 2023). This scarcity often forces analysts to rely on benchmarks from developed markets, which is an approach that does not take into account country-specific differences (Damodaran 2009; Serra and Fávero 2018; Pereiro 2002).
3. **Precedent Transaction Data Scarcity and Inconsistencies**

   If finding comparable companies within public markets is already challenging, sourcing precedent transactions in emerging countries is even harder, as many of these deals involve private companies. Key details are often undisclosed or based on inconsistent criteria, which makes reliable comparisons difficult.
4. **Higher Country Risk**

   As discussed in previous chapters, country risk relates to the additional uncertainty associated with investing in a specific country. In emerging markets, volatility, weaker institutions, and economic instability amplify this risk, which varies from country to country.

   Corporate performance can also be impacted by complex tax frameworks, burdensome bureaucracy, corruption, and inefficient legal systems. Consequently, even well-managed firms remain vulnerable to these broader country characteristics (Damodaran 2009; Guimaraes and Koller 2021).

   Regulatory uncertainty is another risk factor in some countries, as illustrated by a Provisional Measure in Brazil in 2012. This measure established new requirements for the renewal of concessions in the energy sector, such as compulsory tariff reductions without adequate financial compensation. By directly affecting the returns of private concessionaires, this government measure created a temporary perception among market analysts of increased regulatory risk in the country.
5. **Inconsistent Accounting Practices and Disclosure Levels**

   Even after the implementation of IFRS in many countries, the differences in accounting practices remain. Also, the extent of disclosure in emerging markets is often less comprehensive than in developed markets, which makes cross-border comparison even more difficult.

6. **Market Inefficiencies and Limited Liquidity**
   Underdeveloped and inefficient capital markets are common characteristics of emerging economies. Reduced liquidity complicates comparability with multiples from other markets, as less liquid assets are normally traded at discounted prices.
   Market interventions and investor restrictions in countries like China and India lead to disequilibrium in supply and demand, which in turn distorts share prices, as noted by Koller et al. (2020). Another inefficiency is the dominance of retail investors in China, who constitute 75% of holdings, whereas in the United States, institutional investors are the majority shareholders. Retail investors usually lack financial expertise and advanced research capabilities; hence, they tend to show herd behavior, which creates high price volatility. These factors make it even more difficult to align fundamentals with market prices.
7. **Corporate Governance**
   Concentrated family ownership, privileged voting rights, and crossholdings are not uncommon in some emerging markets. All these factors work against managerial accountability and hence increase minority shareholders' risks, as Damodaran (2009) notes.
8. **Nationalization Risks**
   Companies from some emerging markets may be subject to the risk of governmental expropriation or takeover. Past nationalizations suggest that such a risk is more acute in industries with national strategic importance, such as natural resources and energy (Damodaran 2009).

Solutions for Overcoming Challenges

This section examines solutions to overcome the main challenges in carrying out multiples-based valuations in emerging markets.

Widening Benchmarks Across Countries and Industries

As discussed previously, identifying benchmarks from the same industry and country is rather difficult in these markets. According to Damodaran (2009), three approaches may be used to widen the sample:

1. Look for Companies from Different Positions in the Value Chain.
   Assuming that companies within a value chain are subject to similar risks and value drivers, enlarging the industry definition can help analysts find more comparables. For example, if the target company manufactures fish feed, the pool of benchmarks could be expanded to include not only animal feed producers but also aquaculture companies.
   As highlighted earlier, although Damodaran (2012) acknowledges the popularity of same-industry, same-country grouping, he advises against over-reliance

on this approach, as economic fundamentals may differ substantially between companies in the same industry.

2. Same-Sector Benchmarks from Other Countries.

   For the extension of the sample size, benchmark companies from other emerging countries could be used, as theoretically they have similar risk profiles. Seeking comparables from developed markets is also an option to increase the number of benchmarks.

   However, if companies within the same industry and country already show significant differences, these become even more pronounced once a cross-border element is introduced. Valuable work on this theme was developed by Serra and Fávero (2018). They looked into intra-industry variability between Brazilian and US stock exchanges and among firms grouped by their fundamentals, by analyzing eight different valuation multiples between 2011 and 2014. Their research showed so much variability in the average industry-wide multiples between the two countries that they advise against the application of American multiples while valuing a firm in Brazil.

3. Seek Benchmarks with Similar Economic Fundamentals from Other Sectors.

   By clustering companies based on economic fundamentals rather than solely on industry classifications, sample homogeneity and accuracy of the value analysis improve, as benchmarks share key value drivers in intrinsic valuations (Damodaran 2012).

   While Pereiro (2002) also emphasizes the efficacy of clustering benchmarks based on economic fundamentals, he comments that few practitioners are proficient in the statistical testing that needs to be done to carry out and interpret a cluster analysis.

Normalizing Benchmarks' Metrics for Standardization

When applying market multiples across countries, Damodaran (2009) and Pereiro (2002) highlight that accounting standards might vary, which requires normalizing metrics for a like-for-like comparison. While IFRS implementation increased standardization, accounting differences still exist in some countries.

Adjusting Multiples

Depending on how peers are selected, the group may include companies with varying characteristics such as size, ownership control, liquidity or marketability of shares, country risk exposure, and economic fundamentals. Furthermore, in the case of PTA, the dates of precedent transactions can vary widely.

To address such differences, a variety of adjustments and other solutions can be applied, as discussed below.

Main Multiples Adjustments

Cross-Border Adjustments

Pereiro (2002), Serra and Fávero (2018), and Damodaran (2009) agree that overseas benchmarks can be used, as long as they are adjusted for region-specific conditions.

One of the techniques for this adjustment suggested by Damodaran (2009) is to break the sample of intra-industry comparables into two groups: developed and emerging markets. Then, cross-border adjustments can be estimated by taking the ratio of the mean multiples of these two samples. In a similar approach, Pereiro (2002) also uses cross-border adjustment coefficients, but instead of calculating the ratio based on same-industry groups, he relies on country-wide averages.

When importing multiples, it seems obvious that some sort of adjustment would be required to reflect the specific conditions of the target firm's country. The difficulty, however, lies in calculating a reliable adjustment. In our view, the problem with these coefficients is that they are based on an overly simplistic assumption that only country differences are driving variations in valuation ratios and that a linear relationship exists. However, numerous studies indicate that country membership accounts only partially for variation in multiples.

For instance, Serra and Fávero (2018) show that, other than country exposure, industry and firm-specific characteristics are also very relevant in explaining differences in valuation ratios between American and Brazilian public firms.

A study by An et al. (2010) that carried out a statistical analysis on firms based in 33 countries over the period from 1990 to 2006 found that, although country and industry membership do matter, a substantial portion of the variability in valuation ratios is attributable to company-specific factors. Similarly, a study by Norges Bank (2019) evaluating global equity returns from 1975 to 2018 shows that country effects accounted for only 30% of the variance, on average.

The work of Gaio (2009) shows an even less significant role of country factors, which account for no more than 8.5% of the variation in earnings quality within the sample. By studying the determinants of firms' earnings in 38 countries from 1990 to 2003, she found that much of this variation was dominated by firm-level factors.

Guimaraes and Koller (2021) also contributed to this discussion by developing a set of assumptions and calculations to show that stock valuations in some emerging markets do not appear to incorporate a country risk premium at all.

Consequently, despite being intuitive and partially supported by empirical evidence, cross-border adjustments often represent a simplistic assumption that fails to account for all factors driving differences in multiples across borders.

Moreover, since country-risk premiums and cross-border adjustments are often applied uniformly across a nation, the impact of differences between regional markets within a country remains an underexplored area of research.

Regions from a specific country can differ significantly in terms of development, governance, infrastructure, and economic stability. Some areas are wealthier, more urbanized, and backed by stronger institutions, while others face bigger challenges, creating different levels of risk exposure. Even though macroeconomic factors might influence all regions similarly, local conditions can result in very different operational environments. Because of this, applying the same cross-border adjustment everywhere can penalize companies operating in more developed regions.

In light of these complexities, relative valuations in an international setting are extremely difficult to perform. This may help explain why cross-border corrections are not commonly used by practitioners.

Time-based Adjustments

As outlined by Damodaran (2006), valuation multiples of both public and private companies vary over time either because of changes in the fundamentals or in the market perception of risk.

Unlike publicly traded company analyses, where market prices align with the valuation date, the dates of M&A transaction can vary significantly.

As a result, Pratt et al. (2000) and Pereiro (2002) emphasize that multiples derived from precedent transactions occurring at different times should be adjusted to account for changes in market conditions and investors' evolving sentiments. The authors suggest that time-based adjustments can be made by analyzing the variance in the average valuation multiples of public companies from the transaction date to the valuation date. However, because public market data is used to calculate adjustments, this approach has limitations, as the relationship between public market multiples and M&A deal multiples is not fixed over time.

Illiquidity Discounts

Selling publicly traded stocks is usually a straightforward process that can be completed very quickly, at a marginal cost, for a price generally known in advance. In addition, in most cases, it is almost guaranteed that the trade will be completed.

Now compare this with the challenges and significant uncertainties in selling a controlling stake in a private business—a complex process that can easily take many months, without any guarantee of success, and with much higher transaction costs, including advisory and brokerage fees. Add to this the fact that the sale price will be known only at the end of M&A negotiations.

The difficulty, time, and costs associated with selling less liquid assets explain why illiquidity discounts should exist. This should not be confused with the minority interest discount (or lack of control discount), which is a different concept, discussed later in this section.

After understanding the concept of the illiquidity discount, also known as the discount for lack of marketability (DLOM), a practical question is what level of discount should be applied when valuing private companies based on public market multiples?

As Damodaran (2006) explains, it is just not possible to answer this question empirically, considering that such discounts are not directly observable in the case of private companies. In light of this limitation, DLOM estimates can be based on the price differences between restricted stocks and their publicly traded counterparts. In the United States, these discounts range from 25% to 35%, according to Damodaran (2006). Other studies cited by Pratt et al. (2000) and DePamphilis (2019) point out similar discount ranges.

Damodaran (2006) adds that the DLOM can be adjusted based on the specific characteristics of the target company. Furthermore, DePamphilis (2019) provides a helpful list of factors that can be considered to adjust this discount, including company size, liquid assets as a percentage of total assets, financial performance, and leverage.

Control Premium

When buying a controlling stake in a company, many buyers would be willing to pay a control premium related to the economic benefit of making strategic decisions, appointing executives, and influencing dividends distribution.

Based on different works that analyzed acquisition price premiums paid in public market deals, Pratt et al. (2000) explain that measuring the control premium is not easy, as it often also includes synergies. In addition, the range of premiums present high variability and include some below-market value transactions, leading to implied negative control premiums.

According to Damodaran (2006), the value of control is company-specific, being higher for poorly managed companies and lower for well-managed ones. Similarly, DePamphilis (2019) asserts that "if the target business is to be run as currently managed, no control premium should be added (p. 280)."

While control can justify a premium, acquiring a minority interest can be subject to a discount, due to the lack of influence over corporate decisions.

Regression Analysis

Through regression analysis, it is possible to estimate how a dependent variable relates to independent variables, allowing the prediction of their interactions.

Running regression analysis can help identify how market multiples relate to different financial metrics of the benchmark companies. According to many scholars, regression is one of the most effective methods to account for differences in economic fundamentals within the peer group. Damodaran (2006) highlights that multiple linear regression can even be used to control for differences in liquidity, measured by the turnover ratio of comparables.

Even though it may look like a sophisticated solution to the challenges of performing relative valuations, regression analysis has some relevant weaknesses, as outlined by Damodaran (2012). One weakness is multicollinearity, as independent variables such as growth, risk, and payout ratios can be correlated, which hinders the reliability of regression coefficients. Another limitation is that regression models are time-sensitive, given that the influence of variables changes over time. Moreover, "the regression is based on a linear relationship between PE ratios and the fundamentals, and that might not be appropriate" (Damodaran 2012, p. 362).

A Step-by-Step Guide to Relative Valuation

In this section, we introduce a general four-step framework for performing relative-value analysis, with specific adjustments for emerging markets.

Step 1: Analysis and Adjustments of the Target Company's Financials

Before getting into research and market data analysis, understanding the target firm's operations and financials is crucial to guide important decisions ahead in your relative-value analysis. This step can be broken down into the following key activities.

Compilation of Financial Data

Based on the financial statements and management accounts collected from the target company, the valuation process starts with the compilation of financial and non-financial information from previous years.

Data Normalization

For comparability against the benchmark firms, the target company's financials must be adjusted for the following items:

- **Non-Recurring Items:** Adjust reported earnings for extraordinary gains and losses (e.g., asset sales, one-off revenues, tax-credit recoveries from prior periods, litigation settlements, natural disasters).
- **Accounting Standards:** To neutralize differences in accounting practices, analysts should standardize depreciation methods, useful lives of assets, inventory valuation techniques (e.g., FIFO vs. LIFO). This requires understanding the practices adopted in the comparables' financial statements.

- **Non-Operating Assets:** Adjust the influence on earnings of non-operating assets, such as excess cash and equity investments.
- **Taxes:** Normalize taxes for an effective rate, eliminating the effect of non-recurring deferred taxes, tax credit compensations, or loss carryforwards.

In the case of private businesses, specific challenges may arise when applying multiples. Closely held businesses tend to have weaker internal controls and less reliable financial reporting than listed companies, with a higher risk of manipulative accounting by the owners. This can include understated earnings, with the objective of reducing taxable income, or inflated earnings, in anticipation of a financing round or potential sale of the company.

In light of these characteristics of privately held firms, additional adjustments may be needed, including:

- **Owner Expenses:** Eliminate the effect of family perks or use of business assets for personal purposes.
- **Executive Compensation:** When part of the executives' compensation is done through dividends, this needs to be adjusted to industry standards, to allow comparability.
- **Real-Estate Assets**: When the company's balance sheet includes operational real estate assets, it is recommended to impute a market rent expense adjustment to normalize the financial performance of the company for the economic cost of owning property.
- **Misstated Revenues and Expenses:** Find and correct all misstated revenues and/or expenses—an important adjustment to reflect the company's real earnings.

Private company adjustments are widely known by practitioners and extensively discussed in the literature, by authors such as DePamphilis (2019), Pratt et al. (2000), Damodaran (2006, 2012), and Koller et al. (2020).

Data Analysis and Definition of Value Indicators

Following data normalization, the resulting financial metrics must be carefully analyzed to determine: (i) the most appropriate value indicator(s) to perform the relative valuation (i.e., the metrics to be multiplied by the guideline multiple in Step 4) and (ii) the most suitable time period for measuring value indicator(s).

As discussed below, the financial characteristics of the target company will drive the selection of the most appropriate value indicator(s):

- **Positive Earnings:** If the company being valued has consistently positive earnings, is no longer in its early stages, and is not going through a cyclical downturn, then using earnings-based multiples like EV/EBITDA, EV/EBIT, or P/E is generally appropriate. EV/Sales may also be used as a complementary multiple.
- **Asset-Intensive Industries:** For companies that require significant capital expenditure to maintain or replace assets, the EV/EBIT multiple might be more suitable than EV/EBITDA. As EBIT accounts for depreciation, which approximates the

cost to replace assets, this value indicator provides a closer reference to future cash flows.

- **Early-Stage Companies with Negative Earnings:** For early-stage companies with low or negative earnings, using revenue or operating-metric multiples may be the only appropriate option for performing a relative valuation.
- **Companies in Financial Distress:** Given that companies in financial distress fail to meet the going concern assumption, in these cases asset-based approaches or restructuring scenarios would be more appropriate than relative valuation.

The chosen value indicator (e.g., EBITDA, EBIT, Revenues) can be calculated for different time periods, including:

- Last 12 months (LTM)
- Latest fiscal year
- Average of previous years
- Forecasts of future years (which then requires using forward-multiples).

Analyzing the following factors can help identify the most appropriate time period:

- **New Revenues/Expenses Not yet Materialized:** In B2B companies, the loss or win of contracts can substantially affect future earnings. In addition, expenses for the mobilization of these new contracts are typically incurred before the revenue recognition. In these cases, using forecasted value indicator(s) instead of historical figures is recommended to reflect the effect of losing or gaining these contracts. Historical data can also be applied, as long as it is normalized to account for the impact of contract losses or gains.
- **Cyclical Industries:** Performance fluctuations caused by economic cycles and price volatility are not uncommon in some sectors, such as commodities and manufacturing. In such cases, Damodaran (2012) does not recommend using a single year as the time period, as there is a risk of basing the valuation on a peak or a trough within the cycle. Instead, he recommends using the average earnings over an entire business cycle, adjusting for inflation variance throughout the period, especially in emerging markets.
- **Extraordinary Events:** If financial metrics were affected by extraordinary events, these periods should be excluded from the value indicators' calculation. For example, the COVID-19 pandemic severely impacted various sectors, which required careful adjustments for a more accurate representation of the typical performance.

Step 2: Benchmarks Identification and Evaluation

In this step, market data of similar companies is gathered and analyzed to support the selection of the benchmark companies to be used.

Search for Same-Country and Same-Industry Benchmark Companies

As a starting point, you can search for comparable companies and precedent transactions from the same country and industry as the target company. Depending on the number and quality of comparables, this should provide enough data for a reasonably good relative-value analysis.

Expand the Search

If the search provided few comparables, additional benchmark companies may be identified from: (i) the same industry but operating in different countries or (ii) other industries with similar fundamentals.

Normalize and Adjust Benchmark Companies Data

To ensure comparability, many authors recommend adjusting the financial statements of benchmarks, to normalize differences in accounting standards, capital structures, one-off events, non-operating items, among others. This is an activity that seldom analysts do, as it requires digging deeper in the benchmark companies' financial statements. Doing this properly significantly increases the time dedicated to performing the relative valuation.

Prepare Market Data and Select Comparables

Compiling organized tables is key to narrowing down the list, as per the activities below:

- Compile the gathered and normalized market data in tables.
- Keep comparable companies and precedent transactions separate, as they will be subject to different adjustments, as discussed in Step 3.
- Select companies that align most closely with the target company's operational and financial characteristics.
- Based on the value indicator(s) chosen in Step 1 to value the target company, namely, Net Revenues, EBITDA, Net Income or another, analyze such metric in the selected list of benchmark companies compiled.
- Ensure that the multiple is defined consistently and that it is measured uniformly across the firms being compared.
- Complete data gaps, by conducting additional research.

Excluding Outliers

In certain periods, earnings may fall to exceptionally low levels, resulting in disproportionately high earnings multiples. Such outliers can distort the analysis and should be excluded.

Mitigate Potential Earnings Multiples Bias

When using earnings multiples, firms with negative earnings in the peer group are excluded from the multiple calculation, as EV/EBITDA or P/E multiples cannot be computed. In such situations, Damodaran (2012) recommends aggregating the market values of all benchmark companies, including loss-making firms, and calculating multiples based on the combined values.

Calculate a Single Valuation Multiple

After calculating the valuation multiples for each benchmark company, they must be consolidated into a single value. This can be done by calculating the mean and median. For reasonably large samples, Damodaran (2012) emphasizes that median values are generally more representative of the typical firm in the group. Running a regression analysis can also help derive a single value for the multiple.

Validate the Size and Quality of the Sample

The number of comparables required depends on the degree of similarity and data availability. When close matches are available, which is rare, even a small group of four to six companies can be effective, as noted by Damodaran (2012) and Pratt et al. (2000).

Given that the expanded search will most likely produce benchmarks with varying characteristics, adjustments are needed, as detailed in Step 3.

Step 3a: Adjustments to Multiples of Comparable Companies

Once benchmarks have been selected, the single-value multiples calculated in Step 2 should be adjusted before being applied to the target company.

Cross-Border Adjustments

Pereiro's (2002) book provides a table with P/E correction coefficients for eight different emerging markets, calculated against NYSE market data from 1995 to 1999.

Based on data extracted from Bloomberg, Table 2 presents a more up-to-date comparison of the average EV/EBITDA in eight emerging economies relative to the United States, with the corresponding country-wide cross-border corrections, as recommended by Pereiro:

As discussed earlier, these coefficients seem to oversimplify the reasoning behind differences in multiples across countries. For instance, if calculated using Damodaran's (2009) technique, these cross-border adjustments would have resulted in distinct coefficients. Table 3 illustrates the difference between Brazil-wide

Table 2 EV/EBITDA and Cross-border Adjustment Factor

Mean EV/EBITDA									
Year	Argentina	Brazil	Mexico	Turkey	Korea	China	India	S. Africa	U.S.-SPX
2020	3.3x	10.8x	7.2x	6.3x	8.2x	12.1x	12.7x	8.6x	14.5x
2021	3.0x	8.3x	7.9x	6.6x	9.4x	14.4x	17.0x	9.3x	17.6x
2022	2.6x	5.1x	6.5x	5.1x	7.3x	12.9x	16.1x	5.5x	13.4x
2023	4.0x	5.1x	5.9x	4.9x	8.1x	12.8x	15.2x	5.9x	13.7x
2024	10.1x	5.8x	5.5x	5.0x	8.0x	13.0x	16.8x	7.1x	15.9x
Cross-Border Adjustment Factor: Mean EV/EBITDA Emerging Market/U.S Market									
2020	0.23	0.74	0.49	0.43	0.57	0.83	0.87	0.60	1.00
2021	0.17	0.47	0.45	0.38	0.53	0.82	0.97	0.53	1.00
2022	0.19	0.38	0.49	0.38	0.54	0.96	1.20	0.41	1.00
2023	0.29	0.37	0.43	0.36	0.59	0.93	1.10	0.43	1.00
2024	0.64	0.37	0.35	0.31	0.51	0.82	1.06	0.45	1.00
Mean	**0.30**	**0.47**	**0.44**	**0.37**	**0.55**	**0.87**	**1.04**	**0.48**	**1.00**

Source: Bloomberg

Table 3 Cross-border Adjustment Factor Comparison

Market-wide vs Industry-specific Averages Across U.S. and Brazil					
	2020	2021	2022	2023	2024
Country-Wide Cross-border Adjustment	**0.74**	**0.47**	**0.38**	**0.37**	**0.37**
Industry-Specific Cross-border Adjustment between Brazil and the U. S					
Electric	0.55	0.47	0.59	0.66	0.51
Food	0.29	0.38	0.33	0.48	0.33
Paper	0.71	0.57	0.46	0.63	0.47
Steel	0.64	0.71	1.27	0.92	0.64
Software Industry	0.89	0.43	0.70	0.70	0.45

Source: Bloomberg

EV/EBITDA adjustments and NYSE for the period 2020 to 2024, compared to the US/Brazil adjustment for specific industries.

The adjustments proposed by Damodaran were calculated as the ratio of mean multiples for the same industry between Brazil and the United States. In practice, using this technique ends up being mathematically identical to simply relying on Brazil's industry averages to value the target firm, aside from any exclusion of outliers or fine-tuning of the peer group. Therefore, it seems that this approach does not add much value to the analysis.

Applying Illiquidity Discounts and Control Increases

If the valuation ratios of listed companies are used as a reference to value a private company, analysts should apply DLOM. A size adjustment can also be added, if the target company is much smaller than the benchmarks, as noted by Damodaran (2006), Pratt et al. (2000) and explicitly adjusted for by Pereiro (2002).

While seeking country-specific DLOM references would be preferable to using US-based data, local references in emerging economies are often unavailable.

Some non-exhaustive examples of DLOMs and control increases for US and non-US markets are highlighted in Table 4.

Pereiro (2002) recommends applying the multiplicative method, so that the effects of control increases and DLOM are computed in a way that accounts for their combined effect. This will depend on the target company's characteristics relative to each benchmark company.

Table 4 Discount for Lack of Marketability (DLOM) and Control Increases

Adjustment Type	Author	Non-US	US
DLOM	Pereiro (2002)	Small Companies: 67.6%[a]	Small Companies: 52%[a]
		Larger Companies: 34.9%[a]	Larger Companies: 40%[a]
	Damodaran (2006)		25%–35%
	Pratt et al. (2000), summary of empirical studies on restricted stock		23%–45%
	DePamphilis (2019)		5%–35%
	Koeplin et.al, cited by Pereiro (2006)	23%–54%	20.4%
Control Increase	Pereiro (2002)	38.7% (Argentina)	31%–36%

Sources: Damodaran (2006), Pereiro (2002, 2006), Pratt et al. (2000), and DePamphilis (2019)
[a]Combined effect of Illiquidity Discount end Size Increase, applying the multiplicative method, used by Pereiro (2002)

Doing Regressions

As outlined in the previous section, running a regression analysis can be a useful approach to control for differences in risk, growth, and cash flow profiles among comparables. With the resulting regression equation, analysts can account for these differences.

Step 3b: Adjustments to Precedent Transaction Multiples

If the PTA sample includes deals from previous periods, a time-based adjustment should be calculated, based on the change in average valuation multiples of public companies between the comparables' transaction date and the target company's valuation date.

When both the target company and the benchmarks from your PTA group are privately owned businesses, applying DLOM is not needed.

Step 4: Target Company Valuation Based on the Adjusted Multiples

The final step is the simplest one. It basically consists of multiplying the adjusted single-value multiples by the target company's value indicators, as summarized below:

1. **Compile a Summarized Data Table:** Organize in a table the target company's value indicators chosen in Step 1, next to the adjusted single-value multiples calculated in Step 3.
2. **Calculate the Relative Value**: Multiply the target company's adjusted financial indicators (e.g., normalized EBITDA) by the adjusted single-value multiple, keeping PTA and CCA valuation results separate. If for any reason it is important to have a single consolidated valuation result, this can be calculated by assigning weights to the PTA and CCA results.
3. **Cross-Validate the Results**: Compare results of your CCA and PTA work with other valuation approaches and verify if they make sense and align with market realities.

These steps can help analysts address some of the limitations of relative valuations through careful selection and adjustment of comparables and metrics.

Practical Example

This section presents a relative valuation of a fictitious privately owned company from Brazil. This practical case was designed to illustrate real-world challenges and complexities of applying multiples in an international setting.

Target Company Background

Our target company is Teresense Commerce and Apparel Industry Ltd. (Teresense)—a Brazilian privately held company founded in 2012 by two partners. Teresense is a retailer and wholesaler of clothing and accessories, with a portfolio of known brands focused on the men's fashion segment. The company started as a small local brand, exploring elements of their hometown culture and heritage. Gradually Teresense grew into a prominent player in the Brazilian apparel sector, adding other brands to its portfolio.

In line with the model followed by the largest apparel companies in Brazil, Teresense is involved in every stage of the value chain, including the design, production, marketing, and sale of clothing and accessories.

Its main sales channels include multi-brand stores, own retail locations, and an e-commerce platform. With revenues of approximately BRL 440 million in 2024 (approximately USD 81 million), Teresense has been delivering strong growth rates in the past years. Headquartered in the city of Vitória, in Southeastern Brazil, it also boasts distribution centers that facilitate sales all around the country.

As the owners were approached by a larger company interested in acquiring Teresense, this valuation aims to estimate the company's value, assuming a full sale of the business.

Data Analysis and Normalization

The consolidated financial information of the company is summarized in Table 5.

Based on the reported financial data and on information provided by the management team of Teresense, EBITDA from the past 3 years was normalized, as shown in Table 6:

The conducted normalizations and adjustments are described below:

(a) Adjustment for non-recurring revenues of USD 1.6 million in 2024.
(b) A market rent was imputed to its own retail stores to provide a more comparable and accurate representation of Teresense's operating performance.
(c) As the owners' compensation as executives is paid through tax-free dividends, a corresponding expense at market levels was included as an adjustment. This is because dividend is a cash outflow that does not impact EBITDA.

Table 5 Teresence: Key Financial Metrics (All Figures in USD thousand[a])

Income Statement (year ending 31/Dec)	2022	2023	2024
Net Revenues	**46,669**	**70,285**	**81,493**
(−) Cost of goods sold	(14,012)	(19,936)	(21,967)
Gross Profit	**32,657**	**50,349**	**59,526**
(−) Operating Expenses	(20,583)	(31,745)	(38,724)
EBITDA	**12,073**	**18,604**	**20,801**
EBITDA Margin	25.9%	26.5%	25.5%
(−) Depreciation & Amortization	(14,033)	(13,823)	(12,219)
EBIT	**(1960)**	**4781**	**8583**
(+/−) Financial Revenues/Expenses	(4358)	(5068)	(7189)
(+/−) Non Operating Result	1617	3486	4376
PBT	**(4701)**	**3199**	**5769**
(−) Income Tax/Social Contribution	–	(985)	(1742)
Net Income	**(4701)**	**2214**	**4027**
Other Relevant Metrics/ Ratios			
Net Debt	42,505	58,045	44,165
Net Debt/EBITDA	3.5x	3.1x	2.1x
ROIC	−1.4%	3.1%	6.5%

Source: Author

[a]Translated financial information from Brazilian Reais (BRL) to American Dolars (USD), according to international translation standards

Table 6 Normalization of the Target Company's Key Metrics (USD thousand[a])

	2022	**2023**	**2024**
Reported EBITDA	**12,073**	**18,604**	**20,801**
(−) Adjustments	**(550)**	**(611)**	**(1571)**
One-off revenue adjustment [a]	–	–	(1664)
Own stores rent adjustment [b]	(356)	(387)	(388)
Owners' salary adjustment [c]	(195)	(224)	(222)
Non recurring expenses [d]	–	–	333
Expensed Capex [e]	–	–	370
Adjusted EBITDA	**11,523**	**17,993**	**19,230**
Adjusted EBITDA Margin (for 2024, based on normalized net revenues)	24.7%	25.6%	24.1%

[a]Translated financial information from Brazilian Reais (BRL) to American Dolars (USD), according to international translation standards
Source: Author

(d) In 2024, Teresense incurred one-off litigation expenses of USD 0.33 million, related to a dispute with a former supplier. This is clearly an extraordinary item that was adjusted to reflect normalized performance.
(e) A portion of Teresense's capital expenditures was incorrectly recorded as operating expenses in 2024. As this should be subject to depreciation charges, this amount was adjusted and reversed to EBITDA.

Considering that Teresense consistently delivers positive earnings in a sector with well-established processes and a proven business model, the valuation multiples selected were EV/Revenue and EV/EBITDA. EV/EBIT could also have been used.

Comparable Companies Approach (CCA)

Benchmark Identification Within the Brazilian Apparel Sector

As outlined in the previous section's relative valuation guide, the first step in identifying benchmark companies for CCA involves seeking companies listed on the Brazilian Stock Exchange (B3) from the same industry as Teresense.

The apparel sector includes the following six players listed on Brazil's B3, as shown in Table 7.

Table 7 shows that the apparel sector stands out in Brazil, with six listed companies, offering a relatively robust peer group. As discussed previously, it is not very common to find this many industry peers in CCA valuations in emerging economies.

However, as Lojas Marisa was in financial distress at the time, it was excluded, narrowing the sample to five benchmarks. The recalculated average multiples excluding this outlier are presented in Table 8.

Table 7 Brazilian Comparables—B3 (Figures in USD Million[a])

Company Name	Ticker	EV/ EBITDA	EV/ Sales	P/E	EV	Net Revenue	EBITDA Margin	Net Debt/ EBITDA
Lojas Azzas	AZZA3	10.6x	1.7x	9.1x	2071	1185	16.5%	2.4x
Guararapes	GUAR3	4.1x	0.6x	18.2x	1094	1729	15.5%	1.4x
Veste S/A	VSTE3	8.1x	1.5x	n/a	311	201	19.1%	1.3x
Lojas Renner	LREN3	7.3x	1.3x	14.0x	3413	2609	17.9%	0.5x
C&A Modas	CEAB3	3.4x	0.7x	8.8x	937	1366	20.1%	1.3x
Lojas Marisa	AMAR3	32.1x	0.8x	n/a	213	215	3.9%	n/a
Mean		**10.9x**	**1.1x**	**12.5x**	**1340**	**1218**	**15.5%**	**1.4x**
Median		**7.7x**	**1.1x**	**11.5x**	**1015**	**1276**	**17.2%**	**1.3x**

Source: Bloomberg

[a]Financial metrics converted to USD using the exchange rate of BRL 5.40, as per the corresponding quarter. Figures refer to trailing twelve months as of Q3 2024 (September 30, 2024)

Table 8 Brazil's Benchmark Multiples Excluding Outlier

Selected Benchmarks	EV/EBITDA	EV/Sales	P/E
Mean	6.7x	1.2x	12.5x
Median	7.3x	1.3x	11.5x

Source: Bloomberg

The analysis indicates that C&A Modas, Lojas Renner, and Guararapes differ from Teresense in terms of pricing strategy and customer focus. While Teresense targets high-ticket products with a portfolio of premium brands, these benchmarks are retailers that primarily cater to more price-sensitive segments. Additionally, these three peers do not sell through third-party multi-brand stores, which represent a significant portion of Teresense's sales.

These differences likely explain why Teresense has been achieving EBITDA margins higher than its Brazilian peers, which can be seen in Tables 6 and 7.

Despite these differences, given the limited number of comparables within the same industry, all five companies were included in the final peer group.

Expanding the Search Internationally

According to some scholars, expanding the pool of benchmarks to also include firms from other countries can enhance the relevance of the data sample. In this regard, data from US-based apparel companies was sourced, as summarized in Table 9.

By analyzing the data, it becomes clear that the G-III and FIGS multiples are outliers and should be excluded. Recalculated mean and median multiples excluding these outliers are shown in Table 10.

Applying Adjustments to Benchmark Multiples

After calculating the CCA mean multiples, a cross-border correction was applied to the US multiples to account for differences in country-specific factors. Additionally, since the multiples were derived from public companies, and Teresense is a privately held business, a 20% illiquidity discount (DLOM) was applied. These adjustments are detailed in Table 11. No control premium was considered in this analysis.

The correction coefficients of 0.37 and 0.42, used to adjust the US EV/EBITDA and EV/Revenue to Brazil's market conditions, were based on country-level average multiples. The resulting cross-border adjusted multiples as low as 3.6x EBITDA and 0.4x Revenues seem to be significantly misaligned with the market reality of Brazil's apparel sector.

Precedent Transaction Approach (PTA)

Search for Comparable M&A Deals in Brazil

A search for precedent transactions in Brazil's apparel & textile sector identified many M&A transactions; however, only seven provided sufficient information about the implied acquisition multiples, as summarized in Table 12.

Table 9 US Comparables—NYSE and Nasdaq (Figures in USD Million[a])

Company name	Ticker	EV/EBITDA	EV/Sales	P/E	EV	Revenue	EBITDA margin	Net debt/EBITDA
Tapestry	TPR	8.9x	1.9x	12.2x	12,763	6666	19.6%	1.3x
Ralph Lauren	RL	10.9x	1.5x	15.3x	10,053	6740	15.4%	0.9x
VF Corporation	VFC	15.6x	1.3x	0.0x	13,664	9999	3.7%	7.3x
Levi Strauss	LEVI	24.4x	1.5x	14.6x	9404	6158	6.3%	4.3x
PVH Corp.	PVH	6.7x	0.8x	7.7x	7635	8771	13.4%	2.9x
Columbia	COLM	14.9x	1.4x	19.4x	4811	3332	9.7%	0.1x
Under Armour	UAA	7.9x	0.7x	10.7x	4259	5401	4.1%	0.8x
Hanesbrands	HBI	21.6x	1.6x	20.5x	5817	3590	7.5%	12.1x
Carter's Inc.	CRI	9.1x	1.2x	10.9x	3340	2842	12.9%	2.6x
G-III	GII	36.9x	0.5x	7.0x	1671	3106	13.1%	11.1x
FIGS Inc.	FIGS	70.5x	1.7x	131.4x	934	546	6.8%	−17.0x
Jerash Holdings	JRSH	3.3x	0.2x	n/a	19	130	2.1%	−3.3x
Mean		**19.2x**	**1.2x**	**22.7x**	**6198**	**4773**	**9.5%**	**1.9x**
Median		**12.9x**	**1.4x**	**12.2x**	**5314**	**4495**	**8.6%**	**1.9x**

Source: Bloomberg

[a]Figures refer to trailing twelve months as of Q3 2024 (September 30, 2024)

Table 10 US Benchmark Multiples Excluding Outliers

Selected benchmarks	EV/EBITDA	EV/Sales	P/E
Mean	12.4x	1.2x	11.8x
Median	10.0x	1.4x	11.6x

Table 11 Adjustment of CCA Benchmark Companies Multiples

Multiple type	Country	Mean multiple	Cross-border correction coefficient	Multiple adjusted for country difference	DLOM	Multiple adjusted for illiquidity
EV/ EBITDA	Brazil	6.7x		6.7x	20.0%	5.4x
EV/ Revenue	Brazil	1.2x		1.2x	20.0%	0.9x
EV/ EBITDA	USA	12.4x	0.37	4.5x	20.0%	3.6x
EV/ Revenue	USA	1.2x	0.42	0.5x	20.0%	0.4x

Table 12 Precedent Transactions – Brazil (Company Names Withheld)

Transaction	Year	Deal Value (R$'000)	EV/Revenue	EV/EBITDA
Transaction A	2020	210,000	1.2x	7.0x
Transaction B	2020	715,000	1.8x	16.1x
Transaction C	2021	5,100,000	4.8x	21.0x
Transaction D	2021	400,000	1.1x	16.4x
Transaction E	2021	180,000	1.6x	7.0x
Transaction F	2021	105,000	1.2x	–
Transaction G	2023	173,000	2.2x	8.7x
Mean		**983,286**	**2.0x**	**12.7x**
Median		**210,000**	**1.6x**	**12.4x**

Source: News Articles and Disclosure of Material Events by Buyers

Although finding such a large amount of PTA data is not very common in an emerging market, the level of disclosure of the deals above makes it impossible to understand how these multiples were computed.

Time-Difference Adjustments

Most of the transactions identified took place between 2020 and 2021, when Brazil's interest rates were significantly lower and market sentiment was different. Adjusting for these fluctuations can enhance comparability to the market reality in 2024, which is Teresense's valuation date.

By computing the variance in Brazil's B3 average valuation multiples from the date of each transaction to the end of 2024, the following time-related adjustments were calculated, as shown in Table 13.

Table 13 Time-Differences Adjustment on Precedent Transactions (Company Names Withheld)

Transaction	Year	EV/ Revenue	EV/ EBITDA	Time adjustment EV/Revenue	Time adjustment EV/EBITDA	Adjusted EV/Revenue	Adjusted EV/EBITDA
Transaction A	2020	1.2x	7.0x	0.69	0.54	0.9x	3.8x
Transaction B	2020	1.8x	16.1x	0.69	0.54	1.2x	8.7x
Transaction C	2021	4.8x	21.0x	0.69	0.71	3.3x	14.8x
Transaction D	2021	1.1x	16.4x	0.69	0.71	0.7x	11.6x
Transaction E	2021	1.6x	7.0x	0.69	0.71	1.1	4.9x
Transaction F	2021	1.2x	–	0.69	0.71	0.8x	–
Transaction G	2023	2.2x	8.7x	1.07	1.15	2.3x	10.0x
Mean	–	**2.0x**	**12.7x**			**1.5x**	**9.0x**
Excluding large deals							
Mean	–	**1.5x**	**7.6x**			**1.3x**	**6.2x**

Some of the transactions above appear to involve high acquisition premiums, with multiples ranging from 16.1x to 21.0x EBITDA. As these apparel companies were significantly larger than Teresense at the time of each acquisition and had stronger brand equity, they do not seem to be appropriate benchmarks.

Consequently, Table 13 also shows the recalculated PTA mean multiples excluding these non-comparable acquisitions. This adjustment significantly reduces the final adjusted multiple from 9.0x EBITDA to 6.2x EBITDA.

Other Normalizations and Adjustments

Since all of the PTA deals involved the transfer of control, no control premium adjustments are required, as Teresense's deal entails the transfer of 100% of its shares.

Lastly, as already discussed, best practices suggest using standardized accounting methods, consistent transaction price calculations, and adjustments for economic differences. However, in the case of PTA-based valuations, this is nearly impossible due to the limited availability of information about private deals, especially in emerging economies.

Using Adjusted Multiples to Value Teresense

Based on Teresense's normalized 2024 revenues and EBITDA, Table 14 shows the valuation results obtained both for the CCA and PTA.

As discussed, this relative-value analysis was based on US and Brazil-based multiples, adjusted for cross-border corrections, illiquidity discounts, and time-based differences.

Analyzing and Sense-Checking Results

The CCA and PTA valuation, using Brazil and US comparable firms, yielded significantly varied results due to the factors discussed below:

Inconsistent CCA Results

- The CCA valuation was hindered by variation within the peer group, as Teresense differs significantly from public benchmarks in size, brand awareness, customer focus (which affects margins), and sales channels.
- Brazilian comparable companies' valuation multiples in 2024 seem to be discounted in relation to prior years. While this mirrors market sentiment at the

Table 14 Relative Valuation of Teresense Based on the CCA and PTA Approaches (in USD Thousand)

Multiple type	Valuation approach	Benchmark country	Adjusted multiple	(x) Teresense's value indicator	(=) Enterprise value	(−) Net debt	(=) Equity value
EV/Sales	CCA	Brazil	0.9x	79,829	75,626	44,165	31,461
EV/Sales	CCA	USA	0.4x	79,829	32,575	44,165	(11,589)
EV/Sales	PTA	Brazil	1.3x	79,829	101,519	44,165	57,354
EV/EBITDA	CCA	Brazil	5.4x	19,230	102,942	44,165	58,777
EV/EBITDA	CCA	USA	3.6x	19,230	69,771	44,165	25,607
EV/EBITDA	PTA	Brazil	6.2x	19,230	119,866	44,165	75,701
Mean					**83,716**	**44,165**	**39,552**

valuation date, it may also be partially explained by market inefficiencies, which are not uncommon in emerging economies.

- The cross-border corrections applied to the US benchmarks resulted in unrealistic multiples for the Brazilian apparel sector, especially for a company like Teresense, with margins and growth rates higher than those of the CCA benchmarks.
- CCA revenue multiples produced significantly different results compared to the EBITDA multiples, which highlights their inadequacy in capturing Teresense's higher operating profits relative to peers, leading to a skewed valuation.

More Consistent PTA Results, but with Questionable Reliability

- Unlike CCA, which relies on data from public companies that are very different from the target company, PTA focuses on real-world acquisitions of smaller, private companies, and thus more comparable to Teresense. Consequently, at first glance, PTA appears more appropriate for this exercise.
- However, significant issues arise from the lack of transparency in M&A deals. It is simply impossible to reconcile the basis on which precedent transactions were calculated, which hinders reliability and comparability of the data set.
- In addition, many of these M&A deals in the apparel sector included earnouts or stock swaps as part of the payment scheme, which further complicates comparability.
- Lastly, transactions that included high acquisition premiums were excluded from the sample, increasing comparability. If these exclusions had not been made, the discrepancy between the PTA and CCA valuation results would be even greater.

Potential Solutions to Improve Reliability

This practical example highlighted how uncertainty and scarcity of comparables can impact valuation accuracy in emerging markets. The following solutions could be considered:

- **Cluster Analysis:** Instead of grouping benchmark companies from the same industry, they could have been clustered by economic fundamentals, which could improve accuracy. However, as Brazil's B3 has only 344 listed companies, finding firms that are comparable to a medium-sized private company is somewhat challenging.
- **Regression Within the Apparel Sector:** Differences among benchmarks could be addressed via regression analysis, but the small sample of apparel companies in the country limits the application of this solution. One might argue that including US-based apparel companies could increase the sample size for an effective regression. However, simultaneously controlling for economic fundamentals and country risk differences increases the number of variables, adding complexity and reducing reliability.

- **Expanded Sample Regression Analysis:** Using benchmarks from different industries and controlling for differences in economic fundamentals through regression could align relative valuation with intrinsic value drivers. The challenge with this method is that it requires extensive benchmark research, increases complexity, and is unfamiliar to most market practitioners.

Conclusion

Relative-value analysis is the most commonly used valuation method, mainly for its simplicity, speed, and market-based view. However, as extensively discussed in this chapter, the method is not without challenges and limitations, especially in the context of emerging markets.

In these regions, volatility and uncertainty of relative valuations are higher, because of increased country risks. Finding CCA and PTA benchmarks is another challenge, considering the lack of comparables in these countries. In some cases, this may force analysts to import multiples from developed economies. In doing so, some scholars recommend applying cross-border adjustment coefficients and other solutions, but these seem to be an overly simplistic approach. This is because the variation in multiples across countries is only partially explained by differences in country-specific factors, as supported by several studies. Teresense's case illustrated the challenges of performing a relative valuation in an emerging market and showed how generic corrections can be deceptive.

In light of the unique challenges in emerging economies, performing relative valuations in these markets requires greater analytical rigor. By adhering to best practices and exercising sound judgment, practitioners can use multiples in these dynamic regions, either as a primary valuation method or as a tool to sense-check the results of a DCF valuation.

However, the analytical effort and extensive adjustments to effectively apply multiples in emerging markets can take away the method's greatest strengths—its simplicity and speed.

Acknowledgement The author gratefully acknowledges Apex Partners for granting access to databases used in the research of multiples and market information. Special thanks go to Daniel Moraes, Pedro Zordan, and Ronan Bonnemasou for their invaluable contributions to the research and analysis, which were instrumental in the development of this chapter.

Key Terms and Definitions

Benchmark A reference group of companies with similar characteristics used in valuation to derive multiples and compare financial performance or market valuation metrics.

CCA (Comparable Companies Approach) A valuation method that uses publicly traded companies with similar characteristics as benchmarks to estimate the value of a target company.

DCF (Discounted Cash Flow) DCF is a valuation method that estimates the intrinsic value of an asset by projecting its future cash flows and discounting them to present value using an appropriate discount rate.

DLOM (Discount for Lack of Marketability) A valuation adjustment applied to reflect the reduced liquidity of an asset, especially when it cannot be easily sold or converted to cash.

EBITDA (Earnings Before Interest, Taxes, Depreciation, and Amortization) A financial metric used to measure a company's operational profitability before accounting for non-operating expenses.

Equity Value The total value of the equity of a company, which is attributable to its shareholders.

EV (Enterprise Value) The total value of a company, including equity and debt, adjusted for cash and cash equivalents.

IFRS (International Financial Reporting Standards) A set of global accounting standards designed to ensure transparency, consistency, and comparability in financial statements.

Illiquidity The inability of an asset to be quickly converted into cash without significant loss in value.

NOPAT (Net Operating Profit After Tax) represents the after-tax profit generated by a company's core operations, excluding income from non-operating assets or financing expenses such as interest.

PTA (Precedent Transaction Approach) A valuation approach that examines multiples paid in historical mergers and acquisitions to estimate the value of a similar target company.

ROIC (Return on Invested Capital) A profitability ratio that measures the return a company generates on its invested capital, indicating efficiency in capital utilization.

Value Indicator A financial metric, such as revenue, EBITDA, or net income, used as the denominator in multiples to standardize valuation comparisons across firms.

References

An JY, Bhojraj S, Ng D (2010). Country, industry, and idiosyncratic components in valuation ratios (Chapter 3). In JY An (ed) Three essays on international equity returns and valuation ratios (Unpublished Doctoral dissertation). Cornell University, Ithaca, NY

Cole S, Melecky M, Mölders F, Reed T (2020) Long-run returns to private equity in emerging markets. Policy Research Working Paper No. 9366. Development Economics, Development Research Group, Finance, Competitiveness, and Innovation Global Practice, International Finance Corporation. World Bank. https://www.worldbank.org/prwp

Damodaran A (2006) Damodaran on valuation: Security analysis for investment and corporate finance, 2nd edn. Wiley, Hoboken, NJ
Damodaran A (2009) Volatility rules: valuing emerging market companies. Stern School of Business, New York University
Damodaran A (2012) Investment valuation: tools and techniques for determining the value of any asset, 2nd edn. Wiley, Hoboken, NJ
DePamphilis D (2019) Mergers, acquisitions, and other restructuring activities: an integrated approach to process, tools, cases, and solutions, 10th edn. Academic Press, San Diego, CA
Gaio C (2009) The relative importance of firm and country characteristics for earnings quality around the world. Working Paper, ISEC, Lisbon
Guimaraes P, Koller T (2021) Don't overthink your approach to valuation in emerging markets. McKinsey & Company. Retrieved from McKinsey website
International Accounting Standards Board (2011) IFRS 13: fair value measurement. IFRS Foundation
Koller T, Goedhart M, Wessels D (2020) Valuation: measuring and managing the value of companies, 7th edn. Wiley, Hoboken, NJ
Norges Bank (2019) Country and industry effects in global equity returns (Discussion Note No. 01). Retrieved from https://www.nbim.no
Pereiro LE (2002) Valuation of companies in emerging markets: a practical approach. John Wiley & Sons
Pereiro LE (2006) Investment valuation in emerging markets: evidence from Argentina. J Multinatl Financ Manag 16(2):160–183
Pratt SP, Reilly RF, Schweihs RP (2000) Valuing a business: The analysis and appraisal of closely held companies, 4th edn. McGraw-Hill, New York, NY
Serra RG, Fávero LPL (2018) Multiples' valuation: the selection of cross-border comparable firms. Emerg Mark Financ Trade 54(9):1973–1992
Statista (2023) Number of listed companies in the US, Brazil, Mexico and South Africa as of December 2023. Retrieved January 6, 2025, from https://www.statista.com
World Economics (2025) Retrieved January 6, 2025, from https://www.worldeconomics.com/

High Stakes, Higher Rates: An Overview and Step-by-Step Approach to Calculating the Cost of Capital in Emerging Market firms

Adam Patterson

People calculate too much and think too little.—Charlie Munger, Investor, philanthropist and Vice Chairman of Berkshire Hathaway
If there were a contest for the most measured number in finance, the winner would be the cost of capital"—Aswath Damodaran
Is the juice worth the squeeze?—Popular idiom

Abstract The cost of capital in emerging markets is a complex and dynamic concept that requires careful consideration of various factors. This chapter highlights some of the fundamental themes related to the role and computation of the cost of capital in discounted cash flow analysis. We start with a literature review around the development of the cost of capital in valuation before discussing the key approaches, challenges, and solutions in an emerging market context before illustrating a step-by-step example of how to estimate the cost of capital for a privately held emerging market company. It contributes to the academic and professional literature by blending theory and practical themes to a key and often misunderstood component of emerging market valuation analytics. The practical framework also seeks to demystify the use of WACC for emerging markets by illustrating the necessary inputs and financial rationale to develop robust cost of capital estimates.

Keywords Valuation · DCF · Free cash flow · Discount rate · WACC · CAPM · Opportunity cost · Hurdle rate · Risk · Expected return · IRR · Country risk premium

A. Patterson (✉)
Redirection Corporate Advisory, London, UK
e-mail: adam@redirection.com

S. Derindere Köseoğlu, A. Patterson (eds.), *Valuation in Emerging Markets*, Contributions to Finance and Accounting,
https://doi.org/10.1007/978-3-031-93526-8_8

Introduction

At a fundamental level, the building blocks of value are universal: the size of the cash flow, its forecast growth, and discount rate. This is what Damodaran (2002) calls the "philosophical basis" of valuation, whereby every asset has an intrinsic value that can be estimated using these building blocks. Thus, in the discounted cash flow (DCF) approach to valuation, the central axiom is that the intrinsic value of a firm is obtained by discounting expected residual cash flows at the weighted cost of capital. Or, mathematically:

$$\text{Firm Value} = \sum\nolimits_{t=1}^{t=n} \frac{Free\ Cash\ Flows\ to\ Firm}{(1 + WACC)t}$$

Cash flows are discounted to account for the time value of money, which contemplates factors such as inflation, potential interest rates you can earn on other assets and consumer preference to spend today rather than tomorrow unless you are being adequately compensated. Discount rates also function as "risk premiums": investors demand an extra return to compensate for the risk that the future cash flow might not materialize. *Caveat lector*, risk and return are two sides of the same coin. Assorted categories of discount rates such as risk-free rate, cost of equity, or cost of debt, are used contextually in corporate finance and valuation. In general terms, in the former, the discount rate is used as a hurdle rate in capital budgeting and the metric employed in optimizing capital structures, whilst the latter is used to value a company's operating assets. Nonetheless, the principal hypothesis remains the same: the objective of the discount rate is to capture the risk associated with an investment which means that, *ceteris paribus*, riskier investments require higher costs of capital.

In the developing markets space, these concepts become more significant due to the increased risk and volatility factors that are often associated with these markets. Valuation experts face hurdles when assessing emerging markets since determining the cost of capital involves navigating through practical challenges, such as economic uncertainties, lack of corporate information, inflation differentials, which inputs to use, and above all market and regulatory considerations in these regions. This chapter, therefore, examines the historical evolution of the cost of capital and its usage and then delving into the key computation components and guiding principles before concluding by illustrating a specific cost of capital model for a Brazilian firm.

Literature Review: A Brief History of Time (Value of Money)

The concept of the discount rate, central to value estimation, has evolved significantly over time, rooted in early philosophical and economic thought. Indeed, the author would suggest that the concept of risk and reward and as such expected returns are at least as old as Neolithic Civilisation and the birth of agriculture. After all can we not imagine an early farmer loaning seeds or produce to a neighbour until harvest time for the promise of receiving more than he initially loaned?

We know that by the eighteenth century B.C., the Babylonian King Hammurabi— he of the famous law codes—was establishing restrictions on interest rates and in doing so provided the first historical example of limiting potential returns on investment (Homer and Sylla 2005). Classical thinkers such as Aristotle expanded on this discussion by applying the dialectical method on the ethics of lending, introducing the concept of time preference— future value being less attractive and uncertain compared to present value. After all, a bird in the hand is worth two in the bush as the Aesopian proverb states, potentially the world's first fundamentalist investment advice. Early reflections essentially established a foundation for comprehending risk versus return, which is intrinsically tied to discounting concepts.

Fast-forwarding closer to modernity for the sake of brevity, discounted cash flow valuation was already being used in industry as early as the 1700s in the United Kingdom. Around this time, British economic thinkers such as Adam Smith (1723–1790) and John Stuart Mill (1806–1873) were writing about how with limited economic resources borrowing costs reflected risk and time value and that individuals and businesses demanded compensation for deferring consumption or investment, respectively.

The 1930s also saw a new wave of academic interest on this topic. Irving Fisher (1930) formalized his work on interest theory, connecting discount rates to intertemporal choice. His "Fisher equation" defines interest rate expectations, which can influence discount rates and overall valuation metrics. Furthermore, American economist John Burr Williams (1938) helped legitimize the DCF model in his now classic The Theory of Investment Value, published in 1938. Williams was one of the first to logically conclude that the intrinsic value of an asset—dividends, in this instance—had to be projected on the basis of the "rule of present worth" in conjunction with a conservative appropriate interest rate that reflected the investor's opportunity cost of capital and expected return. In his view, calculation of the appropriate interest rate entailed blending observable market rates and more subjective risk premiums, including further adjustments according to the investment's singular circumstances under analysis. The interpretative flexibility of discount rates herein permitted further refinement and modification by successive scholars and their use in several contexts, such as company and sector-specific risk-adjusted rates.

Franco Modigliani and Merton Miller (1958) further refined this thinking by demonstrating the irrelevance of a firm's capital structure under certain conditions, thus laying theoretical foundations for estimating the cost of equity and debt. Sharpe's 1964 innovation, the Capital Asset Pricing Model (for which he would later win a Nobel Prize in Economic Sciences), together with Lintner's 1965 and Mossin's 1966 contributions, pioneered risk-adjusted return frameworks for estimating equity costs. CAPM assumes that systemic risk has to be factored into the discount rate via beta and equity risk premium over a risk-free rate typically derived from government bonds. Scholars such as Damodaran (2011a, 2011b) proposed alternative risk premiums reflecting country-specific risks in response to empirical challenges that questioned how far the CAPM can successfully capture all relevant risks. Such approaches built on Fama and French's seminal 1992 work on "multi-factor" models which sought to expand on the CAPM by introducing additional factors, encompassing firm size, book-to-market values, and excess market returns.

Unlike developed markets, where financial systems tend to be more stable and data more readily available, emerging markets face *sui generis* challenges that necessitate adjustments to traditional cost of capital models. Emerging markets are characterized by greater macroeconomic volatility, data issues, weaker institutions, and higher political and currency risks, which substantially influence discount rates and overall valuation methodologies (Damodaran 2009a, 2009b). According to Damodaran (2002), "Emerging markets are distinct in that they exhibit higher equity risk premiums, and their risk factors, such as political instability, are not captured in standard models".

For instance, while the capital asset pricing model (CAPM) has become a cornerstone—and essentially 'the' go-to framework in valuation—in estimating the cost of equity, its reliance on a single risk factor based on the security market line (SML) assumes market efficiency and integration, premises that can provide challenges in emerging economies. Bekaert and Harvey (1995a, 1995b) emphasized the segmentation of emerging markets, arguing that investors demanded additional premiums to compensate for country-specific risks. This laid the groundwork for incorporating CRPs into cost of capital calculations.

As a result, analysts often add CRP to the traditional CAPM framework to address these challenges, yet disagreements persist regarding its calculation. Damodaran (2002) proposed a systematic approach to estimating CRPs, using sovereign bond spreads as proxies for country risk. This methodology has since been widely adopted as we will see, but it is not without its critics. Fernández (2019) argued that sovereign spreads may not fully capture private sector risks, necessitating additional adjustments.

As EMs and frontier economies gained further prominence in global investment portfolios and broader GDP share from the 1990s, and concepts such as the BRICs (originally Brazil, Russia, India and China) and MINT (Mexico, Indonesia, Nigeria and Turkey) countries emerged in the 2000s–2010s, the need for more nuanced approaches to the cost of capital—going beyond the standard CAPM universe—in these regions intensified. This has led to the development of alternative methods for estimating the cost of equity, including the use of country risk premiums, the Build-Up Method (BUM), and modifications to the traditional CAPM model.

The professional and academic debate also extends to the weighted average cost of capital (WACC). In emerging markets, capital structures are often skewed by reliance on debt and internal cash generation due to underdeveloped equity markets. This introduces complications in estimating the cost of debt, where spreads above LIBOR or SOFR may be significantly higher to reflect additional credit and market risks. Some large EM companies' costs of debt may also be lower than the government's own borrowing costs. What's more, tax shield benefits on debt, a key component of WACC, may also be less predictable due to unstable tax policies or varied enforcement (Pereiro 2002).

This is not just an academic discussion, as it provides the context and evolution of technical thought for professional assessments and calculations as to how to best utilize the existing cost of capital models when we are valuing emerging market firms. However, first let us summarize and define our terms.

Discussion on the Cost of Capital in Valuation: It's WACC

As Damodaran (2016) states: "The cost of capital, in its most basic form, is a weighted average of the costs of raising funding for an investment or a business, with that funding taking the form of either debt or equity".

There are many methods used by valuation professionals to compute the cost of capital, each with its explicit scope and limitations. Let us briefly discuss. The Adjusted Present Value (APV) approach considers the relative value of a firm without debt and the value of the financing decision as two independent components, which are computed and then added together (Myers 1974). This is more advantageous when debt levels have unique characteristics over time. The Flow to Equity (FTE) method however puts more emphasis on the equity as it considers the cash flows to equity holders at the required return on equity after the cash flows have been settled which makes it ideal for firms that are highly leveraged (Damodaran 2002). On the other hand, the world's most famous investor, Warren Buffett, prioritizes the computation of simplified opportunity costs together with broad margins of safety: "We don't discount the future cash flows at 9% or 10%; we use the US treasury rate. We try to deal with things about which we are quite certain. You can't compensate for risk by using a high discount rate (Buffett 1998)".

And yet as both a student of value and a professional valuation advisor, the author would argue that it is difficult to escape the hegemony of the WACC model, despite certain critiques, due to its popularity, versatility, and the potential inertia observed in the corporate finance universe. WACC combines both the cost of equity and the cost of debt, net of tax shields, to consider the overall structure of a firm's capital and its effect on the valuation of the firm. Moreover, at the practical level, in M&A processes, we also need to ensure that our costs of capital are broadly in line with not only market best practices but also advisors on the other side of the table, who will most likely be using WACC for their own calculations. It is then a "WACC world". Furthermore, it has been suggested that WACC is used in almost 80% of professional valuation assignments (Fernández 2019). We will then employ the WACC method as we advance in this chapter. First, however, let us dig deeper into the calculation and discuss some of the principal challenges we face and solutions in our valuation toolkit when discussing cost of capital calculations in emerging markets.

The Basic WACC Formula

$$WACC = \left(\frac{E}{V}x\ Re\right) + \left(\frac{D}{V}x\ Rd\ x\ (1 - Tc)\right)$$

where

E = *Market value of the firm's equity*
D = *Market value of the firm's debt*
V = *E* + *D*
Re = *Cost of equity*
Rd = *Cost of debt*
Tc = *Corporate tax rate*
Cost of Equity via CAPM

$$Re = Rfr + \beta\ x\ (Rm - Rfr)$$

where:

Rfr = *Risk free rate*
β = *Equity beta*
Rm-Rfr = *represents the equity risk premium (ERP)*

Risk-Free Rate (RFR)

The risk-free rate represents the return on an investment without a hypothetical risk of default. Typically, it is approximated using yields on government securities, such as 5–10-year US Treasury bonds. In emerging markets, however, this assumption becomes problematic due to the lack of truly "risk-free" instruments. For instance, local government bonds often carry significant sovereign and reinvestment risk.

Practitioners can use a variety of options, as summarized by Damodaran (2004):

(a) The interest rate on a nominal currency-denominated bond issued by the emerging market government
(b) The interest rate on an inflation-indexed emerging market government bond
(c) The interest rate on a dollar-denominated emerging market government bond
(d) The use of developed market government bonds which would then require further adjustments, *a posteriori*.

In the approach to follow, the author will employ the latter method as such securities can provide a more reliable measure of the pure time value of money, free from significant credit risk, possible liquidity distortions and more directly related to a conceptual "risk-free" rate. At this point, there are three further considerations: which country bond to use, which type of rate, and which period. We will utilize the yield on a US government zero-coupon bond that matches the explicit forecast period of our cash flows. Although technically no investment is ever 100%

free of risk, US government bonds are considered the global benchmark for a risk-free rate proxy due to their minimal default risk, large, traded volume, and high liquidity. Additionally, the zero-coupon structure eliminates reinvestment risk, ensuring that the rate reflects a pure time value of money over the specific period, which is particularly important for valuations where cash flows are explicitly forecasted for a defined horizon. In other words, these bonds are not subject to transient market risk as they are exempt from coupon payments. Moreover, by focusing on the same period as the explicit forecast, the rate ensures temporal consistency between cash flows and discounting, enhancing the accuracy of present value calculations. We can either opt to use a geometric average or median of a recent period of the risk-free rate, such as say 30 or 90 days, to smooth out any short-term noise in yields, or the current rate as an accurate point-in-time measure of the risk-free rate and thus avoid misalignment between the discount rate and current market conditions. However, this approach should be reconsidered if there have been significant structural changes in economic dynamics or monetary policy that materially impact the risk-free rate.

What's more, in DCF, it is essential to distinguish between the cost of capital calculations for the explicit forecast period and the perpetuity period to account for the differences in risk profiles and growth expectations over time. Valuation best practices typically entail a comprehensive and explicit forecasting period of 5 years. Early-stage companies or traditional firms with a more dynamic growth outlook can adopt a three-stage or more growth model. Technically, and top of mind, forecast durations should be linked to the point the company being valued is likely to achieve operational maturity. We should also ask ourselves if it is plausible to estimate a private company operating in perpetuity. Of course, valuation advisors should use their common sense to align theoretical and practical considerations.

The preference for a five-year forecast is—aside from perhaps the previously mentioned inertia in corporate finance—largely due to its ability to strike a balance between accurately predicting near-term operational and financial performance and addressing the escalating uncertainty associated with projections that extend further into the future. In the explicit forecast horizon, risks and returns should be inherently linked with underlying business growth assumptions as well as economic and market realities. This can necessitate a more formal and customized cost of capital that fully reflects these fluctuating factors (Pereiro 2002). Following this forecasting horizon, valuation models tend to transition into a perpetuity to capture the firm's steady-state growth on the assumption that the company will be in a sustainable and mature phase. This is a practice that delivers precision in the short run as well as capturing the realistic method of valuing the long run (Koller et al. 2020a, 2020b).

As such, we extend the same rationale for the risk-free rate over the forecast period to the perpetuity calculation by using a long-term and zero-coupon US government bond, for instance, with a 30-year duration.

Equity Risk Premium (ERP)

The ERP captures the additional return demanded by investors for bearing equity risk over the risk-free rate. Estimating the ERP in emerging markets is contentious due to variability in data quality, market depth, and investor behaviour. Common methods include historical averages, implied equity premiums derived from market prices, and survey-based estimates.

In the author's experience, most practitioners in the investment banking universe use the historical ERP and as such assume that over a long period the equity premium will be in line with, or revert to, the mean. However, this does raise several questions:

- How far back to go? Should we use an 80-year historical timeframe or 30 years? And how do we justify the use of one period over another? This is of extra interest when our periods include, or do not include, atypical performance events or market cycles, think of the dot.com bubble, the great financial crisis or the post-2020 bull market.
- To compute these averages, do we use geometric or arithmetic averages or the median which is less affected by extreme values?
- Should we use rates from Treasury Bills or Treasury Bonds?

One solution to these questions is to use implied ERPs. An implied, forward-looking Equity Risk Premium is typically deemed a more robust measure, indicative of present market conditions, particularly when juxtaposed against a historical premium. The guiding principle is that the price that investors are willing to pay for risky assets is the crucial metric of their desired risk premium on that risky asset which Damodaran (2023) defines as the "watch what I pay not what I say" approach. This methodology aligns with the inherently dynamic nature of valuation by integrating market expectations instead of depending on retrospective averages, which often fail to capture recent economic or structural changes and market transformations. Forward-looking ERPs use current market prices and projections of future cash flows, such as dividends or earnings, to estimate the premium. This approach ensures that the methodology is coherent with the forward-looking essence of cash flow projections utilized in discounted cash flow (DCF) models and can be constantly updated with the most recent market inputs. Additionally, it mitigates the often-substantial standard errors and biases linked to historical premiums.

As always, Damodaran (2023) provides an illustrative example of how the implied ERP is calculated for the S&P500 index in the US market (Fig. 1):

Therefore, we can determine the expected return and forecast cash flows that investors are requesting from a risky asset if we know the price paid for it via reverse engineering. The formula for estimating the equity risk premium is then equal to the difference between the expected market return and the same risk-free rate we have calculated earlier. This implied ERP is also adaptable to economic transition phases, which is particularly crucial in emerging markets. Think about how different Eastern Europe or South Korea are at the present time compared to 40 years ago. After all, we recall that one of the key truisms in investing is that past performance may not

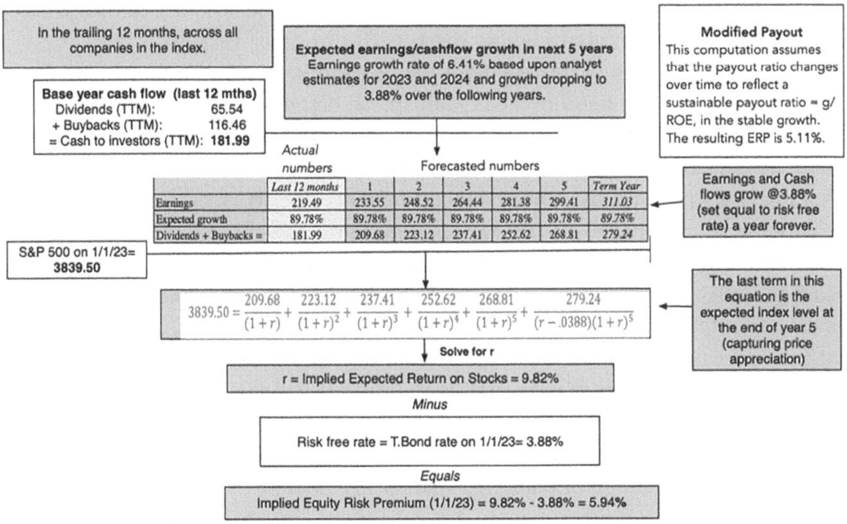

Fig. 1 An implied ERP map. Credit: Damodaran (2023)

accurately predict future risks and returns. To summarize, although the past can offer insights, its relevance may diminish in rapidly evolving contexts because of these inherent limitations. In the example to follow, we will employ the implied ERP for the US market using the same rationale for the use of the US risk-free rate (global benchmark, large liquid markets, greater access to publicly available data, etc.). We could also calculate the ERP for specific EM stock indexes. The same rules apply.

In our example, the author will use the US current implied premium for the explicit projection period and in doing so implicitly assumes that the market is broadly efficient and correct overall and that the valuation standard should reflect market neutrality. A key benefit of the use of the US rate is two-fold: the number is more easily available "off the shelf" and the market inputs used in the formula are arguably more robust. For the long-term ERP in our cost of capital, we will use a mix of the implied premium and historical view and apply the average implied equity risk premium which should smooth out any current mispricing in perpetuity. Again, we can build out our own forward-looking implied premiums for both global and emerging markets.

Country Risk Premium (CRP)

For emerging markets, the ERP often includes a country risk premium (CRP) to account for systemic risks such as political instability and economic uncertainty (see Godfrey and Espinosa 1996 and Damodaran 2016). Moreover, for certain emerging markets with a tradition of higher interest rates, government bonds can sometimes have a long-term return above equity markets (for instance Brazil).

To calculate a specific CRP, we can either use the sovereign Credit Default Swap (CDS) spread for the country or the default spread based on the local currency rating for the country. CDS spreads on emerging market bonds reflect the cost of insuring against default on sovereign or corporate debt in these markets. These spreads are generally higher than those for developed markets due to greater perceived risks, including political instability, weaker legal systems, lower credit ratings, and economic volatility. The resulting "country spread" reflects the additional risk investors associate with the specific emerging market compared to the United States, incorporating sovereign default risk and broader market concerns. These spreads capture real-time investor sentiment and risk perceptions, providing a more dynamic and forward-looking assessment compared to static credit ratings. When adjusted for the US CDS spread, the resulting figure isolates the country-specific premium, aligning it with a globally recognized benchmark. This approach ensures consistency and relevance in the valuation of emerging market investments.

We have one further adjustment to make, to ensure we are capturing total country risk— country ratings only assess default risk after all—which is a function of not only credit risk but also equity risk factors. Again, we employ guidance from Damodaran (2024) who states:

> In the short-term especially, the equity country risk premium is likely to be greater than the country's default spread. You can estimate an adjusted country risk premium by multiplying the default spread by the relative equity market volatility for that market (Standard deviation in country equity market/Standard deviation in country bond). Since government bonds are not available or traded in most countries, [we can] also approximate the relative equity market volatility by estimating the standard deviations in two indices, the S&P emerging market equity index (for equities) and an iShares emerging market government bond ETF (for government bonds) and using that ratio for all countries to estimate the additional country risk premium.

The formulas for these two approaches are then given as follows:

- Equity volatility-based method:

$$Total\ ERP = Risk\ PremiumUS\ x\ Country\ Equity\ (\sigma)\ \ USEquity\ (\sigma)$$

- The "melded" method (Damodaran's term):

$$Total\ ERP = \ Default\ spread\ on\ country\ bond\ x\ Country\ Equity\ (\sigma)\ \ Country\ Bond\ \ (\sigma)$$

As Damodaran's market premium comes from the US market, our starting point will be the country's CDS spread, if available, and then deduct the US CDS spread. This delta then becomes the emerging market spread or the country risk-free rate, we will utilize for our cost of capital calculation.

We would add that other authors have attempted to provide more sophisticated frameworks. For instance, Abuaf (2011 & 2015) proposed estimating equity costs through a multiple return regression based on the return on the S&P 500 Index and the country CDS rate and later refined the method by using CDS changes rather than levels.

Country Risk Exposure

Nonetheless, certain authors such as critics like Erb et al. (1996) suggest that relying solely on sovereign spreads can understate or overstate risks, as these spreads do not always align with corporate conditions or total exposure to country risk. This is a valid point: country risk exposure is not a "one-size-fits-all" factor. For instance, a Mexican company may generate the bulk of its revenue from the US market. This also works in reverse. Think of a developed economy multinational company which sells in multiple emerging markets, and thus, in theory, should incorporate additional country risks. The key point here is how to holistically contemplate risk exposure, be it through revenues, location of production facilities, and connection to political risk. Firms may also employ financial instruments to mitigate certain risks.

Let us get back to our emerging market CRP. We can again apply Damodaran's toolkit (2002) to optimize our cost of capital calculations encompassing these additional factors. We can adjust the CAPM model as follows, quoting directly from the author:

- Approach 1: Assume that every company in the country is equally exposed to country risk. In this case,

$$E(Return) = Riskfree\ Rate + CRP + Beta * (Mature\ ERP)$$

- Approach 2: Assume that a company's exposure to country risk is similar to its exposure to other market risks.

$$E(Return) = Riskfree\ Rate + Beta\ (Mature\ ERP + CRP)$$

- Approach 3: Treat country risk as a separate risk factor and allow firms to have different exposures to country risk (perhaps based upon the proportion of their revenues come from non-domestic sales).

$$E(Return) = Riskfree\ Rate + \quad (Mature\ ERP) + \lambda(CRP)$$

Where the factor "l" measures the relative exposure of a firm to country risk.

Beta (β)

Beta measures a stock's sensitivity to market movements, reflecting its systematic risk. Traditional beta estimation, based on historical regression against a market index, often proves unreliable in these contexts due to unstable correlations and the influence of idiosyncratic events (Estrada 2000). In developed markets, beta estimation generally relies on historical stock price data. However, the higher volatility, lower liquidity, and market inefficiencies of EMs can complicate beta calculations.

Pereiro (2010) sums up the challenge as follows, and it is worth citing in full:

> In principle, the CAPM is universally applicable to investments. In practice though, decision-makers face at least two serious predicaments in applying CAPM logic to emerging market investment assets. The e first is a data predicament—that is, relevant local data may not exist, or it can turn out to be undependable or atypical. If you try to use a pricing model based on local (domestic) industry betas, you may find that some markets simply have no companies quoting in certain industries, and therefore, no industry betas will be available at the domestic level. In other markets, the local price series available to compute betas are unacceptably short—therefore, betas will be unreliable. In still others, even if you do find a reliable industry beta, it may still not fairly reflect the risk of its industry if the sector in question weighs heavily and disproportionately in the local market's capitalization.

Academics have proposed various solutions, including adjusting beta to reflect country-specific risk, using global indices as benchmarks, leveraging peer comparisons in more stable markets (Godfrey and Espinosa 1996) or computing domestic industry betas for a consolidated long list of EMs as a unique asset class. All these solutions bring additional technical challenges. For instance, are betas, and thus industry "risk", as well as sector development stages equivalent across multiple countries? It seems a fair bet to suggest that this is not always the case. Let us then focus our efforts in this section on privately held firms in emerging markets which tend to provide greater estimation challenges. For a broader analysis of the use of beta for listed emerging market firms, please see Pereiro (2002) and Fernandez (2004a, 2004b). Furthermore, for further discussion on the use of beta types and periods, please see Kaplan and Ruback (1995).

Frontier market scholars recommend using global indices to proxy for market returns, arguing these better capture systemic risks faced by international investors (Bekaert and Harvey 1995a, 1995b). For the author, this should often be our starting point for M&A operations and private company valuations in emerging markets. It is true then that for privately held firms' valuation, we do run into certain additional obstacles. As per Damodaran (2004), we can opt to use either accounting beta regressions, fundamental beta regressions based on observable variables, such as earnings growth, debt earnings variances or adopt the bottom-up beta approach, which involves averaging betas from comparable listed firms and adjusting for the capital structure of the company being valued as per industry best practice (more on this on the cost of debt section below). Broadly speaking, the unlevered beta (asset beta) is utilized to neutralize the effects of leverage differences and is then releveled using the firm's target capital structure. The formula is as follows:

Macro (International)		Micro (Local Market)	
US Industry Beta	β	EM Industry Beta	β
Sector Average	0,95	Comparable Company 1	0,95
		Comparable Company 2	1,05
		Comparable Company 3	0,90
		Comparable Company 4	0,97
		Comparable Company 5	0,89
		Average	0,95

Fig. 2 Analysing betas

$$\text{Levered Beta} = \text{Unlevered Beta} \ /[1 + (1 - t)\, x\, D/E]$$

The author's suggested practical approach is to triangulate a synthesis using US or global macro average industry betas—and thus ensure consistency with the other international cost of capital inputs we have previously discussed—and compare with a micro list of emerging market local firms, if available, to assess for alignment. For the latter, we can choose to analyse specific segments, broader related industries or firms with a similar business model, potentially cleaning the data set for firms in financial distress. Furthermore, if a company operates in multiple sectors, or countries, we can use the weighted average— by revenue streams, for instance—to enhance the computation.

For example, a private firm operating in a single sector and country of which there are comparable companies in the local market (Fig. 2):

As a closing point, let us consider the use of Total Beta. Despite certain controversies, the scholarly literature on total beta emphasizes its potential relevance for capturing the potential increased risk levels that less diversified investors could encounter in private company assets. In the CAPM universe, investors can diversify most of the risks peculiar to emerging markets and thus corporate finance theory is clear: the discount rate—should consider only non-diversifiable risk, with diversifiable risk better contemplated in cash flow projections. However, according to practitioners like Damodaran (2011a, 2011b) and Fernández (2019), total beta better captures the realities of private firm valuation by accounting for both systematic and unsystematic risks, making up for the absence of portfolio diversification which could be a key concern in emerging markets. The debate will continue. However, in the author's experience, at the practical level, it often seems self-evident that the result of cost of capital calculations using Total Beta provide more realistic estimates for smaller private firms.

The formula is given as follows:

$$Total\ Beta = \frac{Standard\ Deviation\ of\ Firm's\ Sector\ Returns}{Standard\ Deviation\ of\ Market's\ Returns}$$

We borrow again from Pereiro (2010) who asserts that "we are interested in total beta because it is a most useful risk measure for undiversified investors—e.g., private-firm owners whose wealth is concentrated into a single stock and thus bear the handicap of nil diversification. Also, total beta works well as a maximum extreme reference for partially diversified investors" and can also be adopted to calculate a "true" beta for those investors who hold partially diversified portfolios.

Cost of Debt (Rd)

The cost of debt reflects the effective interest rate a firm pays on its borrowings, adjusted for tax benefits. In emerging markets, high inflation, currency devaluation risks, and limited credit access elevate borrowing costs. Firms may also rely on international debt markets, where they face higher spreads due to perceived country risk. Calculating the cost of debt involves considering the firm's credit rating, the default risk premium, and the tax shield benefits. The choice of tax rate (effective or statutory) can significantly affect borrowing costs.

The academic literature on calculating the cost of debt for emerging market firms emphasizes approaches that adjust for additional risks specific to these markets. We summarize below some key points raised in the literature which we will expand upon below:

- Adjusted Sovereign Spreads: Pereiro (2002) and Bekaert and Harvey (1995a, 1995b) suggest contemplating sovereign spreads (e.g., from Credit Default Swaps or bond yield differentials) to a base risk-free rate, reflecting country-specific risks such as political instability or currency volatility and essentially then, higher borrowing rates for many emerging market companies.
- Local vs. Global Debt Markets: Godfrey and Espinosa (1996) advocate for the use of local currency-denominated yields when available, to better capture the firm's domestic market conditions. In the absence of robust and meaningful local numbers, dollar-denominated or global debt instruments may act as proxies, better encompassing international investors' perceptions of risk.
- Imputed Market Rates: For companies that do not have traded debt, Fernández (2019) recommends imputing the cost of debt from market benchmarks or sector-wide averages, adjusted for company-specific credit ratings or scores.

In summary, when assessing company debt to calculate the cost of capital, we have two main options. We can choose to utilize either the market value or the book value of debt. For publicly listed firms, this is somewhat straightforward as we can assume that book value of debt roughly equals the market value, or we can estimate the market value of debt based on projected interest payments and the face value and maturity of the debt. Logically, what is important is to encompass the current, or rather marginal, cost of debt, and the most up to date corporate lending and risk profile. To calculate the cost of debt for these firms, we can use a synthetic rating based on their interest rate coverage (the proportion of EBIT divided by interest expenses) and use this function to calculate a default rating spread or the yields on bonds issued by these listed firms to arrive at the cost of debt.

Nevertheless, let us again focus on the more challenging space of private company cost of debt and provide some key considerations.

- D/E Ratio: If our starting point is the belief that the balance sheet value of debt for private companies is of limited value, we can propose one of the following approaches:
  - Assume the company possesses debt dynamics similar to the broader sector and thus use the industry average. This method would be especially valid if we are valuing a potential IPO event during the forecast period.
  - After analysis of the company's balance sheet and in discussion with the management team, we can also stipulate a target D/E ratio.
  - Another option is to adjust the industry average beta based on the degree of the firm's operational leverage. Operating leverage is a financial metric that measures a company's ability to increase profits by increasing revenue or put differently the ratio between a company's fixed and variable costs.
- Cost of borrowing:
  - In its simplest form, in local currency terms, we could use the cost of borrowing of the most recent financing terms the private company has as our cost of debt rather than looking at past loans. Once again, the guiding principle is what marginal or future interest rates would look like, not only for the company and sector (certain countries could have subsidized loan rates for specific segments) but the expected monetary dynamics of the emerging market as a whole. For example, if in our emerging market, firms at currently paying an average spread of 5% over the central bank base rate, and this premium is expected to remain stable during our forecasts, we would model the cost of debt as a function of this spread against projections of the interest rate in future periods, assuming of course that debt financing is expected to come via domestic credit markets.
  - In dollar terms, we could employ a similar "synthetic" approach to that of public firms, that is, a spread based on the interest coverage ratio against a stipulated ratings spread and also contemplate a country spread default to arrive at the costs of debt. In this case, we could use as our base, smaller cap listed firms in a similar sector. The following formula provides a guide:

    $$\text{Cost of debt}\,() = \text{Riskfree Rate} + \text{Company Spread} + \text{Country Spread}$$

  - Tax impacts are integral to WACC, as interest expenses are tax-deductible, reducing the effective cost of debt. The final step then in calculating the cost of debt is to incorporate the after-tax cost of debt into valuation to reflect the value of tax shields to account for the actual tax benefits derived from interest expense deductions. Tax shields from cross-border financing structures may require additional adjustments to align with local regulations. In emerging markets, where firms may face inconsistent enforcement of tax laws, differing or dynamic regulations or variations in marginal rates, practitioners often adjust for these inconsistencies by using effective tax rates based on historical data or industry averages. A key theme here is that in emerging markets with differing tax regimes, not all companies will have access to tax shields. For instance, in Brazil, only companies that adhere to the "Real Profit" tax system can legitimately claim to have tax shields. This raises two further points: our cash flow projections should reflect any anticipated changes in the company's tax regime and also any previous losses which can be utilized throughout the explicit projection period. For reasons of conservativism and adherence to local accounting principles, the author would suggest it is best practice to use marginal tax rates even if that equates to a reduction in forecast after tax operating income. Furthermore, if we use effective rates, we are assuming that the company will be able to maintain its tax contributions at the potentially lower level in the future which might not always be the case. A hybrid solution to this question could also involve extrapolating out the tax rate from effective to marginal rates by the end of the cash flow projection period.

- Input consistency: As a final sense check, we need to make sure that the numbers for debt (D/E ratios etc.) we use in our cost of capital calculations are aligned with the debt adjustments we make to arrive at Equity Value from Enterprise Value.

Inflation and Currency Adjustments

The use of inflation rate differentials in capital cost calculations is a key step for valuations in emerging markets. Higher interest rates and inflation are common elements of emerging markets which subsequently impact the cost of both debt and equity. As such, inflation volatility increases uncertainty meaning that higher risk premiums are required. Inflation influences not only the nominal risk-free rate but also potential returns. Godfrey and Espinosa (1996) assert that inflation adjustments are essential for ensuring that valuations incorporate consistent purchasing power parity (PPP) and thus ensures that nominal cash flows and discount rates have comparable characteristics across various currencies and economic contexts. What is important is to ensure alignment between the currency of our cash flow forecasts and the currency in which you estimate your discount rate. The use of nominal rates without inflation-adjusted cash flows can skew valuation results. The name of the game is consistency between currencies, inputs, and between nominal and real cash flows. As an additional point, firms operating across multiple currencies may adopt hedging strategies to stabilize cash flows, but these introduce additional costs that must be reflected valuation model.

Company-Specific Risk Premium

Practitioners often use company-specific risk premiums (CSRP) by adjusting the discount rate in their valuation models to reflect unique firm-level risks. This is because the CAPM model works on the prevailing premise with a well-diversified portfolio of assets, investors should not be "compensated" for unsystematic or diversifiable risk. But can risks and returns be fully explained solely by Beta? Likewise, are all investors in emerging market firms diversified? Or going further, should the marginal investor's degree of diversification impact company valuation? If so, is a two-tier level of cost of capital methodology, academically solid?

Ultimately, in private company valuations experts may include a CSRP to account for supplementary endogenous factors like revenue or earnings quality, limited operational history, governance concerns, or key person risks (Damodaran 2011a, 2011b). Similarly, at the exogenous level, in emerging markets, practitioners might use CSRPs to address political instability, illiquidity, currency volatility, not captured by traditional beta calculations (Pereiro 2002). At the company management level, Claessens and Yurtoglu (2012) argued that better corporate governance leads to higher returns on equity and enhanced efficiency for local firms. However, there is no universal CSRP model, even if some financial and risk advisory firms like Duff & Phelps provide risk premium reporting guidelines to assist in estimating discount rates. Nevertheless, to help illustrate the rationale utilized in such considerations, we can use a similar framework as presented by Gross Mendelsohn, a global financial services and CPA consulting firm (Fig. 3):

In conclusion, let us look a bit more closely at some of these principal-specific qualitative and quantitative risk factors which for emerging market valuations are of greater importance. After all, as we highlighted in the beginning of this chapter, valuations are impacted by risk as one of our key building blocks of intrinsic value. For example:

- Political risk premium: Companies operating in politically unstable regions may add a CSRP, for instance, a range between 0.5% and 2%, depending on the severity of the identified risk. The logic would be that a highly volatile country like Venezuela might see a higher adjustment compared to one in Chile with broadly less instability. Jensen (2008) contended that political instability often leads to higher required returns, as investors demand additional compensation for the uncertainty surrounding policy continuity. One approach to measuring political risk involves using indices such as the International Country Risk Guide (ICRG), which quantifies factors such as government stability and regulatory quality. Another method is scenario analysis, where firms model various political outcomes and their implications on projected cash flow (more on this approach below). Political risk could also manifest as a greater concentration of sales dependent on public sector clients. For certain risks such as nationalization, scenario analysis is the best way to model such uncertainty and the possible impact on value. Simply put, not all risks can be integrated into the WACC framework.

Component	Risk		
	Low	Neutral	High
Specific person			x
Small company			x
Management depth			x
Access to capital	x		
Customer concentration		x	
Product or service diversification		x	
Geographical distribution		x	
Volatility of earnings or cash flow			x
Potential new competitors			x
Pending litigation	x		
Pending regulatory changes	x		

Fig. 3 Qualitatively estimating CSRPs. Credit: Gross Mendelsohn (2022)

- Size premium (SCP): We could devote several chapters alone on this well-discussed and interesting concept but unfortunately a more detailed analysis is out of the scope of this chapter. Suffice to say that the existence, quantification, and causes of the SCP have been endlessly debated. Industry professionals and investors often utilize an additional adjustment of 3–6% to account for the assumed greater risk and return profile of smaller companies. On the surface, it does make sense. According to data from Ibbotson, an investment management company, the annual yield of US small caps beat large cap returns by 1.7% between 1926 and 2022. Cordischi (2024) helps contextualize:

  In 1981, economist Rolf W. Banz showed that the superior relative returns of small caps cannot be explained merely by CAPM beta—there is an additional small cap premium. Further risk factors have been identified over the years. The Fama-French three factor model of 1992 comprises market risk, a small cap premium and a value premium.

  To apply this logic in considering the SCP, analysts usually rely on a formula that looks like this:

$$\text{Expected Return} = \text{Risk free rate} + \text{Beta} * \text{Equity Risk Premium} \\ + \text{Small Cap Premium}$$

This is all very well and good in theory, but the rationale for SCP usage has shaky quantitative foundations. As always, concepts such as "one size fits all" and industry inertia along the lines of "we have always used a SCP" do not necessitate a robust valuation. The author would then agree with Damodaran (2015a, 2015b) — who else?! —who in a succinct analysis suggests that smaller firms are indeed potentially more exposed to certain risks than large firms but that these heightened risk factors, such as capital constraints, bankruptcy, and lack of liquidity—and additionally say greater client concentration and related operational variables, for example—can be better accounted for directly in the composition of cash flow projections and reinvestment capacity via expected values or as an end of valuation lack of liquidity or marketability discount (DLOM).

In practice, these premiums are often determined through qualitative assessments, accumulated experience of use by the valuator, or benchmarking against industry peers facing similar risks, though this approach remains generally subjective and varies amongst professionals, with both points providing valuation challenges. Nonetheless, one is reminded of the aphorism "perfect is the enemy of good". That being said, Kroll (2011), a financial and risk advisory firm, offered a balanced summary which the author feels helps us conclude this section and smoothly transitions into the chapter's final thoughts and WACC calculations:

> There is still no consensus in the professional valuation community or the courts as to the best means of identifying and incorporating company-specific risks into a DCF analyses. What is clear is that purely subjective reasoning will be insufficient in advocating for a higher discount rate to reflect these risks. Valuators should consider all available information and all available alternatives, and avoid vague, unsupportable statements. Instead, analysts should present thoughtful, reasoned, and well-developed analyses. In many cases, risk-adjusting the cash flows directly will produce the most reliable and supportable analyses to reflect company-specific risks.

Closing Thoughts: The Discount Rate Is Not a "Panacea" for all Risk

We have seen that in cash flow valuation models, the discount rate is our principal vehicle for expressing our concerns about risks to our projected cash flows. In synopsis, we use higher discount rates on riskier cash flows and lower discount rates on more predictable cash flows. That being said, it has also been suggested throughout this chapter that the discount rate is not a universal cure-all for every risk industry-analysts encounter during valuation assignments. A number of scholars and professionals have criticized the over-reliance on discount rates as the only source of information about all valuation risks. Copeland et al. (1994) contended that although the cost of capital represents systematic risks, many firm-specific and project-specific uncertainties can be accounted for in cash flow forecasts. Fernandez (2004a, 2004b) also highlighted that rather than inflating the BUM discount rate *ad infinitum,* it is preferable to directly incorporate operational risks management inefficiencies, and other non-systematic factors into cash flow projections. Koller et al. (2020a, 2020b) agree and emphasize that rather than depending only on a higher cost of capital, valuation accuracy increases when risks such as demand variability and regulatory changes are explicitly modelled in cash flows. Damodaran also regularly argues this point in numerous articles and books, so it seems we are on solid academic grounds. The author also recalls Warren Buffet quoting the economist John Maynard Keynes, "I would rather be vaguely right, than precisely wrong", which aptly flags up that financial analysis is not always a precise exercise. Moreover, by compartmentalizing risks—systematic ones in the discount rate and idiosyncratic or operational risks in the cash flows—our valuation narrative becomes more robust and better aligned with real-world dynamics by quantifying specific value drivers or adjustments in our projections.

Indeed, an interesting article from the global consultancy firm McKinsey & Company written by Guimaraes and Koller (2021) even argues that "the risks of investing in emerging markets are real, but it's not necessary to amplify them by adding an extra risk premium to the cost of capital". As such they provide a critique of a one-size-fits-all approach to the use of CRPs. We summarize three key arguments of the paper as follows:

(a) When projecting future performance additional country risk premiums are frequently set too high which can make good projects appear unattractive or paying over the odds. To the authors, the use of typically high WACCs may result in implicitly unrealistic assumptions in growth rates or returns on investment.
(b) They contend that it does not make sense to apply the same risk premium to every company in a country. Some companies in emerging markets may have lower costs of debt than their government. In sum, many companies have investment-grade ratings but whilst the country government may not.
(c) What's more, their research demonstrated that in certain emerging markets, the valuation of stocks does not incorporate a significant country risk premium and that performance factors rather than country risk alone can account for differences.

To your author, such arguments represent coherent academic positions which we can incorporate into our tool kit. As such, every emerging market valuation should capture the specific and unique risk and return profiles of the company being analysed. Many risks in emerging markets are idiosyncratic, meaning they don't apply equally to all companies and sectors. But there is a solution. If as valuators we feel that the inputs we are using to estimate discount rates, such as cost of debt, country exposure *et al*, need to be adjusted upwards or downwards, then that is a key part of the process. At this stage, we can make three macro points. First, it seems apparent that on the whole, the cost of capital of an emerging market company should be different from the cost of capital for a developed market firm (if of course we can make broad generalizations). Second, we should of course treat large

Net present value (NPV) for "business as usual" and "economic distressed" scenarios, identical facilities

Scenario approach

European market
Cash flows in perpetuity[1]

Probability	Scenario	Year 1	2	3	4…
100%	As usual	100	103	106	109
0%	Distressed	–	–	–	–
Expected cash flows		100	103	106	109
Cost of capital					7.5%
Net present value					€2,222

Emerging market
Cash flows in perpetuity[2]

Probability	Scenario	Year 1	2	3	4…
75%	As usual	100	103	106	109
25%	Distressed	45	46	48	49
Expected cash flows		86	89	92	94
Cost of capital					7.5%
Net present value (86% of European NPV)					€1,917

Country-risk-premium approach

European market
Cash flows in perpetuity[1]

Scenario	Year 1	2	3	4…
As usual	100	103	106	109
Cost of capital				7.5%
NPV				€2,222

Emerging market
Cash flows in perpetuity[2]

Scenario	Year 1	2	3	4…
As usual	100	103	106	109
Cost of capital				7.5%
Country risk premium				0.7%
Adjusted cost of capital				8.2%
NPV (86% of European NPV)				€1,917

Fig. 4 Scenario-based approach to DCF: BAU and economic distress. Notes: The authors assume a cash flow growth rate of 3% in perpetuity and the same rate and a recovery "under distress" rate of 45% of cash flows "as usual". Credit: Guimaraes, Leandro, and Koller, Tim, 2021 (a McKinsey & Company publication)

publicly listed EM firms differently from smaller private corporates. Lastly, we need to make sure any adjustments we make for EMs are coherent and in line with financial theory and avoid seeking to "reinvent the [WACC] wheel". We also certainly need to "sense check" and reverse engineer our assumptions to make sure they are realistic throughout the forecast period and in perpetuity.

As a last point, we again borrow from the McKinsey article which the author feels could provide an insightful solution to ensure we do not "overload" our discount rates. We will quote in full and also provide their graphical illustration of the concept (Fig. 4):

> It's all too easy to underestimate the impact that even a small country risk premium has on valuations. Macro analyses can mask a wide variation in P/Es across economies. But that's where the scenario discounted-cash-flow (DCF) approach proves its mettle: it assesses risks based on company-specific factors and tests what the effects of those risks would mean to the business being valued. At a minimum, business leaders should model two scenarios. The first should reflect cash flows that could develop under "business as usual" conditions—for instance, in the absence of major economic distress. The second should reflect cash flows that could develop if one or more emerging-market risks materialize. Exploring different scenarios forces managers to discuss emerging-market risks and their effect on cash flows under realistically conceivable circumstances, thereby gaining more insights than they would from a simple, arbitrary addition to the discount rate.

Putting It All Together: A WACC Example for a Privately Held Brazilian Firm

- In this phase of the valuation, we have built our cash flow model and projected our earnings for a five-year period and then calculated our perpetuity values. Our valuation is a two-stage model.
- Our valuation model will be based on the Free Cash Flow to Firm (FCFF) approach which represents the cash flow from operations based on the operating profit available for distribution after taking account of depreciation expenses, working capital, and capital investments. As such, our discount rate will be the WACC.
- Our cash flows are forecast in local currency—in our case, the Brazilian Real (R $)—and subsequently our WACC will also be calculated in the local currency. In our example, the Brazilian company's sales are concentrated in the domestic market which affects our CRP calculation. We also need to define if our cash flows and discount rate will be in nominal or real terms.
- Moreover, as a small firm with no plans to raise institutional capital or IPO over the forecast period, the marginal investor is undiversified and as a result, we adopt the Total Beta approach.
- As an additional sense check, our professional experience suggests that the resulting WACC is in line with previous similar valuations and current market realities in Brazil, including central bank rates and credit spreads for private firms, even if they seem high by international standards.
- Broader risk factors identified during the valuation process, such as failure or execution risk, liquidity concerns, and earnings adjustments—normalized EBITDA, etc. —will be contemplated either directly in the cash flow forecasts or as direct discounts to resulting enterprise value. This guarantees that we have better visibility of risks and value drivers in our cash flow model (Fig. 5).

Essentially then the WACC illustrates how much the company is remunerating it's capital holders. As we have seen, a high WACC typically signals higher risk associated with business operations, and vice-versa. But then relatively speaking, what is high and what is low?

In the above example, we arrive at a calculated WACC of 21.3% and 20.4% over the explicit forecast period and perpetuity, respectively. Do such discount rates make sense? It is common for the valuator to critically assess the final estimate of WACC, questioning whether it appears too high or too low based on the assumptions and prevailing market conditions. Where risk factors are more complex and interrelated as in emerging market contexts, this level of scrutiny can be beneficial. Refinements can of course be made, but in the end the model drives the result, and adjustments must be made on the basis of sound financial sense and not attempting to arrive at a preconceived conclusion. Let the model do the heavy lifting, after all as we have argued, not all company risk should be contemplated in the discount rate anyway.

Example: Weighted Average Cost of Capital	**Forecast Period**	**Perpetuity**	**Formulas & Notes**
CAPM			
Risk Free Rate (Rfr)	4,00%	4,50%	Forecast Period: Fitted Yield on a 5 Year Zero Coupon Bond (median last 30 days) Perpetuity: Fitted Yield on a 30 Year Zero Coupon Bond
Equity Risk Premium (ERP)	4,50%	4,75%	Forecast Period: Implied ERP - Trailing 12-month cash yield Perpetuity: Forecast long term ERP
Beta	3,16	3,16	
Country Risk Premium (CRP)	3,50%	3,00%	
Volatility Brazilian Stock Exchange	30,00%	30,00%	Based on historical and expected performance we maintain these ratios stable in our example
Volatility Brazilian Government Bond	20,00%	20,00%	
Total CRP	5,25%	4,50%	Forecast Period: Total CRP = Default spread on country bond * (σCountry Equity / σCountry Bond) Forecast Period: Forecast spread * (σCountry Equity / σCountry Bond)
Total ERP	**9,75%**	**9,25%**	
(+) Small-Cap Premium (SCP)	0,00%	0,00%	Not contemplated in this example
(+) Company Specific Risk Premium (CSRP)	0,00%	0,00%	Not contemplated in this example
CAPM in USD	**23,46%**	**24,00%**	
US Inflation	2,00%	2,20%	Forecast Period: Average projected inflation rate per country Perpetuity: Long-term projected inflation rate per country
Brazil Inflation	4,00%	3,50%	
CAPM in BRL	**25,89%**	**25,58%**	
Beta			
Unlevered Beta (βu)	0,95	0,95	We use the same bottom-up beta from the example in the chapter and assess that its determinants will remain stable over both the forecast period and perpetuity
Marginal Tax Rate	34,00%	34,00%	We use the marginal tax rate for Brazilian firms in the "Real Profit" regime
D/E	50,00%	50,00%	Based on market averages of comparable firms. In this example we maintain the D/E stable over the long term
Average Market Correlation	40,00%	40,00%	We will assume that the diversification dynamics will stay the same in our example
Total Unlevered Beta	2,38	2,38	=Market Beta / ρMarket
Total Levered Beta	**3,16**	**3,16**	Total Levered Beta = Totalβu + (D / E) Totalβu (1 – t)
Summary: WACC Estimates			
Equity %	66,67%	66,67%	
Cost of Equity %	25,89%	25,58%	
Debt %	33,33%	33,33%	
Net Cost of Debt %	12,00%	10,00%	We utilize recent company interest rates aligned with the current credit environment adjusted for future market dynamics and discounting the tax shield
WACC in BRL	**21,3%**	**20,4%**	

Fig. 5 Private Brazilian firm WACC computation. Source: Author´s own creation

That said, ensuring consistency with previous valuation exercises and market realities is crucial. A common pitfall is local currency vs. USD mismatches: Is a WACC of nearly 20% believable if the local risk-free rate is 18% in the first place? Forward-looking metrics and market trend analysis can be used to check assumptions as will making sure country risk and local financing dynamics are being adequately considered.

Moreover, to avoid such possible inconsistencies, techniques like sensitivity analysis—checking how the effect of WACC changes on economic value—can often provide a clearer picture. Furthermore, computing WACC in the local currency as an additional sense check can help reveal any potential inconsistencies or result mismatches and enhance confidence in the final cost of capital computations and consequently a market-consistent valuation.

Conclusion

The cost of capital in emerging markets is a complex and dynamic concept that requires careful consideration of various factors. As emerging markets continue to grow and integrate into the global economy, the importance of accurately estimating the cost of capital in these regions will be increasingly important. In this chapter, we have argued that by adjusting our traditional cost of capital estimates to encompass country-specific risks, currency differentials, and market inefficiencies, we can help make sure that they reflect the true risks associated with investing in emerging markets. We have also summarized part of the academic literature to provide a synopsis of challenges and solutions and technical options we have when required to build out adequate emerging market WACCs. We then provided a working model for an emerging market WACC calculation and an adjoining conceptual discussion to help elucidate the discussion. Ultimately, a well-estimated cost of capital is not only a critical component of valuation but also a key determinant of investment decisions in emerging markets, whose risk and return profiles require additional attention, to ensure we can accurately analyse if the "juice is worth the squeeze" in EM valuations.

References

Abuaf (2011 & 2015), quoted in Walker, Eduardo (2016) Cost of capital in emerging markets: bridging gaps between theory and practice. Latin Am J Econ 53(1): 111–147.

Bekaert G, Harvey CR (1995a) Time-varying world market integration. J Financ 50(2):403–444

Bekaert G, Harvey CR (1995b) Emerging equity market volatility. J Financ Econ

Buffett W (1998) Comments on weighted average cost of capital (WACC) during the 1998 Berkshire Hathaway annual meeting. Cited in Seeking Alpha (2013). Available at: https://seekingalpha.com/article/1641702-wacc-is-flawed-use-warren-buffetts-approach-instead

Claessens S, Yurtoglu B (2012) Corporate governance and development: an update. Global Corporate Governance Forum Focus, No. 10. International Finance Corporation, Washington, DC. Published April 23, 2012
Copeland T, Koller T, Murrin J (1994) Valuation: measuring and managing the value of companies. Wiley
Cordischi A (2024) The small-cap premium: down but not out. Available at: https://www.worldfinance.com/banking/the-small-cap-premium-down-but-not-out
Damodaran A (2002) Investment valuation: tools and techniques for determining the value of any asset, 2nd edn. Wiley, New York, NY
Damodaran A (2004) Country risk and company exposure: theory and practice. J Appl Financ
Damodaran A (2009a) The dark side of valuation: Valuing young, distressed, and complex businesses. Pearson Education, Upper Saddle River, NJ
Damodaran A (2009b) The dark side of valuation: valuing young, distressed, and complex businesses. FT Press
Damodaran A (2011a) The little book of valuation: how to value a company, pick a stock, and profit. Wiley, Hoboken, NJ
Damodaran A (2011b) Applied corporate finance. Wiley
Damodaran A (2015a) Putting the D in the DCF: the cost of capital. Available at: https://aswathdamodaran.blogspot.com/2015/01/putting-d-in-dcf-cost-of-capital.html
Damodaran A (2015b) The small cap premium: where is the beef? Available at: https://aswathdamodaran.blogspot.com/2015/04/the-small-cap-premium-fact-fiction-and.html
Damodaran A (2016) The cost of capital: the Swiss army knife of finance. NYU Stern School of Business. Available at: https://www.stern.nyu.edu
Damodaran A (2023) Implied ERP. Available at: https://pages.stern.nyu.edu/~adamodar/pdfiles/eqnotes/webcasts/ERP/ImpliedERP.pdf
Damodaran A (2024) Equity Risk Premiums (ERP): determinants, estimation and implications – the data. Available at: https://pages.stern.nyu.edu/~adamodar/New_Home_Page/datafile/crryprem.htm. Accessed: December 2024.
Erb CB, Harvey CR, Viskanta TE (1996) Expected returns and volatility in 135 countries. J Portf Manag
Estrada J (2000) The cost of equity in emerging markets: a downside risk approach. Emerg Mark Q 4(1):19–30
Fernandez P (2004a) The value of tax shields is NOT equal to the present value of tax shields. J Financ Econ
Fernandez P (2004b) Company valuation methods: the most common errors in valuations. IESE Business School Working Paper. Available at: https://papers.ssrn.com/sol3/papers.cfm?abstract_id=274973
Fernández P (2019) Valuation and common sense, 5th edn. IESE Business School, Madrid
Fisher I (1930) The theory of interest. Macmillan
Godfrey S, Espinosa R (1996) A practical approach to calculating costs of equity for investments in emerging markets. J Appl Corp Financ 9(3):80–89
Gross Mendelsohn (2022) Understanding the company-specific risk premium: a guide for attorneys. Available at: https://www.gma-cpa.com/blog/understanding-the-company-specific-risk-premium-a-guide-for-attorneys
Guimaraes L, Koller T (2021) Don't overthink your approach to valuation in emerging markets. McKinsey & Company. Available at: https://www.mckinsey.com/capabilities/strategy-and-corporate-finance/our-insights/dont-overthink-your-approach-to-valuation-in-emerging-markets
Homer S, Sylla R (2005) A history of interest rates, 4th edn. Rutgers University Press, p 25
Jensen MC (2008) The small-cap premium: reality or illusion? Harvard Business School Working Paper Series
Kaplan SN, Ruback RS (1995) The valuation of cash flow forecasts: an empirical analysis. J Financ

Koller T, Goedhart M, Wessels D (2020a) Valuation: measuring and managing the value of companies. Wiley

Koller T, Goedhart M, Wessels D (2020b) Valuation: measuring and managing the value of companies, 7th edn. McKinsey & Company and Wiley

Kroll (2011) From the parlor to the courtroom: the use of company-specific risk premium in valuations. Available at: https://www.kroll.com/en/insights/publications/expert-services/from-the-parlor-to-the-courtroom-the-use-of-company-specific-risk-premium-in-valuations

Lintner J (1965) The valuation of risk assets and the selection of risky investments in stock portfolios and capital budgets. Rev Econ Stat 47(1):13–37

Modigliani F, Miller MH (1958) The cost of capital, corporation finance, and the theory of investment. Am Econ Rev 48(3):261–297

Mossin J (1966) Equilibrium in a capital asset market. Econometrica 34(4):768–783

Myers SC (1974) Interactions of corporate financing and investment decisions—implications for capital budgeting. J Financ 29(1):1–25. https://doi.org/10.2307/2978188

Pereiro LE (2002) Valuation of companies in emerging markets: a practical approach. Wiley, New York, NY

Pereiro LE (2010) The beta dilemma in emerging markets. J Corp Finan

Sharpe WF (1964) Capital asset prices: a theory of market equilibrium under conditions of risk. J Financ 19(3):425–442

Williams JB (1938) The theory of investment value. Harvard University Press, Cambridge, MA

Estimating Privately Held Capital Asset Values in Emerging Markets Using Certainty-Equivalent Risk Pricing

Malcolm McLelland

Abstract This chapter presents an method alternative to estimating risk-adjusted discount rates used in valuation of privately held capital assets, which is derived directly from post-CAPM asset pricing theory. The method—which can be termed the certainty-equivalent risk pricing method—is particularly useful in estimating values of privately held capital assets in emerging markets because of its conceptual simplicity, objectivity, and transparency. As a means of explaining the optimality of the method, common problems encountered in estimating the value of privately held capital assets are reviewed and how such problems have commonly resulted in the use of subjective, ad hoc methods. Asset pricing theory underlying the certainty-equivalent risk pricing method is briefly explained and the method is then explicitly derived from the theory. Finally, a realistic example of international risk pricing and valuation of a hypothetical Brazilian company that exports manufactured products into the global economy is presented.

Keywords Privately held capital assets · Emerging markets · Valuation · No-arbitrage · Risk pricing

Introduction

A common view among finance professionals is that estimated values of privately held capital assets—enterprises, business units, debt and equity interests not traded in public markets—are necessarily subject to substantial professional judgment and, hence, highly subjective; especially assets exchanged in cross-border, emerging market transactions. Despite ample financial economic theory and supporting evidence to the contrary, business valuation professionals largely continue to hold this belief and suggest such valuation estimates necessarily rely on variety of complex,

M. McLelland (✉)
McLelland Financial Economics LLC, Saint Petersburg, FL, USA
e-mail: mmc@mclelland-financial-economics.com

S. Derindere Köseoğlu, A. Patterson (eds.), *Valuation in Emerging Markets*, Contributions to Finance and Accounting,
https://doi.org/10.1007/978-3-031-93526-8_9

ad hoc professional judgments relating to currency translation, so-called country risk, and illiquidity and non-marketability discounts.

The objective of this chapter is to allow finance professionals to become familiar with the financial economic theory and related methods that allow development of valuation estimates of privately held assets in emerging markets in an accurate, reliable manner with a minimum of subjective judgment and untestable assumptions. In contrast to common existing valuation practice, it is possible and more efficient to use well-known theory and methods that have existed for roughly 40 years, which result in value estimates supported by objective judgment, testable assumptions, and reliable empirical data.

Background

Capital asset values depend on expected cash flows and risk-adjusted discount rates. A relatively few concepts and principles are addressed in this chapter, which are understood at some level by all finance professionals. Such concepts and principles are directly related to the following expression with which all finance professionals are familiar with:

$$\underbrace{FMV_t = \sum_{u=t}^{T} \underbrace{\frac{1}{\left(1+\overline{R}\right)^{u-t}}}_{\substack{\text{risk-adjusted} \\ \text{cash flow} \\ \text{discount factor} \\ \text{for } u=[0,T]}} \cdot \underbrace{CF_u}_{\substack{\text{expected} \\ \text{future} \\ \text{cash flow} \\ \text{at time } u}}}_{\substack{\text{fair market value } (FMV) \text{ of a capital asset is} \\ \text{equal to its expected future cash flows } (CF) \\ \text{discounted at the risk-adjusted expected} \\ \text{rate of return } (\overline{R}) \text{ set in a } \textit{fair market}}}$$

As can be seen in the above expression, there are basically two things required to obtain an estimate of *fair market value* (*FMV*) of a capital asset: Estimates of (1) expected future cash flows (*CF*) obtained from holding the capital asset, and (2) the risk-adjusted expected rate of return for the asset set in a *fair capital market*.

Fair capital markets. Most finance professionals are familiar with the concept of a *fair market* from various professional literature, but the concept will be defined for purposes of this chapter as follows:

A *fair capital market* is a market where *risks* influencing returns to holding capital assets are traded in a competitive manner where both buyers and sellers have open, unrestricted access to trading in the market.

A common perspective is that existing capital markets are anything but fair; largely because of the potential for restricted access to markets, information asymmetries between market participants, and so on *within individual capital markets* (e.g., the New York Stock Exchange). One of the primary implications of modern asset pricing theory (e.g., arbitrage pricing theory and risk-neutral pricing theory), however, is that capital markets facilitate the trading of *risks* via the trading of securities. For example, the risk of the devaluation of the U.S. Dollar at the 1-year horizon is traded not only in primary and secondary markets for U.S. Treasury securities, but across many capital asset classes traded in both public and private market transactions—for example, equity securities, alternative investments, and real estate—as well as globally across countries and a variety of organized securities exchanges. In short, even if trading of individual or certain portfolios of securities is restricted, this does not necessarily render capital markets unfair; it is only unfair to the extent that trading in the underlying *risks* influencing capital asset returns is restricted in a systematic way across markets.

The definition of a *fair capital market* and the discussion here suggests that even if an individual capital market might not be considered *fair—aggregate global capital markets* can accurately be regarded as a fair market for trading risks, if not for individual securities. As will be seen in an example of estimating the value of a privately held enterprise in Brazil, this insight into capital markets is not only important for valuation of capital assets in emerging markets, but for valuation of privately held assets more generally.

Risk factor is defined as any observable factor that influences cash flows associated with holding a capital asset. Accordingly, the FMV of a capital asset, its expected cash flows, and its risk-adjusted rate of return are appropriately regarded as functions of any such risk factors:

$$\underbrace{FMV_t(\mathbf{x}) = \sum_{u=t}^{T} \frac{1}{\left(1+\overline{R}(\mathbf{x})\right)^{u-t}} \cdot CF_u(\mathbf{x}) = \sum_{u=t}^{T} \frac{1}{\left(1+\overline{R}(\mathbf{x})\right)^{u-t}} \cdot (\alpha+\beta_1 x_1+\beta_2 x_2+\ldots+\beta_K x_K)}_{\substack{\text{fair market value } (FMV) \text{ of a capital asset, its expected future cash flows, and it} \\ \text{risk-adjusted expected rate of return as a function of risks } \mathbf{x}=(x_1,x_2,\ldots,x_K)}}$$

From this perspective on capital markets and risk factors, estimating FMV of capital assets reduces to estimating relationships between observable risk factors, cash flows, and capital market returns (and, hence, discount rates), which is generally best accomplished using statistical methods. It is, of course, the case that expected cash flows and risk-adjusted discount rates do not necessarily have linear relationships to risk factors suggested by the above expression. But such linear relationships, when carefully regarded as "local linear approximations," are often sufficiently accurate and reliable for capital asset value estimation. Although the theory and methods discussed in this chapter will be presented in terms of linear models, discussion of non-linear models is avoided only because (i) it is usually possible to modify models to capture non-linearities and (ii) issues relating to non-linearities would obscure the more fundamental ideas being presented and lead to a focus on more advanced aspects of statistical methods rather than on valuation per se.

Expected future cash flows are defined as the expected payoffs measured in monetary units that results from holding a capital asset, where such payoffs come either in the form of expected cash distributions, or expected sales proceeds (net of transaction costs), to the holder of the asset. Such payoffs are generally regarded as *risky*—that is, subject to *uncertainty*—but may be either risky or certain.

Because, circa 2025, there are arguably no coherent theories explaining and predicting how investors form expectations of future cash flows, this aspect of developing valuation estimates will be avoided. The interested reader in such matters is referred to texts that address econometric forecasting (e.g., Wooldridge 2009).

Cross-border currency issues. One aspect of expected future cash flows that should be addressed in emerging market valuation is cross-border currency adjustments. Textbook discussions on international valuation issues suggest the currency in which expected cash flows are denominated must be "matched" to the discount rate used in estimating value. For example, an asset generating cash flows denominated in U.S. Dollars (USD) should not be discounted using a discount rate appropriate for discounting cash flows denominated in Brazilian Real currency (BRL). The idea underlying what might be termed the *currency consistency principle* is that different currencies have different inflation rates, which are best thought of as relative currency devaluation rates.

The apparent logic of the principle, as suggested by textbooks, is that unless expected cash flows and discount rates are matched with respect to currencies, there will generally be errors in the nominal risk-free components of discount rates because of mismatches between (i) expected inflation implicit in expected cash flows and (ii) the expected inflation component of the nominal risk-free rate embedded in the discount rate. Although currency-consistent discount rates seem intuitively reasonable and obvious, its application can be subtle: In the modern, largely highly integrated, global economy, risk factors are inherently international, even in most emerging economies. To see this more clearly, consider the following FMV expression for an enterprise that generates both USD and BRL expected cash flows:

$$FMV_t(\mathbf{x}) = \sum_{u=t}^{T} \frac{1}{\left(\underbrace{1 + \overline{R}(x_{\mathrm{USD}}, x_{\mathrm{BRL}}, \ldots)}_{\substack{\text{risk} - \text{adjusted discount rate} \\ \text{is a function of, and includes,} \\ \text{risk premia for both USD} \\ \text{and BRL devaluation risk}}} \right)^{u-t}} \cdot \left[\underbrace{CF_u^{\mathrm{USD}}(x_{\mathrm{USD}}, x_{\mathrm{BRL}}, \ldots)}_{\substack{\text{USD} - \text{denominated expected} \\ \text{cash flow depending on both} \\ \text{USD and BRL devaluation risk} \\ \text{factors due to internal} \\ \text{enterprise supply chain} \\ \text{dependencies}}} + \underbrace{CF_u^{\mathrm{BRL}}(x_{\mathrm{USD}}, x_{\mathrm{BRL}}, \ldots)}_{\substack{\text{BRL} - \text{denominated expected} \\ \text{cash flow depending on both} \\ \text{USD and BRL devaluation risk} \\ \text{factors due to internal} \\ \text{enterprise supply chain} \\ \text{dependencies}}} \right]$$

The expression suggests that, regardless of the nominal currency in which expected cash flows are denominated, it is necessary to understand and estimate the currency risk sensitivities on which cash flow streams depend; then incorporating such currency risk pricing into risk-adjusted discount rates.

Problems in Emerging Market Asset Value Estimation

Capital Asset Pricing Model Applications Are Generally Considered Invalid

The well-known Capital Asset Pricing Model (CAPM) is quite familiar to substantially all finance professionals and, so, requires neither explanation nor discussion. It is, however, helpful to fix ideas to present the CAPM as a means of later contrasting it to more modern asset pricing theories:

$$\underbrace{\overline{R}_i}_{\substack{\text{expected}\\ \text{rate of}\\ \text{return}}} = \underbrace{R_F}_{\substack{\text{risk}\\ \text{free}\\ \text{rate}}} + \underbrace{\beta_i\left(\overline{R}_M - R_F\right)}_{\substack{\text{capital market}\\ \text{aggregated}\\ \text{risk premium}}}$$

It is perhaps helpful to present an historical perspective on the CAPM provided by the well-known financial economists Eugene Fama and Kenneth French (2006, p. 43):

> The [original] … CAPM … has never been an empirical success. In the early empirical work, the Black (1972) version of the model, which can accommodate a flatter tradeoff of average return for market beta, has some success. But in the late 1970s, research begins to uncover variables like size, various price ratios and momentum that add to the explanation of average returns provided by beta. The problems are serious enough to invalidate most applications of CAPM.

From the perspective of how single period asset pricing theory developed in the mid-1970s, this historical perspective is unsurprising: The newer asset pricing theories such as *arbitrage pricing theory* (Ross 1976) and *risk-neutral pricing theory* (Rubinstein 1976; Ross 1978) were developed specifically to address and remedy the theoretical and empirical deficiencies of CAPM theory.

Most important for the purposes of this chapter is that CAPM assumes *a priori* that the (global) capital market is already in equilibrium. Accordingly, CAPM is silent on how different individual risks—which may or may not become impounded in the global aggregated risk premium—are priced, hedged, or diversified in the capital markets. For this reason, CAPM is at minimum inadequate for use in cross-border valuation settings where it is necessary to estimate the prices of individual risks influencing capital asset cash flows in emerging markets that are not obviously priced in developed economy capital markets.

Arbitrage Pricing Theory Applications Are Not Considered Feasible

Arbitrage Pricing Theory (APT) explains and predicts how individual risks influencing capital asset returns are priced, hedged, and diversified in the capital markets under the single, basic assumption that investors prefer higher returns for accepting greater risk (cf. Ross 1976). One implication of APT is that, unlike CAPM, the risk-adjusted expected rate of return for an asset is the sum of a risk-free rate of return plus a series risk factor premia to which the asset's returns are expected to be sensitive:

$$R_i^* = \underbrace{\underbrace{\lambda_0^*}_{\substack{\text{risk-free}\\ \text{rate}}} + \underbrace{\beta_{i1}\lambda_1 + \beta_{i2}\lambda_2 + \dots + \beta_{iK}\lambda_K}_{\substack{\text{risk premia}\\ \text{for asset } i}}}_{\text{risk-adjusted expected market rate of return for asset } i} = \underbrace{\lambda_0^*}_{\substack{\text{risk-free}\\ \text{rate}}} + \left(\underbrace{\beta_{i1}\ \beta_{i2}\ \dots\ \beta_{iK}}_{\substack{\text{asset } i\\ \text{risk factor}\\ \text{sensitivities}}}\right)\left(\underbrace{\lambda_1\ \lambda_2\ \dots\ \lambda_K}_{\substack{\text{risk}\\ \text{factor}\\ \text{premia}}}\right)'$$

A substantially more important implication of APT is that, again unlike CAPM, expected capital asset return is an empirical issue rather than a theoretical issue: CAPM explicitly suggests all asset returns depend on a single aggregated risk premium, whereas APT suggests expected returns for an asset depend only on the specific risks to which that individual asset is sensitive. This implies that the extent to which a risk factor is priced in the capital markets can be demonstrated using statistical methods; specifically, methods estimating and testing the magnitudes and reliabilities of relationships between capital asset returns and observable risk factors. That is, so-called *systematic risks* are those that have reliably measurable associations to capital asset returns; the concept of the single aggregated risk factor implied by CAPM is essentially irrelevant to risk pricing and asset valuation.

Interpreting APT market risk factor premia. To understand APT and its implications, it is necessary to understand the meaning and interpretation of risk factor premiums—often called risk prices—which can be defined as follows:

$$\lambda_k = \frac{1_k}{\rho_k} - 1 \approx \frac{\text{1 monetary unit of return to holding risk } k \text{ over period } t = [0,1]}{\text{implied current market price of holding 1 monetary unit of return to risk } k \text{ over period } t = [0,1]} - 1$$

While simple, the expression is somewhat abstract and can perhaps be better understood by deriving it from the discounted present value of a single future cash flow:

$$\underbrace{\rho_{kt}}_{\substack{\text{current}\\ \text{market}\\ \text{price of}\\ \text{asset } 1_k}} = \underbrace{\frac{1}{1+\lambda_k}}_{\substack{\text{risk } k\\ \text{discount}\\ \text{factor}}} \cdot \overbrace{\underbrace{CF_{kt+1}}_{\substack{\text{1 monetary}\\ \text{unit payoff}\\ \text{to holding}\\ \text{pure risk k}\\ \text{for one}\\ \text{period}}}}^{1_k} = \frac{1_k}{1+\lambda_k} \Rightarrow \underbrace{\lambda_k = \frac{1_k}{\rho_k} - 1}_{\substack{\text{risk factor premium}\\ \text{for holding pure risk}\\ k \text{ for one period}}}$$

The expression combined with multivariate statistical theory imply that if the marginal effect of a risk factor k on cash flows can be estimated (using statistical methods), this marginal effect represents a single monetary unit payoff from holding pure risk k for one period: 1_k. Further, if the marginal effect of risk factor k on assets traded in the capital market can be estimated (again using statistical methods), then the risk k market price (ρ_k) and factor premium (λ_k) can be extracted from the estimates.

The consensus view on APT. Despite the relative simplicity of extracting risk factor premia from capital market data, experience suggests it is primarily capital asset portfolio managers and hedge funds that develop such information; business valuation professionals rarely do so, as discussed by Hitchner (2017, p. 196):

> APT is not widely used in business valuation assignments for cost of capital determinations due to the unavailability of usable data for the components of the model.

It is apparently true that APT is not widely used in business valuation, but experience suggests that a wide variety of economic risk factor and capital market price data are freely available from public sources (e.g., Federal Reserve Bank of St. Louis in the USA, Banco Central do Brasil, investing.com, finance.yahoo.com, and google.com/finance). Nonetheless, the purpose of this discussion is not to resolve such issues, but rather to explain why and how business valuation professionals have largely adopted subjective, ad hoc methods of estimating risk-adjusted expected rates of return to address perceived shortcomings of CAPM and APT; particularly in the case of emerging market valuation practice.

Resulting Extant Methods Are Ad Hoc and Subjective

A consensus view of the business valuation profession is that, among other conceptually similar methods, it is acceptable or perhaps even necessary to use what is termed the *build-up model* to determine risk-adjusted discount rates (cf. Hitchner, 2017, pp. 194–195):

$$\underbrace{\overline{R}_n}_{\substack{\text{expected}\\ \text{rate of}\\ \text{return for}\\ \text{privately-}\\ \text{held and}\\ \text{-traded}\\ \text{asset } n}} = \underbrace{R_F}_{\substack{\text{risk}\\ \text{free}\\ \text{rate}}} + \underbrace{\underbrace{MRP_n}_{\substack{\text{market}\\ \text{risk}\\ \text{premium}}} + \underbrace{IRP_n}_{\substack{\text{industry}\\ \text{risk}\\ \text{premium}}} + \underbrace{SSRP_n}_{\substack{\text{(small)}\\ \text{size risk}\\ \text{premium}}} + \underbrace{CSRP_n}_{\substack{\text{company}\\ \text{specific risk}\\ \text{premium}}}}_{\substack{\text{build-up method risk premia are not well-defined}\\ \text{and, so, are necessarily subjective}}}$$

The method commonly used to apply the build-up model is summarized as "the discount rate is calculated by adding together the analyst's assessment of the systematic and unsystematic risks associated with a particular subject company or ownership interest" (Hitchner, 2017, pp. 194–195). It should be evident from this statement—as well as the lack of an explanation in the Hitchner (2017) text of how valuation professionals might more objectively apply the model—that the build-up model is generally used in a subjective, ad hoc way: The valuation analyst simply forms a subjective, presumably qualitative, assessment of the risks influencing an asset's returns and then uses subjective judgment to assign the various risk premiums. In summary, standard professional practice at least allows use of subjective assumptions in determining discount rates; suggesting objective estimation is not required or perhaps even common.

The same analysis applies equally to how valuation professionals often determine risk-adjusted discount rates in international and emerging markets valuation contexts. In general, a common approach would be to simply add a *country risk premium*—again based on subjective judgment—intended to account for differences in risks influencing expected cash flows, which differ between developed market economies from which data for market risk and industry risk premia are most often sourced, and the country of domicile for the asset being valued:

$$\underbrace{\overline{R}_n}_{\substack{\text{expected}\\ \text{rate of}\\ \text{return}}} = \underbrace{R_F}_{\substack{\text{risk}\\ \text{free}\\ \text{rate}}} + \underbrace{MRP_n}_{\substack{\text{market}\\ \text{risk}\\ \text{premium}}} + \underbrace{IRP_n}_{\substack{\text{industry}\\ \text{risk}\\ \text{premium}}} + \underbrace{SSRP_n}_{\substack{\text{(small)}\\ \text{size risk}\\ \text{premium}}} + \underbrace{CSRP_n}_{\substack{\text{company}\\ \text{specific risk}\\ \text{premium}}} + \underbrace{\boldsymbol{CRP_n}}_{\substack{\textbf{country}\\ \textbf{risk}\\ \textbf{premium}}}$$

Although application of the above models has wide variation due to the inherently subjective nature of the risk assessments and assigned risk premia, perhaps the most problematic aspect of such methods is that they ignore extant asset pricing theory—even including CAPM—which uniformly suggest risk-adjusted expected rates of return depend on the specific sensitivity of individual asset cash flow streams to risk factor(s). Nonetheless, the ad hoc models shown above remain loosely based on CAPM in that a *market risk premium*, usually based on a broad equity index such as the S&P 500 Index, is included that arguably represents an average of all risks aggregated in the broad equity index returns.

The negative assessment of such subjective, ad hoc models presented here is not particularly controversial as can be seen by considering the following quote from Campbell Harvey, a well-known academic authority and researcher on international cost of capital estimation (Harvey 2005, p. 12):

> There is widespread disagreement as to how to approach the international cost of equity capital. ... In developed, liquid markets it is best to use either a capital asset pricing model or a multifactor model. ... For emerging markets it is not so simple. ... Given that the assumptions of the CAPM do not hold, I avoid using the world version of the CAPM in these markets. ... I will often examine a number of models such as the sovereign spread, Damodaran and the Erb, Harvey, and Viskanta model and average the results. ... There are many other issues that take us well beyond the standard asset pricing frameworks. Stulz (1995, 2005) argues that the variation in the degree of agency costs will induce differences in the cost of capital across countries. This poses a considerable challenge for all of the current models.

In essence, the comments again suggest a substantial lack of theory and empirical evidence for the various CAPM-based methods for estimating international cost of capital. Moreover, the various problematic theoretical and empirical aspects of both CAPM and the related subjective, ad hoc methods suggest there is no clear rationale for using such models and methods; particularly when less (or, perhaps, non-) problematic, alternative theories and methods exist.

Solution for Emerging Market Asset Value Estimation

Certainty-Equivalent Cash Flows Are Appropriately Discounted Using Risk-free Rates

Perhaps the simplest conceptual approach to asset valuation is called *certainty-equivalent valuation* by valuation professionals or *risk-neutral pricing* by financial economists. The approach is well-grounded in post-CAPM asset pricing theory (Rubinstein 1976; Ross 1978), and its application has been clearly described by well-known financial economist Fischer Black in his article titled "A Simple Discounting Rule" (Black 1988). The solution for emerging market asset value estimation presented below is derived directly from this literature.

The certainty-equivalence concept. Certainty-equivalent asset valuation is based on the fundamental concept that a cash flow level exists that is essentially certain, and this relationship to the expected (risky) cash flow level can be most easily understood by examining the following graph of a probability density function over different levels of cash flows (Fig. 1):

The annotation above the certainty-equivalent cash flow level explains a sometimes misunderstood aspect of certainty-equivalent valuation: As can be seen by the non-zero probability to the left of the certainty-equivalent level, the cash flow level is not strictly risk-free or certain; it simply corresponds to the level of cash flow that is equivalent to that of a selected, *so-called* risk-free asset such as a U.S. Treasury security. Applying this concept to valuation simply requires developing a method of estimating the correspondence between risky asset returns and the selected non-risk-asset return.

The valuation implications of certainty-equivalence. Before developing a method for estimating certainty-equivalent asset return and cash flow levels, it is important to recognize that certainty-equivalent valuation is not simply an alternative to the standard discounted cash flow method; the two methods are, *in principle*, equivalent:

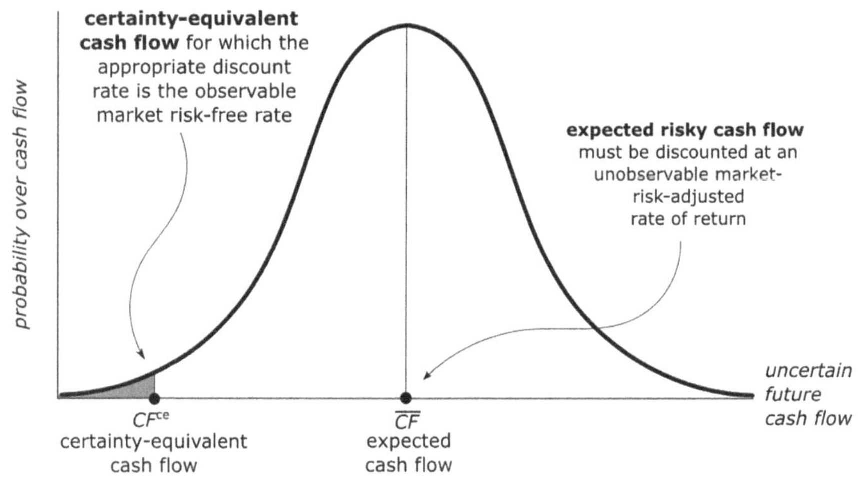

Fig. 1 A graphical representation of the certainty-equivalence concept

$$\underbrace{FMV_t}_{\substack{\text{fair}\\ \text{market}\\ \text{value}}} = \underbrace{\sum_{u=t}^{T} \frac{CF_u}{\left(1+\overline{R}\right)^{u-t}} = \sum_{u=t}^{T} \frac{CF_u^{\mathrm{CE}}}{\left(1+R_F\right)^{u-t}}}_{\text{discounted expected future cash flows under both the standard discounted cash flow method (using a risk-adjusted discount rate) and the certainty-equivalent method are equivalent}}$$

where the first sum is the **expected risky cash flows discounted at an unobservable risk – adjusted rate** and the second sum is the **certainty – equivalent level of cash flows discounted at an observable risk – free rate**.

As suggested, the appropriate discount rate for valuing certainty-equivalent cash flows is the observable yield to maturity on the selected, nominally risk-free asset by which certainty-equivalence is defined. Although a deeper exploration of the theory is beyond the intended scope of the chapter, it should be noted that were value estimates to differ between the standard and certainty-equivalent methods represented above, such differences would be necessarily attributable to the estimates underlying one or both methods; the differences are not the result of an invalid theory or theories.

Certainty-Equivalent Cash Flows Can Be Estimated Using Statistical Methods

Understanding certainty-equivalence risk factor levels. Following the basic intuition of risk-return relationships, and the fundamental assumption underlying APT and risk-neutral pricing theory, it is clear that any risk priced in the capital market would have a statistical association with asset return(s). In this connection, consider a graph of the hypothetical relationship between some observable risk factor (e.g., gross domestic product) and the excess return on an asset *M* traded in a public capital market where *excess return* is defined as asset *M*'s market return minus a (nomimal) risk-free rate of return (Fig. 2):

The points in the graph represent data comprised of joint observations of excess asset returns and the risk factor value. The line drawn through the field of data points represents a *conditional mean function*, which represents the mean (i.e., expectation or probability-weighted average) of excess return conditional on different levels of the risk factor. Such conditional expectation functions can be estimated using standard statistical methods including the least squares method or maximum likelihood method. It can be seen clearly in the graph that there is a risk factor level at

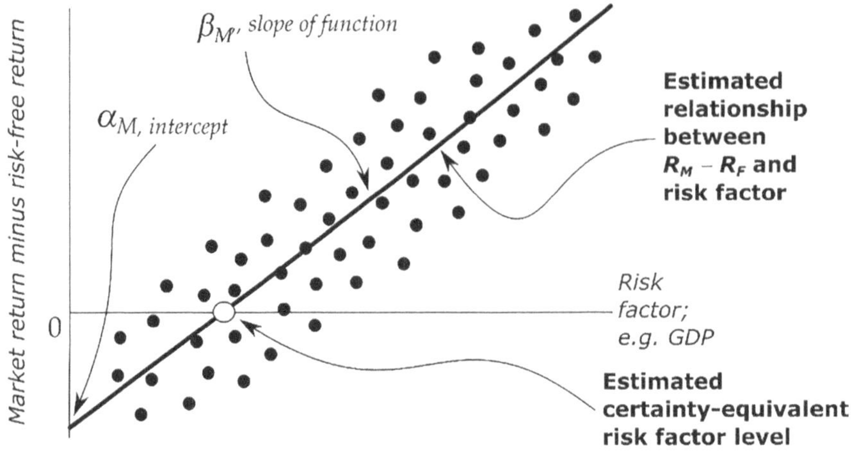

Fig. 2 A graphical representation of the certainty-equivalence concept

which the conditional expectation of excess return is zero. This is the estimated *certainty-equivalent level of the risk factor.*

Calculating certainty-equivalence levels of risk factors. Using parameter notation introduced in Fig. 1, the certainty-equivalence condition and risk factor level can be written in algebraic form as follows:

$$\underbrace{\underbrace{\overbrace{R_M - R_F}^{\substack{ER_{Mt} \\ \text{excess return}}}}_{=\,0} = \underbrace{\alpha_M + \beta_M x}_{\substack{\text{relationship} \\ \text{between } R_M - R_F \\ \text{and risk factor } x}}}_{\substack{\textbf{Certainty - equivalence condition}: \\ \text{Point where market return equals} \\ \text{risk-free return, } R_M - R_F = 0}} \Rightarrow \underbrace{x^{\mathrm{CE}} = -\alpha_M/\beta_M}_{\substack{\text{certainty-} \\ \text{equivalence level} \\ \text{of risk factor } x}}$$

To be clear, the certainty-equivalence level risk factor x, denoted x^{CE}, is the estimated level at which the excess return on the asset is expected to be zero; or, equivalently stated, *the risk factor level at which the expected asset return is equal to the risk-free return.*

Certainty-equivalent levels of cash flow. Basic valuation theory suggests a direct, positive, causal relationship between asset values and expected cash flow levels. Accordingly, such valuation theory suggests a direct causal relationship between estimated certainty-equivalence levels of risk factors and asset expected cash flows. To understand the statistical relationship between asset values, returns, and cash flows, consider the following derivation of the covariance relationship between asset returns and asset cash flows:

$$\underbrace{V_t \equiv V_{t-1} + \pi_t + ET_t^{net}}_{\substack{\text{equity value at time } t \text{ is equal to its} \\ t-1 \text{ value plus economic profit } (\pi) \\ \text{and net equity transactions } (ET)}} \xrightarrow[\substack{ET_t^{net} = 0 \\ \pi_t = cCF_t}]{assume} \underbrace{R_t \equiv \frac{\Delta V_t}{V_{t-1}} = \frac{cCF_t}{V_{t-1}}}_{\substack{\text{equity return is proportional} \\ \text{to equity cash flows}}} \Rightarrow \underbrace{\mathrm{CV}\left(R_t, \mathbf{x}\right) \cong \mathrm{CV}(CF_t, \mathbf{x})}_{\substack{\text{covariances (CV) of} \\ \text{equity returns and equity cash flows} \\ \text{with risk factors } (\mathbf{x}) \text{ are equivalent}}}$$

(The equity value expression is used simply as an example without loss of generality; other more general derivations of asset return and cash flow covariance equality can also be developed that do not rely on this basic framework and the zero net equity transactions assumption.) The crucial assumption underlying the derivation is that economic profit and cash flows to equity holders have a proportional relationship via the constant of proportionality c, which can generally be tested using empirical methods.

It can be shown under this assumption, as well as under the logarithmic transformation of cash flow in the following empirical model, that the covariance equivalence between asset returns, cash flows, and risk factors stated above holds (see, e.g., Wooldridge 2009, pp. 185–187). Accordingly, certainty-equivalent cash flow levels for a privately held asset n can be estimated by (i) estimating parameters of the following logarithmic cash flow function and (ii) substituting the estimated certainty-equivalent risk factor level into the estimated asset n cash flow function as follows:

$$\underbrace{\ln CF_n = \alpha_n + \beta_n x}_{\substack{\text{logarithmic risky} \\ \text{cash flow of asset } n \\ \text{estimated as a} \\ \text{function of risk } x}} \xrightarrow{\substack{\text{substitute} \\ \text{certainty-} \\ \text{equivalent} \\ \text{value of} \\ \text{risk factor} \\ x^{\text{CE}} \text{ for } x}} \underbrace{\begin{aligned} \ln CF_n^{\text{CE}} &= \alpha_n + \beta_n x^{\text{CE}} \\ &= \alpha_n - \beta_n(\alpha_M/\beta_M) \end{aligned}}_{\substack{\text{asset } n \text{ estimated} \\ \text{certainty-equivalent} \\ \text{logarithmic cash flow level}}}$$

The estimated asset n certainty-equivalent, logarithmic cash flow level can then be transformed to its non-logarithmic level by exponentiating the expression:

$$\underbrace{\ln CF_n^{\text{CE}} = \alpha_n - \beta_n(\alpha_M/\beta_M)}_{\substack{\text{certainty-equivalent} \\ \text{logarithmic cash flow level}}} \rightarrow \underbrace{CF_n^{\text{CE}} = \exp\left(\ln CF_n^{\text{CE}}\right) = \exp\left[\alpha_n - \beta_n(\alpha_M/\beta_M)\right]}_{\substack{\text{certainty-equivalent} \\ \text{cash flow level}}}$$

To settle the basic theory it only remains to be shown how the theoretical development presented above applies to more general cases with multiple risk factors, as discussed next.

Multivariate certainty-equivalent cash flow levels. It can be shown that the above theory generalizes directly to the multivariate case where publicly traded and privately held capital asset returns and cash flows are sensitive to an arbitrary number of risk factors:

$$ER_{Mt} = \alpha_M + \beta_{M1}x_{1t} + \beta_{M2}x_{2t} + \dots + \beta_{MK}x_{Kt}$$

$$= \alpha_M + \left(\underbrace{\beta_{M1} \ \beta_{M2} \ \dots \ \beta_{MK}}_{\substack{\text{publicly-traded asset } M \\ \text{(usually a portfolio)} \\ \text{estimated sensitivities to} \\ \text{risk factors } x_1 \ x_2 \ \dots \ x_K}} \right) \left(\underbrace{x_1 \ x_2 \ \dots \ x_K}_{\substack{\text{observable} \\ \text{risk factors}}} \right)'$$

Using the parameter estimates from the above excess return function for publicly traded asset M and parameter estimates for an analogous logarithmic cash flow function for privately held asset n, the following certainty-equivalent level of logarithmic cash flow for asset n can be derived:

$$\ln CF_n^{\text{CE}} = \alpha_n + \beta_{n1}x_1^{\text{CE}} + \beta_{n2}x_2^{\text{CE}} + \dots + \beta_{nK}x_K^{\text{CE}}$$

$$= \alpha_n + (\beta_{n1} \ \beta_{n2} \ \dots \ \beta_{nK})(x_1^{\text{CE}} \ x_2^{\text{CE}} \ \dots \ x_K^{\text{CE}})'$$

$$= \alpha_n + \underbrace{\left(\underbrace{\beta_{n1} \ \beta_{n2} \ \dots \ \beta_{nK}}_{\substack{\text{estimated asset } n \\ \text{risk sensitivities}}} \right) \left(\underbrace{\frac{-\alpha_M}{\beta_{M1}} \ \frac{-\alpha_M}{\beta_{M2}} \ \dots \ \frac{-\alpha_M}{\beta_{MK}}}_{\substack{\text{estimated certainty-equivalent} \\ \text{levels of risk factors } 1,2,\dots,K}} \right)'}_{\textbf{aggregate proportional effect of certainty}-\textbf{equivalent risk levels on cash flow}}$$

The asset n certainty-equivalent cash flow level is then obtained by exponentiating as previously shown:

$$CF_n^{\text{CE}} = \exp\left(\ln CF_n^{\text{CE}}\right) = \exp\left[\underbrace{\alpha_n + \left(\underbrace{\beta_{n1} \ \beta_{n2} \ \dots \ \beta_{nK}}_{\substack{\text{estimated asset } n \\ \text{risk sensitivities}}} \right) \left(\underbrace{\frac{-\alpha_M}{\beta_{M1}} \ \frac{-\alpha_M}{\beta_{M2}} \ \dots \ \frac{-\alpha_M}{\beta_{MK}}}_{\substack{\text{estimated certainty-equivalent} \\ \text{levels of risk factors } 1,2,\dots,K}} \right)'}_{\textbf{estimated certainty}-\textbf{equivalent level as a proportion of cash flow}} \right]$$

This settles the fundamental theory underlying certainty-equivalent valuation. The basic empirical approach associated with applying the theory, and an example of theory application to emerging market valuation, will be presented in the remainder of the chapter.

Relevant Risk Factors Are an Empirical Rather Than Theoretical Issue

It has been a well-established principle of asset pricing and valuation since the acceptance of CAPM, with further support and refinement of the principle from APT and risk-neutral pricing theory, that *only systematic risks are relevant to valuation*. Although the concept of *systematic risk* is arguably irrelevant under post-CAPM asset pricing theory, under such theory risks can be technically characterized as the set of risks perceived to influence expected future asset returns for *at least* one more asset than the number of risks in the set. While this might seem a rather strange definition, it follows directly from APT: Risks can be fully priced and hedged under a no-arbitrage condition when there is at least one more asset sensitive to the set of risks than there are risks. In contrast to CAPM, this implies that risk factors relevant to capital asset pricing are an empirical rather than a theoretical issue.

The discussion of systematic risk here suggests a fundamentally empirical approach to identifying relevant risk factors for estimating capital asset values, in contrast to CAPM which explicitly states there is (only) one relevant risk factor: aggregate capital market risk, most often regarded as being reflected in broad equity index returns as previously discussed. An empirical approach to identifying relevant risks would reasonably involve: (i) forming hypotheses about risk factors expected to influence asset returns and cash flows based on an understanding of the how the asset to be valued generates returns as a function of economic and capital market factors; (ii) obtaining capital market data, financial statement data, and economic data sufficient to test the hypotheses; and (iii) using various statistical methods to test and refine the hypotheses; and, (iv) estimating sensitivities of public-traded asset returns and privately held asset cash flows to the set of risk factors identified as relevant.

A discussion of statistical methods and tests that can be used to apply the empirical procedures discussed here is beyond the intended scope of the chapter; so the interested reader is referred to any standard text on econometrics, which would generally cover all such methods and tests (e.g., Wooldridge 2009). For the purposes of this chapter, it is enough to state the general estimation objectives with respect to the parameters of the publicly traded asset return and privately held asset cash flow empirical models:

$$\overbrace{R_{Mt}}^{\substack{\text{sample of}\\ \text{publicly-}\\ \text{traded}\\ \text{asset}\\ \text{returns}}} = \overbrace{\alpha_M + (\beta_{M1} \;\ldots\; \beta_{MK})}^{\substack{\text{accurate, reliable, stable}\\ \text{parameter estimates}\\ \text{obtained from a sample of}\\ \text{publicly-traded capital assets}\\ M=1,2,\ldots,m \text{ over a relevant}\\ \text{sample period } t=1,2,\ldots,T}} \begin{pmatrix} \overbrace{x_{1t} \;\ldots\; x_{Kt}}^{\substack{\text{relevant}\\ \text{observable}\\ \text{risk factors}}} \end{pmatrix}'$$

$$\underbrace{\ln CF_{nt}}_{\substack{\text{sample of}\\ \text{cash flow}\\ \text{data for}\\ \text{subject}\\ \text{asset } n}} = \underbrace{\alpha_n + (\; \beta_{n1} \;\ldots\; \beta_{nK} \;)}_{\substack{\text{accurate, reliable, stable}\\ \text{paramater estimates}\\ \text{obtained from a sample of}\\ \text{publicly-traded capital assets}\\ M=1,2,\ldots,m \text{ over a relevant}\\ \text{sample period } t=1,2,\ldots,T}} (x_{1t} \;\ldots\; x_{Kt})'$$

With these objectives in mind, some understanding of the empirical procedures and statistical methods can be developed from the following example of capital asset value estimation in an emerging market.

An Example of Emerging Market Capital Asset Value Estimation

Estimating FMV of a Brazilian enterprise. Consider an (hypothetical) example of a privately held Brazilian enterprise engaged in logistics equipment manufacturing—primarily specialized, lightweight, metal shipping containers—the products of which are used in intermodal commercial air, land, and sea freight transportation. The enterprise is domiciled and has all its operations and manufacturing facilities in

Brazil; competitors are mainly located in Asia and North America; and its products are mainly sold in Asia and North America in exchange for U.S. Dollars.

The objective is to estimate the fair market value of the enterprise at 31 December 2024, where the estimate is intended to be used by its owners in negotiating a potential sale. The enterprise is organized as a *sociedade limitada* (similar to a *limited liability company* in the USA) and has zero debt at the valuation date. Working with management, the valuation analyst has developed projections of after-tax operating profit for the 5 years following the valuation date, which reasonably approximates expected cash flows to be available to equity holders (*CF*). The valuation analyst believes the cash flow projections are unbiased and accurate, and the projections include the analyst's estimate of a terminal cash flow at the end of the 5 years representing hypothetical enterprise sale proceeds. The projected operating profit and cash flows—stated in millions of nominal Brazilian Real currency values—are reflected above *CF* in the following expression:

$$FMV_{nt_0} = \sum_{u=t_1}^{t_5} \frac{\overbrace{CF_{nu}}^{\mathbf{1.0}_{t_1},\ \mathbf{2.0}_{t_2},\ \mathbf{3.0}_{t_3},\ \mathbf{4.0}_{t_4},\ \mathbf{10.0}_{t_5}}}{\left(\underbrace{1 + R_n}_{\substack{\text{unobservable} \\ \text{risk-adjusted} \\ \text{expected rate} \\ \text{of return set} \\ \text{in fair market}}}\right)^{u-t}} = \sum_{u=t_1}^{t_5} \frac{\overbrace{CF_{nu}^{\text{CE}}}^{?}}{\left(\underbrace{1 + R_F}_{\substack{\mathbf{.0438} \\ \text{observable} \\ \text{risk-free} \\ \text{yield to} \\ \text{maturity}}}\right)^{u-t}}$$

The annotations suggest the remaining estimation objective is to estimate certainty-equivalent levels of projected cash flows. As will be discussed further, the valuation analyst has already selected the observable yield to maturity available on 5-year maturity U.S. Treasury debt securities at the valuation date of 4.38% as the appropriate nominal risk-free discount rate for the estimated certainty-equivalent cash flow stream.

Identifying relevant risk factors. Discussions between the valuation analyst and enterprise management suggest the hypothesis that enterprise profits, cash flows, and value are mainly influenced by *global economic risk*, *Brazilian economic risk*, *aircraft manufacturing industry risk*, and the *U.S. Dollar-Brazilian Real currency exchange risk*. As shown in Fig. 3, the analyst has chosen a specific observable risk

Identified risk	*Hypothesis*	Observable risk factor
Global economic risk	≈	iShares MSCI All Country World Index ETF (ACWI)
Brazil economic risk	≈	iShares MSCI Brazil Index ETF (EWZ)
Aircraft manufacturing risk	≈	Boeing Company (BA)
US Dollar-Brazilian Real exchange risk	≈	U.S. Dollar - Brazilian Real exchange rate (USDBRL)

Fig. 3 Identified risks and selected observable risk factors

factor as a proxy for each of the identified risks (along with ticker symbols for each risk factor):

As suggested in Fig. 3, the analyst has selected observable risk factors based on the hypothesis that they adequately proxy for the set of relevant risks identified by enterprise management. Accordingly, the analyst obtained the data necessary to test the hypothesis, comprised of 4 years of monthly frequency public capital and money market data (which includes data on the risk factors ACWI, EWZ, BA, and USDBRL) and monthly financial statement data from the privately held enterprise. Included in the public capital market data are equity price and return data on 112 equity securities for companies in the air, land, and sea freight transportation services industries, based on the analyst's general hypothesis that such equities are likely to reliably price the risks identified as relevant to the enterprise being valued.

Public-traded capital asset risk sensitivities and certainty-equivalent risk levels. After selecting 5-year maturity U.S. Treasury securities as the relevant, nominal risk-free asset, the analyst constructed monthly excess returns for the 112 selected equity securities over the 48-month sample period ended 31 December 2024:

$$\left.\begin{aligned} ER_{1t} &= R_{1t} - R_{Ft}^{\text{UST5}} \\ ER_{2t} &= R_{2t} - R_{Ft}^{\text{UST5}} \\ &\vdots \\ ER_{112t} &= R_{112t} - R_{Ft}^{\text{UST5}} \end{aligned}\right\} \begin{array}{l} \text{excess returns constructed from monthly returns} \\ \text{for equities } i = 1, 2, \ldots, 112 \text{ and monthly 5-year US Treasury} \\ \text{buy-and-hold returns over the 48-months ended 31-Dec-2024} \end{array}$$

Similarly, the analyst also constructed one-month holding returns for ACWI, EWZ, BA, and USDBRL as risk factors (risk proxies). The sensitivities of such excess returns to the risk factors were estimated using the following empirical model and a least squares estimation method where observed excess returns were pooled across the 112 equities and the 48 monthly time periods:

$$ER_t = \underbrace{\alpha_M}_{.005} + \underbrace{\beta_{M \cdot ACWI}}_{.521} \underbrace{ACWI_t}_{\substack{\text{Global} \\ \text{economic} \\ \text{risk proxy}}} + \underbrace{\beta_{M \cdot EWZ}}_{.115} \underbrace{EWZ_t}_{\substack{\text{Brazil} \\ \text{economic} \\ \text{risk proxy}}}$$

$$+ \underbrace{\beta_{M \cdot BA}}_{.050} \underbrace{BA_t}_{\substack{\text{Aircraft} \\ \text{mfg risk} \\ \text{proxy}}} + \underbrace{\beta_{M \cdot USDBRL}}_{.097} \underbrace{USDBRL_t}_{\substack{\text{US Dollar-} \\ \text{Brazilian Real} \\ \text{exchange risk}}} \quad \begin{cases} n = 48 \\ R^2 \cong .064 \end{cases}$$

The estimated p-values for the parameter estimates (α_M, $\beta_{M \cdot ACWI}$, $\beta_{M \cdot EWZ}$, …)—not reported here—are all “statistically significant” at conventional levels. Based on such p-values and other statistical tests, the analyst has concluded that the model parameters are accurately and reliably estimated. On this basis, certainty-equivalent risk factor levels are then constructed from the parameter estimates as follows:

$$ACWI_t^{CE} = -\left(\underbrace{\alpha_M}_{.005} / \underbrace{\beta_{M \cdot ACWI}}_{.521} \right) \cong -.0096$$

$$EWZ_t^{CE} = -\left(\underbrace{\alpha_M}_{.005} / \underbrace{\beta_{M \cdot EWZ}}_{.115} \right) \cong -.0435$$

$$BA_t^{CE} = -\left(\underbrace{\alpha_M}_{.005} / \underbrace{\beta_{M \cdot BA}}_{.050} \right) \cong -.0100$$

$$USDBRL_t^{CE} = -\left(\underbrace{\alpha_M}_{.005} / \underbrace{\beta_{M \cdot USDBRL}}_{.097} \right) \cong -.0515$$

Privately traded capital asset risk sensitivities and certainty-equivalent cash flows. The valuation analyst then extracts monthly operating profit data—which, again, closely approximates cash flow available to equity holders—from financial statements of the privately held Brazilian enterprise, applies a logarithmic transformation, and estimates the following model using the least squares method:

$$\ln CF_{nt} = \underbrace{\alpha_n}_{.011} + \underbrace{\beta_{n \cdot ACWI}}_{.736} \underbrace{ACWI_t}_{\substack{\text{Global}\\\text{economic}\\\text{risk proxy}}} + \underbrace{\beta_{n \cdot EWZ}}_{.390} \underbrace{EWZ_t}_{\substack{\text{Brazil}\\\text{economic}\\\text{risk proxy}}} + \underbrace{\beta_{n \cdot BA}}_{.448} \underbrace{BA_t}_{\substack{\text{Aircraft}\\\text{mfg risk}\\\text{proxy}}} + \underbrace{\beta_{n \cdot USDBRL}}_{096} \underbrace{USDBRL_t}_{\substack{\text{US Dollar-}\\\text{Brazilian Real}\\\text{exchange risk}}} \quad \begin{cases} n = 48 \\ R^2 \cong .529 \end{cases}$$

The analyst noted that all estimated p-values for the parameter estimates (α_n, $\beta_{n\text{-}ACWI}$, $\beta_{n\text{-}EWZ}$, …)— not reported here—are all statistically significant at conventional levels with the exception of the USDBRL parameter; suggesting the USDBRL risk sensitivity might not be reliably estimated. After discussion with enterprise management, the analyst concluded that the apparent lack of statistical significance resulted from the enterprise using USDBRL hedging activities sporadically, resulting in variation in sensitivity to the risk factor over the sample period. With this understanding the analyst concludes the estimated USDBRL risk sensitivity estimate is adequately reliable in the sense that USDBRL hedging activities are assumed to be optimal. Finally, the analyst notes that the square root of the model R^2 statistic of 0.529 implies that the four identified risk factors explain an estimated 73% of the variation in enterprise cash flows; suggesting other risk factors or random variation account for 27% of cash flow variation.

Based on prior experience in similar models of equity return and cash flow sensitivities to risk factors, the analyst concludes the risk factors represent substantially all relevant risks influencing enterprise cash flows, which is equivalent to assuming other risks would be irrelevant to the enterprise and diversified rather than priced by potential buyers.

Based on the estimated cash flow model parameters and the certainty-equivalent risk factor levels previously estimated, as well as the assumption that all significant risks to enterprise cash flows are included in the models, the valuation analyst constructs certainty-equivalent cash flow levels for the 5-year cash flow projection period. Because the enterprise cash flow model was estimated in logarithmic form using monthly data, the model represents the estimated *aggregate proportional effects* of risk factor on *monthly* cash flows. Accordingly, to derive the *annual cash flow level as proportion of risk factor effects*, the analyst must (i) multiply the estimated model by 12 to convert to an annual basis, (ii) exponentiate the expression to convert to estimated cash flow level effects, and (iii) multiply the resulting expression by projected expected future cash flow levels. Then by substituting the estimated certainty-equivalent risk factor levels into the expression, the analyst obtains certainty-equivalent levels of projected cash flows for the enterprise:

$$CF_{nt_1}^{\mathrm{CE}} = \underbrace{CF_{t_1}}_{1.000} \cdot \exp\left[12\left(\underbrace{\alpha_n}_{.011} + \underbrace{\beta_{n\cdot ACWI}}_{.736}\underbrace{ACWI^{\mathrm{CE}}}_{-.0096} + \underbrace{\beta_{n\cdot EWZ}}_{.390}\underbrace{EWZ^{\mathrm{CE}}}_{-.0435} + \underbrace{\beta_{n\cdot BA}}_{.448}\underbrace{BA^{\mathrm{CE}}}_{-.0100} + \underbrace{\beta_{n\cdot USDBRL}}_{096}\underbrace{USDBRL^{\mathrm{CE}}}_{-.0515}\right)\right] \cong .764$$

$$CF_{nt_2}^{\mathrm{CE}} = \underbrace{CF_{t_2}}_{2.000} \cdot \exp\left[12\left(\underbrace{\alpha_n}_{.011} + \underbrace{\beta_{n\cdot ACWI}}_{.736}\underbrace{ACWI^{\mathrm{CE}}}_{-.0096} + \underbrace{\beta_{n\cdot EWZ}}_{.390}\underbrace{EWZ^{\mathrm{CE}}}_{-.0435} + \underbrace{\beta_{n\cdot BA}}_{.448}\underbrace{BA^{\mathrm{CE}}}_{-.0100} + \underbrace{\beta_{n\cdot USDBRL}}_{096}\underbrace{USDBRL^{\mathrm{CE}}}_{-.0515}\right)\right] \cong 1.528$$

$$CF_{nt_3}^{\mathrm{CE}} = \underbrace{CF_{t_3}}_{3.000} \cdot \exp\left[12\left(\underbrace{\alpha_n}_{.011} + \underbrace{\beta_{n\cdot ACWI}}_{.736}\underbrace{ACWI^{\mathrm{CE}}}_{-.0096} + \underbrace{\beta_{n\cdot EWZ}}_{.390}\underbrace{EWZ^{\mathrm{CE}}}_{-.0435} + \underbrace{\beta_{n\cdot BA}}_{.448}\underbrace{BA^{\mathrm{CE}}}_{-.0100} + \underbrace{\beta_{n\cdot USDBRL}}_{096}\underbrace{USDBRL^{\mathrm{CE}}}_{-.0515}\right)\right] \cong 2.291$$

$$CF_{nt_4}^{\mathrm{CE}} = \underbrace{CF_{t_4}}_{4.000} \cdot \exp\left[12\left(\underbrace{\alpha_n}_{.011} + \underbrace{\beta_{n\cdot ACWI}}_{.736}\underbrace{ACWI^{\mathrm{CE}}}_{-.0096} + \underbrace{\beta_{n\cdot EWZ}}_{.390}\underbrace{EWZ^{\mathrm{CE}}}_{-.0435} + \underbrace{\beta_{n\cdot BA}}_{.448}\underbrace{BA^{\mathrm{CE}}}_{-.0100} + \underbrace{\beta_{n\cdot USDBRL}}_{096}\underbrace{USDBRL^{\mathrm{CE}}}_{-.0515}\right)\right] \cong 3.055$$

$$CF_{nt_5}^{\mathrm{CE}} = \underbrace{CF_{t_5}}_{10.000} \cdot \underbrace{\exp\left[\underbrace{12\left(\underbrace{\alpha_n}_{.011} + \underbrace{\underbrace{\beta_{n\cdot ACWI}}_{.736}\underbrace{ACWI^{\mathrm{CE}}}_{-.0096} + \underbrace{\beta_{n\cdot EWZ}}_{.390}\underbrace{EWZ^{\mathrm{CE}}}_{-.0435} + \underbrace{\beta_{n\cdot BA}}_{.448}\underbrace{BA^{\mathrm{CE}}}_{-.0100} + \underbrace{\beta_{n\cdot USDBRL}}_{096}\underbrace{USDBRL^{\mathrm{CE}}}_{-.0515}}_{-\mathbf{.0335}}\right)}_{-\mathbf{.2695}}\right]}_{\mathbf{.7638}} \cong 7.638$$

Estimated fair market value ignoring transaction costs. Because certainty-equivalent levels of projected cash flows were estimated using capital market data generated in open, competitive markets arguably meeting the definition of *fair markets*, then it follows that—ignoring transaction costs—the FMV of the 100% equity interest in the privately held Brazilian enterprise can be appropriately calculated using such certainty-equivalent projected cash flow levels and the selected, observable yield to maturity on 5-year U.S. Treasury securities at the valuation date:

$$FMV_{t_0} = \sum_{u=t_1}^{t_5} \frac{CF_u^{\text{CE}}}{(1+R_F)^{u-t}} = \overbrace{\underbrace{\frac{.764}{1.0438^1}+\frac{1.528}{1.0438^2}+\frac{2.291}{1.0438^3}+\frac{3.055}{1.0438^4}+\frac{7.638}{1.0438^5}}_{\substack{\text{discount factors based on observable 4.38\% yield to maturity on}\\ \text{5-year US Treasury security at the valuation date}}}}^{\substack{\text{estimated certainty-equivalent}\\ \text{projected future cash flows}}} \cong \underbrace{\text{R\$ 12.887}}_{\substack{12.887\\ \text{million}\\ \text{Brazilian}\\ \text{Real}}}$$

It is important to note that: (i) the risk-free rate used to discount projected cash flows logically must correspond to the same risk-free securities used to define excess returns with which certainty-equivalent risk factor levels are estimated; (ii) even though the selected risk-free asset is denominated in U.S. Dollars, there is no logical necessity to restate projected cash flows stated in nominal Brazilian Real currency units because estimated certainty-equivalent risk factor and cash flow levels are based on and adjusted for enterprise cash flow stream sensitivity to USDBRL risk; and, (iii) because the FMV estimate shown above is based on certainty-equivalent risk levels estimated from open, competitive markets with *transaction costs*—that is, the costs of trading risk via trading capital assets—that are likely to be substantially different than the market in which a privately held Brazilian equity interest would trade, it would generally be necessary to adjust the estimate for such transaction costs as discussed next.

Estimated fair market value considering transaction costs. Although the essentials of certainty-equivalent risk pricing theory and its application have been fully presented above, it is important to briefly address one final aspect of capital asset value estimation relevant in emerging markets. It is common for valuation professionals to apply so-called *illiquidity and non-marketability discounts* to adjust valuation estimates for differences in transaction costs between public and private capital market transactions.

As discussed in Goodman and McLelland (2024), private capital market transaction costs essentially represent the *shadow price of liquidity risk*; the price of liquidity risk were it explicitly traded in the capital markets. Alternatively stated, private capital market transaction costs comprised of brokerage commissions, transaction advisory services fees, legal fees, etc. are incurred for the purpose of facilitating and executing private market transaction; they are incurred for the explicit purpose of *accessing liquidity*. In this connection, transaction cost differences also exist across countries and geographic regions for a variety of reasons and, accordingly, such differences should generally be incorporated into valuation estimates.

To see the issue more clearly, consider the following relationship between observable transaction price, FMV, and transaction costs in the context of the certainty-equivalent valuation method:

$$\underbrace{PRICE = FMV - TRANSACTION\ COSTS}_{\substack{\text{Observable transaction price}\\ \text{equals unobservable FMV}\\ \text{minus transaction costs}}} \rightarrow \begin{array}{c}\text{Capital asset with single}\\ \text{certainty-equivalent expected CF}\\ \text{of \$1 at } t+1 \text{ sold in the}\\ \text{presence of non-zero}\\ \text{transaction costs that are}\\ \text{proportional to FMV}\end{array} \quad \underbrace{\underbrace{\frac{1^{\mathrm{CE}}}{1+R_F^*}}_{\substack{\text{net price}\\ \text{received}\\ \text{by seller}\\ (P)}} = \underbrace{\frac{1^{\mathrm{CE}}}{1+R_F}}_{\substack{\text{gross}\\ \text{price paid}\\ \text{by buyer}\\ (FMV)}} \cdot \underbrace{(1 - tc)}_{\substack{\text{transaction}\\ \text{cost}\\ \text{factor}}}}_{\substack{\text{Relationship between observable price}\\ \text{and unobservable FMV}}}$$

Understanding the relationship is particularly important in emerging market valuation because—as suggested by the example presented above—fair market and certainty-equivalent basis risk prices are most often estimated using data from developed economy capital markets, where transaction costs can differ substantially from those in emerging market economies. Although a complete exposition of the theory and method for adjusting for transaction cost differences is beyond the intended scope of the chapter, the fundamental concepts and relationships can be summarized in the following expressions (where OCC denotes opportunity cost of capital):

$$\underbrace{R_F^* = \frac{\overbrace{1 + R_F}^{\substack{\text{buyer OCC}\\\text{for certainty-}\\\text{equivalent}\\\text{cash stream}}}}{\underbrace{1 - tc(FMV)}_{\substack{\text{IPCPL theory of}\\\text{private market}\\\text{transaction costs}}}} - 1}_{\substack{\text{private market seller OCC for}\\\text{certainty-equivalent cash flow}\\\text{stream based on IPCPL theory}}} \rightarrow FMV_t = \sum_{u=t}^{T} \frac{CF_u^{\text{CE}}}{\underbrace{(1 + R_F^*)^{u-t}}_{\substack{\text{certainty-}\\\text{equivalent}\\\text{discountfactor}\\\text{adjustedfor}\\\text{transaction}\\\text{costs}}}}$$

Similar to the certainty-equivalent risk pricing theory and method presented in this chapter, the theory summarized in the above expressions—which has been termed *Implied Private Company Pricing Line* (IPCPL) theory; see, for example, Goodman and McLelland (2024)—leads directly to the use of explicit, objective estimates of adjustments for private capital market transaction costs; thus avoiding the problematic aspects of using subjective, ad hoc judgments with respect to illiquidity and non-marketability discounts related to private-capital market transactions.

The interested reader is referred to Goodman and McLelland (2024) for a complete exposition of the theory, as well as a discussion of the evidence supporting the theory, and an example of its application.

Conclusion

This chapter has presented the derivation of a valuation method directly from post-CAPM asset pricing theory. The theory and method can most accurately be termed *certainty-equivalent risk pricing theory and methods* and is most directly attributable to Black (1988). The formal underlying theory has come to be known as risk-neutral pricing theory, which has existed since the 1970s, was developed specifically to remedy theoretical and empirical problems inherent in CAPM. The theory and method presented in this chapter has obvious benefits to business valuation practice, especially in the context of emerging market valuation practice. In particular, valuation practice has often adopted and continued to use ad hoc methods of determining risk-adjusted cash flow discount rates that are neither well-grounded in existing asset pricing theory nor objective; instead relying on the subjective judgment of valuation professionals. As discussed in this chapter, such practices are perhaps more prevalent in emerging market economy valuations than in asset valuations conducted in developed economies. As a means of mitigating such problems, the theory and method presented in this chapter allow valuation professionals to mitigate such subjectivity and focus on developing more objective valuation estimates that are supported by testable assumptions, empirical data, and explicit empirical methods.

References

Black F (1988) A simple discounting rule. Financ Manag 17(Summer):7–11

Fama E, French K (2006) The capital asset pricing model: theory and evidence. J Econ Perspect 18(3):25–46

Goodman D, McLelland M (2024) Understanding IPCPL theory, evidence, and application. Retrieved from https://quickreadbuzz.com/2024/07/10/business-valuation-goodman-mclelland-understanding-ipcpl-theory-evidence-and-application-2/

Harvey C (2005) 12 Ways to calculate the international cost of capital. Retrieved from http://faculty.fuqua.duke.edu/~charvey/Teaching/BA456_2006/Harvey_12_ways_to.pdf

Hitchner J (2017) *Financial Valuation: Applications and Models 4th Edition* (Wiley, Hoboken):196

Ross S (1976) The arbitrage theory of capital asset pricing. J Econ Theory 13:341–360

Ross S (1978) A simple approach to the valuation of risky streams. J Bus 51(3):453–475

Rubinstein M (1976) The valuation of uncertain income streams and the pricing of options. Bell J Econ 7:407–425

Stulz R (1995) Does the cost of capital differ across countries? An agency perspective. Eur Financ Manag 2:11–22

Stulz R (2005) The limits of financial globalization, J Financ 60:1595–1638

Wooldridge J (2009) Introductory econometrics 4e. South-Western, Mason, OH

The Practical Application of Discounted Cash Flow in Emerging Markets: A Case Study of a Brazilian Privately Held Company

Guilherme Vanzin

Abstract This chapter provides a practical step-by-step view on private enterprise value in an emerging market context, presenting a case study of a hypothetical Brazilian company and adds real examples of financial modelling techniques which both valuation practitioners and corporate finance students can benefit from. The chapter utilizes Discounted Cash Flow as the main methodology to estimate the intrinsic value of the firm and integrates macroeconomic factors such as inflation, interest rates, and country risk, which play a major role in valuation in emerging market countries. Market multiples and sensitivity analyses are used to corroborate the outcome and assess the risks associated with valuation. This should provide a framework for readers, whereby they can evaluate and determine the fair value of a private enterprise operating within emerging markets. The contribution of this piece is in offering a no-nonsense, common-sense approach to asset valuation for companies in these interesting and important markets.

Keywords Private enterprise valuation · DCF · Valuation in emerging markets · Macroeconomic factors · Risks in emerging countries · Market multiples · Sensitivity analysis

Introduction

To estimate economic value for private enterprises operating within emerging markets, traditional valuation techniques need to be adjusted to capture additional risk and return factors. Overall, we can argue that these firms have weaker financial reporting standards, lower transparency, and less effective regulatory enforcement (Ngwu et al. 2016). Moreover, Christensen et al. (2013) examine the impact of mandatory International Financial Reporting Standards (IFRS) reporting and enforcement changes, highlighting that even though there has been significant

G. Vanzin (✉)
Nob Hill Consultoria Ltda., Curitiba, Brazil
e-mail: guilherme@nobhill.com.br

S. Derindere Köseoğlu, A. Patterson (eds.), *Valuation in Emerging Markets*, Contributions to Finance and Accounting,
https://doi.org/10.1007/978-3-031-93526-8_10

convergence in international reporting standards over the last few decades, the mere adoption of international standards does not automatically lead to improved financial reporting quality.

A key challenge then is corporate governance—family crossholdings, additional corporate structures to generate tax benefits, off-balance sheet cash flows and liabilities and generally reliable financial statements all bring hurdles for the valuator. Furthermore, market factors such as greater volatility, currency and country risk and inflationary pressures impact not just on corporate returns, revenue and earnings, but also on the risk side of the ledger, and as such cost of capital estimates. WACC calculations, for instance, also provide technical obstacles for beta computation, risk free rates and equity premiums (Damodaran 2012). We can go on: multiple authors have also argued how often underdeveloped equity markets in these economies can lead to questions arising on further liquidity and marketability adjustments and discounts to economic value.

In summary, the valuation of private companies in emerging markets is not a technical exercise alone but one that requires detailed knowledge of local economic drivers, industry-specific risks, and legal frameworks to estimate assertive and robust value estimates. At the practical level, however, as for all private non-listed company valuations, we do confront issues in efficient and reliable data gathering compounded especially in EMs by the fact that with less developed equity markets as flagged up above it can also be harder to understand industry performance dynamics and financial trends.

All that being said, these issues are not insurmountable. By applying well-calibrated adjustments to our number crunching and forecasting, using appropriate discount rates, and incorporating sensitivity and scenario analysis, practitioners can certainly develop robust valuations that reflect economic realities as many other authors have demonstrated in this book.

We will now move to a practical example, demonstrating how these challenges can be addressed with real, straightforward solutions. Through this case study, we will illustrate how to adapt standard valuation methodologies to emerging market conditions using as an example a privately traded middle-market company in Brazil.

Initial Considerations

A significant differential in the valuation of companies in mature markets, such as the United States and Europe, compared to emerging markets like Brazil, is related to additional adjustments for macroeconomic variables.

In the Brazilian context, we can make some preliminary considerations:

- Inflation and Price Indices: Adjustments should be made for the official Brazilian inflation indices, such as IPCA (Broad Consumer Price Index) and IGP-M (General Market Price Index), which make a difference in cost estimates and, therefore, pricing forecasts. Analysts should also identify whether a sector follows a standard index or applies independent price adjustments and adjust revenue and cost projections, accordingly, ensuring a realistic valuation model. Historical price trends, industry benchmarks, and supplier contract structures can be analysed to calibrate revenue and expense forecasts. It is common for projections to include 'real' adjustments above standard inflation estimates. Analysts have to define though if forecasts will be in nominal or real terms.

- Foreign Exchange (Forex) Adjustments: Companies in the import and export business must consider the potential impact of currency fluctuations in their financial statements which can also include hedge instruments and the impact on COGS and net working capital. For instance, between 2022 and 2025 the daily USD/BRL exchange rate had a standard deviation of around 33,8%, more than ten times the volatility of the USD/EUR which was calculated at 3,0%. Analysts can incorporate stress testing and scenario analysis for currency fluctuations and company specific exposure. A decision has to be made regarding the 'valuation currency'.
- Country Risk Premiums: To accurately estimate the cost of capital, valuation models must include country risk premiums (CRP), which reflect the additional economic and political risk of investing in Brazil compared to developed markets. This adjustment typically includes the credit default swap (CDS) spread and sovereign bond yields, reflecting economic and political uncertainties. Considering Brazil's past exposure to fiscal policy changes, risks on foreign debt, and political instability, analysts must carefully evaluate risk premiums and adjust discount rates in order to represent country-specific risks appropriately.
- Changes to CAPM and WACC: High domestic interest rates ('SELIC' in Brazil), equity risk premium, liquidity risks factored in the calculations of the cost of capital. For instance, real interest rates in Brazil between 2022 and 2025 were 7,1%, significantly impacting debt financing costs and risk-free rate assumptions. These factors necessitate potential amendments to standard Capital Asset Pricing Model (CAPM) calculations, ensuring that the cost of equity captures both domestic and international risk components. Here we will adopt the build-up approach to CAPM to include:
  - An industry-specific risk premium, often derived from publicly traded peers.
  - A size premium, reflecting the increased illiquidity and business risk of private firms, specifically in an EM context where firm size categorizations are often different form developed economies, where firms are on average typically smaller.
  - A country risk premium, adjusted for sovereign bond yields and CDS spreads.

Indeed, Gnap (2023) outlined the build-up method as an alternative to CAPM, highlighting its flexibility in unstable economic conditions and the ability to consider the specific risks characteristic of emerging economies. The author will also flag here that for the costs of debt for private companies, which obviously aren't traded, firms resort to bank debt and private credit rather than bonds, which must be adjusted to local lending levels, spreads and credit risk profiles, and access of the firm to external financing. All these factors will be integrated in the valuation process for an

Year	IPCA (IBGE) %	IGP-M (FGV) %	Central Bank Target Rate % (SELIC)	CDI % (December)
2025	4.9	5.4	14.8	14.8
2026	3.0	4.4	11.3	11.2
2027	3.0	4.2	9.5	9.4
2028	3.0	4.2	9.5	9.4
2029	3.0	4.2	9.5	9.4

Fig. 1 Economic forecasts in Brazil ('Projeções de Longo Prazo'). Source: Author's own creation

appropriate reflection of the private company value within an evolving market framework.

In summary, to integrate the economic outlook in Brazil, we will include the main macroeconomic projections of a fictious bank, *Banco Brasileirasso*, according to the information presented below (Fig. 1).

These economic factors will influence the valuation inputs-inflation adjustments, interest rate assumptions, and risk premiums. To facilitate the walkthrough, the income statement and balance sheet for SampleCo from 2022 to 2024 are reproduced below, supplemented by estimates for 2025–2029 based on the assumptions outlined.

The Valuation Method

- Purpose of the Valuation: This valuation has been prepared to approximate the fair value of SampleCo, a Brazilian privately held fashion retail company, in line with IFRS 13—Fair Value Measurement. The valuation is for internal decision-making and strategic planning and takes a market participant view, considering the difficulties of valuing private companies in more volatile and less liquid markets.
- Valuation Methodology: The Discounted Cash Flow (DCF) method has been applied as the principal method—'income approach'—given that it produces a company-specific estimate of value based on future performance expectations. The method is particularly appropriate for private companies operating in frontier markets, where publicly traded equity and debt securities to make direct comparison of prices may be challenging to obtain or simply unavailable.
- Period of Projection: Financial projections will span from 2025 to 2029 based on management projections, valuator insights and estimates, and calibrated for macroeconomic conditions, industry trends, and company-specific risk. A terminal value, based on the Gordon Growth Model, is calculated after 2029 to approximate the value of the company over the long run.
- Basis of Value: The valuation is based on fair value, assuming an orderly market sale between market participants.
- The valuation aims to be in accordance with IFRS 13's fair value hierarchy and based primarily on Level 3 inputs, given the absence of directly observable

market prices. In these cases, economic value estimates can be impacted by political and economic uncertainty, the quality of the company's financial controls, and management forecasts. Cross-checking will be performed using market multiples (normalized for private company status) and precedent transactions where available. Market multiples will thereafter be employed at the conclusion of the exercise to validate and corroborate the DCF-based valuation range.

Introducing SampleCo

SampleCo is a Brazilian fashion retail company that started its operations in 1997 in São Paulo. The company operates 50 flagship stores located in the main cities of the country. In 2024, the company had Gross Revenue of R$694,8 million and EBITDA of R$133,6 million, a margin of 21,3% (Fig. 2).

We note two additional points, firstly, to streamline our walk through we will focus on just Net Revenue. In doing so we assume that the tax rate will be constant—it may not be, or a company may change tax regime—and that devolutions will remain at 1,5% (the percentage in 2024 and the average of the two prior years). Secondly, we assume that EBITDA in our example is already in the adjusted view, which includes the removal of various one-time, irregular, and non-recurring items. For Brazilian firms this usually includes adjusting partner salaries, bringing rent costs to market values, gains or losses from asset sales and off the book items (Fig. 3).

Revenue has grown at a CAGR of 11,9% between 2022 and 2024 and EBITDA at 5,1%, both growth rates well above official inflation. Based on Fig. 2 we can breakdown revenue into the unit economics of each store. On average each of the 50 stores has R$13,9 million in sales which equates to monthly sales of R$1,17 million, a monthly sales volume of close to 12.000 items and average sale ticket of just below R$100.

Item	2022	2023	2024
Gross Revenue	**560.9**	**626.7**	**702.7**
Total Deductions from Sales	10.9%	10.7%	10.8%
Devolutions	1.60%	1.40%	1.50%
Taxes on Sales	9.25%	9.25%	9.25%
Net Revenue	**500.0**	**560.0**	**627.2**
EBITDA	**121.0**	**129.9**	**133.6**
Margin (NR %)	24.2%	23.2%	21.3%

Fig. 2 Performance summary. Source: Author's own creation

Item	2024
Gross Revenue (MR$)	**702.7**
# Stores	50
Revenue /Store (year, R$ M)	14.05
Revenue /Store (month, R$ M)	1.17
Avg. monthly sales volume / store	11,667
Avg. annual Ticket / store (R$)	100.4

Fig. 3 Last year's Revenue Breakdown. Source: Author's own creation

Forecasting Future Financial Performance

Ideally, we would break down all the key accounting lines in a detailed micro view, looking at each individually to align up future projections in a consolidated forecast model. Nevertheless, for simplicity's sake in this example, we will focus on the most important macro-level lines that impact the valuation. For all the projection assumptions to follow, it is also implicit that they are based on a combination of factors, including our analysis of market trends, management estimates, and our own insights of the business. This approach, therefore, focuses more on the 'how' of valuation rather than the 'what' of each operational assumption and makes sure that while the model remains accessible to follow in this chapter, it still reflects the underlying assumptions driving the company's future performance and value.

- Net Revenue: At the practical level we would forecast sales based on the unit economics breakdown presented above—will the company launch new stores? How will the product offering, sales volumes and average tickets change in the future?—but we will streamline here and just focus on the macro number with a separate growth rate each year. We project net revenue to grow at IPCA (the Brazilian consumer price index) plus an additional rate between 2025 and 2029 (9,9% in 2025, 8,1% in 2026—when sector demand is expected to be impacted in the short term by a new regulation—9,0% in 2027, 9,0% in 2028 and 9,0% in 2029). That equates to an average growth rate of 9,0% each year (and around an average 5,6% real growth rate), lower than recent historic growth but in line with market analysts estimates for the sector over the coming years, as it faces increased competition from imports and evolving consumer habits.
- COGS: We forecast the cost margin, at 44% in 2024, to reduce by 0,5% each year to arrive at 41,5% by 2029. This assumption is principally based on the firm's strategy to scale, optimize the supply chain, generate efficiencies with suppliers (for instance with the development of consortiums for raw material purchases) and reduce logistics costs. Our analysis also suggests that the sector average is also around 41%.
- Expenses:

  - Based on market best practices and the current contract, rents should increase in line with the general market price index at around 4,5% a year. Note that if we were forecasting more or larger stores, we would also need to adjust rent accordingly.
  - We expect the current staff structure to remain stable over the next 5 years, helped in part by greater automation and self-service options. SampleCo will continue investing in technology as a hedge against wage pressures and thus aim to keep the workforce stable. As such we just forecast salary growth at the consumer price index of 3,5% on average over the forecast period plus 2% to cover real wage growth. At the practical level we would use HR staff controls to forecast growth in the number of collaborators per year and the expected salary growth based on individual staff members or departments (not all increases may be uniform). We would also need to be aware of legal, tax, and labour obligations. In particular, the Brazilian employment law is stringent and often leads to labour claims via courts (which also need to be provisioned and budgeted for).
  - We assume that technology and innovation expenses remain at 1,8% of revenue as per historical performance over previous years and broader market averages. This means that in absolute terms, growing sales will require increased tech expenditure, in line with the above strategy to keep constraints on staff number growth.
  - We apply a similar assumption for other fixed costs which are expected to remain at 15% of revenue over the forecast period, or in other words, they should grow in line with revenue. Fixed costs as well as technological investments are therefore proportional to increases in revenue. In general, a company should aim to grow its revenue faster than its expenses and thus look for increased profitability. Expenses are usually projected to grow at a set rate each year, although some SG&A expenses, such as marketing can indeed be linked to revenue forecasts.

- Taxes: The corporate tax rate in Brazil stands at 34% for larger companies who adhere to the 'Real Profit' tax regime. No major changes are expected over the next few years so we leave flat.

Based on these assumptions we can put together a projected income statement for SampleCo with projections commencing from 2025. Note that we will discuss Depreciation in the section on Reinvestment below. We also highlight that in this example, 'Adjusted EBITDA' is presented directly as the net result after necessary adjustments. While the specific adjustments are not detailed here, they have already been applied to ensure consistency with the DCF framework. The idea being that this approach maintains clarity for illustration purposes while focusing on the core valuation process.

Revenue is expected to reach R$ 964,8 million and adjusted EBITDA at R$ 258,5 million (Fig. 4).

Item	2022	2023	2024	2025E	2026E	2027E	2028E	2029E
Net Revenue	**500,0**	**560,0**	**627,2**	**689,3**	**745,1**	**812,1**	**885,2**	**964,8**
Cost of Goods Sold	-210,0	-238,0	-276,0	-299,8	-320,4	-345,1	-371,8	-400,4
Gross Profit	**290,0**	**322,0**	**351,2**	**389,5**	**424,7**	**467,0**	**513,4**	**564,4**
Rent	-30,0	-33,6	-37,6	-39,6	-41,4	-43,1	-44,9	-46,8
Wages	-55,0	-64,4	-74,6	-79,7	-83,7	-87,9	-92,3	-96,9
Technology Investment	-9,0	-10,1	-11,3	-12,4	-13,4	-14,6	-15,9	-17,4
Other Fixed Costs	-75,0	-84,0	-94,1	-102,7	-111,9	-121,9	-132,8	-144,8
Adj. EBITDA	**121,0**	**129,9**	**133,6**	**155,0**	**174,3**	**199,4**	**227,4**	**258,5**
Depreciation & Amort.	-50,0	-56	-62,7	-64,8	-65,6	-66,6	-68,2	-68,5
Adj. EBIT	**71,0**	**73,9**	**70,9**	**90,2**	**108,7**	**132,8**	**159,3**	**190,0**

HA%	2023	2024	2025	2026	2027	2028	2029
Net Revenue	**12,0%**	**12,0%**	**9,9%**	**8,1%**	**9,0%**	**9,0%**	**9,0%**
Cost of Goods Sold	13,3%	16,0%	8,7%	6,9%	7,7%	7,7%	7,7%
Gross Profit	**11,0%**	**9,1%**	**10,9%**	**9,1%**	**9,9%**	**9,9%**	**9,9%**
Rent	12,0%	11,9%	5,4%	4,4%	4,2%	4,2%	4,2%
Wages	17,1%	15,8%	6,9%	5,0%	5,0%	5,0%	5,0%
Technology Investment	12,2%	11,9%	9,8%	8,1%	9,0%	9,0%	9,0%
Other Fixed Costs	12,0%	12,0%	9,1%	9,0%	8,9%	8,9%	9,0%
Adj. EBITDA	**7,4%**	**2,9%**	**16,0%**	**12,5%**	**14,4%**	**14,1%**	**13,7%**
Depreciation & Amort.	12,0%	12,0%	3,3%	1,2%	1,6%	2,4%	0,5%
Adj. EBIT	**4,1%**	**-4,0%**	**27,2%**	**20,6%**	**22,2%**	**19,9%**	**19,3%**

VA%	2022	2023	2024	2025	2026	2027	2028	2029
Net Revenue	**100,0%**	**100,0%**	**100,0%**	**100,0%**	**100,0%**	**100,0%**	**100,0%**	**100,0%**
Cost of Goods Sold	-42,0%	-42,5%	-44,0%	-43,5%	-43,0%	-42,5%	-42,0%	-41,5%
Gross Profit	**58,0%**	**57,5%**	**56,0%**	**56,5%**	**57,0%**	**57,5%**	**58,0%**	**58,5%**
Rent	-6,0%	-6,0%	-6,0%	-5,7%	-5,6%	-5,3%	-5,1%	-4,9%
Wages	-11,0%	-11,5%	-11,9%	-11,6%	-11,2%	-10,8%	-10,4%	-10,0%
Technology Investment	-1,8%	-1,8%	-1,8%	-1,8%	-1,8%	-1,8%	-1,8%	-1,8%
Other Fixed Costs	-15,0%	-15,0%	-15,0%	-14,9%	-15,0%	-15,0%	-15,0%	-15,0%
Adj. EBITDA	**24,2%**	**23,2%**	**21,3%**	**22,5%**	**23,4%**	**24,6%**	**25,7%**	**26,8%**
Depreciation & Amort.	-10,0%	-10,0%	-10,0%	-9,4%	-8,8%	-8,2%	-7,7%	-7,1%
Adj. EBIT	**14,2%**	**13,2%**	**11,3%**	**13,1%**	**14,6%**	**16,4%**	**18,0%**	**19,7%**

Fig. 4 SampleCo P&L 2022–2029, horizontal analysis and vertical analysis. Source: Author's own creation

Calculation of Free Cash Flow to Firm (FCFF)

Free Cash Flow to the Firm (FCFF) is the amount of cash that is available to all providers of capital, that is, both debt and equity providers, after accounting for operating expenses, tax, and reinvestment needs of the firm (which are capital spending and working capital net of depreciation). FCFF is one of the valuation measures that quantify the firm's ability to generate cash independently of its capital structure.

FCFF is often preferred in emerging markets valuation because it provides a more stable and reliable measure of a company's intrinsic value, especially in environments characterized by volatile interest rates, fluctuating leverage, and uncertain access to financing. It, therefore, better reflects a firm's operating performance by distinguishing cash flows from financing decisions, which is significant in economies with diversified sources of finance. EMs are likely to employ diversified sources of finance (e.g., government-guaranteed credit, development banks, or private loans). It also removes distortions due to interest rate risk, as these risks are incorporated into the WACC rather than the cash flows themselves. Lastly, FCFF is well-suited for firms with limited access to equity markets, as it accounts for both debt and equity holders, making it a more prudent valuation approach.

We arrive at FCFF based on the following formula:

FCFF = EBIT × (1−t) (+/−) Depreciation & Amortization—Capex (+/−) Variation in Net Working Capital.

where:

- EBIT is Earnings Before Interest and Taxes.
- t = Taxes,
- Add back Depreciation and Amortization as it is a non-cash expense.
- Subtract Capital Expenditures (CapEx) or investment in fixed assets as this directly impacts cash flow.
- Subtract Changes in Net Working Capital (NWC) (Accounts Receivable + Inventory − Accounts Payable).

Reinvestment Assumptions

We analyse the net working capital cycle of SampleCo and, in discussion with the management and analysing market averages, we project out the cash conversion cycle (given as Accounts Receivable + Inventory—Accounts Payable). Based on this forecast cycle we can forecast the financial amounts in R$. We note that the cash operating cycle components are typically scaled as follows:

- Accounts Receivable Days → Revenue (since receivables arise from sales).
- Inventory Days → COGS (as inventory is consumed in production or sales).
- Accounts Payable Days → COGS (since payables are linked to supplier costs).

However, scaling the working capital days against revenue can simplify forecasting and make it more consistent from company to company and period to period. Furthermore, since revenue drives most business activity, scaling receivables, inventory, and payables to revenue gives it consistency in forecast, particularly for companies with fluctuating margins or cost structures. This approach also aligns with financial modelling best practices, where working capital is forecasted as a percentage of revenue to stay proportional to growth. That being, we can use the formulas in our modelling based on a two-step process (Figs. 5 and 6).

Step 1. Calculating Days Outstanding: These formulas express the number of days each working capital component takes relative to revenue:

- Accounts Receivable Days = (Accounts Receivable / Revenue) × 365.
- Inventory Days = (Inventory / COGS) × 365.
- Accounts Payable Days = (Accounts Payable / COGS) × 365.

Operating Current Assets	2022	2023	2024	2025E	2026E	2027E	2028E	2029E
Accounts Receivable	30	30	30	30	30	30	30	30
Inventory	25	25	26	26	25	24	23	22
Operating Current Liabilities	**2022**	**2023**	**2024**	**2025E**	**2026E**	**2027E**	**2028E**	**2029E**
Accounts Payable	13	13	13	13	13	13	13	12
Cash Operating Cycle (Days)	**43**	**43**	**44**	**43**	**42**	**41**	**40**	**39**

Fig. 5 SampleCo net working capital analysis. Source: Author's own creation. Please note that some numbers are rounded up

Year	Acc. Receivable	Inventory	Acc. Payable	Net Working Capital	Change in NWC
2025	56.7	49.3	-24.6	81.4	6.5
2026	61.3	50.9	-26.4	85.8	4.4
2027	66.8	53.0	-28.3	91.4	5.6
2028	72.5	55.0	-30.6	96.9	5.6
2029	79.4	57.0	-33.0	103.5	6.5

Fig. 6 SampleCo net working capital (2025–2029, R$ Million). Source: Author's own creation

Year	EBIT	Taxes	Depreciation & Amort.	CapEx	Change in NWC	FCFF
2025	90.2	-30.7	64.8	-14.9	-6.5	**102.9**
2026	108.7	-37.0	65.6	-16.1	-4.4	**116.8**
2027	132.8	-45.2	66.6	-17.5	-5.6	**131.1**
2028	159.3	-54.2	68.2	-19.1	-5.6	**148.6**
2029	190.0	-64.6	68.5	-20.8	-6.5	**166.5**

Fig. 7 FCFF calculation (2025–2029, R$ Million). Source: Author's Own Creation

Step 2. Projecting Future Financial Amounts: Once you estimate the future days outstanding, you can project the balance sheet amounts using:

- Projected Accounts Receivable = (AR Days / 365) × Projected Revenue.
- Projected Inventory = (Inventory Days / 365) × Projected COGS.
- Projected Accounts Payable = (AP Days / 365) × Projected COGS.

On average, we forecast that the NWC will be 11,2% of net sales and the change in NWC to be 0.7% between 2025 and 2029. Once more, we note that these numbers are in line with market averages.

To close our reinvestment estimates, for depreciation and amortization (D&A) we project the depreciation schedule for existing assets over the five-year forecast period and add in D&A generated from new investments. In doing so, we project that D&A will fall from 10.0% to 7,1% of revenues by 2029, as SampleCo doesn't foresee large investments in new stores or extensive refitting at the same rate as in previous years. Putting all this together we can now forecast our free cash flow over the next 5 years. FCFF is projected to grow from R$102,9 million in 2025 to R$166,5 million by 2029, a CAGR of 12,8% over the period and an average free cash flow margin of 16,2% (Fig. 7).

Weighted Average Cost of Capital (WACC)

With our FCFF forecast ready, we will now calculate the cost of capital. For an emerging market such as Brazil, the weighted average cost of capital (WACC) needs additional adjustments for country risk, inflation, and macroeconomic factors. Here we will overtly simplify multiple steps and explanations. For a more in depth look at this topic the reader can consult analysis from other scholars including Aguilar and Moya (2016), Pereiro (2010), and Godfrey and Espinosa (1996). Moreover, this book volume also has an excellent chapter on the theoretical overview of the cost of capital and computation process in EMs which the author strongly recommends readers consult.

In our illustration we will utilize the capital asset pricing model (CAPM) to estimate the cost of equity and further break this down into a five-year period and perpetuity to align up with our dual growth stage valuation. If the economic context in the EM is volatile, we could calculate an annual CAPM for each year for the projection period (Damodaran 2024). We will do this for our cost of debt as we estimate an acute reduction in interest rates in the country by 2027.

We will quickly reiterate the standard formulas:

Capital Asset Pricing Model (CAPM)

$$COE = Rf + \beta \times ERP + CRP$$

where:

- **COE** = Cost of Equity.
- **RfR** = Risk-Free Rate (typically based on government bonds).
- **β** = Systematic risk measure of the firm relative to the market.
- **ERP** = Equity Risk Premium (expected return of the market above the risk-free rate).
- **CRP** = Country Risk Premium (additional risk for operating in an emerging market, if applicable).

$$WACC = \left(\frac{E}{E+D} * COE\right) + \left(\frac{D}{E+D} * Cost\ of\ Debt * (1-t)\right)$$

where:

- **WACC** = Weighted Average Cost of Capital.
- **EEE** = Market value of equity.
- **DDD** = Market value of debt.
- **COE** = Cost of Equity (from CAPM).

- **Cost of Debt** = Cost of Debt (estimated using company bonds, synthetic credit rating, comparable company analysis, or bank loan spreads).
- t = Corporate Tax Rate (applied to debt to reflect interest tax shield).

Thus, for our CAPM inputs we assume that:

- Capital Structure: SampleCo's capital structure consists of 60% equity and 40% debt.
- Cost of Equity: The cost of equity is determined using the Capital Asset Pricing Model and comprises of
  - Risk-Free Rate: 10,5%, derived from a five-year zero-coupon government bond in Brazil.
  - Beta: 0,95 from the unlevered beta (industry-adjusted) for retail in Brazil adjusted to SampleCo's debt levels.
  - Equity Risk Premium (ERP): 8,99%, market risk premium for Brazil.
  - Country Risk Premium (CRP): Not considered (if you are using a Brazilian risk-free rate in BRL, you do not need to add a CRP separately).

With these inputs, SampleCo's cost of equity is expected to be 19,05% in the local currency over the forecast period.

The cost of debt is estimated by the CDI rate, adjusted for SampleCo's credit risk premium. The effective cost of debt is deduced after allowing for the corporation tax rate of 34%. In EMs, debt is often expensive and can be challenging to obtain. Indeed, simple business loans frequently become more complex credit operations. For a private firm in an emerging market, the cost of debt (Kd) should be estimated using a market-based approach rather than relying on reported interest expense. This being so, best practices include adopting a synthetic credit rating approach, bank loan benchmarking or the risk-free rate plus a default spread. We will use the latter method based on our, and management's, expectations of the cost of future marginal lending.

Assumptions Relating to the Cost of Debt

- The cost of debt is estimated based on the benchmark SELIC rate and SampleCo's credit risk premium. The forecast SELIC rate is used as the base risk-free rate, reflecting the cost of borrowing in local currency, while the company-specific credit spread accounts for the firm's default risk, ensuring a more accurate representation of its true cost of debt.
- The rate for the period 2025–2029 ranges from 14,8% in 2025 to 9,50% in 2029.
- Credit Spread: 2,0% benchmark for SampleCo in the retail industry.
- The Pre-Tax Effective Cost of Debt in 2025 is given as 16,83% for 2025 and decreases further over succeeding years.
- Corporate Tax Rate: 34%, used to find out the after-tax cost of debt.

SampleCo's after-tax cost of debt will thus be as follows (Fig. 8):

The projected WACC for 2025, based on SampleCo's capital structure weights, cost of equity, and after-tax cost of debt, is **15,85% and should decrease over time to 14,47%** (Fig. 9).

Year	SELIC Target Rate %	+ 2% Spread	Tax Rate	After Tax Debt Cost
2025	14.75	16.75	0.34	11.06
2026	11.25	13.25	0.34	8.75
2027	9.5	11.5	0.34	7.59
2028	9.5	11.5	0.34	7.59
2029	9.5	11.5	0.34	7.59

Fig. 8 Estimating the cost of debt. Source: Author's own creation

Fig. 9 SampleCo WACC. Source: Author's own creation

Year	WACC (%)
2025	15,85%
2026	14,93%
2027	14,47%
2028	14,47%
2029	14,47%

Value Is What You Get

We can now project out our discounted cash flow to 2029 using the standard intrinsic value formulas:

Discounted Cash Flow (DCF) Formula with Terminal Value:

$$EV = \sum_{t=1}^{n} + \frac{FCFFt}{(1 + WACC)t} + \frac{TVt}{(1 + WACC)t}$$

where:

- **EV** = Enterprise Value (Present Value of the Firm).
- **FCFFt** = Free Cash Flow to the Firm in year *t*.
- **WACC** = Weighted Average Cost of Capital.
- **TV** = Terminal Value (value of the firm beyond forecast period).
- **n** = Number of forecasted years (5 in our example, using the end of year convention).

Terminal Value (TV) Calculation using the Gordon Growth Model (Perpetuity Growth Method):

$$TVn = \frac{FCFFn + 1}{WACC - g}$$

where:

- **FCFFn + 1** = Free Cash Flow to the Firm in the first year after the projection period (forecast based on the long-term growth rate, or 'g')
- **g** = Long-term growth rate of free cash flows

Year	FCFF (R$ MM)	WACC	Discount Factor	Present Value of FCFF (R$ MM)
2025	102,9	15,85%	0,86	**88,9**
2026	116,8	14,93%	0,76	**88,4**
2027	131,1	14,47%	0,67	**87,4**
2028	148,6	14,47%	0,58	**86,6**
2029	166,5	14,47%	0,51	**84,7**

Fig. 10 Discounting cash flows. Source: Author's own creation

While EMs may have higher short-term growth, long-term sustainable growth should align with GDP growth projections (often lower than developed markets expect). Analysts need to take care when using nominal or real growth rates (Fig. 10).

Total Present Value of FCFF (2025–2029) = **R$ 436,0 million**.

Given that SampleCo is anticipated to be operational beyond 2029, we calculate its Terminal Value (TV), signifying the future worth of all Free Cash Flow to the Firm (FCFF) beyond the forecast period. We employ the Gordon Growth Model (Perpetuity Growth Method), which posits that SampleCo's Free Cash Flow to the Firm (FCFF) will perpetually increase at a constant pace.

Assumptions for Calculating Terminal Value

- FCFF for the first year after the explicit forecast period is calculated by estimating the long-term growth rate of the Brazilian economy of 4,0%.
- Instead of applying a growth rate to estimate perpetual cash flows we could also reassess long term fundamental reinvestment needs and returns on capital to ensure that projected free cash flows better reflect actual capital needs, sustainable growth capacity, and market averages. EM firms often face higher reinvestment needs due to infrastructure gaps, higher costs of capital, and less efficient marketplaces and asset usage, making a direct link between growth, reinvestment, and return on invested capital (ROIC) a more realistic and risk-adjusted way to estimate long-term cash flows. However, for the sake of simplicity in this example we will project the perpetual cash flow based on a uniform growth rate on year five cash flows.
- We update our WACC inputs for the long-term and arrive at a cost of capital of 14% which we will utilize for the perpetuity calculation.

With the assumptions above, we arrive at the following results:

- FCFF in perpetuity: **R$ 173,2 million**
- Undiscounted Terminal Value: **R$ 1.732,0 million**.
- Present Value of Terminal Value: **R$ 881,4 million**.
- Enterprise Value: **R$ 1.317,4 million (R$ 436,0 million + R$ 881,4 million)**

To convert EV to equity value, we now subtract net debt. When arriving at equity value in an emerging market (EM) valuation, it is important that all debt, such as instruments and liabilities, are considered. Such items commonly include off-balance sheet debt, labour and tax liabilities, and crossholdings.

First, we will calculate Net Debt, which is the company's total debt minus cash and cash equivalents. For the year 2024:

- Total Debt (Short-Term and Long-Term Debt): R$ 125,3 million.
- Cash Balance: R$ 119,2 million.
- Net debt: R$ 6,1 million.

This results in an Equity Value of **R$ 1.311,3 million.**

Applying the Finishing Touches

Depending on the objective of the valuation exercise, liquidity adjustments can be utilized. In valuation, a discount for liquidity or lack of marketability (DLOM) is a percentage deducted from the value of an asset to account for its reduced liquidity. This incorporates their reduced liquidity compared to publicly traded stocks, making valuations for non-listed companies more realistic. They can be especially important in emerging economies because these markets, on average, tend to have lower liquidity due to less developed financial markets, greater risks and volatility, and less transparency, all of which can make it more difficult—to greater or lesser degrees—to buy or sell equity. These factors increase the cost of liquidity and the risk of illiquid investments, which investors can account for by applying a discount to the equity value in M&A and other valuation models. The liquidity adjustment can be calculated via restricted stock studies, pre-IPO trading, option-based models and transaction comparables. Such discounts often range between 20–40% (Damodaran 2012). In this chapter, we will not seek to model specifically but we can summarize the potential impact, as below (Fig. 11):

Once Equity Value has been calculated, we benchmark SampleCo's valuation against that of publicly traded retail companies using market multiples. This step helps validate the DCF results and ensures that SampleCo's valuation is justifiable and coherent based on how similar assets are being priced in the Brazilian market. Relative valuation in emerging markets (EMs) can be more challenging due to the lack of comparable companies in key sectors. Analysts often rely on international firms and apply further adjustments for country or company-specific risks.

Fig. 11 Adjusted equity value. Source: Author's own creation

Adjusted Equity Value	DLOM
1.049,0	20,0%
983,5	25,0%
917,9	30,0%
852,3	35,0%
786,8	40,0%

Metric	Industry Median	Industry Range
EV/EBITDA	9.5x	8.0x - 12.0x
EV/Revenue	2.0x	1.8x - 2.4x

Fig. 12 Comparable multiples. Source: Author's own creation

Scenario	EV (R$ Million)	% of Base case	EV/EBITDA	Within industry range?
Upside	1.542,7	117,1%	11,5	Yes
Base case	1.317,4	100,0%	9,9	Yes
Downside	1.205,4	91,5%	9,0	Yes

Fig. 13 Scenario analysis—EV results. Source: Author's own creation

Based on current data we gather from market analysis, we put together valuation multiples for comparable public traded companies after adjusting for liquidity and size factors. We focus here on EV/EBITDA and EV/Revenue. We could also use M&A transactions, but they are generally harder to obtain in EMs (Fig. 12).

Based on SampleCo's EBITDA and Revenue in 2024 (the most recent reporting results) we estimate the implicit multiples which we compute as:

- EV/EBITDA: 9,9 × (3,8% above the industry median).
- EV/Sales 2,1 × (5,0% above the industry median).

In summary, SampleCo's DCF valuation is broadly in line with the market but slightly higher than comparable multiples due to higher-than-average financial metrics (let us say in unit economics and margins). This external relative valuation view is a sure-fire way to validate our value estimates.

Sensitivity analysis also allows us to check the robustness of SampleCo's valuation by changing the critical assumptions to understand their impact on economic value results, thus helping investors understand the sensitivity of valuation to changes in key inputs like WACC, revenue growth, and terminal growth rates.

We can run sensitivity analysis on our own valuation assumptions (WACC and long-term growth etc.) or on operational assumptions (growth rates and margin in the explicit forecast period). We demonstrate below how hypothetically we could structure this sensitivity analysis:

Sensitivity Analysis—Scenario 1:

- WACC: ± 1,0%.
- Terminal Growth Rate: ± 0,5%.

Sensitivity Analysis—Scenario 2:

- Annual Revenue Growth: ± 1,0% of point-estimate.
- Annual EBITDA Margin: ± 0,5% of point-estimate.

We also build out specific scenarios based on internal drivers such as revenue growth, profitability, and reinvestment rates and external factors such as broader GDP performance and interest rates and estimate the following results (Fig. 13):

Valuation Method	Estimated Value (R$ MM)
DCF Valuation (Base Case)	**1.317,4**
CVM Ranges	**1254.8 - 1380.0**
Market Multiple Ranges (EV/EBITDA & EV/Revenue)	**1205.4 - 1543.7**
Scenario Ranges	**1069.1 - 1603.6**

Fig. 14 Scenario analysis—EV results. Source: Author's own creation

To close out, we illustrate here an overview of the valuation results and estimation ranges from the above exercises. Note as well that we include an additional range based on accepted practice in the Brazilian market and required by the national securities exchange commission ('CMV') whereby a range of 4,75% in relation to the midpoint—base case—so that the range of minimum and maximum values does not exceed 10%, as required in CVM Resolution 85. Such local regulation and best practices are important to consider when we are dealing with international valuations (Fig. 14).

Conclusion

Valuation of a private company in emerging markets, as exemplified in this chapter by a Brazilian company case study, requires a method that integrates financial modelling, macroeconomic factors, and market validation. In this chapter, we have applied real valuation methods to SampleCo, indicating how an investor can navigate emerging market environments and apply coherent corporate finance valuation methods.

The DCF method is the most reliable valuation tool for private companies, as it encapsulates expected growth, cost efficiency, and macroeconomic factors in a fundamental and holistic view. This is the same for emerging market firms as for developed companies. We also validated our results with relative analysis of local listed firms in the Brazilian marketplace.

The significance of macroeconomic adjustments cannot be overstated. Inflation indices (IPCA, IGP-M) directly influence revenue and cost projections; CDI/SELIC rates determine the cost of capital, impacting SampleCo's discount rate (WACC); and country risk (CDS spreads) are essential adjustments for international investors evaluating Brazilian assets. Furthermore, if we were conducting our valuation in, for example, US Dollars, we would also need to be mindful of exchange rate volatility.

We have also illustrated how sensitivity and scenario analysis are particularly important in EM valuation owing to increased economic volatility, political risk, and currency fluctuations, which have the potential to affect key drivers of valuation such as growth rates, discount rates, and cash flows. Sensitivity analysis assists in probing the impact on valuation caused by small variations in assumptions (e.g., WACC, terminal growth rate), whereas scenario analysis simulates alternate macroeconomic and business conditions (e.g., high inflation versus stable growth).

Implications for Private Company Valuations in Emerging Economies

Investors need to combine financial modelling with qualitative analysis, especially in the case of private companies that have limited public disclosures. Valuation is a dynamic and strategic tool to assist stakeholders in making informed decisions about financial planning, investments, M&A, and capital deployment.

Valuation of private enterprises therefore requires deep understanding of the economic environment and of the specifics of the subject business, this is especially the case in EMs which all have their specific characteristics and subsequently local challenges and solution from a valuation perspective.

References

Aguilar M, Moya J (2016) Cost of capital in emerging markets: a review and future directions. J Econ Financ Adm Sci 21(40):3–17. https://www.scielo.cl/scielo.php?script=sci_arttext&pid=S0719-04332016000100006. Accessed 20 Feb 2025

Christensen HB, Hail L, Leuz C (2013) Mandatory IFRS reporting and changes in enforcement. J Account Econ 56(2–3):147–177

Damodaran A (2012) Investment valuation: methods and instruments for assessing the worth of any asset. Wiley

Damodaran A (2024) Equity risk premiums in emerging markets. https://pages.stern.nyu.edu/~adamodar/New_Home_Page/datafile/ctryprem.html

Gnap M (2023) The build-up approach. Could it be an alternative to the CAPM? Studia Prawno-Ekonomiczne 126:89–104. https://doi.org/10.26485/SPE/2023/126/5

Godfrey S, Espinosa R (1996) Cost of capital in emerging markets, *Research Gate*. https://www.researchgate.net/publication/256038376_Cost_of_Capital_in_Emerging_Markets. Accessed 20 Feb 2025

Ngwu F, Osuji O, Stephen F (eds) (2016) Corporate governance in developing and emerging markets, 1st edn. Routledge. https://doi.org/10.4324/9781315666020

Pereiro LE (2010) The practice of investment valuation in emerging markets: evidence from Argentina. J Multinatl Financ Manag 20(3–4):181–206. https://core.ac.uk/download/pdf/231073761.pdf. Accessed 20 Feb 2025

The Art of (Valuing) the Deal: Valuation Best Practices in Emerging Markets M&A

Adam Patterson

"M&A activity with emerging markets involvement totalled US$677.5 billion during full year 2023. [Of this] Cross-border emerging markets M&A activity totalled US$285.3 billion".
—LSEG, 2024
"Acquisitions fail for different reasons, but one recurrent theme is that acquirers overpay for the target".
—Ferris and Petitt (2002)

Abstract Valuation plays a central role in mergers and acquisitions (M&A), influencing deal structuring, negotiations, and capital allocation. In emerging markets (EMs), however, M&A processes are often complicated by the same endogenous and exogenesis uncertainty factors which impact solid value estimates—namely economic regulatory uncertainty, currency risks, information asymmetry, and corporate governance issues. In this chapter we provide a review of some of the key challenges, propose theoretical solutions, and then offer practical examples of some of the main valuation approaches and considerations for EM M&A which include accretion/dilatation analysis, synergy quantification and how earnouts and other mechanisms can help bridge value gaps between both sides of the table. The chapter seeks to contribute to the literature by blending theory and practice around valuation and value-related deal components in the interesting nexus of EM M&A transactions.

Keywords Mergers and acquisitions · Challenges · Governance · Tax · Liabilities · Accretion · Dilution · Equity · Debt · Previsability · Value versus pricing · Due diligence · Control · Synergies · Earnouts

---

A. Patterson (✉)
Redirection Corporate Advisory, London, UK
e-mail: adam@redirection.com

S. Derindere Köseoğlu, A. Patterson (eds.), *Valuation in Emerging Markets*, Contributions to Finance and Accounting,
https://doi.org/10.1007/978-3-031-93526-8_11

Introduction

Corporate development ("CorpDev"), which encompasses mergers and acquisitions (M&A), joint venture (JV), and business partnerships and divestitures, has become part of the growth and globalization narrative of EMs. This has a dual focus: Firstly, at the inbound level, multinational corporations from developed markets are pursuing expansion opportunities in faster growing and potentially more profitable geographies and, secondly, over the last few years, EM firms have been active at the outbound level, executing M&A processes in developed economies. M&A activity is increasingly important in EM regions as highlighted by the headline numbers presented in the introductory quotes above, driven by economic liberalization, income growth, consumer preferences, and maturing industries which together offer fertile ground for both cross-border and domestic deals. A central aspect of M&A transactions, valuation typically underpins buyer and seller alignment, fair value definition and goodwill accounting, negotiations and deal structuring as well as capital raising. And yet, as other authors have argued throughout this book, valuation processes, often complex by nature, can be especially so in EMs due to a basket of potential factors such as market volatility and lack of visibility, currency risks, regulatory uncertainties and reduced operational and governance transparency. In such a context then, how do corporate finance professionals deal with and navigate value and pricing estimates in M&A deal making? And how about other components of value such as synergies and earnouts? Providing some explanatory insight and best practices is therefore the focus of this chapter by using examples and discussing some of the key issues, approaches and considerations involved with EM M&A.

Literature Review and Context

There are multiple purposes and justifications for M&A dealmaking from amplifying market share, geographical reach, enhancing product portfolio, economies of scale, solidifying supply chains and acquiring new resources. In a nutshell, it's about growth and competitive advantages. We recall the oft used expression that it's "easier to buy than build". This is especially the case in EMs where large MNCs can quickly gain access to the market via acquisitions without having to start from scratch in a potentially unfamiliar and more challenging marketplace.

Moreover, most M&A deals are also designed to generate those famous "synergies". Synergies are achieved when the merged value of both firms or assets post-merger is greater than the pre-merger value of the individual entities. This axiom is frequently elucidated in mathematical terms as $2 + 2 = 5$, whereby the increase in value is a function of synergies. In modern business, there are a myriad of possible and targeted synergies. For the sake of conciseness, we can however summarize in three main groupings, aligned with the P&L sequence:

- Revenue synergies: combined top line growth, new markets (complementary geographies and clients), new product and service offerings, and cross-selling/ improved sales channels.
- Cost synergies: which aim for lower operating costs, efficiencies, scaling capacity, and better bargaining power with suppliers and distributors.
- Financial synergies: increased debt capacity and better payment terms, optimized cost of capital and tax benefits.

In emerging markets, these goals often overlap with the intent to reach underpenetrated consumer bases, exploit regional advantages, and reduce supply chain vulnerabilities. According to Damodaran (2009), M&A is also a means for firms to obtain capabilities—technological, managerial, or human capital—that would be more difficult or time-consuming to build organically. M&A dealmaking can also be opportunistic, particularly in EMs where global firms can take advantage of attractive forex, valuation or economic scenarios. In terms of theses, common strategies include vertical, horizontal, conglomerate, concentric or leveraged buy-out acquisitions. Indeed, EM firms, after years of cross border dealmaking focusing on strategic and natural resources and capability gaps (technology and know-how), are "increasingly looking to penetrate new markets—just like multinationals in developed markets do" (McKinsey & Company 2015).

For all these M&A strategies, it becomes clear how valuation is a critical step in decision making. Indeed, company and asset valuation in M&A processes, is arguably one of the most debated and interesting topics in corporate finance. And yet, the literature on M&A focused valuation in EMs is arguably somewhat light and thus we seek to amplify knowledge in the field by summarizing key concepts and complement with practical professional experience and insights.

Damodaran (2003) argues that the issues of control and synergy create additional complexities in M&A valuation processes which require approaches that go beyond merely quantifying the value of an acquisition target. He explains how the value of control is based on estimates of how a better managed firm can improve performance in the M&A target than the as-is scenario. For synergies he argues that synergies exist if the "target firm controls a specialized resource that becomes more valuable if combined with the bidding firm's resources". The effect of such synergies can be built into projected cash flows and growth with the combined entity revalued to contemplate such synergies. He summarizes the key valuation points around these themes as follows, which we quote in full (Fig. 1):

It seems intuitive that M&A and valuations in any country are impacted by macroeconomic variables, stock market activity and firm specific factors (Choi and Jeon 2011). There will then obviously be differences between developed and emerging economies. Thus, the consensus seems to suggest that M&A valuation is generally more straightforward in developed markets as a result of greater market and regulatory stability, asset liquidity, and higher corporate governance levels. EMs on the other hand introduce several differential factors for the practitioner: inconsistent and timely company financial reporting, greater exposure to political and economic volatility, regulatory complexity, and more acute cultural and

Component	Valuation Guidelines	Should you pay?
Synergy	*1.* Value the combined firm with synergy built in. This may include a. a higher growth rate in revenues: growth synergy b. higher margins, because of economies of scale c. lower taxes, because of tax benefits: tax synergy d. lower cost of debt: financing synergy e. higher debt ratio because of lower risk: debt capacity *2.* Subtract the value of the target firm (with control premium) + value of the bidding firm (pre-acquisition). This is the value of the synergy.	Which firm is indispensable for the synergy? If it is the target, you should be willing to pay up to the synergy. If it is the bidder, you should not.
Control Premium	Value the company as if optimally managed. This will usually mean that investment, financing and dividend policy will be altered: Investment Policy: Higher returns on projects and divesting unproductive projects. Financing Policy: Move to a better financing structure, eg. optimal capital structure Dividend Policy: Return unused cash Practically, 1. Look at industry averages for optimal (if lazy) 2. Do a full-fledged corporate financial analysis	If motive is control or in a stand-alone valuation, this is the maximum you should pay.
Status Quo Valuation	Value the company as is, with existing inputs for investment, financing and dividend policy.	If motive is undervaluation, this is the maximum you should pay.

Fig. 1 Valuing an acquisition. Source: Damodaran (2003), Acquisition Valuation, page 7

organizational differences, which can create integration challenges. Information asymmetry could also be greater and lead to value estimate discrepancies.

The academic literature, including this volume, has recognized and discussed such challenges. As Godfrey and Espinosa (1996) argue, traditional approaches to valuation, such as the DCF model, require adjustments by adding a country risk premium and scenario analysis reflecting the high volatility of emerging market environments. Recent literature also shows an increasing use of advanced approaches, such as real options analysis and Monte Carlo simulations, to capture the additional uncertainty and dynamic nature of the markets in emerging economies (Koller et al. 2020).

Furthermore, Bruner (2004) suggests that the valuation of EM M&A should be more focused on qualitative factors, such as regulatory risks and cultural integration, which can materially affect transaction outcomes. Recent studies, such as that by McKinsey & Company (2020), have also discussed the relationship between valuation and pricing, postulating that while valuation may underpin or anchor initial viewpoints, the actual dynamics of negotiation, market mood and synergy identification often lead to the final pricing of the transaction. In the author's opinion, this is one of the core concepts in M&A. The price is the result of negotiations between the buyer and seller, and it doesn't always match intrinsic value estimates. It can be higher or lower. Value can be contemplated as a sustainable utility driven by

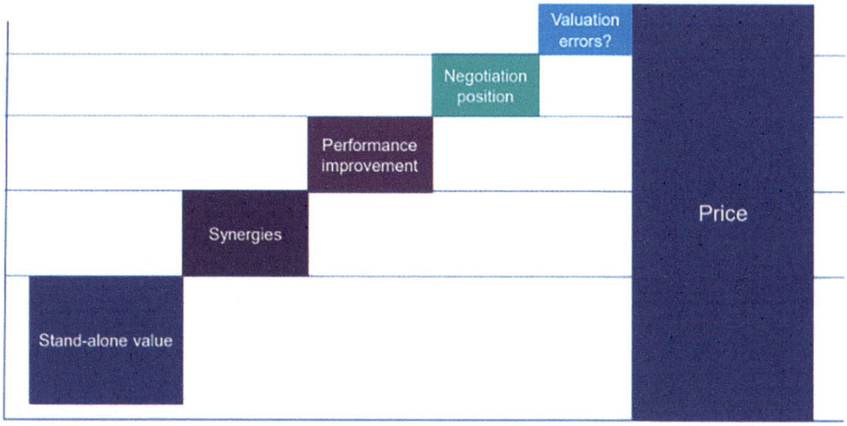

Fig. 2 Price versus value. Source: KPMG (2022)

economic and business fundamentals whilst price is a function of additional factors, market sentiment and subjective opinions. Fair market value (FMV) is the price at which an asset would sell in an open market under certain conditions. Figure 2 from KPMG helps elucidate these concepts in an M&A scenario:

Essentially then, there needs to be overlap between how much the seller can maximize value and the bidder can reduce the potential purchase price. Price can exceed value when the buyer pays an acquisition premium through strategic rationale, market pressures or competitive M&A processes or it can be less based on the interests of both parties. It is often said in M&A that the market defines valuation. Overall, the literature converges on the view that valuation in M&A is both a craft and a science, especially in EMs which often require more nuanced, flexible and adaptive processes. The human element of stakeholder alignment, relationship building, and negotiation skill often come to the fore. This does not mean that valuation is optional in M&A processes but rather it serves as a framework for aligning expectations, influencing deal structure, and the negotiation dynamics at play during the transaction.

Valuation Approaches in EM M&A

For your author, fundamental, intrinsic valuation in both M&A contexts and EMs utilizes the same guiding principles and corporate finance theory as in developed markets, however, with certain adjustments to methods and how the results are used. In other words, the processes are analogous, but the toolkits are broader. Or as Pereiro (2002) noted, the context depends "on what is being valued, for whom, for what purpose, and how".

As always, there are multiple ways to value a company, but what truly matters is constructing a clear narrative, making solid and well-founded assumptions, and ensuring that the analysis, methods used, and data is coherent and aligned with the specific circumstances of the transaction and market. Below we synopsise some of the main methods and approach adjustments potentially required for M&A based valuation in EMs, with the caveat that EMs are not all homogenous where a one-size-fits-all approach to valuation will automatically work (Fig. 3).

Valuation Approach	Challenges	Solutions
Discounted Cash Flow (DCF)	- Potentially increased volatility and lack of predictability in cash flow projections due to greater market instability.	- Incorporate scenario and sensitivity analyses. Use data driven forecasts based on unit economics/key variables. Extensive analysis of value drivers and commercial contracts. On the buy side, estimate factors based on own-company metrics, governance and expected outlook.
	- Lack of reliable financial or operational data and transparency. Accounting numbers may also not reflect the operating reality.	- Adjust projections using local expertise and industry insights. Normalize KPIs and earnings. Utilize market or own-firm inputs for buy-side analyses and audited financial statements where possible.
	- Difficulty in estimating post-merger synergies due to operational and cultural integration risks.	- Develop detailed integration scenarios to model synergies realistically. Adopt micro analysis of contracts, supplier base, staff, commercial processes, technology capabilities, inventory and physical spaces to estimate specific synergies and timings.
	- Country-specific risks make it harder to predict long-term performance for cross-border M&A. Challenges in estimating local costs of capital, changes over time and incremental impacts on acquiring company WACC.	- Add country risk premiums and stress test forecasts for robustness. Integrate country level macroeconomic numbers into forecasts. On the buy-side the company estimates the WACC for the target company to assess its standalone valuation and also evaluates the impact on its own cost of capital of the combined entity post deal.
Comparable Company Analysis (CCA)	- Lack of relevant listed peer companies in similar sectors or local markets. Sample sizes can be smaller. There may be greater liquidity differences between larger and smaller cap firms in EMs.	- Expand peer groups by including broader but related sectors including at different industry stages. We could also focus on the whole equity universe in the EM and use regression analysis to control for differences (looking at the fundamental valuation drivers of risk and return).
	- Issues in utilizing global firms with potentially different accounting standards, currencies, macroeconomic differences and other country or broader risk factors. Market inefficiencies may distort valuation multiples when apply developed market firms for EM assets.	- Use adjusted multiples or regression analysis to control for endogenous and exogenous differences.

Fig. 3 M&A valuation in M&A: Approaches, challenges and solutions. Source: Author's own creation

Precedent Transactions	- Scarcity of updated publicly available M&A transactions in EM markets (result of less M&A deals, less data providers and reduced corporate reporting).	- Build out a database of global regional precedent transactions and apply adjustments. Track broader transactions and pricing trends in the national market to understand value narratives. Micro analyse or reverse engineer investor relations reporting, specialist news or accounting statements from listed firms who have been active in M&A. Utilize global and regional databases. Rely on comparable company valuations in public markets to understand trends.
	- Incomplete or undisclosed deal terms - or even strategic premiums - can obscure effective transaction valuations.	- Adjust for potential premiums and undisclosed terms using proxies from other markets or deep dive into company reporting statements for additional deal insights. Premiums paid in public M&A transaction multiples can estimated by comparing the price paid by the acquirer to the target company's historical trading prices. For private M&A transactions global advisors can work with local advisors and networks to fill gaps in transaction details and knowledge (and thus combine analytical techniques with qualitative research).
Merger Model Accretion/Dilution Analysis	- Exchange rate volatility, less detailed or reliable financial disclosures and regulatory and tax uncertainties complicate accretion/dilution forecasts for cross-border transactions.	- Integrate exchange rate sensitivity into pro forma models for cross-border M&A and adjust financial disclosures, flagging up and dealing with any gaps and unknowns.
	- Enhanced uncertainty around synergy realization - for instance cultural, regulatory, tax and OTB liabilities - could impact analysis.	- Use conservative assumptions for synergies and validate with enhanced due diligence and third-party audits auditing. Employ multiple scenarios to account for potential regulatory changes and tax implications. Incorporate contingency planning. Use alternative valuation approaches, such as EBITDA multiples or cash flow analysis, to validate accretion/dilution results.
	- Mismatched accounting, reporting and governance standards between buyer and target could hinder reliable pro forma financial projections.	- Standardize financial statements and Reconcile accounting practices to align buyer and target financials. Where possible hire independent local advisors for any knowledge gaps.

Fig. 3 (continued)

What is universal in an M&A valuation context is that the value exercise is just one part of the process. On the sell-side, the valuation serves as baseline to align expectations with the client via an exercise of intrinsic and relative valuation which we highlight is primarily for internal stakeholder consumption. Arguably more essential than the specific "number" per se, is firstly, understanding company performance, its business model and the intricacies of financial reporting and, secondly, gathering detailed institutional, operational and accounting data for the Q&A and due diligence stage. Valuation models are there to guide discussions and are less about finding a theoretical “true value”—if one exists—and more about creating a defensible value and range that will keep both sides at the negotiation table. Furthermore, an M&A advisor will expect that a competitive process will ultimately result in a higher acquisition premium—and better contractual terms—for the business. On the buy-side, there is a similar focus for valuation exercises which look to value the financial profile of the combined potential firm and estimate possible price ranges. The main objectives are to understand where (or if) value can be added, where the possible synergies are, how well the company is run—corporate governance and accounting risks—and what is its future potential. For listed firm acquisitions, a major valuation question is how much of a control premium should be paid. Valuation is consequently a tool to justify decisions based on acquirer strategy, cultural fit, competitive pressures, and market positioning. The market—and advisor skill—do help set the final transaction pricing, but the final price almost always comes down to leverage, timing, and market dynamics, and how badly both parties want to close the deal. We will now briefly explore a few key analytical methods we have in our tool kit for M&A valuations.

Practical M&A Valuation Examples

M&A Accretion and Dilution Analysis

In M&A modelling, accretion/dilution analysis is performed in the pre-deal phase to analyse the effect of the transaction on shareholder value, to evaluate the financial feasibility and advantages of a proposed deal. The main goal of the model is to assess the financial impact of an acquisition on the profitability of the acquiring firm, usually measured by the earnings per share (EPS), and if this metric for the acquirer is expected to grow (“accretion”) or decrease (“dilution”) post-closing. Nonetheless, this metric has its drawbacks and has been the subject of critiques over the last few years. For instance, a research paper from McKinsey & Company (2016) contends that:

> *Of all the measures of a company’s performance, EPS, may be the most visible. It’s quite literally the “bottom line” on a company’s income statement… But for all the attention EPS receives, it is highly overrated as a barometer of value creation. The fallacy is believing that anything that improves EPS will have the same effect on value creation and TRS [Total Return to Shareholders].*

As such it may not be a completely optimal tool to reflect the strategic or long-term financial advantages of a transaction, impact on sustainable cash flow, value generation and the return on investment. The EPS approach does however provide a useful and well-known framework to build on for public-to-public firm M&As which we can then ideate around calibrating further for EM valuations. We will, therefore, employ a simplified merger model—merely for illustration purposes—for two developed market firms based on accretion/dilution analytics and discuss potential EM adjustments as we move forward.

A Step-by-Step Merger Model Example

A large, listed developed market firm is looking at acquiring a smaller but also listed firm in a related sector in its home country. We need to build a merger model to advise on the transaction. We start by looking at the headline financial metrics of both companies on the day the analysis is conducted. Financial or monetary data is to be shown in a generic local currency unit format (or "¤"). We highlight assumptions in grey painted cells (Fig. 4).

We observe that the Acquirer's stock price is 50.00 with 800 million shares outstanding whilst the Target's stock price is 18.00 with 200 million shares outstanding. There are no outstanding options. The relative equity values are therefore 40 billion and 3.6 billion, respectively. We input the EPS for each company. Here, EPS can be extracted from the most recent reporting period (quarterly or annual), LTM or forecast numbers. This then gives us our implied P/E multiples. It is noted that the differential valuation multiples can create a "value arbitrage" that potentially could make the deal accretive to the acquirer's shareholders (Fig. 5).

In our example, a control premium—the "excess" paid over an acquisition target's share price, of 25% is paid by the buyer firm in order to gain a controlling interest and thus incentivize and motivate current shareholders to liquidate their positions. Thus, based on this offer price the acquiring firm intends to pay 22.5 to close the deal. In effect, this premium adds up to 900 million in absolute terms. We then calculate the EV of the target firm including this premium, total net debt, and additional liabilities. We define that the transaction will be financed half by cash—via debt—and half in acquirer stock, compute advisor fees, and estimate deal

Key Numbers of M&A parties	
Acquirer Co.	
Fully diluted shares outstanding (FDSO in M)	800
Current stock price	50,0
Equity Value	**40.000**
Estimated Earnings Per Share (EPS)	5,0
P/E Multiple	**10,0x**
Target Co.	
Fully diluted shares outstanding (FDSO in M)	200
Current stock price	18,0
Equity Value	**3.600**
Estimated Earnings Per Share (EPS)	3,0
P/E Multiple	**6,0x**

Fig. 4 Financial overview of acquiring and target firms. Source: Author's own creation

Transaction Assumptions	
Offer Price Per Share	22,50
% Offer Premium	25,0%
Premium	900
Target Co. acquisition equity value (+ premium)	4.500
Target Co. existing debt	200,0
Target Co. existing cash and cash equivalents	50,0
Target Co. existing net debt	150,0
Additional adjustments /liabilities	50,0
Total acquisition EV	**4.700**
% Stock	50,0%
% Cash (via debt financing)	50,0%
Expected annual net synergies	350
Deal Fee (%EV)	47,0
Transaction fees %	1,0%

Fig. 5 Offer rice and deal assumptions. Source: Author's own creation

Funding Consideration (Sources and Uses)	
Target Co. acquisition equity value (+ premium)	4.500
Net debt + adjustments /liabilities (+/-)	200
Working capital adjustment (+/-)	15
Fees	47
Total uses of funds	**4.762**
Debt funding	2.512
Equity funding	2.250
Total	**4.762**
Deal Financing	
Total Transaction Value	5.825
Total Debt Financing	**2.512**
Borrowing period	5 Years
% Interest	6,47%
Annual interest expense	**162,5**
Equity funding	**2.250**
New share issuance	45
Total Shares post issue	845
New share issue (% total)	5,3%

Fig. 6 Deal consideration and financing. Source: Author's own creation

Deal accounting/PPA Assumptions	
Transaction EV	5.825
(-) Book Value	(2.000)
Purchase price premium	**3.825**
(-) PP&E adjustment ("write-up")	(765)
(-) Intangibles adjustment ("write-up")	(191)
(+) Deferred tax	263
Estimated goodwill	**3.132**
% Allocation to PP&E	20,0%
% Allocation to Intangibles	5,0%
Useful life period	20 Years
Annual depreciation	$38
Annual amortization	$10

Fig. 7 Purchase price accounting (PPA). Source: Author's own creation

synergies ("deal consideration"). Based on a thorough analysis of the target's client base, staff and physical asset usage as well as the operational integration and incremental costs involved, we forecast annual net synergies at 350 million each year (Fig. 6).

We calculate working capital adjustments and the cost and terms of borrowing. Please note that the debt component is effectively larger than equity due to the additional costs being contemplated in this line item. The new share issuance is computed as a function of the equity consideration ("Equity funding") divided by the current acquirer firm stock price (or 2.250 / 50 = 45 million new shares). The new stock issue equates to 5.3% of the new total diluted shares (Fig. 7).

To account for goodwill and adjusted fair value—the delta between transaction price and balance sheet figures—we input book value and allocations for PPE and intangibles to estimate D&A expenses. PP&E and intangibles create a deferred tax liability which we compute by multiplying the tangible and intangible write-ups by the corporate tax rate of 27.5%. This computation allows us to analyse consolidated operating performance for a baseline 12-month view. We arrive at the implied Net Profit by multiplying FDSO by EPS for each company and EBT by calculating the effective tax rate across both companies (NI / (1-t)). We subtract new interest expenses, D&A and one-time charges to compute Adjusted EBT (Fig. 8). Adjusted EBT less corporate tax returns Proforma Net Income ((6.397*(1−27.5%) = 4.638)).

Let us now analyse the key results. If we divide proforma net income by FDSO it gives us a Proforma EPS for the acquirer of 5.49 (4.638/845) which equates to an accretion of 9.8%, calculated as the new EPS divided by the Proforma EPS (or 5.49/ 5.0 minus 1). We can also create a simplified perpetuity estimate of the annual benefit of synergies, calculated as 2917−900 = 2917.

Consolidation Analytics	
Acquirer Co. implied Net Profit	4.000
% Corporate tax	27,5%
Earnings Before Taxes (EBT)	**5.517**
Target Co. implied Net Profit	600
% Corporate tax	27,5%
Earnings Before Taxes (EBT)	**828**

Consolidated Pro Forma Numbers - Current View	
Consolidated EBT	6.345
(-) Incremental interest expenses	(163)
(-) Transaction fees	(47)
(-) Incremental D&A	(48)
(-) One-time cpsts and integration impacts	(40)
(+) Annual synergies	350
Adjusted EBT	**6.397**
(-) Corporate tax	(1.759)
ProForma Net Profit	**4.638**
ProForma FDSO (post deal)	845

Fig. 8 Bottom-line and consolidated financials. Source: Author's own creation

$$EPS = + \frac{Pro\ Forma\ Net\ Profit}{Pro\ Forma\ FDSO} + \frac{4,638}{845} = 5.49$$

$$PV = + \frac{Annual\ Net\ Synergies}{WACC} + \frac{350}{0.12} = 2,917$$

$$ROIC = \frac{Adjustd\ Incremental\ NOPAT}{Invested\ Capital} \mid \frac{1,068}{4,762} - 22.4\%$$

The adjusted incremental NOPAT of 1068, derived from incremental EBIT and net synergies, results in a return on invested capital (ROIC) of 22.4% (Fig. 9). This is significantly above the post-deal WACC of 12.0%, indicating that the deal is accretive, with a value creation spread, that is ROIC less WACC, of 10.4%.

This basic approach to merger analysis can also serve as a model for M&A valuation in EMs. However, as in standard valuation, EMs analyses can require certain additional adjustments. That being so, we list a categorized summary of some of the key considerations and adjustments to the traditional accretion/dilution merger model in an EM context:

- **Currency Risk:**
  - Define exchange rate methodology during the financial modelling. Will you use spot rates, average rates, forward exchange rates or hedged rates?

Summary: Accredtion/Dilution Analytics	
Pro Forma EPS	**5,49**
% Accretion/Dilution (+/-)	9,8%
Acquirer Co. WACC (post deal)	12,0%
Present Value of net synergies	2.917
Equity value premium	900
Simplified LT value added (+/-)	**2.017**

Summary: ROI Aquisition Analytics	
Incremental EBT	828
Incremental interest expense	163
Incremental EBIT	990
Incremental NOPAT	718
(+) Annual net synergies	350
Adjusted incremental NOPAT	1.068
Invested Capital (EV + WC + Fees + OT costs)	4.762
ROIC	22,4%
% Above/(below) WACC	86,9%
% Value added (ROIC - WACC)	10,4%

Fig. 9 Bottom-line and consolidated financials. Source: Author's own creation

- For consistency, use the same methodology across the entire model. Build the model in both local and international reference currency(ies). For example, a Swedish firm's acquisition in Brazil can be modelled in the Brazilian Real, Swedish Krona, and the US Dollar. The analyst should maintain a detailed local currency view for the target company's financials to preserve accuracy. Be aware of International Accounting Standards and the "conversion effect", meaning the difference resulting from converting a given number of units of one currency into another currency at different exchange rates.
- EM currencies are often volatile. We should account for this exchange rate volatility for our forward-looking numbers. Perform sensitivity or Monte Carlo analysis and stress testing using high/low exchange rate scenarios to comprehend the potential impact on forecasted performance, valuation and deal outcomes. Consider historical trends and macroeconomic factors when making projections. Use credible data sources for financial assumptions.
- We can include hedging operations (forward contracts, swaps, or options, for example) to manage exchange rate volatility between the developed market currency and the EM currency. The hedged rates and additional costs would then need to be contemplated into our number crunching. We would also need to align the hedging settlement schedule with key cash flow milestones and

reflect how hedging impacts the financial statements such as Mark-to-Market Adjustments and hedging accounting. Consider integrating FX hedging strategies into the deal structure to mitigate post-transaction currency risks.

- **Debt Financing:**
  - Assess whether to use local currency debt, foreign currency debt, or a mix. Foreign debt sources may have lower interest rates but add FX exposure. Local currency may have higher interest rates and shorter maturities. Are rates fixed or floating?
  - Integrate debt refinancing and maturity assumptions.
  - We can model debt service coverage ratio (DSCR) and interest coverage ratio on interest rates in pro-forma financials.
  - Incorporate local debt and capital mechanics in post-deal WACC structure to reflect the risk profile of the combined entity, including the EM exposure. Be mindful of sovereign credit ratings and interest rate differentials.
- **Deal Accounting/Purchase Price Allocation (PPA):**
  - Ensure the target's profit is adjusted to align with the acquirer's accounting standards both pre- and post-deal financial reporting. Also, it may be necessary to convert from local GAAP to IFRS/US GAAP where applicable. Normalize accounting results if required.
  - In our example we illustrate with a single consolidated pro-forma view at a single point in time. At a practical level we would utilize multi-period projections to estimate financial impact (e.g., accretion/dilution effects, debt servicing) utilizing inputs from our broader valuation model. Best modelling practices also suggest we again work with scenario analysis and sensitivity analysis on key value impact variables.
  - Tax: Incorporate complexities in EM tax regimes, such as differing corporate tax rates, withholding taxes, transfer pricing adjustments and tax rate scenarios post-acquisition. Recognize deferred tax liabilities created by fair value adjustments on assets. Tax restructuring and optimization, such as the impact of acquisition vehicle selection (onshore versus offshore) and any applicable tax treaties that may affect withholding tax rates should also be considered. Post-acquisition tax integration (e.g., use of tax loss carry forwards, potential tax synergies) can also be modelled.
  - EPS Contribution: Convert the target's projected EPS into the acquirer's reporting currency. Adjust for post-deal depreciation, amortization (from purchase price allocation), and incremental financing costs. Normalize for one-time items, inflation and FX translation. We also note that forex considerations do not just involve simple conversions but also currency risk adjustments—particularly in volatile EMs where FX hedging may be necessary.
  - Goodwill: Reflect any discrepancies in valuation standards for PP&E and intangibles. EMs often have less developed intangible asset recognition

frameworks, requiring more conservative assumptions. Account for potentially higher goodwill write-offs due to perceived risks. Understand the impact of impairment testing under IFRS/US GAAP and how higher discount rates or market volatility may trigger impairments faster in EMs. Allocate purchase price fairly, including reflecting conservative assumptions for intangible amortization.

- **Working Capital Adjustment/Target:** In the context of an M&A deal, it's generally expected that the target company will maintain a sufficient level of working capital (WC) to support its short-term operations. Transaction parties need to agree on the working capital definition and how it is measured based on local realities (what is included and what is excluded?). Trend and seasonality analysis are essential. If the actual working capital on the reference date deviates from this agreed-upon "sufficient" level, the purchase price will be adjusted accordingly. As such the purchase price can be significantly impacted by the working capital adjustment mechanism. In EMs, additional attention should be given to the effect of existing personal relationship on the operating cycle (payment terms for instance), local industry norms, tax considerations, receivables quality and inventory calculations. Analysts should also evaluate whether an additional WC cushion is warranted especially given any potential uncertainties around WC verification. Participants should reassess WC levels at closing.
- **ROI Acquisition Analytics:**
  - Synergies: When modelling synergies in an EM M&A milieu, it's crucial to take a conservative, scenario-based and run-rate approach, particularly for revenue synergies, due to market conditions, regulatory and legal hurdles, cultural differences and integration challenges. A probability-weighted approach can also add value in synergy computation. It is often surprising to global M&A teams how different operating realities, processes and cost structures can be in EMs. Cost synergies such as procurement efficiency, supply chain integration or operational optimization (e.g., staff, technology, and marketing costs) are likely to be easier to generate. We can stress-test scenarios to factor in political, economic, and currency risks as well as unexpected liabilities and costs, as well as prioritize local expertise to ensure realistic assumptions and execution feasibility. In our synergy modelling, we can incorporate time-based phases (short-term, medium-term, and long-term) for synergy realization. A micro-view of synergy visibility should be employed based on specific contracts and cost lines. Furthermore, as mentioned above in the accounting section, for accretion/dilution analytics it is advisable to build out the longer-term impact of the transaction. This is especially so since many acquisitions are dilutive in the first year due to acquisition premiums paid and transaction expenses but can become accretive thereafter when synergies come online. We would also highlight that although EPS is an important metric, buy-side stakeholders should prioritize deal execution and integration plans. Is there a clear narrative about the acquisition?

The fundamental basis of M&A is that the value of returns and synergies from the deal exceeds any premium paid.

- **WACC:** In addition to quantifying how debt exposure in EM impacts debt financing costs and amounts, it is important to apply country-specific risk premiums and tax effects when discounting future cash flows to calculate value creation metrics. Ceteris paribus, synergies should be discounted at higher rates reflecting a potentially higher risk-adjusted WACC of the combined entity. Thus, a merger model for EMs should be based on risk-adjusted discount rates, the impact of currency movements and on effective financing costs.

In summary, in emerging markets M&A, especially, a broader analytical approach rather than just the EPS framework would be recommended to get to a more holistic assessment of value creation. Cash Flow Per Share (CFPS) generally represents a far more reliable earnings and liquidity measure than does EPS, especially in markets with widespread distortions in accounting. In addition, currency-adjusted return and debt sustainability measures are crucial given the high and volatile borrowing costs and foreign exchange volatility. For instance, forex-adjusted IRRs can be utilized to account for currency depreciation risks. Analysis of Total Shareholder Return (TSR) over an extended period can provide a clear indication of market validation post-acquisition. As such, synergies, sustainable cash flow, and long-term profitability provide a broader framework for assessing deals (see, e.g., Damodaran 2009; Bruner 2004).

Private Firm M&A Valuation: Quantifying Those (Famous) Synergies

We have briefly examined merger valuation models based on the traditional EPS accretion/dilution approach, regularly used for larger cap M&A transactions. Now let us extend our analytical focus to estimate in more detail the value of synergies which can be used more broadly. Here, as a starting point, we can expand upon the previous graphic illustrated in figure two above breaking down the role of synergies, additional costs, and value creation in an M&A transaction (Fig. 10).

Thus, valuation in M&A is a mix of numbers and narrative and in the negotiation stage a combination of value and pricing dynamics. Ultimately, the market sets the transaction price, not the spreadsheet—valuation is just a way to make sure you're not completely off-base before the deal terms and negotiations take over.

The main objective on the buy-side is to also understand where (or if) value can be added, how their acquirer's profit and cash flow metrics will be higher or lower, how their competitive position will be affected and what is the purchase price range. For private targets the key question is how much the strategic gains or synergies are worth and for public firm acquisition, how much of a control premium should be paid.

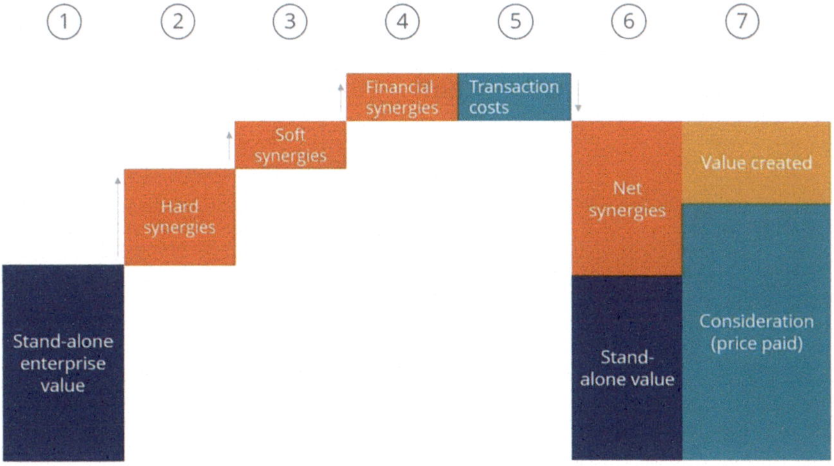

Fig. 10 Analysing Mergers and acquisitions. Source: Corporate Finance Institute (2022)

In this section, we will conduct valuation via DCF on potential transaction synergies. First though, let us recap some of the points we raised in our introductory sections. There is a difference between the value of synergies and control, both of which should be valued separately. Damodaran (2005) explains the rationale and helps contextualize the discussion:

> *First, we ensure that there is no double counting. Second, we can devise strategies for acquisition bidding that can differentiate between control and synergy value. We may be willing to pay close to 100% of the control value (arguing that the target firm could have made the changes on its own) but only a portion of synergy value (since it could not have been created without the acquiring firm). Talking about paying for synergy also should highlight the importance of not only valuing control and synergy, but of paying the right price for a target firm.*

For the author, that's the key point—valuation here serves as a strategic tool for the acquirer to understand how much the target asset is worth and how far they would be willing to go to ensure deal completion. Again, we would flag up potential exogenous factors at play. In an explicit competitive process, transaction pricing dynamics can rise well above fundamental value, for example. We again borrow from Damodaran (2005) to conclude our initial talking points:

> *A fair value acquisition, which would leave the acquiring firm neither better nor worse off, would require that the total price be equal to the consolidated value with the synergy and control benefits built in. Note also the irrelevance of the accountant's estimate of goodwill (which is the difference between market and book value) to any of this discussion.*

Let us now jump into a simplified practical example. These are the macro steps we will employ:

1. Value the target and acquiring company separately.
2. Consolidate both companies' financials and run a consolidated valuation.

Fig. 11 Target Co. headline numbers. Source: Author's own creation

in millions EM LCU	Last Year
Net Revenue	440,0
EBIT	121,0
Op. Margin (%)	27,5%
Adjustments to EBIT	-17,5
Adjusted EBIT	103,5
Adjusted Op. Margin (%)	23,5%
Tax rate	30,0%
NOPAT	72,45
Net Reinvestment	-25,9
Reinvestment (%)	-25,0%
FCFF	46,575

3. Estimate the how, why, what, when and where (from) of synergies. Compute into financial terms.
4. Integrate these synergies into the consolidated firm valuation as a new scenario.
5. The delta between steps two and four is the total value of synergies. This number acts as a potential maximum takeover premium the firm should be willing to pay.

We will value the potential synergies in a cross-border M&A transaction on the buy-side, side of the table. We value the target company as a going concern. The first step is to value the two firms independently. *Caveat lector*, we aim to deliberately simplify several steps and fully pass by others for brevity in order to illustrate the broad process and emphasize a few crucial issues in EM M&A.

A consumer goods company from the United States is analysing an acquisition opportunity in an unnamed emerging market (EM) where it already operates, for the sake of broad-based application in the methodology. As such, the local subsidiary will be the direct acquiring party, with the parent firm providing funding, guarantees, and strategic oversight.

Throughout the Q&A and due diligence process the target has provided extensive operating and financial information. The objective at this stage is for the buy-side team to conduct a valuation analysis based on current metrics and forward-looking projections. The target firm closed out last year with net revenue of 440 million in local currency and operating earnings of 121 million. The key financial indicators are summarized in Fig. 11.

Based on our analysis we estimate that normalized EBIT would be 103.5 million if we adjust for owner expenses, freelancer tax obligations as per local legislation, non-operating items, the market value of rent and other IFRS aligned accounting adjustments (adjustments then equate to 17.5 million). We consolidated the financial statements to include other related subsidiaries of the company which had been operated for, legally questionable, fiscal benefits, computed the actual tax rate as well as contemplated off-balance sheet items, sales and charges. Such practices can be common occurrences in certain EMs—the challenge is to accurately drill down on the quality of earnings and therefore the quality of the valuation. Please note that we are focusing on the last full year period rather than LTM or next year projections as we are conducting our valuation close to the beginning of the following year.

We will now build out our forward-looking model starting with top line growth. In general terms we have a few options in our toolbox:

Method	What It Does	Why Good for EMs?	Formulas	Key Considerations
PERT (Program Evaluation and Review Technique)	Assigns three-point estimates (Optimistic, Most Likely, Pessimistic) and weights them to create an adjusted expected value.	Helps account for high uncertainty and data gaps in EM financial projections.	The PERT three-point estimate formula is given as: (O + 4M +P) / 6 *where:* Optimistic (O) = optimistic scenario, (M) = Most Likely and (P) = Pessimistic	Works best when risks are symmetric but can be adjusted for skewed risks.
Monte Carlo Simulation	Runs thousands of simulations using random input variables to create a probability distribution of outcomes.	Captures volatile macroeconomic conditions (e.g., currency fluctuations, inflation shocks). Useful for M&A synergy projections in uncertain EMs.	∑P(Xi)×Outcome	Requires defining probability distributions (Normal, Lognormal, etc.) for key variables like FX, inflation, or revenue growth.
Regression Analysis	Uses historical data to find relationships between dependent and independent variables.	Helps identify key indicators and the data relationships that drive performance. Useful for variable linked revenue growth modelling.	Y = a + bX + ϵ ... Where: Y – Dependent variable; X – Independent variable; a – Intercept; b – Slope; ϵ – Residual (error).	Requires sufficient historical data on both the market and company side, which can be a challenge in EMs.
Bayesian Forecasting	Updates probability estimates dynamically as new information becomes available.	Adapts to policy changes, geopolitical shifts, and real-time economic trends, which are common in EMs.	The formula for Bayesian forecasting is based on Bayes' Theorem, given as: $P(A\|B)=P(B\|A)P(A)/P(B)$.	Particularly useful for emerging markets because it enables dynamic updates to forecasting as new information becomes available.

Fig. 12 Summary of some key forecasting methods. Source: Author's own creation

Real Options Analysis (ROA)	Adjusts forecasts based on the ability to delay, expand, or exit an investment depending on market conditions.	Ideal for high-risk, uncertain investment environments in EMs. Useful for M&A synergy valuation where acquirers can phase investments.	C=Se−δtN(d1)−Xe−rtN(d2) *where:* C: The theoretical value of the call option S: The price of the stock or underlying asset E: The exercise or strike price R: The risk-free interest rate σ^2: The variance of the stock's or underlying asset's return t: The time to expiration of the option $N(d_1)$: The cumulative normal probability value of d_1 $N(d_2)$: The cumulative normal probability value of d_2	Uses the Black-Scholes model for valuing options. Highly relevant for emerging market modelling when required for uncertainty and volatility analysis and to estimate the value of investment opportunities that are contingent on certain outcomes over medium or longer terms.
Copula Models	Models interdependent risks by capturing the joint distribution of multiple risk factors (e.g., FX & inflation).	Useful in EMs where economic risks are correlated (e.g., high inflation driving FX devaluation). Captures dependency between variables.	C(u1,u2,...,un)=ΦΣ(Φ−1(u1),...,Φ−1(un)) *where:* ΦΣ\Phi_{\Sigma}ΦΣ is the multivariate normal distribution with correlation matrix Σ\SigmaΣ, and Φ−1(u)\Phi^{-1}(u)Φ−1(u) is the inverse normal distribution.	Allows for tail dependence modelling, which is critical for shock based and extreme volatility scenarios which may occur in EMs.

Fig. 12 (continued)

- The target company's recent historical performance.
- Target company management expectations.
- External market forecasts.
- Our own estimation based on our analysis target company's financials and a broad sector outlook.

We can also rely on advanced statistical approaches to enhance our forecasting. We summarize some of the principal ones in Fig. 12:

We forecast a 5.5% annual growth in net revenue over the five-year projection period. Note that we focus on net revenue in this example due to often high taxes on sales in EMs. Nonetheless, in doing so, we do need to be aware of any potential tax code changes over the forecast period. We believe that current operating profitability—adjusted margin of 23.5%—is close to the company's historic average and market averages and will thus use for our projections. We would highlight three additional points at this stage. Although we are using the adjusted margin directly for future forecasts in this example, at a practical level we would (a) forecast costs and expenses to arrive at profit indirectly, (b) we would project both accounting earnings and adjustments each year for greater accuracy and visibility and (c) we would also

in millions EM LCU	Last Year	Year 1	Year 2	Year 3	Year 4	Year 5
Net Revenue	440,0	464,2	489,7	516,7	545,1	575,1
EBIT	121,0					
Op. Margin (%)	27,5%					
Adjustments to EBIT	-17,5					
Adjusted EBIT	103,5	109,2	115,2	121,5	128,2	135,3
Adjusted Op. Margin (%)	23,5%	23,5%	23,5%	23,5%	23,5%	23,5%
Tax rate	30,0%	30,0%	30,0%	30,0%	30,0%	30,0%
NOPAT	72,45	76,4	80,6	85,1	89,8	94,7
Reinvestment	-25,9	-27,3	-28,8	-30,4	-32,1	-33,8
Reinvestment (%)	-25,0%	-25,0%	-25,0%	-25,0%	-25,0%	-25,0%
FCFF	46,6	49,1	51,8	54,7	57,7	60,9

Fig. 13 Target Co. five-year financial map in local currency. Source: Author's own creation

		Year 1	Year 2	Year 3	Year 4	Year 5
FX spot USD/EM LCU	3,05	3,10	3,20	3,40	3,50	3,50
Local inflation forecast		4,0%	3,8%	3,8%	3,8%	3,8%
US inflation forecast		2,5%	2,2%	2,2%	2,2%	2,2%
Relative Inflation Factor		98,6%	98,5%	98,5%	98,5%	98,5%
PPP-Adjusted FX Rate		3,06	3,15	3,35	3,45	3,45

Fig. 14 USD/EM LCU conversion. Source: Author's own creation

usually employ probability weighted forward looking views rather than "point estimates" but will intentionally simplify here. As a final consideration, we compute the effective marginal tax rate and assume a flat reinvestment rate, which has remained stable over the last few years. This approach implicitly bypasses fundamental forecasts regarding the relationship between investment and capital efficiency, and vice versa. Here reinvestment contemplates depreciation expense and is thus internally consistent with the free cash flow build-up method (Fig. 13).

We now convert our projections into US dollars using the PPP-Adjusted Exchange Rate approach to encompass forward forex rates and inflation differentials—suitable for fundamental valuation when assessing intrinsic value over time, given by the following formula:

$$FX_{PPP-\text{adjusted},t} = FX_{\text{base},t} \times \left(\frac{1 + \text{Inflation}_{\text{domestic},t}}{1 + \text{Inflation}_{\text{foreign},t}} \right)$$

For short-term cash flows in an acquisition or financial structure we could also use also forward rates which may be better aligned with current market pricing (Figs. 14 and 15).

Based on these inputs we can value the company using the standard DCF approach:

in millions USD	Last Year	Year 1	Year 2	Year 3	Year 4	Year 5
Net Revenue	144,3	151,9	155,4	154,3	158,2	166,9
EBIT	39,7					
Op. Margin (%)	27,5%					
Adjustments to EBIT	-5,7					
Adjusted EBIT	33,9	35,7	36,6	36,3	37,2	39,3
Adjusted Op. Margin (%)	23,5%	23,5%	23,5%	23,5%	23,5%	23,5%
Tax rate	30%	30,0%	30,0%	30,0%	30,0%	30,0%
NOPAT	23,75	25,0	25,6	25,4	26,0	27,5
Net Reinvestimentos	-8,5	-8,9	-9,1	-9,1	-9,3	-9,8
Reinvestment (%)	-25,0%	-25,0%	-25,0%	-25,0%	-25,0%	-25,0%
FCFF	15,3	16,1	16,5	16,3	16,7	17,7

Fig. 15 Target Co. five-year financial map in USD. Source: Author's own creation

Fig. 16 Target Co. Valuation. Source: Author's own creation

Valuation Results (USD)	
Growth (g)	3,8%
WACC (USD)	10,0%
Operating Value	66,0
Cash Flow$_n$	18,3
Perpetuity	183,4
Present Value Perpetuity	119,4
Enterprise Value	185,4
EV/Adj. EBIT	5,5
EV/Adj. EBIT NTM	5,2

$$Instrinsic\ Value = \overbrace{\frac{FCFF^1}{(1+WACC)^1} + \ldots \frac{FCFF^5}{(1+WACC)^{4.5}}}^{\text{Forecast Period}} + \overbrace{\left[\frac{\left(\frac{FCFF^5 \times (1+g) = Cash\ Flow_n}{WACC}\right)}{(1+WACC)^{4.5}}\right]}^{\text{Perpetuity}}$$

We compute a single WACC in US dollars (we overtly simplify here for illustrative purposes, please see chapter seven in this book, also written by your author, for more information on this topic) and arrive at an EV of $185.4 million. We utilize the mid-year discounting convention. Moreover, for conservatism, we calculate the perpetuity without super-economic growth, or in other words, that over the long term the cost of capital is equal to the return on capital. We also intentionally focus just on firm value rather than the equity view and also detour around potential additional liquidity or working capital adjustments. The implicit adjusted EV/EBIT multiple is 5.5x, which is in line with comparative market averages for recent multiples in M&A transactions of the same size and adjusted listed firm multiples (discounted for liquidity size and performance factors, for example) (Fig. 16).

in millions USD	Last Year	Year 1	Year 2	Year 3	Year 4	Year 5
Net Revenue	389,5	414,8	441,8	470,5	501,1	533,7
EBIT	105,2	112,0	119,3	127,0	135,3	144,1
Op. Margin (%)	27,0%	27,0%	27,0%	27,0%	27,0%	27,0%
Tax rate	30%	30,0%	30,0%	30,0%	30,0%	30,0%
NOPAT	73,6	78,4	83,5	88,9	94,7	100,9
Net Reinvestment	-26,3	-28,0	-29,8	-31,8	-33,8	-36,0
Reinvestment (%)	-25,0%	-25,0%	-25,0%	-25,0%	-25,0%	-25,0%
FCFF	47,3	50,4	53,7	57,2	60,9	64,8

Fig. 17 Acquiring Co. five-year financial map in USD. Source: Author's own creation

Fig. 18 Acquiring Co. Valuation. Source: Author's own creation

Valuation Results (USD)	
Growth (g)	3,8%
WACC (USD)	9,0%
Operating Value	225,5
Cash $Flow_n$	67,3
Perpetuity	747,8
Present Value Perpetuity	507,4
Enterprise Value	732,9
EV/EBIT NTM	6,5

For a comparative foundation to build out synergy mapping we now need to value the acquiring firm and consolidate the financials. The value of the combined firm is the sum of the firms valued independently. We start with the stand-alone valuation of the acquiring firm.

Revenue growth is forecast at 6.5% over the projection period. Assume as well that the firm has a higher effective operating margin (with adjustments not being required in this case) of 27%, which is expected to remain stable over the coming years, but that tax and reinvestment rates are the same. The computed WACC is slightly lower, and we will use the same assumptions for long term growth and cash flow estimation and capital returns in perpetuity as for the target firm. Note that the company's implicit EV/EBIT over the next 12 months is also greater, potentially highlighting the potential for "multiple arbitrage". In the consolidated view we calculate a slightly higher combined WACC from the acquiring firm's perspective to account for the target firm's integration (Figs. 17, 18 and 19).

For robust synergy forecasts, it is crucial to incorporate deep micro-view operational analyses; clear and realistic implementation time schedules and risk-adjusted expectation values. In this example, we use PERT estimates on the summarized value drivers we have highlighted so far. Assume that our synergy forecast is the result of a detailed review of individual client contracts, including opportunities for cross-selling, reduced churn, and enhanced pricing strategies. Such information should be provided in the due diligence phase. Cost structure synergies are hard

in millions USD	Last Year	Year 1	Year 2	Year 3	Year 4	Year 5
Net Revenue	533,8	566,8	597,2	624,8	659,3	700,5
EBIT	139,1	147,7	155,8	163,3	172,5	183,3
Op. Margin (%)	26,1%	26,1%	26,1%	26,1%	26,2%	26,2%
Tax rate	30%	30,0%	30,0%	30,0%	30,0%	30,0%
NOPAT	97,4	103,4	109,1	114,3	120,8	128,3
Net Reinvestment	-34,8	-36,9	-39,0	-40,8	-43,1	-45,8
Reinvestment (%)	-25,0%	-25,0%	-25,0%	-25,0%	-25,0%	-25,0%
FCFF	62,6	66,5	70,1	73,5	77,6	82,5

Valuation Results (USD)	
Growth (g)	3,8%
WACC (USD)	9,5%
Operating Value	291,4
Cash $Flow_n$	85,6
Perpetuity	901,5
Present Value Perpetuity	599,2
Enterprise Value	890,7
EV/EBIT NTM	6,4

Fig. 19 Combined firm's five-year financial map in USD and valuation. Source: Author's own creation

efficiencies and can come online much quicker than potential (soft) revenue gains. For COGS we contemplated an improvement in procurement efficiencies, increased volume discounts, and optimized price points. Our expense-side synergies are underpinned by a thorough staffing efficiency review, streamlining technology usage and optimization of marketing spend. Additional cost savings were mapped from physical space consolidations, lowered reinvestment needs and an improvement in the working capital cycle that should decrease short- and long-term investment requirements while improving cash flow dynamics. We also include initial implementation costs. We would also need to be aware of how much, if any, of any synergy value will be capitalized versus expensed. Our forecast net synergies in the PERT approach, increase from 7.3 million in the first year to 45.1 million by year 5 (Fig. 20).

We now add these synergies to our five-year financial map and value the combined firm post synergy accretion. Assume in this example that synergies have been adequately adjusted for tax treatment (e.g., on the revenue side) and that by the last year of the forecast period the synergies are sustainable. Here we add net revenue synergies to net revenue, cost, and expense synergies to EBIT—whilst also subtracting implementation costs—and reduce effective reinvestment by netting reinvestment synergies. On the latter point, although for purposes of simplicity we maintain stable in this exercise, please bear in mind that at a practical level we could also model increases in marginal return on capital on incremental investments or increase the reinvestment rate to take account of greater investment opportunities post-merger (Fig. 21).

		Year 1	Year 2	Year 3	Year 4	Year 5
Total Net Revenue Synergies						
Upside		3,0	10,5	21,9	26,5	34,3
Basecase		1,9	6,7	14,1	17,1	22,1
Downside		0,9	3,0	6,2	7,6	9,8
PERT		1,9	6,7	14,1	17,1	22,1
Total Cost Synergies						
Upside		11,3	11,9	12,5	13,2	14,0
Basecase		9,6	10,2	10,6	11,2	11,9
Downside		3,2	3,4	3,6	3,8	4,0
PERT		8,9	9,3	9,8	10,3	10,9
Total Expense Synergies						
Upside		12,3	13,0	13,6	14,3	15,2
Basecase		10,0	10,6	11,1	11,7	12,4
Downside		5,8	6,1	6,4	6,8	7,2
PERT		9,7	10,2	10,7	11,3	12,0
Total Reinvestment Synergies						
Upside		0,0	5,0	5,3	5,5	5,8
Basecase		0,0	4,6	4,8	5,1	5,3
Downside		0,0	2,5	2,7	2,8	2,9
PERT		0,0	4,3	4,5	4,8	5,0
Total Synergies						
Upside		26,6	35,4	48,0	54,1	63,6
Basecase		26,2	27,5	35,8	40,0	46,4
Downside		9,9	12,5	16,2	18,1	21,0
PERT		23,5	26,3	34,5	38,7	45,1
Total Incremental Costs						
Upside		12,5	9,375	0,5	0,0	0,0
Basecase		15,0	13,5	2,5	0,0	0,0
Downside		25,0	20,0	7,0	0,0	0,0
PERT		16,3	13,9	2,9	0,0	0,0
Total Net Synergies						
PERT		7,3	12,4	31,6	38,7	45,1
Total Net Synergies % Total Net Revenue						
PERT		1,3%	2,1%	5,1%	5,9%	6,4%

Fig. 20 Synergy forecasts (in millions). Source: Author's own creation

The key takeaways are that both revenue and the operating profit margin are higher in the synergy scenario—period average of 27.7% compared to 26.1%, even after profitability is impacted in the first years due to one-time implementation costs—and relative reinvestment is lower. As such cash flow is positively impacted. We maintain WACC and perpetuity inputs stable. Enterprise Value is given as $1094 million, although we note with caution a greater proportion of value in the perpetuity phase. Further sensitivity analysis and senses checks on growth assumptions as well as costs/returns on capital could be recommended. Nevertheless, we can see that the post-merger EV/EBIT multiple is expected to be higher against the "as-is" level for the acquiring firm (7.3x against 6.4x). Figure 22 summarizes the key value driver impacts each year. We see that synergies are expected to ramp up each

in millions USD		Year 1	Year 2	Year 3	Year 4	Year 5
Net Revenue		568,7	603,9	638,9	676,3	722,6
EBIT		150,0	161,5	180,9	194,1	206,3
Op. Margin (%)		26,4%	26,7%	28,3%	28,7%	28,6%
Tax rate		30,0%	30,0%	30,0%	30,0%	30,0%
NOPAT		105,0	113,1	126,6	135,9	144,4
Net Reinvestment		-36,9	-34,7	-36,3	-38,4	-40,8
Reinvestment (%)		-24,6%	-21,5%	-20,1%	-19,8%	-19,8%
FCFF		68,1	78,4	90,3	97,5	103,6

Valuation Results (USD)	
Growth	*3,8%*
WACC (USD)	*9,5%*
Operating Value	*341,4*
Cash Flow$_n$	*107,6*
Perpetuity	*1132,2*
Present Value Perpetuity	*752,6*
Enterprise Value	*1.094,0*
EV/EBIT NTM	*7,3*

Fig. 21 Combined firm's five-year financial map in USD and valuation with synergies. Source: Author's own creation

Annual synergy delta (+/-) in millions USD or incremental margin %	*Year 1*	*Year 2*	*Year 3*	*Year 4*	*Year 5*	*Average*
Net Revenue	*1,9*	*6,7*	*14,1*	*17,1*	*22,1*	*12,4*
EBIT	*2,3*	*5,7*	*17,6*	*21,6*	*23,0*	*14,0*
Op. Margin (%)	*0,3%*	*0,6%*	*2,2%*	*2,5%*	*2,4%*	*1,6%*
Reinvestment	*0,0*	*4,3*	*4,5*	*4,8*	*5,0*	*3,7*
FCFF	*1,6*	*8,3*	*16,8*	*19,9*	*21,1*	*13,5*

Synergies: At a glance (USD)	
EV Combined Firm	890,7
EV Combined + Synergies	1.094,0
Delta = Value of Synergies	203,3
Present Value of Synergies	135,2

Fig. 22 The value of synergies. Source: Author's own creation

year. The value of synergies is quantified at $203.3 million, calculated as the difference between the combined firm valuation with and without synergies. The present value of these synergies based on the same WACC is computed as $135.2 million assuming a simplified single five-year period (PV can also be calculated annually like any cash flow). This analysis—assuming the robustness of the exercise—therefore, helps the acquiring firm evaluate their potential flexibility in transaction pricing dynamics. Or, put differently, to understand how much they can justify paying above the target's standalone value purely based on fundamental shareholder value (there may of course be other considerations at play). In general, the acquirer expects to retain a significant proportion of synergies.

Before we close out this section, we highlight a few final considerations for M&A valuations in EMs:

- Be consistent in the use of real or nominal projections. Compare forecasts against local sector averages and operating realities as well as the historical performance and capacity of the target firm. Moreover, validate implicit multiples against local benchmarks.
- Ensure solid analysis on normalized and quality-based net working capital metrics both for cash flow projections and final price adjustments. Working capital should be adjusted for seasonality, one-off items, or aggressive accounting treatments. Many emerging market firms face higher reinvestment needs due to supply chain issues, infrastructure deficits, and currency fluctuations affecting imported capital goods. Confirm reinvestment levels align with sustainable long-term growth expectations in the local economy.
- Extend the detailed forecast horizon if growth and profitability patterns, scaling, technology use and reinvestment dynamics are still evolving. Analysts don't need to always rigidly stick with a five-year forecast period.
- Pay special attention to tax regime and regulatory requirements. Emerging markets often have volatile tax policies, government interventions, and fiscal risks that could impact future cash flows. Do not underestimate potential future volatility in forex markets and the impact on sales, earnings, and cash flows.
- Understand potential liabilities on the legal, labour and tax levels which are critical to compute not only Equity values but broader business risk. Adjust for legal disputes, pension obligations, contingent liabilities, and underreported debts, including any hidden liabilities or off-balance sheet items.
- Where possible use audited financial statements and multiple scenario-adjusted valuation approaches.
- Ensure costs of capital include additional risk factors such as CRPs, CSRPS, and currency-adjusted discount rates. Where possible compute in both the local currency and that of the acquiring firm for a further sense check.
- Unlike public companies, private firms have higher liquidity risk and may require a discount for lack of marketability (DLOM). We can assume that EMs may often have lower market liquidity than developed economies.
- For synergy modelling, ensure a clear distinction between control value and synergy value. Synergy represents the additional value generated by integrating the target with the acquirer's existing business. We have significantly simplified multiple steps in our example. Nonetheless, as Damodaran (2005) argued at the beginning of this section, both factors should be quantified separately to avoid any double counting, where synergies could be mistaken for the standalone control premium. After all, control represents the value gained by the acquirer through operational, financial, or strategic improvements to the target.
- After valuation, assess the purchase price allocation (PPA) in transaction modelling, ensuring that any excess purchase price is properly allocated between

tangible and intangible assets and tax treatment is optimized for local EM legislation.

Closing Thoughts: Bridging Valuation Gaps with Earnouts

Let us briefly review the Earnout framework in M&A. We summarize the approach here to add some additional insight of practical deal tools in EM M&A. For a fuller assessment see Rosenbaum and Pearl (2020) or Gaughan (2017).

Earnouts are a typical structuring tool in private M&A transactions in both developed and emerging markets, in which buyers and sellers are able to bridge valuation gaps and manage additional risks by offering contingent compensation if a business meets certain performance goals after an acquisition. Essentially then, dynamic endogenous and exogenous factors increase the relative uncertainty around future cash flows so as to move the needle on both buyer and seller views on valuation outside the "zones of agreement". Due to such a dynamic, analysis cited by Pfeiffer (2024), a global corporate finance advisory firm, highlights the wide usage of earnouts in the space, which we will quote:

- *33% of deals included an earnout (based on data from the 2024 SRS Acquiom M&A Deal Terms Study)*
- *Approximately 50%–80% of earnouts use either EBITDA or revenue as the main earnout metric.*
- *The median earnout potential was 32% of the closing payment.*
- *The median earnout length was 24 months.*

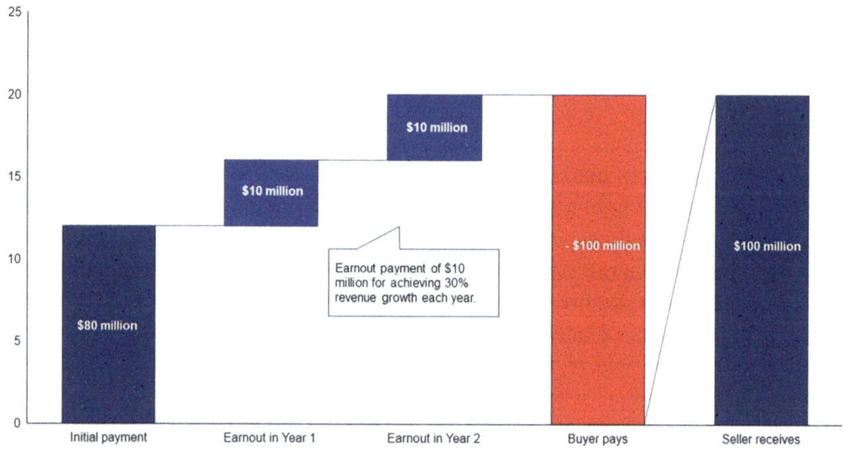

Fig. 23 Earnouts in M&A: Breaking the impasse. Source*:* Aventis Advisors (2024)

- *Over 58% of earnouts include an indemnity set-off right against future earnout payments.*

Earnouts allow buyers to defer a portion of the purchase price, connecting it with the post-closing financial or operational performance of the target. This mechanism serves to align both parties' incentives while limiting the downside risk to the buyer. Considering the myriad additional uncertainties regarding M&A in EMs—high growth and volatile markets—that we have discussed, such structures can make sense for EM M&A operations. Indeed, research by Aquino et al. (2023) revealed that in Brazil, the use of earnouts increased from 18% between 2016 and 2018 to a significant 78% between 2019 and 2020, higher than global averages (Fig. 23).

In practical terms, earnouts serve as instruments to align the company's surplus value expectations negotiated between buyers and sellers, on the grounds of the uncertainty of estimated future results. As a strategy that seeks to reduce valuation uncertainty—and resolve negotiation impasses—it is thus a proxy for expectations differences between buyers and sellers. For instance, they are effective when a target demands a higher price, allowing the buyer to shift some performance risk back to the seller.

One of the primary risks in using earnouts in emerging markets is disputes over performance metrics and business management during the earnout period. EBITDA or revenue calculations can be more susceptible to interpretation, if not manipulation. Whilst operational control in the earnout period can be contentious, robust earnout agreements will consequently include comprehensive financial reporting requirements, pre-agreed budgets, and mechanisms such as independent third-party audits. A standard earnout has three principal components, the linked performance metric (or metrics), the earnout formula and the earnout period. Earnouts periods are longer when valuation uncertainty is likely to resolve over a longer period, which are common in emerging markets due to slower judicial and regulatory processes and labour legislation. Hence, beyond pure valuation factors, earnouts can also help mitigate potential liabilities, they can be intertwined with escrow

Assumptions

Item	Value
Maximum Transaction Price	65.000.000
Transaction price (Upfront)	50.000.000
Earn-out Period	3 Years
Target Revenue (Yr 1)	80.000.000
Target Revenue (Yr 2)	90.000.000
Target Revenue (Yr 3)	100.000.000
Earn-out % (Revenue)	5%
Maximum Earn-out Cap	15.000.000

Assumptions - Earnout Payout Calculation (Based on Revenue Targets)

Year	Actual Revenue	Revenue Target	Payout %	Earn-out Payout
1	82.000.000	80.000.000	5%	4.100.000
2	85.000.000	90.000.000	5%	-
3	102.000.000	100.000.000	5%	5.100.000

Total Earn-out Payout Summary

Total Potential Earn-out	15.000.000
Total Earn-out Paid	9.200.000
Shortfall	5.800.000
Total Paid	59.200.000
Total Paid (% Price)	91%

Sensitivity Analysis (Impact of Revenue Performance on Earn-out Payout)

Revenue Achievement (%)	Earn-out Payout	
80%	6.000.000	
90%	9.000.000	
100%	12.000.000	
110%	15.000.000	*(Cap Reached)*

Fig. 24 A simple Earnout model (USD). Source: Author's own creation

structures, withholding contingent payments pending the attainment of certain milestones. They do, however, require enforceability, financial transparency, and dispute resolution mechanisms. Contingent payment tools such as escrows, hold-backs, and clawbacks, often represent the only tools to break the negotiations deadlock. On the sell-side they provide an opportunity for the seller to "prove" financial performance and the buyer the opportunity to better measure risk and returns post deal completion.

In Fig. 24, we flag up the basic mechanics of an earnout component in M&A. The model projects the earnout payment for 3 years of revenue performance of the target company, using the 5% actual earnout rate on revenues if targets are reached. In this example revenue is utilized due to difficult negotiations on EBITDA composition, the easier verification methods for sales and the greater interests of the acquirer in purchasing the target's client portfolio rather than the accompanying operational structure. While the maximum potential earnout is $15 M, payment was only $9.2 M due to missed targets in the second year. Earnout payments are made annually based on performance instead of a lump sum at the end to reduce risk for the seller and are usually secured via an escrow account to ensure seller compensation if these performance thresholds are met. We perform sensitivity analysis showing how different revenue achievements change the total earnout paid and illustrate that the cap is reached at 110% of target performance over this period. As a result, the final transaction price was $59.2 M, equivalent to 91% of the total potential value.

For earnouts in EMs we would make some further considerations:

- Adjustments and procedures for macroeconomic shocks, currency fluctuations and inflation volatility in emerging markets can be contemplated. Milestones can even be linked to External benchmarks or industry-adjusted performance measures to enhance coherence and robustness.
- Like other financial projections, earnouts can be modelled with advanced sensitivity, scenario and other statistical tools. Advisors should also work with appropriate risk-adjusted discount rates that reflects the country, sector, and counterparty risk to bring metrics to present value views.
- Holistic and enhanced due diligence on the financial, operational, tax, regulatory and environmental sides are important for detailed number crunching and value estimates.
- Apart from financial metrics, earnouts can also represent broader liability management and the reduction of potential risks over the period (which may require a larger time frame to align with local regulatory, fiscal, or labour dispute legalization).

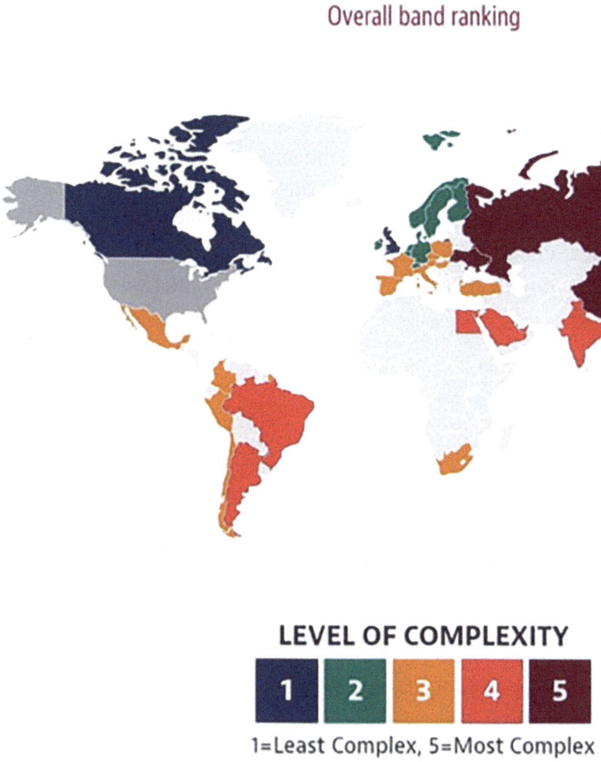

Fig. 25 Ranking of 49 jurisdictions according to the complexity and challenges of carrying out a cross-border acquisition involving that jurisdiction. Source: Baker & McKenzie

Conclusion

EM M&A can provide extensive opportunities for global firms, but such strategies also come with associated risks and challenges. It is often said that in EMs value is a long-term game. Global firms should not underestimate cultural, information, regulatory, or infrastructure questions. Indeed, analysis from Baker McKenzie (2025) clearly highlights that cross-border acquisitions in EM jurisdictions are generally more complex and challenging (Fig. 25).

In this chapter, we have shown that the principles of valuation and related concepts in emerging markets—such as accretion/dilution modelling, synergy estimation, and earnout structures—are largely the same as in developed markets. However, key adjustments must be made to account for the increased market and corporate uncertainties inherent in emerging economies (as illustrated in the above figure). Or put simply, the theoretical foundation of our analyses must be consistent with the real-life marketplace factors in EMs. Moreover, once again, for financial projections probability weighted estimates, advanced statistical tools and scenarios are essential. As is comprehension of local accounting, operational and regulatory standards and dynamics. No valuation model or approaches captures the reality of market sentiment, strategic fit, or competitive pressure, but they help you tell a story that not only resonates with stakeholders but also make sense and are plausible for an EM context given local nuance. As a closing point, the author would argue that value cannot entirely be measured by price which can be construed as merely the overlap between buyer and seller perspectives and zones of agreement. Nonetheless, understanding the methodologies, challenges, and best practices outlined in this chapter can help firms and advisors navigate the complexities of M&A valuation in EMs and potentially unlock value.

References

Aquino CEM, Dower FC, Dal-Ri Murcia F, Lopes IC, Anhesini Souza R (2023) Earnout in M&A operations in Brazil and their impact on equity valuation. Revista Academia & Negocios 10(1): 16–35. Universidad de Concepción. https://www.redalyc.org/journal/5608/560876830002/html/. Accessed February 2025

Baker McKenzie (2025) M&A and corporate governance map: timing and complexity of cross-border acquisitions. https://www.bakermckenzie.com/Maps/MA/index.html. Accessed 19 Mar 2025

Bruner RF (2004) Applied mergers and acquisitions. John Wiley & Sons, New York

Choi J, Jeon S (2011) The impact of M&A on firm performance: evidence from emerging markets. Emerg Mark Rev 12(3):222–244

Corporate Finance Institute (2022) Mergers & Acquisitions (M&A) Process. https://corporatefinanceinstitute.com/resources/valuation/mergers-acquisitions-ma-process/. Accessed 25 Jan 2025

Damodaran A (2003) Investment valuation: tools and techniques for determining the value of any asset, 2nd edn. John Wiley & Sons, New York

Damodaran A (2005) The value of synergy, SSRN Scholarly Paper, NYU Stern. https://pages.stern.nyu.edu/~adamodar/pdfiles/papers/synergy.pdf. Accessed Jan 2025

Damodaran A (2009) The dark side of valuation: valuing young, distressed, and complex businesses, 2nd edn. FT Press, New York

Emerging Markets M&A Review Full Year 2023–2024, LSEG Data & Analytics (2024). https://thesource.lseg.com/TheSource/getfile/download/2557d98b-a84d-4b2a-8f0b-5fdd92914e44. Accessed Jan 2025

Ferris KR, Petitt B (2002) Valuation: avoiding the winner's curse, 1st edn. FT Press, New York

Gaughan PA (2017) Mergers, acquisitions, and corporate restructurings, 7th edn. Wiley, Hoboken, NJ

Godfrey S, Espinosa R (1996) A practical approach to calculating costs of equity for investments in emerging markets. J Appl Corp Financ 9(3):80–89

Koller T, Goedhart M, Wessels D (2020) Valuation: measuring and managing the value of companies, 7th edn. John Wiley & Sons, New York

KPMG (2022) Introduction to valuation methods and requirements. https://assets.kpmg.com/content/dam/kpmg/kh/pdf/events/kpmg%2D%2D-kicpaa/(%20With%20Remarks%20Disclaimer)%20Introductions%20to%20Valuation%20Methods%20and%20Requirements%20.pdf. Accessed Jan 2025

McKinsey & Company (2015) Why emerging market companies acquire abroad. https://www.mckinsey.com/~/media/McKinsey/Business%20Functions/Strategy%20and%20Corporate%20Finance/Our%20Insights/Why%20emerging%20market%20companies%20acquire%20abroad/Why%20emerging%20market%20companies%20acquire%20abroad.pdf. Accessed Jan 2025

McKinsey & Company (2016) How share repurchases boost earnings without improving returns. https://www.mckinsey.com/capabilities/strategy-and-corporate-finance/our-insights/how-share-repurchases-boost-earnings-without-improving-returns#/auth-signin. Accessed Jan 2025

McKinsey & Company (2020) Valuation: measuring and managing the value of companies, 7th edn. John Wiley & Sons, New York

Pereiro LE (2002) Valuation of companies in emerging markets: a practical approach. John Wiley & Sons, New York

Pfeiffer T (2024) Earn-outs in M&A: key deal tool or source of post-closing disputes?, Kroll, 5 November. https://www.kroll.com/en/insights/publications/expert-services/earn-outs-m-and-a-key-deal-tool-source-post-closing-disputes. Accessed 25 Jan 2025

Rosenbaum J, Pearl J (2020) Investment banking: valuation, leveraged buyouts, and Mergers & Acquisitions, 3rd edn. Wiley, Hoboken, NJ

Beyond Valuation: Legal, Regulatory, and Corporate Governance Issues in Emerging Market M&A

Mauricio Ribeiro Maciel

Abstract There are many gaps in the literature regarding emerging market mergers and acquisitions ("EM M&A"). In particular, there is sparse research on specific subjects within this nexus, which lack a more practical perspective and insights into parties acquiring, or advising an acquirer, in EM companies and assets. As such, this chapter proposes to combine a summary of the existing literature together with the author's professional experience (a Brazilian lawyer's perspective), to present a practical view oriented to fuller and richer assessments of EM M&A. Although valuation is one of the main steps in any M&A transaction, risk assessment is also an important and challenging part of it. The author focuses on legal, regulatory, and corporate governance issues and how they affect due diligence before the deal and the negotiation of a share purchase agreement and a shareholders' agreement. Broader but related issues other than legal, regulatory, and corporate governance are also discussed. This chapter is not intended to present a comprehensive guide or even to provide an exhaustive list of every issue on the subject and will instead center its focus on the main common concerns to EM M&A more generally. The author concludes that historical context, the rule of law and ownership concentration in EM are distinct from developed markets and thus suggests that successful acquisition depends on adequate due diligence that also contemplates pre and post policy and regulatory risks as well as addressing contractual protections considering country practice on interpretation and enforcement of contracts. All issues which can impact final asset transaction pricing.

Keywords Emerging markets · Mergers and acquisitions · Corporate governance · Due diligence · Legal issues · Regulatory issues · Best practices · Rule of law · Practical insights · Advisor experience

M. R. Maciel (✉)
Marins Bertoldi Law Firm, Curitiba, Brazil
e-mail: mrm@marinsbertoldi.com.br

S. Derindere Köseoğlu, A. Patterson (eds.), *Valuation in Emerging Markets*, Contributions to Finance and Accounting,
https://doi.org/10.1007/978-3-031-93526-8_12

Introduction

In any merger or acquisition transaction, valuation is one of the first and crucial steps. Essentially, both parties, the seller and the acquirer, will proceed with negotiations only if both can (broadly) agree on how much the target is worth. If the acquirer arrives at a result within the range of what the seller would accept, the M&A process continues: the parties sign a letter of intent, or a memorandum of understanding, and the acquirer traditionally commences the due diligence process to assess the risks of acquiring the target before negotiating the terms of a share purchase agreement and/or other agreements. It is a truism that many deals are not concluded because of the risks the acquirer discovers during due diligence or because the parties did not reach an agreement on the consequences and mechanisms to protect the acquirer over such risks. Moreover, many other deals are concluded but lead to undesirable outcomes due to risks that were or were not identified and/or to disputes on the interpretation of the transaction agreements which subsequently can reduce transaction value.

Thus, from a lawyer's perspective, although the parties tend to assume the deal is concluded once the price is agreed, an M&A transaction is significantly broader than the target's valuation. A legal advisor must understand what the valuation assumptions are and assess whether any legal, regulatory and/or corporate governance issues might affect them. For instance, if part of the target's economic value resides on an existing patent or innovation, on certain clients or distribution agreements, or on some key executives, the legal advisor must confirm whether this patent is proprietary, whether there may be any dispute over that patent, whether such innovation can be legally protected, whether such clients and/or distribution agreements are enforceable, and negotiate contractual protections to assure such protections and to bind the relationship with said key persons for a minimum additional period. Also, the legal advisor must advise on which of the identified risks may be contractually allocated and/or mitigated and which would not be remedied and would be potential deal breakers.

Thus, legal, regulatory and governance issues that affect the valuation may lead to renegotiation on the price and/or a negotiation on contractual mechanisms for price adjustments and/or earnouts after confirmation of the target's performance over a determined period. They will also be essential in the negotiation of collaterals, representations, warranties, and indemnities clauses to allocate the risks to the seller and avoid any loss to the acquirer regarding the risks which did not lead to any discount on the transaction consideration. Values may be retained by the acquirer or in an escrow account until all contingencies and liabilities are resolved and the major valuation assumptions are proved to be accurate. On the other hand, tax efficiencies to both parties and governance enhancements may present opportunities of negotiating an improved valuation.

Once the acquisition is closed, multiple situations may arise to confirm whether the deal was successful or not. Most of the disputes arising from M&A transactions are caused by interpretation or enforcement issues, or risks that were not previously identified and adequately allocated by the transaction agreements. That is why it is important to invest in legal advisory for assessing risks and negotiating the agreements. This task becomes even more complex and challenging when the transaction is cross border, especially in emerging markets.

When studying emerging market mergers and acquisitions, one can find many gaps in the literature. There are a few studies on cross-border M&A, but not specifically related to emerging markets (and mostly cover cross-border transactions between developed countries). Furthermore, whilst there are some studies on the performance of EM M&A, they are not necessarily focused on the legal and risk perspective. Wiedemann et al. (2024), after extensive research on the literature on cross-border M&A, highlighted the gap on due diligence in cross-border M&A despite its obvious importance. And yet, a cross-border acquisition in an EM is presumably more complex than any domestic or cross-border acquisition in developed markets. Wiedemann et al. (2024) also suggests further research on corporate governance related to M&A. There is indeed some research on corporate governance, however much of the focus is on a policy perspective rather than evaluating how an acquirer could deal with corporate governance risks and what corporate governance mechanisms could be effectively contracted by an acquirer to mitigate such risks.

By better understanding EM related risks and how to evaluate and mitigate them, it could increase the probability and quantity of successful EM M&A deals. It would thus be beneficial to acquirers and also for broader market development.

This chapter proposes to combine some research on existing literature and the authors' professional experience (a Brazilian lawyer's perspective), to present a practical view oriented to the assessment of EM M&A. We focus on legal, regulatory, and corporate governance issues and how it should affect the due diligence before the deal and the negotiation of a share purchase agreement and a shareholders' agreement. As such it provides a qualitative legal opinion counterpoint to the chapter on valuation methods in M&A. Wider-related issues other than legal, regulatory, and corporate governance are also discussed. This chapter is not intended to present a comprehensive guide or even to provide an exhaustive list of every issue on the subject and will instead center its focus on the main common concerns to EM M&A more generally. The objectives are to highlight the main differences between M&A in developed and developing markets, that should be considered by any acquirer and their advisors to expand risk evaluation in comparison to usual due diligence practices in developed economies and to suggest some possible solutions to overcome identified risks.

Section "Understanding Some Key Characteristics of Emerging Markets, the Rule of Law, Corporate Governance and Corruption Issues" aims at understanding key characteristics of EM, how the rule of law is evolving, what the literature and previous research present in terms of its difference from developed economies as well as the main corporate governance issues and challenges. Section "How Emerging Markets Characteristics Impact Inbound M&A Risks" intends to answer how EM rule of law and corporate governance characteristics affect or may affect the risk assessment of an EM M&A transaction. Previous research, personal expert views and factual examples from the news and media reporting contributes to attempts to illustrate the principal and common issues based on experience and common perception. Section "How EM Risks Should Be Addressed in Due Diligence" aims to draw some conclusions on, based on Sects. "Understanding Some Key Characteristics of Emerging Markets, the Rule of Law, Corporate Governance and Corruption Issues" and "How Emerging Markets Characteristics Impact Inbound M&A Risks" and based on our experience, how EM risks should be addressed in due diligence besides the standard approaches and practices in global marketplaces. Section "EM Risk-related Best Practices in Defining Deal Structure and Negotiating and Drafting Its Agreements" aims to propose EM risk-related best practices in defining deal structure and negotiating and drafting its agreements, especially the share purchase agreement and the shareholders agreement. Section "Conclusion" concludes the chapter by discussing the role of the rule of law, contractual enforcement and corporate governance can enhance both risk mitigation and opportunities in EM M&A.

Understanding Some Key Characteristics of Emerging Markets, the Rule of Law, Corporate Governance and Corruption Issues

This section will present EM characteristics in terms of the rule of law, corruption and ownership structure. Concentrated ownership structures with defined control leads to controlling versus minority conflict rather than agent versus owner. Distinct kinds of conflict (in relation to some developed markets) require different corporate governance practices. Differing levels of the rule of law require enforcement factors to make corporate governance and anti-corruption practices more effective.

One interesting factor about studying EMs is that there are some characteristics that appear to be common among them despite the vast difference in almost every other aspect of each country. Pargendler (2014), when teaching corporate governance in emerging markets, first suggests caution in generalizing since its learnings, best practices and overall results cannot be accurate for each country. In fact, their differences are more evident than their similarities. Taking the BRICS (Brazil, Russia, India, China, and South Africa) bloc for example, they are in very different geographic locations, they have very different histories, very different cultures and political realities. Notwithstanding that, they have some similar challenges, especially in terms of the rule of law, from which many other challenges derive. Thus, dealing with their similarities does not mean that the outcomes will be the same, but that every EM will require attention to some similar aspects which should then be further evaluated on a country-based (and firm-based) level.

For instance, according to Tapia-Hoffmann (2021), the historical context of colonialism led to a culture of relying on elected officials to overcome injustice and inequalities in Latin America. This culture leads to power and authority in the hands of certain individuals or groups based on relationships instead of the law. The subsequent result is a lack of the rule of law, that is, lack of a legal-based predictable, stable, and trustworthy system that could enable every person to clearly foresee the consequences of her acts. Where the rule of law is strong, people (even foreign investors) can understand the law and trust it will be executed as expected and that there are institutions to preserve the rule of law. On the other hand, where the rule of law is weak, law and regulations are not clear and may constantly change, its interpretation is unpredictable, it may not be enforced or it could be costly and slow, people do not trust in the legal system, the level of corruption and abuse of power is high, people do not trust in government policies and promises and as such all these issues are self-perpetuated since authorities tend to use their power to maintain such a system.

Comparing 2023 World Bank rule of law and corruption perception indexes related to five EMs (Brazil, Russia, India, China, and South Africa) and four developed markets (France, Germany, United Kingdom, and the United States) provides a broad understanding on the gap between each country. On a scale from 0 (low) to 1 (high), these countries ranked in the following order regarding the rule of law: Russia 0.12, China 0.24, India 0.42, South Africa 0.7, Brazil 0.81, France 0.96, United Kingdom 0.96, United States 0.97, and Germany 0.99. On a scale from 0 (corrupt) to 100 (clean), these countries ranked in the following order regarding corruption perception: Russia 26, Brazil 36, India 39, South Africa 41, China 42, United States 69, France 71, United Kingdom 71, and Germany 78.

The same comparison under the 2023 Worldwide Governance Indicator presents slightly different results with major difference regarding the Brazilian position in the rule of law index. On a scale from −2.5 (low) to +2.5 (high), these countries ranked in the following order regarding rule of law: Russia −1.2, Brazil −0.3, China 0.0, South Africa 0.1, India 0.2, France 1.2, United States 1.3, United Kingdom 1.4, and Germany 1.6. Also, on a scale from −2.5 (corrupt) to +2.5 (clean), these countries ranked in the following order regarding corruption perception: Russia −1.1, Brazil −0.5, India −0.4, South Africa −0.3, China 0.0, United States 1.1, France 1.2, United Kingdom 1.5, and Germany 1.7.

Pargendler (2014) and Oman et al. (2003) link the low rule of law of emerging markets to their typical ownership structures. Under a weak enforcement of laws and contracts, relationship-based governance prevails. Companies can be directly or indirectly controlled by the State (quite common in China for instance) or by powerful families. Even where they do not own the majority of company stock, both maintain their power through a dual class of shares (one class giving more rights and powers, other class with restricted voting rights) or pyramidal structures (with many layers of holding companies that allows an indirect controlling shareholder with less equity investment). Also, so-called "crony capitalism" may be observed, where authorities are also influenced by State interest on State owned enterprises and by powerful controlling shareholders, who use their political and economic power in their self-interest leading to a tendency of perpetuation of these structures.

Where companies have controlling shareholders, there are less conflicts of interest between owners and (directly controlled) agents, but more conflicts between controlling and minority shareholders. Controlling shareholders may control other formally independent companies as well, allowing them to obtain synergies but also leading to expropriation risk, where one company's resources are diverted in other company's interest in detriment to former's minority shareholders. Since controlling shareholders directly manage or exert their control over management, it tends to be less transparent and less accountable.

However, corporate growth requires more investment, which in turn requires better corporate governance. In the attempt to develop their markets and following some global tendencies, some EM implemented legal and regulatory reforms based on developed market systems. Although the results in expanding their capital markets, mere legal transplantations proved to be ineffective without tackling controlling minority conflicts and enforcement issues. Donaggio (2014) analyses two Brazilian cases after the creation of "Novo Mercado", a legal transplant from the German Neuer Markt consisting of a self-regulated listing that requires strict governance rules. Both cases analyzed by the author were related to companies listed in Novo Mercado and notwithstanding that, both failed to fully protect their investors. Donaggio (2014) concludes that the reasons for the failure were: the lack of enforcement of the rules, which derived from a formalistic interpretation (different from interpretation practices from Germany) and potential regulatory capture, and an inadequate oversight structure with the necessary budgets as well as human and technical resources. Nonetheless, even though the legal transplantations were not effective, in Brazil they led to an expansion of its market, followed by other legal and regulatory reforms that improved the rule of law and protection, especially on regulatory level, as observed by Donaggio (2014), Pargendler (2014), and Santana (2013).

Similarly, in relation to corruption, Windsor (2014) concluded that the adoption of corporate governance and anti-corruption measures are not effective where agents lack integrity. Thus, again, such issues observed in EM must be tackled considering their context and potential impact not only on the structural paradigm of how asset valuation is conducted but also on the completion of M&A transactions.

Looking at Brazil, the main challenges remain on the enforcement side by its judicial system since the Brazilian Securities Commission (equivalent to the US SEC) can only impose penalties directly on companies and not compensation for harmed shareholders. Santana (2013) lists the crucial issues of the Brazilian judicial system: slow pace, high costs, little jurisprudence on corporate matters (since the slow pace leads to arbitration or to agreements before rulings in most cases), low expertise or knowledge on corporate law. The same issues are observed in the Indian judicial system, contrasting the reforms on the Securities and Exchange Board. Also in Asia, the main challenges from an enforcement perspective, where even in regulatory agencies the lack of resources, lack of practical independence, lack of transparency and arbitrary regulations are all observed according to the OECD Organisation for Economic Co-operation and Development (2007).

Despite the differences between EM in terms of rule of law, corporate governance, and corruption, they all tend to have weaker levels in comparison to developed markets and this affects the efficacy of any practice that ignores these issues. More optimal than trying to simply transplant developed market solutions or even to create an "equal" solution for all EMs, these matters should be better evaluated at the country and firm level to address adequate and focused solutions based on local realities and enforcement mechanisms.

It is also important to consider that EMs tend to seek, and are partially defined by, economic growth and development. This development is also seen in the regulatory landscape which is constantly changing and going through reforms. Thus, their levels of corruption, rule of law and corporate governance can be dynamic. In an M&A context then, we would caution against expecting the future in terms of laws and governance to be necessarily path dependent. As such, to paraphrase an often used expression from financial markets: past performance is not indicative of future performance. The "gamblers fallacy"—the mistaken belief that the outcome of a random event is always influenced by previous outcomes—does, to a lesser degree, also comes to mind.

How Emerging Markets Characteristics Impact Inbound M&A Risks

We have discussed how EMs require more attention than developed markets when it comes to the rule of law, especially regarding enforcement and interpretation, and to relationship-based governance that can lead to influence and corruption, this section will then analyze specifically if and how much such factors affect inbound M&A in EMs (i.e. acquisition of an EM company by a non-EM company). When acquiring a company in EMs, these characteristics may lead to failure before completion or to losses and low performance after completion.

Zhou et al. (2016) researched inbound and outbound M&A transactions in Brazil, Russia, India, and China and focused on patterns regarding whether each announced transaction was completed or terminated early. They found a solid impact of country-level level risks (rule of law) to inbound M&A completion while causation from firm-level differences (corporate governance issues) could only be identified in relation to outbound and not to inbound transactions. They conclude that not only were the country-level risks relevant, but the extent of their differences in relation to the acquirer's country, that is, the greater the difference, the higher the termination risk. The pattern is justified by the difficulties of pre-evaluating the risks, interpretating the complexities and anticipating regulatory changes when the acquirer is less familiar with these issues.

Interestingly, Thenmozhi and Narayanan (2016) found apparently opposite patterns when researching post-acquisition performance of EM acquisitions: the greater the difference between target and acquirer country-based rule of law, the higher the post-acquisition performance. However, they also conclude that this pattern is only factual for targets where country-level rule of law is not significantly low, since no target with too low rule of law appeared in the research, therefore leading to the conclusion that they are not even being targeted by developed countries (or, then, in connection with Zhou et al. (2016), they are terminated before completion). Their research sample comprised EM countries with a rule of law index from −1.0055 on a scale from −2.5 to +2.5 according to the Worldwide Governance Indicator dataset. They suggest that beyond a threshold in the country-based level of rule of law an acquirer could effectively enforce better practices at a firm-level and the target could benefit from it.

Also highlighted by Zhou et al. (2016), were some detailed examples which illustrate the required concerns regarding country-based rule of law when acquiring an EM target. In 2007, for instance, Vodafone entered the Indian market by acquiring from a Chinese seller two thirds of Hutchison Essar shares. After the acquisition, Indian authorities charged Vodafone with a tax in the billions on the capital gains merit. According to Denyer and Lakshmi (2011), the authority's interpretation of tax law used to justify this charge was unprecedented and led to retroactive tax investigations. Many foreign investors complained about the lack of clarity in Indian laws, unpredictability of Indian policies, and corruption. In 2012, the instability worsened as according to Nam (2012), a new tax provision confirmed authorities' power to retroactively tax the indirect transfer of assets.

In our experience in EM M&A, an acquirer should be prepared to deal with some complexities when assessing the risks related to the target. Risks may be country-based, due to external factors and over which the target has control, or can be firm-based, which can be due to internal or external factors. They may also be related to responsibilities from past actions (usually resulting in financial losses, or even in temporary or definitive ban, besides reputational losses), or to transaction terms and structure, or to post acquisition performance. The instability and uncertainty caused by low country levels of rule of law, the dynamics of power and influence, and corruption may affect an acquisition in many ways. Some risks may be added and linked to the EM characteristics referred to in Sect. "Understanding Some Key Characteristics of Emerging Markets, the Rule of Law, Corporate Governance and Corruption Issues". Based on that, we organize a list and comment on each item specifically regarding its impact on acquisition.

1. **Legal issues:** Issues regarding understanding and enforcement of the law and enforcement of contracts.

   (a) Complex legislation. Usually, in EMs, there are many laws, and they are usually unclear, what makes difficult for any company to be certain about its compliance. In Brazil, for instance, tax law is so complex that it makes it the country in the world where the highest number of hours (1501 h per year) are needed to fulfil all tax obligations including related bureaucracy according to World Bank data. Furthermore, tax laws frequently change. Many issues regarding the interpretation of tax (and every other) law are submitted to judicial review, but the judicial process often requires years to resolve disputes and, until a final Supreme Court decision is decreed, there may be opposite judicial precedents to similar situations, and court interpretations may change from time to time. As commentators in the country say, "in Brazil not even the past is certain". We can assume that this is broadly the case in multiple EMs as well. For an acquisition, this means uncertainty regarding potential losses from incompliance prior and after completion.

(b) Risk of revision by courts, annulment, and weak enforcement of contracts. In some EM more than others, there may be reduced certainty regarding the enforcement of contracts with government or with third parties. They may be misinterpreted, changed, or annulled by courts for economic or political reasons or due to dubious interpretation of the applicable law. As reported by Henisz and Zelner (2010), the financial crisis in Asia in 1997 led to some contracts being renegotiated or terminated. This signifies the risks of applicable penalties, inexecution and future performance failure of target's contracts and of the share purchase agreement between acquirer and seller.

(c) Slow legal processes. The long time taken for dispute resolution leads to various consequences. The longer a lawsuit takes to be settled, the more it costs in terms of legal fees and due interest rates on penalties and damages, the more the risk of being ineffective at the time of the settlement, and the more the pressure and incentives to negotiate and settle the dispute with an extrajudicial agreement. It affects the target's contracts and the share purchase agreement.

(d) Lack of independence, and political and economic influence on courts' decisions. This is a typical characteristic of the weak rule of law. People cannot rely on laws when there may be certain political or economic interest from government or a powerful group. It leads to uncertainty about compliance and enforcement of laws and contracts and can reflect on losses and penalties and the share purchase agreement. As an example, recently in Brazilian tax disputes, where the courts ruled against the State and tax authorities, they modulated the effects of the decision to avoid significant losses to the State. Therefore, even when the companies receive confirmation that they did comply with the law, they may be subject to losses.

(e) Protective labor, employment, consumer and environmental law and enforcement and exceptions to limited liability. Social concerns in EM cause companies, officers, directors, and shareholders to bear a higher liability in relation to certain matters. In Brazil, for instance, they may be personally charged for any damages and penalties due to labor, employment, consumer, or environmental violations caused by the company. It means the acquirer and its local representatives may be personally liable for the target's previous or futures violations.

2. **Regulatory issues:** Issues regarding lack, change, understanding and enforcement of regulations.

   (a) Complex or lack of regulations. The same issues of complexity, lack of clarity and weak enforcement of laws apply to regulations as well. Additionally, certain matters can also lack regulations (not only for capital markets, but regulations in general, especially in industries and activities the State tends to regulate, e.g., health, infrastructure, telecommunications), causing uncertainty about whether some practices will be considered lawful or not. This can mean risks of applicable penalties, or a temporary or definitive ban impacting future performance of the target.

(b) Constant change. New regulations and changes in existing ones are common in EMs since in some cases they are still going through institutional and regulatory development. It can also be a consequence of changes in government. It causes uncertainty as well since there may be new and sometimes unpredictable restrictions that may affect future performance or even prohibit foreign investments in certain sectors. Uncertainty can impact valuations.

(c) Liquidity. In countries where capital markets are still not developed, with few public companies and few transactions, it may be more difficult to sell the acquired shares in the future when willing to divest or to issue more shares in capitalization. Even if the target is not a public company when the acquisition is closed, it affects the possibility of going public. In case the acquisition is not over 100% of the shares, the risk may be higher, and the acquirer should better understand divestment options in different scenarios, including a possible shareholders conflict. Liquidity is a key factor that can impact asset valuation.

(d) Direct or indirect expropriation (without adequate compensation or no compensation at all), currency control and restrictions on repatriation. Although higher in developing than emerging markets, foreign assets may be subject to these risks during an economic crisis and/or political instability (see, for instance, see Akhtaruzzaman et al. 2017 and Lint and Alisont, 1994). It means direct losses and absence of future performance (or of access to its returns) to a foreign acquirer.

(e) Weak regulatory supervision. It weakens investor protection, failing to avoid abuses from the management and/or controlling shareholders.

(f) Antitrust. It is also important to understand antitrust regulations, since they may restrict the acquisition and (in case of a weak antitrust regulation) fail to protect the target against cartels and other companies abusing of their economic power, therefore affecting target's future performance.

(g) Labor unions. Besides protective labor and employment law, labor unions may also have and exert power over companies elevating their expenses and risks.

(h) Tax breaks. While attempting to provide incentives to grow investment, EM may offer tax breaks to some companies. It may cause a competitive advantage to its beneficiaries in detriment of its competitors.

3. **Corporate governance issues:** Issues regarding internal conflicts, controls, and processes.
   (a) Distinct types of conflict of interest: not only agency conflict but mainly controlling versus minority shareholders conflicts due to common EM ownership structures, that is, State-owned enterprises and powerful family-owned businesses. Thus, any foreign acquirer's interests may be harmed and not adequately protected whenever in conflict with State or powerful families' interests.
   (b) Ineffective board of directors. It may be due to the lack of adequate enforcement and/or the State and/or controlling shareholders' influences on them. It results in difficulties in evaluating risks from past activities and in overseeing the management.
   (c) Lack of adequate transparency. A lack of regulation or firm practice and/or different general accepted accounting principles from developed markets standards may affect the understanding of the target's reports. Some reports may be voluntary and lack in many companies. It leads to more difficulties in reducing asymmetry of information and overseeing the management.
   (d) Unreliable financial statements. This may result in fraud, which the management and/or controlling shareholders cause and hide the target's losses. It may also result from a cultural practice of deliberated violating the law not for personal benefit, but for the target's benefit when there is a belief that the law and taxes are extremely restrictive and make entrepreneurial activity not viable. In this case, the target may maintain some informal practices and informal contractual or employment relationships, resulting in difficulties evaluating risks and compliance.
   (e) Lack of internal processes and controls. The concentrated ownership structure provides less incentives for adopting internal controls since controlling shareholders tend to exert direct control over management. It results in difficulties for any acquirer in evaluating risks from the past and ensuring compliance after acquisition.
   (f) Related party transactions and expropriation. Target's resources may be diverted to other controlling shareholders companies to the detriment of the target's interests (see Saurabh 2023). It may result in losses to the target and/or difficulties in evaluating how it affects the target's performance.
   (g) Corruption (and FCPA and other applicable foreign law compliance) and money laundering. EMs weaker rule of law tends to provide authorities with more discretionary power and influence. Some authorities may impose unfair discretionary restrictions and charge bribes to lift them. It may cause reputational risks to acquirers, monetary penalties, and difficulties in conducting business free from corruption.

Besides global common due diligence practices, understanding specific country risks, and adding attention to above-listed issues is important to better evaluate risks to an acquisition and barriers to future performance in an EM.

How EM Risks Should Be Addressed in Due Diligence

Once verified that EM requires more attention to the rule of law than developed markets do, the challenge is to adequately evaluate and address these risks. An adequate assessment allows the acquirer to decide whether to withdraw the transaction before completion or to adopt precautions to increase the probability of a successful deal.

First and foremost, it is hard to conceive a proper assessment without the assistance of local advisors, since they will comprehend and be duly updated to the latest political, economic, legal, and regulatory country issues and status. Second, it might be more efficient to evaluate country-level risks before evaluating firm-level risks.

As argued in Sect. "How Emerging Markets Characteristics Impact Inbound M&A Risks", it is important to understand how weak the rule of law in that country is, since below a threshold it may be unfeasible to take advantage of the acquirer's strengths and to perform, while a low level above this threshold may reflect a great opportunity of higher performance levels. Some questions to ask are: what is the country's level of corruption? What role do relationships play in the enforcement of rules and authorities acts? How clear or unclear are the laws and regulations? Could any authority or agency be consulted regarding any interpretation before investment is made? Would in this case their answer bind any future interpretation by authorities? This could be an interesting way to overcome some uncertainties if their answer provides legal certainty that the agency/authority cannot enforce a different interpretation in the future. However, if legal certainty cannot be provided, one should analyze whether such consultation could be a valuable risk mitigator or it would only start authorities' unnecessary investigation and increase the risk of resulting in penalties.

The more a country's governance is relationship-based, the higher the risk of unfair competition. What barriers could be to fair competition with local companies? How powerful are State-owned enterprises and family-owned enterprises and how do they exert their power over competition and minority shareholders? What are the tax breaks in place and how are they granted? How likely a better tax break be granted to a competitor?

Another aspect that should be understood is how open the country is to foreign investments and whether foreign investors may or may not have bargaining power over the agencies. Some questions to ask are: are there current restrictions on foreign investment? What does the country's current political, economic, and social status say about interests and incentives to grow foreign investments? And what could such incentives be? What conditions could be negotiable? How discretionary is the power of the authorities to negotiate such incentives and how effectively they could reduce or even eliminate some uncertainties (especially but not necessarily exclusively regulatory uncertainties)? Are there specific protections to foreign investments? Which international treaties are applicable and enforceable in this country? How do law and regulation protect any foreign or domestic investor and target from agents and from controlling shareholders abuses? It is also important to understand the effectiveness of regulatory supervision, enforcement costs and time length of regulatory and judicial processes.

A country-level due diligence should aim not only at understanding current issues but also at the probability of relevant changes occurring. As Tapia-Hoffmann (2021) emphasizes, the legislative process of a country and the ease or difficulty to create and amend laws indicate how stable and credible their current laws are. Thus, some questions that should be answered are: is it easy or difficult to change laws and regulations? How frequently have they changed in recent history? Were these changes in the same direction or were they revolutionary and unpredictable? What facts in the country's recent history may indicate specific risks, for example, expropriation? What are the current social, political, and economic concerns in the country that can lead to changes? Are there political and economic instabilities that could lead to risks to investment, including the risk of expropriation? What are the government's promises and policies and does the government usually fulfill their promises or not? How likely is a change of government? How strong are institutions? How likely is that a change of government causes significant and harmful changes in law and regulation? May a new law in the country have retroactive effects? All these questions may help understanding not how the future laws and regulations will be but how unpredictable they can be. The more unpredictable, the higher the risks of investing in that country.

Before evaluating firm-level risks, the acquirer should also understand how effective firm-level practices (related to corporate governance, to contract enforcement, to corruption, to compliance) can be and which firm practices are, and which are not effective given country-based rule of law. It should direct what agreements and practices may take place regarding the acquisition, to the relationship between acquirer and seller and to the target's future governance. Section "EM Risk-related Best Practices in Defining Deal Structure and Negotiating and Drafting Its Agreements" will address these issues further.

After country-level evaluation, if the risks of investing in that country are acceptable, the acquirer should proceed to the firm-level risk assessment. All the understanding regarding the country's business environment should help to better interpret and understand the targets practices and documents. Notwithstanding that, firm-level risk assessment brings many challenges.

The first challenge may be gathering information. The information gathered during the usual due diligence practices may be incomplete. Since the governance in EM is relationship-based (or still transitioning to rule-based), some vital information may have no documents to prove and support it. Some relationships with employees and/or third parties may be informal. If the acquirer does not have access to this information, significant risks may be ignored. And even if this information is gathered, the lack of documents harms its accuracy. On the one hand, it may cause difficulties in interpreting and enforcing some obligations. On the other hand, it may cause unpredictable claims. In some countries, when there is no written proof, the courts may rule according to other evidence that may lead to behavior and expectations of each party. Therefore, one question should be asked: how do courts and authorities rule when there are no written documents? Understanding the answer, the acquirer should investigate beyond documents, talking to key persons, making questions, finding omissions, auditing inventory, auditing practices in person, sending advisors to visit the plant and finding risks that may be unknown even to seller. Assume the seller may be negligent and do not have enough controls in place. Understand how business is done by the target. Is there any key person who is determinant to target's success? What makes this a key person, is it any relationship, any personal influence, being part of a powerful family or any other nontransferable asset? Understand the target's organizational culture.

Challenge number two would be assessing information. Even when documented, it may be inaccurately interpreted. Misinterpretation may derive from different reasons: documents may be unclear, the law governing those documents may be unclear, reports may be uncompliant with some standards or may follow other than developed markets standards, there may be opposite judicial precedents to similar situations, court interpretations may change from time to time, or lack of regulations and precedents may cause uncertainty on the possible interpretations to some situation.

Even when assisted by local advisors, the acquirer should aim to understand differences in reporting, standards, general local practices, and principles to be able to better understand the outputs and compare them to global practices. An adequate assessment must allow the acquirer to understand how difficult post-acquisition integration will be and what losses may arise from past firm practices (legacy liabilities). Some risks may be inevitable because of the country-level rule of law and its uncertainties. Thus, it should be interpreted considering how acceptable and usual such risk taking in the country is. What were the risks taken by the target? Were they higher than average risk taking in the country? How could it be avoided? What financial losses may arise from them? How are court interpretations regarding the subject and how clear or uncertain are the law and court rulings on the subject? Which risks are limited to the target, and which may directly affect the acquirer? Which risks taken by the target may cause a violation in the acquirer's country? How can uncertainties be reduced or not by consulting agencies and authorities (without leading to corruption)? Which relationships target maintain with government and authorities that may increase the risk of corruption?

Once the risks are identified, challenge number three would be quantifying their potential financial impact and assessing reputational risks. When the laws and regulations are unclear, penalties may be subject to some discretionary calculation besides the difficulties of calculating damages.

After assessing risks and their potential impacts, challenge number four would be assessing viability of mitigating them in relation to past actions and post-acquisition. Some actions may be taken prior or after the acquisition to mitigate them. However, since laws and regulations tend to be unclear and interpretation to be uncertain, it is probable that no risks may be eliminated. It will not be a simple task of identifying violations and correcting them. They might be reduced through a more conservative approach, but this may not always be the best approach since it can mean assuming more costs and expenses in relation to competitors. It would be recommended a careful analysis, understanding the risks, the uncertainties in their interpretation, the actions that might be taken to mitigate them and the impacts, costs and other risks that may result from such actions.

Challenge number five would be estimating integration costs. Integration is one of the main phases of any acquisition. It is where synergies can be achieved, and the acquirer may increase the target's performance. If integration is not well planned and finds more barriers than expected, the transaction may destroy value instead of generating it. The higher the differences in culture and standards between the target and the acquirer, the higher the positive impact the acquirer may exert, but the higher the costs and difficulties for the integration.

Finally, challenge number six would be assessing the risk of deal annulment and other litigation that may arise in relation to the acquisition. What are common issues that arise from M&A transactions in the target country and how did the courts rule?

This section does not intend to present a complete list of issues but to highlight the importance of amplifying the scope of due diligence in any inbound cross-border acquisition in EM. The usual global due diligence checklist will also apply in addition to the issues above. When it is not the first acquisition of an acquirer in the target country, it should be easier to comprehend all the issues, but even in this case, it would be recommended to ask similar questions since EM may be subject to constant political, economic, regulatory, and legal changes.

EM Risk-related Best Practices in Defining Deal Structure and Negotiating and Drafting Its Agreements

One of the main objectives of due diligence is to assess risks. The other should be assisting with the integration. The first must prevent the acquirer from supporting more losses than expected from past action. The second must guarantee estimated synergies and performance will happen. However, even when these steps are carefully conducted, a deal might be unsuccessful because of litigation arising from the relationship between acquirer and seller. Thus, deal structure, deal agreements and the target's governance after completion are also important once the parties decide to sign and close the deal. And, as in legal structure from developed markets to EMs, where the outputs are different if not adapted, deal structure, deal agreements and the target's governance should not be just transplanted from developed markets (although which commonly occurs).

When evaluating and defining the deal structure, both acquirer and seller tend to negotiate the percentage of equity to be acquired, type of consideration (cash, equity, or a combination of both) and other conditions that may allow for tax efficiency. Research shows that a cash deal in the acquisition of majority control decreases the probability of failure before completion and increases the probability of enhancing the target's performance after completion. As Zhou et al. (2016) observes, a cash deal is less complex than a stock deal and other types of consideration that could lead to further negotiation on the valuation of the acquirer's shares. Besides, they suggest the EM targets need or preference for cash may incentivize them to concentrate more efforts in closing the deal.

Tesar et al. (2010) established that acquisition of control of EM target from developed market acquirer significantly improved performance of the target in comparison to acquisition of minority equity. They conclude that such an increase in performance is a result of the acquirer transfer of intangible assets, enhanced governance, and access to cheaper capital. They suggest a lower percentage of acquiring shares would deter the acquirer from sharing intangible assets and imposing better corporate governance practices. Thus, an acquisition of control allows the acquirer to add more value to the target, especially in industries where intangible assets provide more competitive advantages.

In addition to what the research demonstrates, both the percentage of acquiring equity and the consideration affect the transaction agreements, the corporate governance practices after completion and the risks of litigation over transaction terms or over the relationship between the acquirer and the seller. A full cash acquisition tends to leave less margin for misinterpretation while a stock acquisition should demand a more complex agreement subject to different interpretations and possibly some difficulties to enforce. Acquiring 100% of the target shares avoids majority control versus minority conflicts and issues. On the other hand, it makes the acquirer-seller relationship purely transactional, what might decrease some incentives for extrajudicially resolving any disputes regarding the transaction agreements.

Acquiring majority control in an EM target may provide the acquirer with powers to impose any governance practices, however it may raise some issues regarding the relationship with minority shareholders after the acquisition. Since EM tends to have concerns about majority-minority conflicts of interests, there are laws and regulations protecting minority interests, which may be unclear and lead to different interpretations and some strike suits by minority shareholders. Notwithstanding that, being the minority shareholder after an acquisition of a lower percentage would recommend a negotiation of a shareholders agreement guaranteeing some rights and governance practices in addition to legal and regulatory provisions to protect the acquirer's interests. Lastly, in the case of a 50% acquisition, or a merger of equals, the higher challenge would be to negotiate robust rules to overcome deadlock situations.

Each of these deal structures requires the acquirer to consider how agreements are interpreted and enforced, and which corporate governance practices are effective in the target country, what may differ from developed markets. Haroon and Zaka (2023) compared studies in EM and in developed markets and concluded that few practices have the potential to be universal, while most of them have different outcomes in terms of performance and earnings management. Some practices are more effective in EMs while not effective or even detrimental in developed countries. It is justified by the already mentioned differences in ownership structures and majority control versus minority conflicts.

Potential universal practices are board gender and ethnic diversity, family management and equity-based compensation. Indeed, the convergence in corporate governance regulations in EM firms has generated gains in reducing agency costs, improving accounting standards and reporting quality and also market valuations. However, while these practices can be effective in increasing EM corporate performance, they are not always effective in reducing or eliminating what is termed "earnings management", or a firm's deliberate manipulation of its financial numbers to meet expectations or to portray a selected narrative. This can be legal, but at the same time excessive or deceptive practices can violate regulations and good faith negotiations in M&A. This leads to the conclusion that such practices should be applied to EM, but with concerns around auditing and checking the accuracy of financial reports and results. Some practices are certainly effective in terms of performance for EM but not necessarily for developed markets: external directors (in EM effective in performance, not conclusive for earnings management; in developed markets ineffective in performance and effective in earnings management), larger boards (performance, but leads to higher earnings management), non-management block holders and institutional investors (not effective for earnings management). We of course generalize here: country, sector, and firm specifics should always be taken into consideration in M&A discussions.

When negotiating the agreements, the first thing is to define applicable law and jurisdiction. Usually, they are composed in EM law and jurisdiction. These will directly affect how the agreement should be drafted. EM and developed markets may differ in terms of language, interpretation and enforcement and it would change the outcome of the same clauses. In some developed countries, for instance, courts cannot consider any condition that is not written in the agreement while in some EM countries courts may consider every kind of proof (even not written in the agreement) to understand the context and assist interpretation. In Brazil, agreements must be interpreted according to good faith, common local practices, parties' behavior, and what should be their most reasonable intention according to every information they had. Therefore, recitals and representations and warranties sections should be carefully drafted to present the relevant context of the negotiation.

Given the risks identified in the due diligence, all the uncertainties related to the firm or to the country and the lengthy judicial processes, some worldwide common clauses may need more attention and negotiation. Covenants and restrictive covenants should aim to mitigate some risks before closing. Material adverse change clauses should allow the termination of the agreement before closing if any unexpected material change occurs. Representations and warranties and indemnification clauses should address the seller's liability regarding all previous acts. Earn-out mechanisms may protect the acquirer from both unexpected bad performance and legacy liability; however, their complexity demands careful negotiation and drafting since it can often result in litigation. Types of collateral in favor of the acquirer may be especially important as well to avoid the need of the legal system to enforce the agreement regarding the seller's liability: contingent payments, escrow accounts, and insurance are the most common instruments used in this context.

Conclusion

A common conclusion from every study related to EM and from experts practice is that there is no universal practice that may result in uniform outcomes in acquisitions. Even generalization among emerging markets must be measured since each market has its own history and issues. What is common among them, as we have seen. is that they tend to have weak rule of law, although at differing low levels. Furthermore, this is the main characteristic that leads to all the risks and issues that developed markets are not familiar with.

Indeed, weak rule of law leads to many uncertainties, which makes every due diligence more challenging. Risks are more difficult to identify, evaluate, and mitigate. Weak enforcement leads to higher importance of majority control or full control and other structures or mechanisms that make the acquirer less dependent on the legal system. A different ownership structure leads to different challenges in corporate governance practices. Uncertain interpretation leads to more careful agreement drafting. Notwithstanding that (or actually because of all that) the impact that a developed market acquirer can have on an EM target, adding better governance, access to cheaper capital and access to more intangible assets lead to great business opportunities.

Understanding the rule of law of the market in question to better evaluate all country-based and firm-based legal, regulatory, and corporate governance issues should guide the acquirer to better navigate the complexities of an EM and enhance the probability of successful M&A dealmaking. As we have argued, valuation is a fundamental part of the M&A process, but especially in an EM context, solid understanding, analysis, and assessment of legal, regulatory, and corporate governance pillars are also of the utmost importance.

References

Akhtaruzzaman M, Berg N, Hajzler C (2017) Expropriation risk and FDI in developing countries: does return of capital dominate return on capital? Eur J Polit Econ 49:84–107. https://doi.org/10.1016/j.ejpoleco.2017.01.001

Denyer S, Lakshmi R (2011) India frustrates foreign investors with its unpredictable tax policies. https://www.washingtonpost.com/world/india-frustrates-foreign-investors-with-its-unpredictable-tax-policies/2011/03/17/AFVpacLC_story.html

Donaggio A (2014) Limitations of legal transplants and convergence to corporate governance practices in emerging markets: the Brazilian case. In: Boubaker S, Nguyen D (eds) Corporate governance in emerging markets. CSR, sustainability, ethics & governance. Springer, pp 399–418. https://doi.org/10.1007/978-3-642-44955-0_19

Haroon O, Zaka M (2023) A review of corporate governance effectiveness: developed vs emerging markets. Corp Law Gov Rev 5(1):38–62. https://doi.org/10.22495/clgrv5i1p4

Henisz WJ, Zelner BA (2010) The hidden risks in emerging markets. Harv Bus Rev 88(4):88–95

Lint L, Alisont JR (1994) An analysis of expropriation and nationalization risk in China. Yale J Int Law 19(1):135–162

Nam R (2012) *Foreign investors complain at India tax provisions*. https://www.reuters.com/article/business/foreign-investors-complain-at-india-tax-provisions-idUSL3E8ET0ZN

Oman C, Fries S, Buiter W (2003) Corporate governance in developing, transition and emerging-market economies. *OECD Development Centre Policy Brief No. 23*. OECD Publishing

Organisation for Economic Co-operation and Development (2007) Corporate governance in emerging markets: Enforcement of corporate governance in Asia – The unfinished agenda. OECD Publishing.

Pargendler M (2014) Corporate governance in emerging markets. In: Gordon JN, Ringe W-G (eds) *Oxford handbook of corporate law and governance* (forthcoming). FGV Direito SP Research Paper Series No. 17. https://ssrn.com/abstract=2417994

Santana MH (2013) Brazil: the corporate governance framework and practices relating to supervision and enforcement. In: Supervision and enforcement in corporate governance. OECD Publishing, pp 123–145

Saurabh K (2023) Expropriation mechanisms, corporate governance, and cross-border acquisitions by Indian firms. Int J Discl Gov 20:395–409. https://doi.org/10.1057/s41310-023-00183-7

Tapia-Hoffmann AL (2021) Legal certainty and central bank autonomy in Latin American emerging markets. In: *European yearbook of international economic law*, vol 15. Springer, pp 45–67. https://doi.org/10.1007/978-3-030-70986-0_2

Tesar L, Chari A, Ouimet P (2010) The value of control in emerging markets. Rev Financ Stud 23(4):1741–1770. https://doi.org/10.1093/rfs/hhp090

Thenmozhi M, Narayanan PC (2016) Rule of law or country level corporate governance: what matters more in emerging market acquisitions? Res Int Bus Financ 37:448–463. https://doi.org/10.1016/j.ribaf.2016.01.008

Wiedemann M, zu Knyphausen-Aufseß D, Ippendorf N (2024) Revisiting Shimizu et al. (2004): what do we know and what should we know about cross-border mergers and acquisitions? Rev Manag Sci. https://doi.org/10.1007/s11846-024-00813-6

Windsor D (2014) Corporate governance as an antidote to corruption in emerging markets. In: Boubaker S, Nguyen D (eds) Corporate governance in emerging markets. CSR, sustainability, ethics & governance. Springer, pp 365–382. https://doi.org/10.1007/978-3-642-44955-0_17

Zhou C, Xie J, Wang Q (2016) Failure to complete cross-border M&As: "to" vs. "from" emerging markets. J Int Bus Stud 47:1077–1105. https://doi.org/10.1057/s41267-016-0027-y

Liquidity in Equity Markets

Theory and Practice for Emerging Markets

Breno Pavao

The price paid for a company is determined based on not only the characteristics of the company but also by the market in which the company trades (Covrig and McConaughy 2014)

Abstract This chapter examines the concept of liquidity in developed and emerging markets, focusing on its role in equity valuation frameworks. It begins by defining liquidity as the ease of executing asset transactions with minimal price impact and highlights its abstract nature, driven by a combination of intrinsic and external factors. The author explores the intrinsic relationship between liquidity and market efficiency, positing that both are influenced by the same underlying variables, such as the number of participants and information availability.

Keywords DLOM discount for lack of liquidity · Market structure · Market efficiency · Trading costs · Private firm valuation · CAPM · Cash flow yield · Earnings yield

Introduction

This chapter explores the concept of liquidity in markets, particularly in equity markets, and how it directly and indirectly impacts asset prices and valuation frameworks. Given the inherent abstract nature of liquidity, the chapter first reviews available literature in order to get a better understanding of what liquidity really means. In essence, liquidity is merely a reflection of numerous factors impacting the functioning of a specific market. While it's intuitive and correct to think of liquidity as influenced by laws, regulations, and other exogenous factors, what really dictates a market as having greater or less liquidity is a more intrinsic aspect of each market: the number of market participants, the availability of relevant goods and services, and the willingness of participants to trade. These rather rudimentary factors are

B. Pavao (✉)
Curitiba, Brazil

S. Derindere Köseoğlu, A. Patterson (eds.), *Valuation in Emerging Markets*, Contributions to Finance and Accounting,
https://doi.org/10.1007/978-3-031-93526-8_13

indeed what make markets, to a greater or lesser degree, liquid in their most basic form, with exogenous factors such as regulation or technology simply increasing or decreasing the level of liquidity. With that in mind, the author traces a parallel between what is known as market liquidity and market efficiency. The objective of such a comparison is to provide a better understanding of liquidity and what drives it, as the same factors that are usually accepted as influencing the level of efficiency in markets are also the building blocks for market liquidity. As it will be discussed, the concept of market efficiency and market liquidity are, in the author's view, intrinsically connected.

Even though liquidity is an abstract concept, there is a vast literature on how to quantify it. This chapter briefly reviews known methods for quantifying liquidity (or isolating a liquidity premium), with a focus on private versus public firms. Although the author focuses on the different levels of liquidity specific to private equity markets versus public equity markets, liquidity is a universal concept applied individually to each asset, within and between each market (e.g., different asset classes or regions). We note that liquidity is usually a relative measure. Each asset has its own liquidity level, which is not constant and not necessarily similar to other assets in the same market. Take for example the liquidity premium that is often attributed to longer dated treasury securities vs. government bills, illustrating that liquidity is not uniform within assets classes nor markets. Nonetheless, the author proposes a simple exercise to extract a liquidity premium based on observed market prices, which can be presented as an annualized rate and used in a build-up cost of equity method.

Background

Liquidity is inherently an abstract concept. The simplest way to think about it is to consider it the cost of buyers' remorse: basically, the cost of reversing an asset trade almost instantaneously after making it (Damodaran, New York University—Stern School of Business 2006). Put differently, liquidity refers to how easily an asset can be bought or sold, without impacting its price, or having a low-price impact risk. Different markets present different levels of liquidity, which is influenced by many factors, and the combination of these multiple factors is reflected in a more or less liquid market (as redundant as it sounds, this is how liquidity usually works, with some feedback loop dynamics). Therefore, assuming that liquidity reflects the influence of various factors, it becomes a challenging task to attribute a "liquidity" premium to any single factor. Moreover, isolating individual risk premiums, including one specifically tied to varying liquidity levels in markets, is equally difficult. Take for example the commonly used small cap premium. The small cap premium isolates the excess return that investors demand for holding shares of smaller companies, often quantified based on their total market capitalization. "The size premium is the historical tendency for the stocks of firms with smaller market capitalizations to outperform the stocks of firms with larger market capitalizations"

(Wrotenbery 2013). What is often overlooked, however, is that the historically stronger performance of smaller companies can also be viewed as a liquidity premium for holding stocks that are less liquid, as Damodaran implies: "the key is to avoid double counting the cost of illiquidity since some of the small premium may be compensation for the illiquidity of small cap companies" (Damodaran, Marketability and Value: Measuring Illiquidity Discount 2005). Amihud also showed that at least part of the premiums received by smaller companies can be explained by insufficient liquidity (i.e., reduced market value) (Amihud, Illiquidity and Stock Returns: Cross-section and Time Series Effects, 2002). As we will discuss further on, liquidity is heavily influenced by the number of market participants. In a risk-aversion framework, the inherently riskier nature of smaller companies compared to larger, more consolidated ones tends to deter investors. Consequently, it becomes difficult to determine how much of the premium is attributable to the company's inherent risk and how much stems from the risk of failing to find a potential buyer or seller, a core aspect of liquidity.

Similarly, it's important to differentiate the definitions of liquidity and marketability. Even though these terms are often considered to be synonyms, the former is related to the conversion of an asset into cash while the latter concerns legal issues in the transfer of an asset. By the definition, it's reasonable to assume that even though these are different concepts, marketability influences liquidity. In fact, any characteristic that makes it more difficult or easier to accomplish a transaction without impacting market prices can be understood as decreasing or increasing liquidity, including the size of the company. Building on this perspective, by adding any other premium rather than a liquidity discount, there's a significant probability of double counting, since it can be viewed as the sum of many different risk characteristics observed for a given company that influence its trading volume. Therefore, the author contends that all excess return demanded by investors for holding stocks of privately versus publicly held firms, as observed in market prices, is entirely driven by a "liquidity" risk premium. The author's definition of this premium is as follows: "the liquidity risk premium reflects the excess return implied by observed market prices of privately vs. publicly held firms, which in turn reflects numerous other factors that combined make market transactions for privately held firms relatively less frequent". Note that the same concept is valid when analyzing differences in equity market prices between developed and emerging markets. Emerging markets are normally less liquid than developed ones, which is reflected in usually lower valuation multiples in these economies.

Different asset classes typically exhibit varying risk levels. Traditional and safer markets often attract a broader pool of marginal investors, which aligns with the concept that the equity risk premium is partially influenced by a liquidity premium. However, liquidity differences alone do not explain every market spread. When analyzing liquidity premiums driven by market structure, it is important to compare similar assets. In such cases, price differences are likely to be influenced primarily by variations in market structure, such as between private and public equity markets.

The author's definition of liquidity implies that investors still require risk premiums that are shared by public and private equity markets. Put in CAPM terms, it assumes that investors require the same risk free rate, and equity risk premium for public and private companies, but that usually lower multiples in private equity markets reflect the additional risks inherent to this market, other than the differences in assets, which would result in the spread between the equity risk premium observed for the private and the public company. For example, this logic implies that, if two companies are theoretically identical, but one is privately held while the other is publicly traded in a stock exchange, the transactional risks which are naturally higher for private firms would demand a premium, and would result in a lower price and, consequently, lower valuation multiple for the private firm.

In order to understand what makes a market to a greater or lesser extent liquid, it's crucial to understand how liquidity is created. Something that is obvious but imperative to mention, is that "markets" are simply a conglomeration of people trading goods. At the most basic of levels, markets would only need people and goods to start providing some functioning liquidity—other additional factors could of course increase liquidity, but liquidity is originally created by just market participants and goods. Markets are more or less liquid in part because of the number of participants in them. Reasons around why there are more transactions in one market compared to another can be explained by laws, regulations or restrictions—the market microstructure—but the original aspect of liquidity is the number of market participants, goods and their willingness to trade. Some markets are more active than others and some stock exchanges are considered to be more efficient than others. This is easily observed in the differences in trading volumes from equity markets in developed economies compared with emerging ones. "These illiquid assets are shunned by the frequent traders and are heavily discounted by them. [...] And, in equilibrium, liquid assets are held by frequently-trading investors while the illiquid assets are held by investors with long expected holding periods" (Amihud et al. 2005). The number of market participants provides safety for future liquidation, which is priced at present value and is related to the price impact (the impact a transaction has on the price of the asset being traded) factor of illiquidity. For public markets, the price impact is generally lower due to a usually larger pool of possible counter-party trades. This is not true for private markets where assets are very unique and other market participants are harder to find. Additionally, information asymmetry of private business by definition increases the influence one can have over prices, increasing overall volatility and further driving away investors, and decreasing market liquidity.

The level of liquidity in a market is also often associated with its efficiency. The factors increasing and decreasing market efficiency are the number of participants, information availability, financial disclosure, and limits to trading. For markets to be efficient, prices should adjust quickly and rationally to the release of new information. In other words, prices of assets in an efficient market should "fully reflect" all information. Financial markets, however, are generally not classified at the two extremes as either completely inefficient or completely efficient but, rather, as exhibiting various degrees of efficiency. In other words, market efficiency should be viewed as falling on a continuum between extremes of completely efficient, at one end, and completely inefficient, at the other. The degree of efficiency also varies

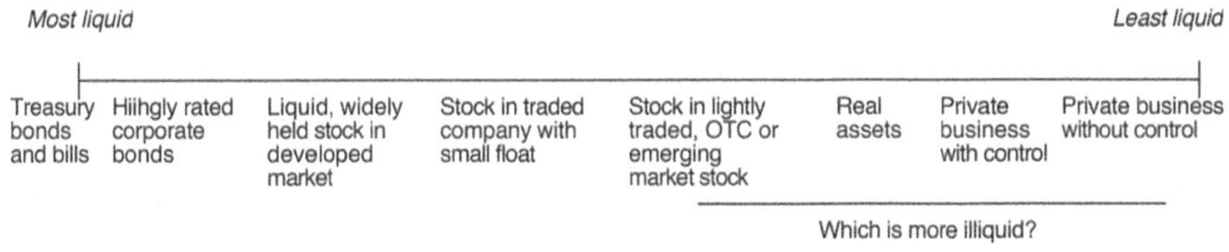

Fig. 1 Markets ranked from most to least liquid. *Source*: Aswath Damodaran (2009) Available at: http://people.stern.nyu.edu/adamodar/pdfiles/country/illiquidity.pdf

through time, across geographical markets, and the type of market (CFA Institute 2019). Naturally, some markets are more efficient than others because they present different characteristics and structures. The same idea applies when comparing privately and publicly traded companies, and emerging and developed economies. Looking closer at the factors that contribute to market efficiency, it's evident that these different markets present different degrees of efficiency. Indeed, one of the most critical factors contributing to the degree of efficiency in a market is the number of market participants. A large number of investors follow the major financial markets closely on a daily basis, and if there are mis-pricings in these markets, investors will act so that these mis-pricings disappear quickly. Information availability (e.g., an active financial news media) and financial disclosure should promote market efficiency. Moreover, information trading activity and traded companies in such markets as the New York Stock Exchange, the London Stock Exchange, and the Tokyo Stock Exchange is readily available (CFA Institute 2019).

While it's not common to attribute a risk premium to a more inefficient market, it's intuitive to think that an investor would require a premium for assets traded in such an environment. As is the case for the concept of efficiency, liquidity in markets is best analyzed as a value falling within a range, it's never completely illiquid or liquid. Defined thus, all assets are illiquid. The difference is really a continuum, with some assets being less illiquid than others (Damodaran, New York University—Stern School of Business 2006). Figure 1 ranks different markets by their liquidity levels according to their trading costs (bid-ask spread). Private placements are among the most illiquid markets, while treasury bonds and bills are among the most liquid ones. The spreads in U.S. government securities are much lower than the spreads on traded stocks in the United States. For instance, the typical bid-ask spread on a Treasury bill is less than 0.1% of the price. The spreads on corporate bonds tend to be larger than the spreads on government bonds, with safer (higher rated) and more liquid corporate bonds having lower spreads than riskier (lower rated) and less liquid corporate bonds. The spreads in non-U.S. equity markets are generally much higher than the spreads on U.S. markets, reflecting the lower liquidity in those markets and the smaller market capitalization of the traded firms. While the spreads in the traded commodity markets are similar to those in the financial asset markets, the spreads in other real asset markets (real estate and art, for instance) tend to be much larger (Damodaran, New York University - Stern School of Business 2006).

It is interesting to note the strong correlation between market efficiency and liquidity, which supports the idea that liquidity differences contribute to the additional risks inherent in private markets compared to public ones. In Fig. 1, assets are ranked from more to less liquid, and it is reasonable to assume the same order would apply if ranked by market efficiency—defined as the degree to which prices reflect all available information.

For example, Treasury bonds are considered risk-free because virtually all information affecting their prices is known. Key attributes, such as maturity, coupon, face value, and, most importantly, default probability, are either known or assumed with high confidence. In contrast, corporate bonds involve greater uncertainty due to their non-zero default probability, but they still offer more certainty than equities, where factors like earnings results are less predictable.

Emerging market equities often experience higher volatility, which deters more risk-averse investors, reduces market participation, and consequently decreases liquidity. This dynamic is observed across the liquidity spectrum, with less risky asset classes typically exhibiting higher trading volumes. Amihud attributes liquidity to explain part of the equity risk premium puzzle: "it follows that liquidity can help explain a number of puzzles, such as why equity commanding high required returns (the equity risk premium puzzle), why liquid risk-free treasuries have low required returns (the risk-free rate puzzle), and why small stocks that are typically illiquid earn high returns (the small firm effect)" (Amihud et al. 2005).

In private markets, the amount and reliability of information decrease significantly, leading to more frequent mispricing and reduced market efficiency. However, it is important to note that the key difference between private and public companies lies in transaction-related uncertainty rather than the underlying security. For instance, while an investor might have access to comparable financial information for both private and public companies, the process of transferring equity ownership in private placements is far less transparent and predictable.

Liquidity is usually measured by higher or lower transaction costs and often represented by the bid-ask spread, but this measurement is an ordinal scale, the order of the values is what's important and significant, but the differences between each one is not really known (Market Research Methods 2020). This means that markets can be ranked as more or less liquid according to the bid-ask spread as a percentage of the asset price, but this does not tell how much more or less liquid markets are, and because of that it's not possible, from this measurement, to come up with an interval scale for the liquidity premium. Furthermore, while it's possible to rank higher and lower transaction costs as a percentage of asset price, it wouldn't reflect the risk premium itself, at least not in terms of an annualized rate, which could be used in build-up risk models such as the CAPM. To calculate such a premium, a better approach would be to focus directly on price differences that are caused by these higher transaction costs. For this, a few approaches are common.

There are three approaches typically used to estimate the premium for illiquid assets. Empirical approaches, theoretical approaches and others that are not classified as either theoretical or empirical, but that utilize specific characteristics of the

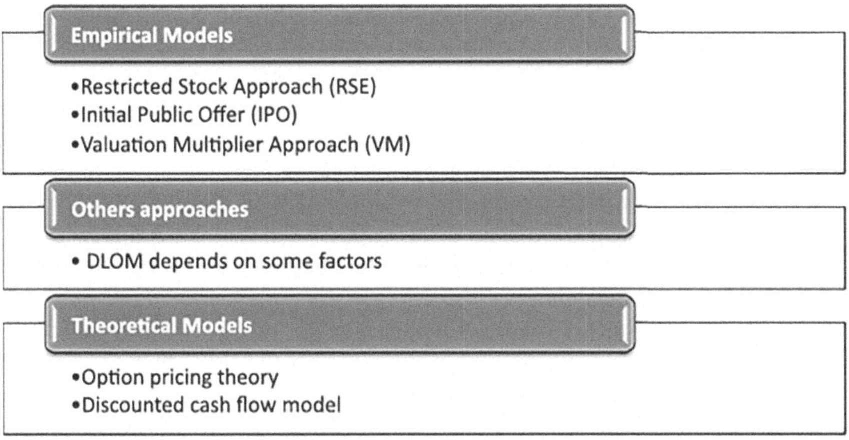

Fig. 2 Different methods for estimating the illiquidity premium. *Source*: The Discount Rate in Valuing Privately Held Companies - Juana Alonso Can˜adas, PhD, and Alfonso A. Rojo Ramirez, PhD, Business Valuation Review—2011

transaction to come up with the best estimation of higher transaction costs (Canadas and Ramirez 2011) (Fig. 2).

Empirical approaches, as the name describes, are based on observed data and it's more consistent with the definition of liquidity being the price impact that reflects the extra risk of these illiquid markets. There are three main types of empirical approaches to estimate the liquidity differences that should yield the premium:

- **IPO (Initial Public Offering) Approach**: this approach relies on the different market characteristics that private and public companies are traded on. The assumption is that the price differential of a company before and after going public should reflect the higher liquidity brought by trading on a market with a higher degree of efficiency. It's basically a comparison of the share price before and after the IPO. After all, it's the exact same company, but trading on a different market, so it should reflect only the risk differences brought by the new market environment. IPOs are considered to be liquidity events and an exit strategy for an illiquid investment—that is, for equity that has little or no market to trade on. Founders of a firm, naturally, push toward a liquidity event and the investors along the way—venture capital firms, angel investors or private equity firms—hope for or expect one within a reasonable amount of time after initially making an investment (Chen 2019). Taken from this perspective, it's natural that this approach might not be the optimal one to represent the liquidity differences because lots of other factors are in play during such events, and the conflict of interest between investors, investment banks, owners or any stakeholders whatsoever might distort prices and the difference observed might not reflect a liquidity level one would expect for private company's transactions. Prof. Damodaran points out the limitation of this approach, supporting the idea of being an ambiguous premium, "the first [limitation] is the sheer size of the discount suggests that there may be something else going on in these transactions. In particular, these might not be arms-length transactions, and the sellers of these shares may be getting compensating benefits elsewhere" (Damodaran, New York University - Stern School of Business 2006). This can be confirmed looking at the results from searches that point to a "discount of almost 45% (Emory 1981) and ranges between 32% and 55% (Damodaran, Marketability and Value: Measuring Illiquidity Discount 2005), compared to differences in other approaches that suggest a 20% discount (Koeplin et al. 2000) (Canadas and Ramirez 2011). IPO approach tends to be more volatile than other approaches and this can be explained by this limitation.

- **RSE (Restricted Stock Exchange) Approach**: Restricted securities are securities issued by a company, but not registered with the SEC, that can be sold through private placements to investors. However, these securities cannot be resold in the open market for a one-year holding period, and limited amounts can be sold thereafter. Restricted securities trade at significant discounts on publicly traded shares in the same company (Damodaran, New York University - Stern School of Business 2006). What is more, following the idea of comparing realizable prices in different markets to yield a premium representing the liquidity differences, as in other empirical approaches. RSE may not have the same limitation of the IPO approach because this is not technically a liquidity event, therefore other pressures that are affecting the price should be normalized over time and present a more appropriate price for privately held companies in normal market conditions. Nevertheless, unlike truly private firms, RSE have an expiration date on its liquidity premium. "According to empirical research, we can conclude that the RSE approach shows a high variability range (Sheeler 2004) with an average between 35% and 45%, although there is a tendency for it to be reduced over time (Damodaran, Marketability and Value: Measuring Illiquidity Discount 2005)" (Canadas and Ramirez 2011). Maher examined restricted stock purchases made by four mutual funds in the period 1969–1973 and concluded that they traded an average discount of 35.43% on publicly traded stock in the same companies. Moroney reported a mean discount of 35% for acquisitions of 146 restricted stock issues by 10 investment companies, using data from 1970. In a recent study of this phenomenon, Silber finds that the median discount for restricted stock is 33.75%. Many of these older studies were done when the restriction stretched to two years. More recent studies since the change in the holding period come back with lower values for the discount (20–25%) (Damodaran, New York University - Stern School of Business 2006).
- **VM (Valuation Multiplier) Approach**: This approach is similar to the RSE, where the liquidity difference comes from the price differential of companies being traded in different markets, but while the RSE focuses on placements that cannot be traded during certain periods, incurring a higher degree of illiquidity, VM focuses on companies that are private and are available for trading. The higher difficulty in finding a buyer or seller drives the overall relative price down. Thus, different from RSE, VM represents the price differential paid for a private company in normal market conditions. The difference between the relative prices

(measured by price multipliers such as price-to-earnings) represent the liquidity differences and this approach is consistent with the concept of liquidity as being caused by the sum of additional risk factors that make this market relatively more illiquid. "One such approach [...] is to find a set of comparable transactions—that is, acquisitions of companies in similar industries at around the same time—and then calculate the purchase price multiples of various relevant financial parameters, such as sales or earnings. The estimated multiples are then applied to the values of these parameters for the company being valued" (Koeplin et al. 2005). The difference found using this approach is nearly 20% (Koeplin et al. 2000).

There are two main theoretical approaches, which are not based on market data, but supported only by conceptual definitions and assumptions. One way is to consider liquidity as a "put option for the period when an investor is restricted from trading. Thus, the illiquidity discount on value for an asset where the owner is restricted from trading for 2 years would be modeled as a 2-year at-the-money put option. The problem with this is that liquidity does not give you the right to sell a stock at today's market price anytime over the next 2 years. What it does give you is the right to sell at the prevailing market price anytime over the next 2 years" (Damodaran, New York University - Stern School of Business 2006). The other theoretical approach tries to adjust the liquidity in the fundamentals of discounted cash flow. "First, (Tabak 2002) suggests a model based on the CAPM and the equity risk premium. Second, (Mercer 2003) designs the Quantitative Marketability Discount Model (QMDM) to employ the basic discounted cash flow model to value illiquid interests of PHC [privately held companies] in the context of appraisals of the relevant business companies" (Canadas and Ramirez 2011).

Overall, there are two main options to include a liquidity discount in an asset price. The first would be a direct deduction on the present value of future cash flows, the intrinsic value. This is quite a simple approach and the assumption is as follows: more illiquid assets are traded at a lower price than more liquid ones, so a reduction on the final price must be made to reflect this price differential. The value of the asset can be computed as if it were liquid and then adjusted for illiquidity at the end (as a discount or "haircut") (Damodaran, New York University - Stern School of Business 2006). A second approach would be to increase the discount rate through a liquidity premium, which is actually based on the price differential. The difference is that premium is the annualized rate that yields the difference in market prices. This approach considers illiquidity as being a function of holding period and transaction costs. Amihud and Mendelson make the interesting argument that when you pay for an asset today, it incorporates the present value of all expected future transactions costs on that asset (Damodaran, New York University - Stern School of Business 2006). Or, in other words, "the buyer anticipates further costs upon sales, and so on, throughout the life of the security" (Amihud et al. 2005). Therefore, the premium should be added into the discount rate and it will vary according to the expected holding period.

Quantifying Liquidity

How to Isolate the Liquidity Risk Premium Embedded in Private Firms Prices

This section proposes a simplified method for extracting and quantifying the liquidity risk premium embedded in asset prices in private equity markets. The method relies on the spread on the cash flow yields implied in market prices from private versus public equity markets. It assumes that additional risks related to the market structure (i.e., lower liquidity) command a lower valuation multiple than similar private peers. Lower average multiples in private equity markets are thus driven by lower liquidity in these markets, which in turn is driven by several factors, but most importantly, the much smaller number of market participants compared with publicly traded peers' market. The smaller number of participants makes it harder to find potential buyers and sellers, which in turn drives prices lower as a liquidity premium is actively or passively added by investors through lower average valuation multiples.

Before presenting a theoretical example, it is important to emphasize that while liquidity is described as a combination of various factors influencing higher or lower prices across different asset classes, prices are not determined solely by liquidity. When isolating a 'liquidity' risk premium—defined as the additional premium demanded due to the relative difficulty of buying or selling an asset without impacting its value—it is not reasonable to compare yields across vastly different asset classes. The greater the difference in risk and return characteristics between assets, the more factors come into play, influencing trade volumes and complicating direct comparisons. Put simply, when comparing similar assets that are traded in different markets, such as private and public firms, or emerging and developed economies' equity, price differences are more likely to be driven by the difference in liquidity level between these markets.

The below table shows a theoretical example of how to extract the liquidity risk premium for private companies, which should follow the following steps:

Step 1: Take a sample of private companies that were recently acquired, and a sample of comparable public peers. It's important to highlight that peers should be similar here, at least in terms of industry, so that only the private vs. public characteristic remains as a differential.

Step 2: Calculate the cash flow yield implied by the acquisition price for each of these private transactions and calculate the cash flow yield of each of the public peers based on current market prices.

Step 3: Based on the assumptions presented in this chapter, the spread between the cash flow yield from private companies vs. similar public peers represents the liquidity premium. This spread reflects the liquidity risk premium that's embedded in private companies' valuation. Note that the P/E multiple is lower for private companies (Fig. 3).

R$mn	Market	Price paid	Earnings	Cash flow	P/E	Earnings yield	Cash flow yield
Private company A	Developed	300	46	35	6.5x	15.3%	11.7%
Private company B	Developed	400	55	50	7.3x	13.8%	12.5%
Private company C	Developed	600	80	70	7.5x	13.3%	11.7%
...	...	...	...	...	...	...	...
Median		**na**	**na**	**na**	**7.3x**	**13.8%**	**11.7%**

R$mn		Market Cap	Earnings	Cash flow	P/E	Earnings yield	Cash flow yield
Public company A	Developed	300	40	30	7.5x	13.3%	10.1%
Public company B	Developed	400	50	45	8.0x	12.5%	11.4%
Public company C	Developed	600	60	53	10.0x	10.0%	8.8%
...	...	...	...	...	...	...	...
Median		**na**	**na**	**na**	**8.0x**	**12.5%**	**10.1%**

Liquidity risk premium in developed private equity markets -> *1.5%*

R$mn	Market	Price paid	Earnings	Cash flow	P/E	Earnings yield	Cash flow yield
Private company A	Emerging market	275	46	35	6.0x	16.7%	12.7%
Private company B	Emerging market	375	55	50	6.8x	14.7%	13.3%
Private company C	Emerging market	575	80	70	7.2x	13.9%	12.2%
...	...	...	...	...	...	...	...
Median		**na**	**na**	**na**	**6.8x**	**14.7%**	**12.7%**

R$mn		Market Cap	Earnings	Cash flow	P/E	Earnings yield	Cash flow yield
Public company A	Emerging market	350	46	40	7.6x	13.1%	11.4%
Public company B	Emerging market	475	55	50	8.6x	11.6%	10.5%
Public company C	Emerging market	675	80	70	8.4x	11.9%	10.4%
...	...	...	...	...	...	...	...
Median		**na**	**na**	**na**	**8.4x**	**11.9%**	**10.5%**

Liquidity risk premium in emerging private equity markets -> *2.2%*

Fig. 3 Theoretical example on isolating the liquidity risk premium. *Source*: Author

In the second table above, a theoretical example illustrates how this method could be applied to extract the liquidity risk premium for private equity in emerging markets. It's important to note that the example is identical to that for developing economies. While it might be tempting to compare the hypothetical cash flow of 10.1% from the developed public equity markets with the 10.5% for emerging economies, assuming that the 0.4% spread reflects lower liquidity in emerging markets—this approach is not recommended.

The examples are intentionally identical to emphasize that assets must be very similar to isolate the risk premium directly and indirectly associated with lower liquidity environments. As discussed further below, including a practical example, whole economies are too dissimilar to justify price differentials solely based on liquidity, even within the same asset class. Factors such as cultural differences, tax structures, risk-free rates, and inflation expectations significantly influence asset risk, which cannot be attributed purely to liquidity.

As outlined in the background section, higher risks often deter investors, leading to lower liquidity for certain asset classes or markets. However, when comparing economies, additional complexities arise. Investors are rarely international, a challenge compounded by the home bias. Consequently, even relatively riskier economies can exhibit higher liquidity levels, complicating the extraction of liquidity premiums and impairing direct comparisons between economies.

This method proposes that the liquidity risk premium could then by applied to a build-up model, such as the CAPM, in order to value privately held firms for a specific industry (which is based on the peers' sample). While this sounds like a simple method for solving a complex issue, the author recognizes that it would be naïve to assume that is a practical solution considering the amount of information availability for private firms. Nonetheless, the exercise remains valid, and it can be an informative analytical framework when information availability allows.

It can't be emphasized enough that this method is highly reliant on its inputs, which means that in order to extract only the excess returns that are related specifically to liquidity, it's imperative that the samples contain similar companies. Note that it is implied that private companies should trade at lower multiples than public peers, which is more often than not, untrue. Start-ups are a good reminder that valuation of private firms often present much higher multiples than public peers. The issue again is related to the similarity between the private and public companies' samples. A start-up that's valued at several times its earnings could be understood as a firm with a robust future outlook, and thus having very unique cash flow expectations. Additionally, the unique nature of these companies creates a pool of potential investors, such as private equity funds, larger public companies, sovereign funds and so on. Therefore, the "liquidity" premium wouldn't be as high as it's for other more homogenic private firms.

While it may be tempting to apply the same framework and method to compare different equity markets, empirical data often diverges from theoretical expectations. For example, as shown below, the P/E ratio for the Mexican equity index, Mexbol, has been materially higher than Brazil's Ibovespa over the past ten years. Interestingly, Brazil is ranked as the fourth-largest fund industry in the world, according to IOSCO data, yet it trades at a significant discount to Mexico in terms of P/E. While many factors explain this discrepancy, liquidity is unlikely to be onc of them. The larger size of Brazil's market should, in theory, imply a lower liquidity premium compared to Mexico. This observation highlights the importance of comparing similar assets when analyzing liquidity premiums. Brazil's lower P/E ratio compared to Mexico, despite its greater market liquidity, reflects other factors, particularly opportunity cost. For instance, Brazil's much higher real interest rate creates a higher baseline for investor returns, meaning investors require a greater risk-free rate. This translates into a higher cost of equity and, consequently, a lower valuation multiple. One way to isolate the "excess risk-free rate" to better understand the liquidity premium is by adjusting for these factors. However, as noted earlier in the chapter, there is a significant risk of double-counting when attributing risks in such analyses (Fig. 4).

Conversely, the difference in P/E multiples between the U.S. equity market (e.g., S&P 500) and the global market (e.g., MSCI World Index) is largely attributable to liquidity differentials. Since both markets use the same risk-free rate (the U.-S. Treasury long-term yield), the primary driver of the cost of equity difference is

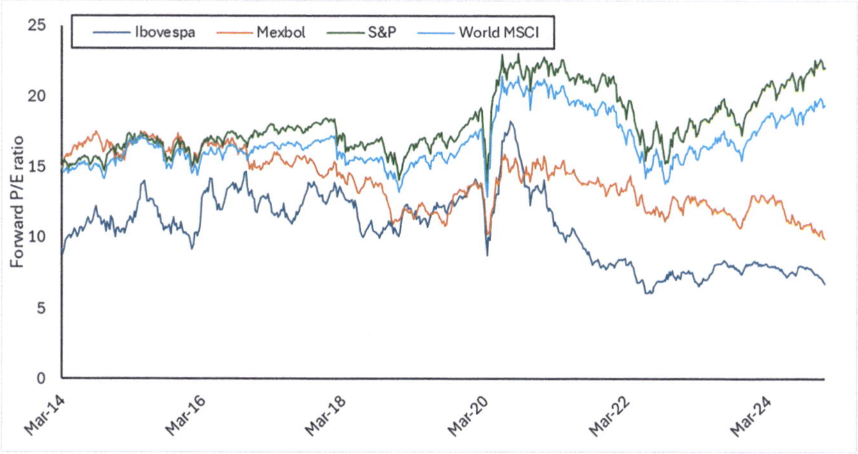

Fig. 4 Forward P/E ratios for Brazil, Mexico, USA, and World. *Source*: Bloomberg

in the "remaining risks", the equity risk premium (since the focus is on equity markets). Specifically, the U.S. equity risk premium is lower than the global equity risk premium, assuming, for the sake of simplicity, that expected growth rates are similar.

According to the analytical framework presented in this chapter, the world equity risk premium would apply to both markets. However, a liquidity risk discount (as opposed to a premium) would be applied to U.S. companies, reflecting their more liquid market environment. The average liquidity discount for U.S. markets during the period 2014–2024 was around 0.4%, although having recently increased above 0.6%, and are, thus, generally fairly stable.

Looking specifically at emerging markets, we summarize some of the main drivers of greater liquidity in these economies (Fig. 5).

Conclusion

As discussed in this chapter, liquidity, defined as the ease of transacting assets, varies significantly across markets. Different asset classes, such as fixed income and equities, or different geographies, like emerging and developed markets, exhibit varying levels of liquidity for several reasons. These differences ultimately influence the number of market participants, which is the primary driver of higher or lower liquidity.

Higher-risk assets or markets typically attract fewer investors due to risk aversion. This lower participation reduces liquidity, making it harder to find buyers or sellers, thereby increasing both transactional risk and the price impact of trades. Emerging markets, for example, are inherently riskier than developed markets due to factors

Driver of Reduced Liquidity in EMs	Summary	References & further reading
Market Depth & Trading Volume	In EMs, liquidity tends to be lower, due to smaller investor bases, more limited financial products and higher transaction costs. EMs also often face challenges around the availability, diversity, and pricing of capital. Moreover, trading technology, financial data and market-maker schemes also add additional challenges. In larger EMs, there may also be additional factors which reduce regional market development. Such market imperfections can also lead to higher broker costs and more price uncertainty.	Lesmond (2008), Bekaert et al. (2003)
Concentration of Ownership and Reduced Float Level	Share ownership is typically more concentrated within the vast majority of emerging markets. Generally, liquidity tends to be higher when the level of free float is greater, as the more shares available for trading can lead to enhanced price discovery. Institutional investors are particularly sensitive to free float levels as they require liquidity in order to efficiently move in and out of positions. Additionally, governments in emerging markets have a larger role in the economy and listed national 'champions', and institutional investors may avoid strongly government-owned shares due to concerns over political influence and corporate governance. For example, Banco do Brasil is quoted at a discount compared to its private-sector equivalents in Brazil due to such concerns over the perceived potential for political interference. Furthermore, in emerging markets, it is common for founding families or key shareholders to retain majority ownership even after an IPO, limiting the available market float. This can decrease stock liquidity, affect corporate governance, and affect valuation multiples.	IOSCO Emerging Markets Committee (2007)
Regulatory Framework & Investor Protection	Emerging markets can have weaker legal and regulatory frameworks, less investor protection and more challenging market access, all of which can impact on liquidity metrics.	Shleifer & Wolfenzon (2002), La Porta et al. (1998)

Fig. 5 Drivers of Liquidity in EMs

such as weaker institutions, less robust property rights, and heightened political risks. As a result, emerging markets attract fewer international investors, who often demand a premium to compensate for these risks. This premium reflects both the inherent risks and the relatively lower liquidity of these markets.

When valuing firms in less liquid markets—whether private versus public equities or emerging versus developed markets—it is reasonable to incorporate a liquidity premium. This premium reflects the relative difficulty in trading assets, driven by the lower number of market participants. As discussed in the chapter, this premium can be estimated by comparing assets with similar risk-return profiles but traded in different market environments. For private firms, the exercise is relatively straightforward since it is often possible to identify public peers, with price differentials primarily reflecting lower liquidity in private placements. However, for emerging markets, as demonstrated in the comparison between Brazil and Mexico, the analysis becomes more complex because finding comparable peers at the economy-wide level is challenging. In such cases, it is necessary to isolate other risk factors that contribute to price differentials.

One potential method to extract the liquidity premium in emerging equity markets (relative to developed ones, as liquidity is inherently a relative concept) is to compare the price differentials of the same company's stocks traded in two different markets. For example, the price of a Brazilian company's stock traded domestically can be compared with its American Depositary Receipts (ADRs) traded in the U.S. market. Since the U.S. market generally has more participants and higher liquidity, the ADR should trade at a premium to the local stock. The implied yield differential, based on metrics such as cash flow, dividends, or earnings, could then represent the liquidity premium for the stock traded in Brazil.

References

Amihud Y (2002) Illiquidity and stock returns: cross-section and time series effects. J Financ Mark:31–56

Amihud Y, Pedersen HM, Heje L (2005) Liquidity and asset prices. Financ Trends Finance:269–364

Bekaert G, Harvey CR, Lundblad C (2003) Liquidity and expected returns: lessons from emerging markets. Rev Financ Stud 16(3):659–704

Canadas JA, Ramirez AA (2011) The discount rate in valuing privately held companies. Bus Valuat Rev:70–81

CFA Institute (2019) CFA curriculum level I - equity and fixed income. John Wiley & Sons, Charlottesville

Chen J (2019, June 07). Investopedia. Retrieved from www.investopedia.com: https://www.investopedia.com/terms/l/liquidity_event.asp

Covrig V, McConaughy D (2014) Public versus private market participants and the prices paid for private companies. J Bus Valuat Econ Loss Anal:77–97

Damodaran A (2005) Marketability and value: measuring illiquidity discount. New York University - Stern School of Business, New York

Damodaran A (2006, December 05) New York University - Stern School of Business. Retrieved from New York University - Stern School of Business: http://people.stern.nyu.edu/adamodar/pdfiles/country/illiquidity.pdf

Emory JD (1981) A professional appraiser's approach to fair market valuation of closely-held securities. Estate Plan 8:228–232

IOSCO Emerging Markets Committee 2007. Factors influencing liquidity in emerging markets. International Organization of Securities Commissions (IOSCO). Available at: https://www.iosco.org [Accessed Jan 2025]

Koeplin J, Sarin A, Shapiro AC (2000) The private company discounts. J Appl Corp Finance:94–104

Koeplin J, Sarin A, Shapiro AC (2005) The private company discount. J Appl Corp Finance:94–101

La Porta R, Lopez-de-Silanes F, Shleifer A, Vishny RW (1998) Law and finance. J Polit Econ 106(6):1113–1155

Lesmond DA (2008) Liquidity of emerging markets. J Financ Econ 92(3):466–491

Market Research Methods (2020, March 03) Market Research Methods. Retrieved from https://www.mymarketresearchmethods.com/: https://www.mymarketresearchmethods.com/types-of-data-nominal-ordinal-interval-ratio/

Mercer CZ (2003) A primer on the quantitative marketability discount model. CPA J 73:66–68

Sheeler CL (2004) Empirical support for illiquidity discount levels: is it time for a new road map. Valuat Strat:26–47

Shleifer A, Wolfenzon D (2002) Investor protection and equity markets. J Financ Econ 66(1):3–27

Tabak D (2002) A CAPM-based approach to calculating illiquidity discounts. Marsh & McLennan Companies

Wrotenbery K (2013, December 30) Seeking Alpha. Retrieved from www.seekingalpha.com: https://seekingalpha.com/article/1921171-examining-the-size-premium

Estimating Liquidity Risk Pricing and Transaction Costs in the Valuation of Privately Held Capital Assets in Emerging Markets

Malcolm McLelland

Abstract This chapter presents an objective method of estimating the price of liquidity risk in private capital markets—commonly termed discount for lack of marketability ('DLOM')—in the context of estimating the value of privately held capital assets. The method is derived from basic financial economic theory, the intimate logical relationship between liquidity risk and private capital market transaction costs, historical practices of transaction broker-advisor practices, and empirical data on merger and acquisition transaction fees. Transaction cost functions representing estimates of the price of liquidity risk in private capital markets are estimated for both a highly developed market economy and an (arguably) emerging market economy. An example of applying the method in the context of estimating the value of a privately held capital asset in Brazil is presented and, finally, the method is compared briefly to existing, subjective DLOM estimation methods.

Keywords Privately held capital assets · Emerging markets · Valuation · Liquidity risk · Transaction costs

Introduction

The relationship between the price of liquidity risk—alternatively called a *liquidity risk premium*—and transaction costs is apparently not well understood in the corporate finance and valuation literature, but will be shown in this chapter to be intimately related; and this is especially true in private capital markets and emerging markets. In this connection, the objective of this chapter is to allow finance professionals to become familiar with this relationship in terms of basic financial economic theory, empirical evidence, and the development of a method for estimating fair market values of capital assets in emerging economy private market transactions. More specifically, the objective is to provide professionals with theory,

M. McLelland (✉)
McLelland Financial Economics LLC, Saint Petersburg, FL, USA
e-mail: mmc@mclelland-financial-economics.com

S. Derindere Köseoğlu, A. Patterson (eds.), *Valuation in Emerging Markets*, Contributions to Finance and Accounting,
https://doi.org/10.1007/978-3-031-93526-8_14

evidence, and methods for estimating the value of privately held capital assets in emerging markets in the presence of non-zero liquidity risk and transaction costs.

Background

Observable market prices do not represent fair market values. Careful analysis of modern asset pricing theory (e.g., arbitrage pricing theory, Ross 1976) implies that there is generally a difference between observable transaction prices and what is termed *fair market value* (*FMV*) in the valuation literature. Under the no-risk-arbitrage assumption inherent in such theory—most easily thought of as the *law of one risk price*—prices of risk across fair market venues must be equivalent, implying any difference between prices of capital assets across the market venues must be attributable to transaction costs:

$$\underbrace{TRANSACTION\ \ PRICE}_{\substack{\textbf{observable}\\ \text{transaction}\\ \text{price}}} = \underbrace{FMV}_{\substack{\textbf{unobservable}\\ \text{fair market}\\ \text{value}}} - \underbrace{TRANSACTION\ COSTS}_{\substack{\textbf{generally unobservable}\\ \text{transaction}\\ \text{costs}}}$$

The easiest way to understand this relationship in an intuitive way is to think of the extreme—though unrealistic—case where a certain *fair market*, as commonly defined, has zero transaction costs. In this special case, any capital asset not trading in this zero-transaction-cost market is potentially subject to a variety of transaction costs: brokerage commissions, advisory fees, legal fees, and so on. Observable prices in a *non*-zero-cost market would necessarily be net of any transaction costs because, logically, traders would only trade in the *non*-zero-cost market if they cannot access zero-cost market, for whatever reason.

At a more practical level, International Valuation Standards (promulgated by the International Valuation Standards Council) and other valuation standards generally state that FMV represents the hypothetical transaction price that would be observed in a fair market *before transaction costs*. The rationale presented in such standards is based on the idea that transaction costs are a function of the specific asset and transaction setting and, accordingly, represent something specific about the asset and transaction rather than about how assets are generally priced in fair markets.

Because FMV is not directly observable, the discussion suggests FMV must be estimated from observable data on capital market transaction prices and transaction costs. It is not immediately obvious, however, how transaction costs estimates can be developed.

Fair market value estimates require estimates of risk prices set in fair markets. Most finance professionals are familiar with the following expressions for the FMV of a capital asset and, relatedly, the risk-adjusted expected rate of return for an asset with expected future cash flows influenced by an arbitrary set of risk factors, $\mathbf{x} = (x_1, x_2, \ldots, x_K)$:

$$\underbrace{FMV_t(\mathbf{x}) = \sum_{u=t}^{T} \frac{CF_u(\mathbf{x})}{\left(1+\overline{R}(\mathbf{x})\right)^{u-t}}}_{\substack{\text{fair market value } (FMV) \text{ of a capital asset,} \\ \text{its expected future cash flows } (CF) \text{, and its} \\ \text{risk-adjusted expected rate of return } (\overline{R}) \text{ are} \\ \text{functions of } risk\,factors,\, \mathbf{x}=(x_1,x_2,\ldots,x_K)}} \leftrightarrow \begin{array}{c} \overline{R}(\mathbf{x}) = \lambda_0 + \beta_1\lambda_{x_1} + \beta_2\lambda_{x_2} + \ldots + \beta_K\lambda_{x_K} \\ = \lambda_0 + \left(\begin{array}{c} \underbrace{\beta_1\beta_2\ldots\beta_K} \\ \text{sensitivity of asset} \\ \text{to risk factors} \\ \mathbf{x}=(x_1,x_2,\ldots,x_K) \end{array}\right)\left(\begin{array}{c} \underbrace{\lambda_1\lambda_2\ldots\lambda_K} \\ \text{prices of risk factors} \\ \mathbf{x}=(x_1,x_2,\ldots,x_K) \\ \text{set in a } fair\ market \end{array}\right)' \end{array}$$

Familiarity with *risk factor premiums*—commonly called *risk factor prices* $(\lambda_1\lambda_2\ldots\lambda_K)$—is less common, although they can be easily understood as follows:

$$\lambda_k = \frac{1_k}{\rho_k} - 1 \approx \frac{\text{1 monetary unit of return to holding risk } k \text{ over 1 period}}{\text{implied current market price of holding 1 monetary unit of return to risk } k \text{ over 1 period}} - 1$$

For purposes of this chapter, it is important to recognize that when estimating FMV of a capital asset, it is necessary that such risk factors are estimated using data obtained from capital markets appropriately characterized as *fair markets*. Most finance professionals tend to think of the highly liquid capital markets in developed economies as meeting the definition of fair markets.

Liquidity is a risk priced in the capital markets. An interesting aspect of asset pricing theory and empirical asset pricing is that there seems little consensus on precisely how investors and traders estimate, price, hedge, and trade *liquidity risk*. One aspect of the problem is that liquidity risk is somewhat difficult to define rigorously, but will be defined for purposes of this chapter as follows:

> *Liquidity risk* is uncertainty over the extent to which buyers and sellers are willing and able to compete in a capital market to buy and sell assets sensitive to a particular risk or set of risks.

For example, liquidity risk with respect to maritime transportation equity securities might exist resulting from high levels of uncertainty over a lack of security in major maritime shipping routes. That is, investors might be unwilling to buy, or unable to sell, maritime transportation equities because of such uncertainties. So, such liquidity risk represents uncertainty over the conditions under which buyers provide liquidity to a capital market. Setting aside the complexities of risk factor interactions suggested by this discussion, it is reasonable to hypothesize that liquidity risks are priced in fair capital markets, for example,

$$\overline{R} = \lambda_0 + \beta_1\lambda_1 + \ldots + \underbrace{\beta_{LIQ}\lambda_{LIQ}}_{\substack{\text{liquidity}\\ \text{risk}}} + \underbrace{\beta_{MTR}\lambda_{MTR}}_{\substack{\text{maritime}\\ \text{transportation}\\ \text{risk}}} + \ldots + \beta_K\lambda_K$$

Importantly, it is possible (and common) to estimate and test hypothetical relationships about risk factor sensitivities and risk prices suggested by the above expression. In this chapter, it will be sufficient to simply assume that liquidity risk associated with the aggregated set of risks to which a particular capital asset is sensitive are priced in fair markets.

Private market transaction costs are the shadow price of liquidity risk. Finance professionals generally apply so-called *illiquidity and non-marketability discounts* to adjust valuation estimates for differences in transaction costs between public and private capital market transactions. Unfortunately, it is common to use subjective assumptions to determine such discounts, rather than developing explicit, objective estimates. Goodman and McLelland (2024) present theory implying that private capital market transaction costs essentially represent the *shadow price of liquidity risk* in private capital markets; that is, the price of liquidity risk if it were explicitly traded in such private markets. Private capital market transaction costs comprise brokerage commissions, transaction advisory fees, legal fees, accounting, and auditing fees, and such costs are incurred for the specific purpose of facilitating and executing such transactions. This means that *private capital market transaction costs are incurred for the explicit purpose of accessing liquidity.* In this connection, it is important to note that transaction cost differences also exist across countries and geographic regions for a variety of reasons and, accordingly, such differences should generally be incorporated into valuation estimates.

Private market transaction costs influence opportunity cost of capital. The valuation literature indicates that the appropriate risk-adjusted discount to use in estimating FMV represents an *opportunity cost of capital* (OCC). In general, there is a difference between the buyer's and seller's OCCs, and the difference results from transaction costs:

$$\underbrace{PRICE = FMV - TC}_{\substack{\text{observable transaction price}\\ \text{equals unobservable FMV}\\ \text{minus transaction costs}}} \quad \xrightarrow{\substack{\text{Capital asset with single}\\ \text{certainty-equivalent expected CF}\\ \text{of \$1 at } t+1 \text{ sold in the}}} \quad \underbrace{\underbrace{\frac{1^{CE}}{1+R^*}}_{\substack{\text{net price}\\ \text{received}\\ \text{by seller}\\ (P)}} = \underbrace{\frac{1^{CE}}{1+\overline{R}}}_{\substack{\text{gross}\\ \text{price paid}\\ \text{by buyer}\\ (FMV)}} \cdot \underbrace{(1-tc)}_{\substack{\text{transaction}\\ \text{cost}\\ \text{factor}}}}_{\substack{\text{Relationship between observable price}\\ \text{and unobservable FMV}}}$$

(presence of non-zero transaction costs that are proportional to FMV)

As discussed, private capital market transaction costs comprise a variety of costs including, but not limited to, the following:

Cost description	Cost explicitly incurred by
Brokerage commissions	Seller
Transaction advisory fees	Seller and buyer
Legal fees	Seller and buyer
Due diligence services fees	Buyer

While such costs are typically thought of in terms of which party—buyer or seller—explicitly makes the payments for each cost, it turns out that, in principle, it is the seller who essentially bears the costs by accepting (or not) the transaction price net of all-in transaction costs.

Buyer and seller opportunity costs of capital. In the context of private and emerging market transactions, it is best to regard buyer OCC ($\overline{R}$) as being determined by capital asset prices set in well-developed, competitive capital markets (e.g., US, UK, and EU markets), while seller OCC depends on both buyer OCC and private market transaction costs:

$$\underbrace{R^* = \frac{\overbrace{1+\overline{R}}^{\substack{\text{buyer OCC}\\ \text{estimated from}\\ \text{fair market data}}}}{\underbrace{1-tc(FMV)}_{\substack{\text{adjustment for}\\ \text{private market}\\ \text{transaction costs}}}}}_{\text{private market seller OCC}} - 1 \rightarrow FMV_t = \underbrace{\sum_{u=t}^{T} \frac{CF_u}{(1+R^*)^{u-t}}}_{\substack{\text{risky expected future}\\ \text{cash flow stream}\\ \text{discounted using}\\ \text{seller OCC}}}$$

The notation $tc(FMV)$ indicates that transaction costs as a proportion of the FMV depend on the FMV, as will be discussed further below. Interested readers are referred to Goodman and McLelland (2024) for a complete exposition of the theory, as well as a discussion of evidence supporting the theory.

Estimation Objective

The Lehman Formula

Experience suggests a large portion of private capital market transaction costs comprise brokerage commissions and transaction advisory services fees, which are often a decreasing, convex function of transaction price (where price is closely related to FMV as suggested by equations above). This characteristic of brokerage and advisory services fees apparently traces to what is called the *Lehman formula* used by Lehman Brothers in their investment banking business as a means for setting brokerage and advisory fees, which was then widely adopted and modified by other broker-advisors. The original formula was based on $1 million U.S. Dollar increments of transaction price, which has since been modified to be based on a generalized decreasing fee schedule that is most often negotiated with clients on a case-by-case basis:

$$\left.\begin{array}{l}5\%\text{for first }\$1\text{M of transaction price}\\4\%\text{for next }\$1\text{M of transaction price}\\3\%\text{for next }\$1\text{M of transaction price}\\2\%\text{for next }\$1\text{M of transaction price}\\1\%\text{for transaction price}>\$4\text{M}\end{array}\right\}\xrightarrow[\substack{\text{Lehman}\\ \text{formula}}]{\text{generalized}}\left\{\begin{array}{l}f_1\%\text{for first transaction price increment}\\f_2\%\text{for next transaction price increment}\\f_3\%\text{for next transaction price increment}\\\vdots\\f_I\%\text{for }I\text{th transaction price increment}\end{array}\right.$$

While informal surveys of investment bankers and merger and acquisition (M&A) advisors suggest that brokerage and advisory contracts are often not negotiated with reference to a decreasing fee schedule as suggested above, it is nonetheless an empirical fact that the fees pursuant to such contracts are consistent with the hypothesis that *brokerage and advisory services fees are a decreasing convex function of transaction price and value*. Accordingly, generalized Lehman formulas represent a reasonable basis for estimating (a portion of) private capital market transaction cost functions.

A Non-linear Approximation to the Lehman Formula

Consistent with the hypothesis that the largest portion of private market transaction costs are a decreasing, convex function of transaction price and value, the relationship between proportional transaction costs (TC) and transaction price (P) can be written using a natural logarithmic transformation of transaction price, ln(P):

$$\overbrace{TC/P}^{tc} = \delta_f - \delta_v \ln(P)\begin{cases}\delta_f : tc \text{ independent of } \ln(P)\\ \delta_v : \text{marginal effect of } \ln(P) \text{ on } tc\end{cases}$$

Figure 1 shows how this non-linear function approximates three versions of the Lehman Formula (*LF*):

$$\underbrace{\begin{aligned} LFpct_{200} &= .2793 - .0256\ \ln(P) \\ LFpct_{150} &= .2100 - .0193\ \ln(P) \\ LFpct_{100} &= .1398 - .0128\ \ln(P) \end{aligned}}_{\text{Logarithmic approximations to Lehman formula fee percentages}}$$

As seen in Fig. 1, the logarithmic function fits various Lehman formulas quite closely, again suggesting it adequately represents the contractual relationships between investment bankers or M&A advisors and their clients. Actual empirical evidence supporting this hypothesis is shown in the following section.

Estimation Method

Unbiased Estimation Theory

Obtaining unbiased estimates of the logarithmic approximation to a generalized Lehman formula, discussed above, requires consideration of the following conditional expectation function (CEF):

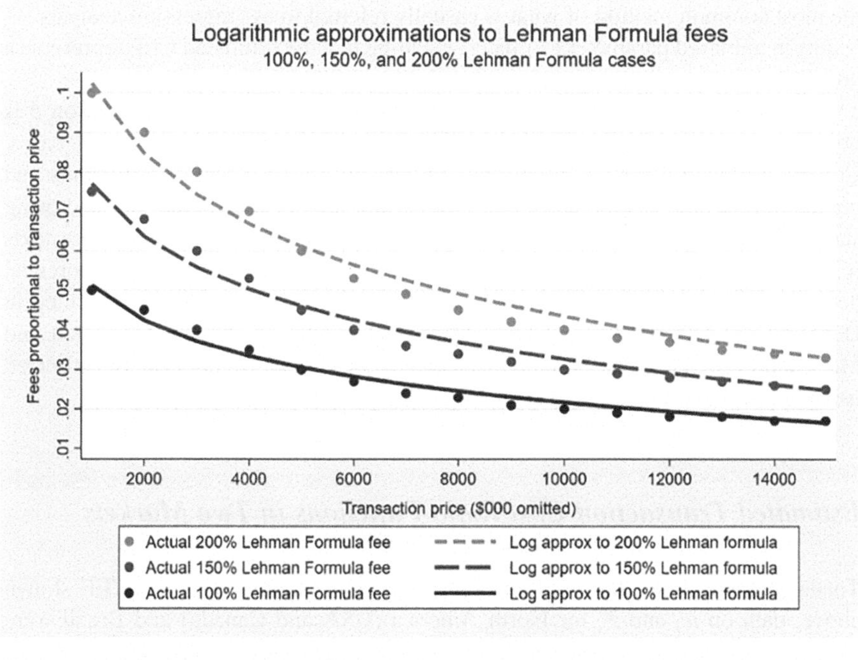

Fig. 1 Logarithmic approximations to Lehman Formula fees

$$\underbrace{\mathrm{E}(tc_i P_i) = \delta_f + \delta_v \ln(P_i) \quad i = 1, 2, \ldots, N}_{\substack{\textbf{conditional expectation function}: \\ \text{expectation of } TC_i/P_i \text{conditional on} P_i \text{with parameters} \\ \delta_f \text{and } \delta_v \text{in the population } i=1,2,\ldots,N}}$$

Multivariate statistical theory, specifically the *Gauss-Markov Theorem*, implies that unbiased estimates of the CEF parameters can be obtained from empirical data under the following conditions (cf. Wooldridge 2009, p. 57):

Condition 1—The CEF shown above is *linear in parameters* in the relevant population, implying the expectation of tc_i changes linearly across $\ln(P_i)$ in the population; that is, the relationship is linear in expectation.

Condition 2—A random sample of data on tc_i and P_i is obtained from the population for which Assumption 1 holds.

Condition 3—The random sample referred to in Assumption 2 includes observations for which there is variation in the independent variable, transaction price P_i.

Condition 4—Deviations between individual tc_i values and their conditional expectation do not depend on the value of the independent variable $\ln(P_i)$; that is, distance between tc_i and its conditional expectation is independent of the value of $\ln(P_i)$ or, equivalently, there are *no independent variables omitted from the conditional expectation function that are correlated with* $\ln(P_i)$.

If the conditions hold in the CEF and population, then *least squares estimation*—the most common method of what is casually referred to as "regression analysis"—results in unbiased parameter estimates, meaning that the estimated CEF represents a probability-weighted average of tc_i at each level of $\ln(P_i)$.

Because Condition 2 holds when data is collected properly and Condition 3 is observable after collecting data, these conditions generally hold in most cases. Conditions 1 and 4 tend to hold when underlying theory accurately explains and predicts real world relationships. Moreover, Conditions 1 and 4 can be tested using standard multivariate hypothesis testing methods discussed in econometrics texts (e.g., Wooldridge 2009). Accordingly, based on this discussion, and the theoretical development and empirical evidence consistent with the above CEF presented in Dohmeyer and Butler (2012), Dohmeyer et al. (2013, 2014) and Goodman and McLelland (2024), it can be concluded that the CEF can be unbiasedly estimated using appropriate data on tc_i and P_i.

Estimated Transaction Cost Ratio Functions in Two Markets

To demonstrate both the empirical properties and estimation of the CEF shown above, data on tc_i and P_i for North America (USA and Canada) and Brazil were obtained from the 2018–2019 update of an annual survey of M&A transaction fees

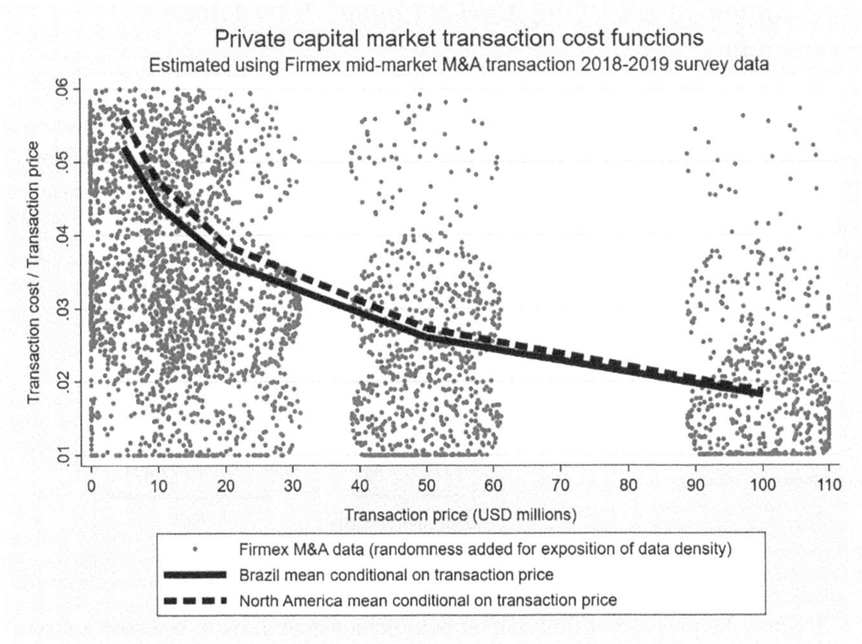

Fig. 2 Estimated private capital market transaction cost functions

conducted by Divestopedia and Firmex (2019). Using this data and the least squares estimation method, Fig. 2 presents the following graph constructed from the M&A transaction data and the CEFs estimated and tested for each of the two geographic regions:

$$\text{Estimated CEFs}: \underbrace{tc_i^{BR} = \underset{(<.001)}{.0703} - \underset{(<.001)}{.0113} \ln\left(P_i^{BR}\right)}_{\textbf{Brazil}: n=100,\, R^2 \cong .465} \quad \underbrace{tc_i^{NA} = \underset{(<.001)}{.0763} - \underset{(<.001)}{.0125} \ln\left(P_i^{NA}\right)}_{\textbf{North America}: n=1262,\, R^2 \cong .367}$$

The graph and estimated CEFs show that (i) the data are consistent with the hypothesis—derived from the generalized Lehman formula—that private capital market transaction costs are a decreasing, convex function of transaction price or value, and (ii) the parameters of the estimated CEFs are estimated reliably as demonstrated by the small p-values shown in parentheses below each parameter estimate.

It should be noted that the Divestopedia-Firmex survey data represents a combination of private market brokerage and transaction advisory fees only. So, to estimate the OCC for capital asset sellers in private market transactions, it is necessary to augment the CEF estimate(s) for other types of transaction costs as shown in the following example.

An Example of Emerging Market Capital Asset Value Estimation

An example from Brazil. To demonstrate how to apply the theory, method, and estimates presented above, consider now an example from a Brazilian mid-market transaction negotiated circa 2019 where an estimate of FMV of the sellers' business was used to advise the sellers on pricing and structuring the transaction. In this connection, as suggested in the background discussion above, the seller's OCC estimation objective can be stated in terms of the following expression:

$$R^* = \frac{1+\overline{R}}{1-tc(FMV)} - 1 = \frac{1+\overline{R}}{1-\left[\underbrace{OTC/FMV}_{\substack{\text{other transaction}\\ \text{cost ratio}}} + \underbrace{\delta_f - \delta_f \ln(FMV)}_{tc(FMV)}\right]} - 1$$

Because the purpose of this chapter is to demonstrate how to estimate a private capital market seller's OCC in the presence of transaction costs, how estimates of expected future cash flows of the sellers' business and the hypothetical buyer's OCC ($\overline{R}$) will not be shown. Rather such estimates will simply be substituted into the above expression, while the estimated transaction cost adjustment to obtain the sellers' OCC and FMV will be explicitly derived here.

Using previously estimated expected future cash flows (stated in millions of U.S. Dollars) and the estimated buyer's OCC associated with the sellers' business of 17.5%, shown in bold numerals, only the *transaction cost adjustment* remains to be estimated:

$$FMV_{t=0} = \sum_{t=1}^{t=5} \frac{\underbrace{(\mathbf{5.0}_{t=1}, \mathbf{7.5}_{t=2}, \mathbf{10.0}_{t=3}, \mathbf{12.5}_{t=4}, \mathbf{45.0}_{t=5})}_{CF_t}}{\left[\underbrace{\frac{1+\overbrace{\overline{R}}^{.175}}{1-\left(\underbrace{OTC/FMV_{t=0}}_{\substack{\text{non-}tc(FMV)\\ \text{transaction costs}}} + \underbrace{\delta_f - \delta_f \ln(FMV_{t=0})}_{tc(FMV)}\right)}}_{\text{transaction cost adjustment}}\right]^t}$$

Because FMV is estimated circa 2019 for a business to be sold through a private capital market transaction in Brazil, the estimated CEF shown in Fig. 2 for Brazil can be used as the estimate of *tc*(*FMV*). Further, based on discussions with management of the sellers' business regarding various legal, auditing, and other professional services associated with the expected sale, an estimate of \$400,000 (\$.400 million) of costs other than brokerage and advisory services was developed. Substituting such estimates into the FMV expression results in the following equation, which represents one non-linear equation with one unknown value; that is, the FMV of the sellers' business:

$$FMV_{t=0} = \underbrace{\sum_{t=1}^{t=5} \frac{\overbrace{(5.0_{t=1}, 7.5_{t=2}, 10.0_{t=3}, 12.5_{t=4}, 45.0_{t=5})}^{CF_t}}{\left[\frac{1+.175}{1-(.400/FMV_{t=0}+.0703-.0113\ln(FMV_{t=0}))}\right]^t}}_{\equiv PV(FMV_{t=0})}$$

This non-linear equation can be solved using numerical methods using standard quantitative spreadsheet software—for example, the Microsoft Excel *GoalSeek* function—based conceptually on the following expression:

$$\Delta FMV_{t=0} = FMV_{t=0} - PV(FMV_{t=0}) = 0$$

Specifically, the expressions immediately above are used to solve for FMV, as shown in Fig. 3, using a Microsoft Excel spreadsheet and the Excel *GoalSeek* function. The present value factor (*PVF*) formulas on Lines 12–16, the results of which are the present value factor values on Line 7, include the transaction cost adjustment, and all the numerical inputs are obtained from the expressions above:

The resulting FMV solution shown in Fig. 3 stated in the form of the discounted present value equation can be written as:

$$FMV_{t=0} = \sum_{t=1}^{t=5} \frac{CF_{it}}{\left\{\left(1+\underbrace{\overline{R}}_{.175}\right)\Big/\left[1-\left(\underbrace{OTC}_{.400}/\underbrace{FMV_{t=0}}_{36.404}+\underbrace{\delta_f}_{.0703}-\underbrace{\delta_v}_{.0113}\ln\underbrace{FMV_{t=0}}_{36.404}\right)\right]\right\}^t} \cong \mathbf{\$36.404\ M}$$

The resulting estimate of the seller's OCC, based on the estimated hypothetical buyer's OCC and estimated Brazilian private market transaction costs, can be written as:

	A	B	C	D	E	F	G
1	R_i =	**0.1750**					
2	*legal & prof* =	**0.4000**					
3	δ_f =	**0.0703**					
4	δ_v =	**0.0113**					
5	t =	**0**	**1**	**2**	**3**	**4**	**5**
6	CF_{it} =		**5.0**	**7.5**	**10.0**	**12.5**	**45.0**
7	PVF_t =		0.8165	0.6666	0.5442	0.4443	0.3628
8	$PV(FMV)$ =	36.404	4.082	4.999	5.442	5.554	16.326
9	$-FMV$ =	36.404					
10	ΔFMV =	0.000	<= set to zero by changing FMV cell (B9)				
11							
12	$PVF_{t=1}$ = ((1 + B1) / (1 - (B2/B9 + B3 - B4*ln(B9))))^-C5						
13	$PVF_{t=2}$ = ((1 + B1) / (1 - (B2/B9 + B3 - B4*ln(B9))))^-D5						
14	$PVF_{t=3}$ = ((1 + B1) / (1 - (B2/B9 + B3 - B4*ln(B9))))^-E5						
15	$PVF_{t=4}$ = ((1 + B1) / (1 - (B2/B9 + B3 - B4*ln(B9))))^-F5						
16	$PVF_{t=5}$ = ((1 + B1) / (1 - (B2/B9 + B3 - B4*ln(B9))))^-G5						

Fig. 3 Solving for FMV in the presence of transaction costs

$$R^* = \underbrace{\overbrace{\left(1+\underbrace{\bar{R}}_{.175}\right)}^{\text{estimated hypothetical buyer OCC}} \Big/ \left[1-\left(\underbrace{OTC}_{.400}/\underbrace{FMV_{t=0}}_{36.404}+\underbrace{\delta_f}_{.0703}-\underbrace{\delta_v}_{.0113}\ln\underbrace{FMV_{t=0}}_{36.404}\right)\right]-1}_{\text{estimated seller OCC}} \cong \mathbf{.2248(22.5\%)}$$

Importantly, estimates of the seller's OCC and the underlying transaction cost estimates are empirically based and, therefore, objective. The method requires only minimal subjective assumptions, which can however be—and, indeed, were—tested using statistical methods as shown in Fig. 2.

Standard valuation practice. It is helpful to consider how the method of estimating FMV presented above differs from standard valuation practice is most often based on (subjectively) assumed discounts for illiquidity and lack of marketability; usually referred to by the acronym DLOM for *discount for lack of marketability*. Most succinctly, standard valuation practice involves estimating FMV using public capital market data and then multiplying that by a DLOM factor to reduce it to an estimate of private market FMV:

$$\underbrace{FMV^{\text{private}}}_{\substack{\text{estimated } FMV \\ \text{in a private} \\ \text{market} \\ \text{transaction}}} = \underbrace{FMV^{\text{public}}}_{\substack{\text{estimated } FMV \\ \text{using public} \\ \text{market data}}} \cdot \left(\underbrace{1 - DLOM}_{\substack{\text{discount for} \\ \text{illiquidity} \\ \text{and lack of} \\ \text{marketability}}} \right)$$

While the expression makes intuitive sense to most finance professionals, understanding the deficiencies in the approach can perhaps be seen most clearly in the following quote addressing DLOM in Hitchner (2017, pp. 413–414):

> The privately held company experiences uncertainty not only of the time required for sale but also of the eventual sales price. Selling a business also requires transaction costs, relative to the size of the company, typically including preparation of due diligence, business valuation services, and accounting and legal costs. Furthermore, it is quite likely the sale will not transact for cash but will include some contingent earnout, deferred payments, or notes, assuming the buyer will not back out at the last minute.
>
> Proponents of a DLOM on controlling interests observe that the costs and risks of selling a controlling interest greatly exceed the cost of normal transfers of publicly held stock, which justifies a marketability discount. Hence, discounts for lack of marketability exist, even in the absence of empirical data.
>
> While many experts agree, in theory, on the need for a discount for lack of marketability/liquidity on controlling interests in a privately held company, no direct empirical evidence is available to support such a discount. The initial public offering and restricted stock studies used to develop discounts for lack of marketability are based on minority interests, not controlling interests.

This passage arguably illustrates a lack of rigor in addressing liquidity risk and marketability in estimating FMV in private capital markets: Liquidity risk and private market transaction costs are both conflated and aggregated into one apparently ill-defined concept termed DLOM for which, the passage asserts, there is no empirical evidence. The theory and method presented in this chapter does not suffer from these problems.

Conclusion

This brief chapter has presented theory and empirical evidence supporting the theory, that underlie a method for estimating private capital market transaction costs representing the shadow price of liquidity risk in the private capital markets; that is, the price of liquidity risk were it explicitly and observably traded in the private capital market. Such theory and evidence resolve a long-existing lack of clarity and objectivity with respect to estimating liquidity risk, transaction costs, and so-called lack of marketability discounts (DLOMs) in private capital markets. These matters are especially relevant to estimating the value of privately held capital assets in emerging markets because of the common—and often necessary—practice of estimating the prices of non-liquidity risk using capital market data obtained from highly liquid markets in highly developed economies: Liquidity risks must be estimated in the private markets in which the specific asset would sell, while other risks must be estimated in *fair markets*. Perhaps, most importantly, the theory and method presented in this chapter clearly show how more objective estimates of the fair market value of privately held capital assets can be developed in emerging markets. Such objectivity and the transparency it implies are particularly important in emerging markets where trust between counterparties is often a deciding factor in the success of private capital market transactions.

References

Divestopedia & Firmex (2019) M&A fee guide 2018-2019. Firmex, Toronto, Ontario (CA)

Dohmeyer R, Butler P (2012) The implied private company pricing line. Bus Valuat Rev 31(1): 35–47

Dohmeyer R, Burkert R, Butler P (2013) The implied private company pricing line 2.0: K0 = (FCFF1 / P) + g. Bus Valuat Update 19(9):1–9

Dohmeyer R, Burkert R, Butler P (2014) The implied private company pricing model: K0 = (FCFF1 / P) + g. Bus Valuat Update 20(3):1–11

Goodman, D., & McLelland, M. (2024). Understanding IPCPL Theory, Evidence, and Application. Retrieved from https://quickreadbuzz.com/2024/07/10/business-valuation-goodman-mclelland-understanding-ipcpl-theory-evidence-and-application-2/

Hitchner J (2017) Financial valuation: applications and models, 4th edn. Wiley, Hoboken

Ross S (1976) The arbitrage theory of capital asset pricing. J Econ Theory 13:341–360

Wooldridge J (2009) Introductory econometrics, 4th edn. South Western, Mason

Technology and Financial Innovation in Emerging Markets: Impacts on Value Creation

Anna Sung

Abstract This chapter examines the transformative impact of technology and financial innovation on value creation in emerging markets. It outlines the evolution of financial technology ("FinTech") through phases marked by advancements such as ATMs, blockchain, and mobile payments, showcasing their role in enhancing efficiency, security, and accessibility. The discussion highlights how FinTech addresses financial inclusion challenges in emerging markets through AI, mobile payments, lending, and green finance, with examples like Kenya's M-Pesa and India's AI-driven agriculture platforms. It also addresses barriers such as regulatory challenges and digital literacy gaps while exploring future trends like decentralized finance and quantum computing. The chapter emphasizes FinTech's critical role in fostering economic growth, improving financial inclusion, and reshaping industries in developing economies, positioning it as a key driver of sustainable development and innovation.

Keywords Financial technology · FinTech · Financial inclusion · Blockchain · Mobile payments · Sustainable development · Economic value

Technology and Financial Technology

Nowadays, technology is often associated with digital advancements, it is not necessarily limited to them. In history, technology has influenced the business world for centuries, even in its earliest forms. The invention of writing and record-keeping around 3000 BCE can certainly be considered a technological advancement. The development of writing systems in Mesopotamia (cuneiform) and Egypt (hieroglyphs) revolutionized trade by enabling accurate record-keeping. This innovation allowed merchants to track debts, contracts, and transactions, reducing disputes and improving economic organization.

A. Sung (✉)
University of Chester, Chester, UK
e-mail: a.sung@chester.ac.uk

S. Derindere Köseoğlu, A. Patterson (eds.), *Valuation in Emerging Markets*, Contributions to Finance and Accounting,
https://doi.org/10.1007/978-3-031-93526-8_15

As per Leong and Sung (2018), the development of Financial Technology has progressed through distinct phases, each shaped by key technological advancements. The first phase, known as FinTech 1.0 (1866–1987), marked the earliest adoption of technology in financial services. A significant event during this period was the installation of the Trans-Atlantic telegraph cable in 1866, which greatly reduced communication time between North America and Europe from ten days to just 17 hours. This breakthrough facilitated the global exchange of financial information, improving international trade and banking. Later, in the 1970s, mainframe computers played a crucial role in automating financial transactions, further enhancing efficiency in financial institutions. In 1973, the establishment of the Society for Worldwide Interbank Financial Telecommunications (SWIFT) introduced a secure and standardized messaging system for international banking transactions. Another major milestone was the introduction of Automated Teller Machines (ATMs) in 1967, with Barclays Bank in London being the first to install an ATM, making banking services more accessible and convenient for customers.

The second phase, FinTech 2.0 (1987–2008), witnessed the digital transformation of financial services, driven by the rise of the internet and advancements in computing. The 1990s saw the emergence of online banking, allowing customers to access their accounts remotely, perform transactions, and pay bills online. This innovation significantly reduced operational costs for banks while enhancing accessibility for users. The early 2000s marked the rapid growth of e-commerce and digital payment platforms, with companies like PayPal pioneering secure online transactions. The widespread use of credit and debit cards further accelerated the transition from cash-based to electronic payments. Additionally, the increasing interconnectivity of devices, known as the Internet of Things (IoT), played a role in enhancing financial data tracking, improving transaction processing, and strengthening fraud detection mechanisms.

The third phase, FinTech 3.0 (2008–present), was catalysed by the global financial crisis of 2008, which led to the rise of FinTech start-ups and the development of alternative financial solutions. A defining moment of this period was the launch of Bitcoin in 2009, introducing blockchain technology as a decentralized and secure system for financial transactions. Cryptocurrencies challenged the traditional financial system by eliminating intermediaries and offering greater transparency. Artificial Intelligence (AI) and Big Data analytics also became prominent during this phase, leading to the rise of robo-advisors that provide automated financial planning and investment management. AI-powered systems improved fraud detection and risk management, enhancing the overall efficiency of financial institutions. The widespread adoption of mobile payment solutions such as Apple Pay, Google Wallet, and WeChat Pay further advanced the shift towards a cashless society, enabling seamless transactions. Another crucial development during this period was the growth of Regulatory Technology ("RegTech"), which leveraged AI and automation to help financial institutions comply with regulations efficiently, reducing compliance costs and strengthening security measures.

With reference to each of these phases, a key driver of FinTech's progress is technological advancements, which have continuously enhanced the efficiency, security, and accessibility of financial services.

How FinTech Creates Business Value

FinTech has revolutionized the way businesses operate by integrating financial services with modern technological advancements. As businesses increasingly adopt digital financial solutions, the role of FinTech in creating business value has become more significant. For instance, digital payment platforms, such as PayPal, have enabled businesses to accept payments seamlessly from customers worldwide, reducing transaction friction and enhancing customer experience. Similarly, blockchain-based solutions like smart contracts and decentralized finance (DeFi) applications have transformed transactions by increasing transparency, reducing fraud, and eliminating intermediaries. Moreover, artificial intelligence (AI)-powered financial analytics tools help businesses gain valuable insights into spending patterns, risk management, and financial forecasting. Companies offer AI-driven expense management platforms that automate budgeting and spending controls, leading to better financial decision-making. Additionally, the rise of robo-advisors has also revolutionized investment management for businesses and individuals by offering automated, algorithm-driven financial planning services at lower costs.

In fact, financial innovation is often closely linked to value creation. For example, Square (now Block) acquired Afterpay, a leading "Buy Now, Pay Later" (BNPL) provider, for $29 billion. This acquisition enabled Square to integrate BNPL into its ecosystem, enhancing its services for both merchants and consumers. The deal demonstrated how FinTech innovation can generate higher valuation multiples by expanding revenue streams and capturing market share in the rapidly growing digital payments sector. Similarly, Morgan Stanley acquired E*TRADE, a digital brokerage platform, for $13 billion. This allowed Morgan Stanley to leverage E*TRADE's digital-first customer base and advanced trading tools, adding value by strengthening its wealth management services and achieving greater scalability. Another notable example is UBS's acquisition of Wealthfront for $1.4 billion. By integrating Wealthfront's digital wealth management platform, UBS enhanced its offerings to appeal to younger, tech-savvy investors. This move highlighted how FinTech innovation can add value to traditional financial services by improving operational efficiency and broadening customer reach.

FinTech and Emerging Markets

As FinTech continues to revolutionize businesses by integrating financial services with modern technology, its impact is becoming increasingly significant in emerging markets. These regions, characterized by rapid digital adoption and financial inclusion challenges, are now at the forefront of FinTech innovation. With traditional banking infrastructure unable to serve vast populations effectively, technology-driven financial solutions are stepping in to bridge the gap and redefine economic landscapes.

In fact, emerging markets present an enormous opportunity for FinTech innovation due to their large, underbanked populations, rapid smartphone penetration, and increasing internet connectivity. Countries in regions such as Latin America, Africa, and Southeast Asia are witnessing a surge in digital financial adoption, driven by the need for inclusive financial solutions.

How FinTech Impacts Financial Services in Emerging Markets

FinTech is transforming financial services in emerging markets in various ways. Below are some notable ways in which FinTech is driving change in these regions.

AI in Emerging Markets

Artificial Intelligence (AI) is changing industries and economies worldwide. It is also becoming important in emerging markets, which include parts of Asia, Africa, Latin America, and Eastern Europe.

AI is important in emerging markets because it helps solve problems and improve efficiency. Many of these countries have limited resources and old systems that slow down progress. AI-powered tools can make processes faster, reduce costs, and improve decision-making. For example, AI can help farmers predict weather and soil conditions, leading to better crop production. In finance, AI makes banking easier for people who do not have access to traditional banks by offering mobile banking and digital payments.

AI can also help emerging markets grow by creating jobs, supporting new businesses, and making industries more competitive. In manufacturing, AI-powered machines help increase production and reduce waste. In banking, AI detects fraud, improves risk assessment, and provides customer support through chatbots. In healthcare, AI helps doctors diagnose diseases and provide remote medical services. All these benefits help strengthen economies and make them more competitive in the global market.

What Is Driving AI Growth in Emerging Markets?

Many factors are pushing AI growth in emerging markets. One big reason is technology leapfrogging, which means skipping old technologies and directly using the latest ones. A good example is mobile banking in Africa, where many people use digital payments instead of traditional banking. Another reason is that cloud computing makes AI tools affordable and easy to use. Disruptive innovation is also important because it creates new business models to solve local problems. Many governments in these markets are supporting AI by making policies and funding technology projects. The increasing availability of Big Data also helps businesses make better decisions using AI.

Real-World Example: AI in Indian Agriculture

A good example of AI's impact in emerging markets is its role in Indian agriculture. Farming in India faces many problems, such as unpredictable weather and outdated methods. AI is helping farmers by providing real-time weather updates, soil analysis, and crop health reports. Companies like Microsoft and Indian start-ups are using AI to give farmers advice on when to plant and harvest crops (Microsoft 2017). AI is also improving supply chains by connecting farmers with buyers, reducing waste, and ensuring fair prices. This use of AI is helping farmers earn more and improve food production in the country.

Challenges of AI in Emerging Markets

Despite its benefits, AI adoption in emerging markets has many challenges. One major issue is the lack of internet access and electricity in remote areas, making it difficult to use AI. Another challenge is the shortage of skilled AI professionals, as many countries do not have enough AI experts. Small businesses struggle to afford AI technology and do not always understand its benefits. Ethical concerns, such as data privacy and AI bias, also need attention. In addition, unclear government policies in some countries make it hard for companies to invest in AI.

Future Trends of AI in Emerging Markets

As mentioned above, the future of AI in emerging markets looks bright. More small- and medium-sized businesses in emerging markets can use AI to compete with larger companies. AI in finance will expand as well, helping more people access banking and credit. As AI continues to grow, ethical AI development, such as its potential gender bias (Leong and Sung 2024), will be a key challenge.

Mobile Payment in Emerging Markets

Mobile payment is becoming a major part of financial transactions in emerging markets. These regions have seen rapid growth in digital payment systems. Traditionally, many people in these markets do not have access to traditional banks, making mobile payment an important tool for financial inclusion. With the rise of smartphones and internet access, mobile payment provides financial services to people who do not have access to banks. Many people in these regions rely on cash transactions, which can be unsafe and inconvenient. Mobile payment allows users to store money digitally and make transactions using their phones. This system is useful for small businesses, farmers, and workers who receive wages.

Mobile payment also makes it easier for governments to distribute financial aid and subsidies. The ability to make quick and secure payments helps improve the overall economy and encourages digital transformation. Furthermore, many small businesses and street vendors in these markets now accept mobile payments, which helps them attract more customers. Digital payment systems also reduce the costs associated with handling cash and improve record-keeping. In rural areas, farmers can receive payments directly through their phones, reducing the risk of fraud and delays. Mobile payment also enables cross-border transactions, allowing businesses to expand beyond their local markets. As more people adopt mobile payment, economies become stronger and more connected to the global financial system.

What Is Driving Mobile Payment Growth in Emerging Markets?

Several factors are driving the growth of mobile payment in emerging markets. One of the main reasons is the high penetration of mobile phones. Even in remote areas, many people own mobile phones, making digital payments accessible. Another important factor is the lack of traditional banking infrastructure. Since many people do not have bank accounts, mobile payment provides an alternative way to save and transfer money. Governments and financial institutions are also promoting digital payments by offering incentives and creating regulations that support mobile transactions. Additionally, FinTech companies are developing new mobile payment solutions that are affordable and easy to use. These factors together are making mobile payment a popular choice in emerging economies.

Real-World Example: Mobile Payment Success in Kenya

A famous example of mobile payment success in an emerging market is M-Pesa in Kenya (Stadler 2024). M-Pesa, launched by Safaricom, allows users to store money, send payments, and pay bills using their mobile phones. Since its introduction, M-Pesa has transformed the way people in Kenya handle money. Many people, especially those in rural areas, do not have access to banks, but they can use M-Pesa for daily transactions. The service has also helped small businesses grow by providing a secure and convenient payment option. M-Pesa's success has inspired similar mobile payment systems in other countries, proving that mobile payment can be a powerful tool for economic development.

Challenges of Mobile Payment in Emerging Markets

Despite its many benefits, mobile payment faces challenges in emerging markets. One major issue is the lack of reliable internet and mobile network coverage in some areas. Without proper connectivity, it becomes difficult for people to use digital payment services. Another challenge is cybersecurity. As mobile payment grows, so does the risk of fraud and hacking. Many users also struggle with a lack of digital literacy, making it harder for them to adopt and trust mobile payment systems. Regulatory challenges can also slow down the growth of mobile payment. In some countries, financial policies are not clear or do not support digital payment solutions.

Future Trends of Mobile Payment in Emerging Markets

One major trend of mobile payment in emerging markets is the increased use of mobile wallets, where users can store money digitally and make transactions easily. More businesses and governments are expected to adopt mobile payment solutions, making digital transactions more common. The rise of artificial intelligence and blockchain technology will also improve the security and efficiency of mobile payments. Biometric authentication, such as fingerprint and facial recognition, will make mobile payments more secure and convenient. Additionally, partnerships between telecom companies, banks, and FinTech start-ups will help expand mobile payment services to more people. As technology continues to evolve, mobile payment will play an even bigger role in the financial landscape of emerging markets.

Lending and Microfinance in Emerging Markets

Like mobile payments, lending and microfinance play a crucial role in emerging markets by providing financial services to individuals and small businesses that do not have access to traditional banks. In many parts of emerging markets, formal banking systems are either too expensive or difficult to reach. Microfinance institutions and alternative lending services help bridge this gap by offering small loans, credit facilities, and financial support to low-income individuals, farmers, and entrepreneurs. These financial solutions help boost economic development, reduce poverty, and encourage entrepreneurship through improving financial inclusion for millions of people who lack access to banking services. For example, a previous study (Abebe and Kegne 2023) had discussed how microfinance plays a key role in empowering women by providing them with financial opportunities to start and grow businesses, ultimately strengthening communities and improving living conditions.

What Is Driving the Growth of Lending and Microfinance in Emerging Markets?

Several factors are driving the growth of lending and microfinance in emerging markets. One key factor is the high demand for financial services among underserved populations. Millions of people in these markets lack access to formal banking, creating a strong need for alternative financial solutions. Technological advancements, such as mobile banking and digital lending platforms, are also helping expand microfinance services. Many people now can use mobile devices to access financial services, making it easier to apply for and receive loans. Additionally, impact investors and social enterprises are investing in microfinance institutions to promote financial inclusion and economic development.

Real-World Example: Microfinance Success in Bangladesh

A well-known example of microfinance success in an emerging market is the Grameen Bank in Bangladesh (https://grameenbank.org.bd/). Founded by Professor Muhammad Yunus, a Nobel Peace Prize winner, Grameen Bank provides small loans to poor individuals, especially women, to help them start businesses and improve their lives. The bank follows a group lending model, where borrowers form small groups to support each other in loan repayment. This approach has led to high repayment rates and positive social impact. Over the years, Grameen Bank has helped millions of people escape poverty by providing them with access to credit and financial literacy programs. The success of Grameen Bank has inspired similar microfinance initiatives in other countries, demonstrating the power of lending and financial inclusion in driving economic growth.

Challenges of Lending and Microfinance in Emerging Markets

Despite its benefits, lending and microfinance face several challenges in emerging markets. One major issue is the high cost of lending. Microfinance institutions often struggle with high operational costs, making it difficult to offer affordable loans. Interest rates can sometimes be high, leading to concerns about debt burdens on borrowers. Another challenge is the risk of loan defaults. Many borrowers lack stable income sources, making it difficult for them to repay loans on time. Fraud and lack of transparency in some microfinance institutions also create trust issues. Additionally, regulatory challenges and inconsistent government policies can limit the growth of microfinance services. Addressing these challenges requires improved financial education, better risk assessment tools, and stronger regulatory frameworks to protect both lenders and borrowers.

Future Trends of Lending and Microfinance in Emerging Markets

A future trend of lending and microfinance in emerging markets is the rise of digital lending platforms, which use technology to provide fast and easy access to credit. Mobile banking and FinTech solutions are expected to play a bigger role in expanding financial services to underserved populations. Another trend is the growth of peer-to-peer (P2P) lending, where individuals and small businesses can borrow directly from investors through online platforms. As financial technologies continue to evolve, lending and microfinance will become more accessible, efficient, and impactful in emerging markets.

Agri-FinTech in Emerging Markets

Agri-FinTech is transforming agriculture in emerging markets by providing financial solutions tailored to farmers and agribusinesses. Many rural areas have limited banking infrastructure, making it difficult for farmers to get loans or manage their finances. Agri-FinTech platforms offer digital financial services, allowing farmers to access credit, make payments, and buy farming supplies using mobile phones. These financial tools help farmers improve productivity, reduce risks, and increase their income. As agriculture is a major contributor to the economy in many emerging markets, improving financial access for farmers leads to overall economic development and food security.

What Is Driving the Growth of Agri-FinTech in Emerging Markets?

Several factors are driving the growth of Agri-FinTech in emerging markets. One of the reasons, amongst others, is that traditional banks often view farming as a high-risk sector, making it difficult for farmers to obtain loans. Agri-FinTech solutions use data analytics and artificial intelligence to assess creditworthiness and offer customized financial products. Government support and policies promoting digital finance and agricultural innovation also contribute to the growth of Agri-FinTech. Additionally, investment from FinTech companies and venture capitalists is helping expand Agri-FinTech services in emerging markets.

Real-World Example: Agri-FinTech Success

A notable example of Agri-FinTech in an emerging market is Ant Group's "Zhima Credit" (Sesame Credit) and MyBank's Rural Finance Initiative in China. Smallholder farmers in China often struggle to access traditional bank loans due to a lack of credit history and collateral. To address this, MyBank, a digital bank under the Ant Financial Services Group (Alibaba's FinTech arm), leverages Big Data and AI technology to assess farmers' creditworthiness and provide instant microloans. In addition, MyBank also used remote sensing technologies on farmlands, based on factors such as crop growth and variety to access risks and make decisions on credit extension (The Ant Group 2022).

Through Zhima Credit (Sesame Credit), a digital credit scoring system linked to Alipay's transaction data, MyBank evaluates farmers' financial behaviour and agricultural activity to approve loans instantly—loan application to be processed in 3 minutes with 1 second money transferal and without human interaction (3-1-0 model). This process eliminates paperwork and speeds up funding, making credit more accessible (IFC 2020). Additionally, MyBank partners with Taobao and other e-commerce platforms to help farmers sell their produce directly to consumers, boosting their income (Liu 2016). The success of MyBank's initiative shows how Agri-FinTech can improve financial access, support rural development, and help farmers grow their businesses in digital economy.

Challenges of Agri-FinTech in Emerging Markets

Despite its benefits, Agri-FinTech faces several challenges in emerging markets. For example, many smallholder farmers are not familiar with using mobile apps and digital financial tools, making it difficult for them to adopt Agri-FinTech solutions. Another challenge is unreliable internet and mobile network connectivity in rural areas, which limits access to digital financial services. Additionally, trust issues and resistance to new financial technologies can slow down adoption among farmers. Regulatory challenges also pose a barrier to the growth of Agri-FinTech. In some emerging markets, financial regulations do not fully support digital lending and FinTech solutions, creating uncertainty for Agri-FinTech companies. Furthermore, financial risks such as loan defaults and market volatility can impact the sustainability of Agri-FinTech platforms.

Future Trends of Agri-FinTech in Emerging Markets

Several key trends shaping the future of Agri-FinTech in emerging. The use of blockchain technology is expected to increase, improving transparency and security in agricultural transactions. More Agri-FinTech start-ups are focusing on integrating artificial intelligence and Big Data analytics to assess credit risks and provide customized financial solutions to farmers.

Another important trend is the rise of agricultural insurance solutions. More Agri-FinTech platforms are offering micro-insurance products to protect farmers from losses due to climate change and natural disasters. Looking ahead, the growth of Agri-FinTech plays an important role in sustainable agriculture and economic growth in emerging markets.

Green and Sustainable FinTech in Emerging Markets

Green and sustainable FinTech is playing an essential role in emerging markets by promoting financial solutions that support environmental sustainability and economic growth. These financial technologies focus on reducing carbon footprints, promoting green investments, and improving financial inclusion. Many emerging markets face challenges related to climate change, deforestation, and pollution, making sustainable FinTech solutions even more important. By integrating digital finance with sustainability initiatives, green FinTech is helping businesses and individuals adopt eco-friendly practices.

In fact, many developing countries are vulnerable to environmental risks such as droughts, floods, and air pollution. Green FinTech solutions, such as carbon credit trading platforms, digital green bonds, and climate risk assessment tools, help businesses and individuals transition to more sustainable practices. FinTech also plays a key role in financing renewable energy projects, promoting eco-friendly agriculture, and supporting circular economies.

What Is Driving the Growth of Green and Sustainable FinTech in Emerging Markets?

The increasing awareness of climate change and environmental risks is one of the key factors that drive the growth of green and sustainable FinTech in emerging markets. Governments, businesses, and individuals are recognizing the importance of sustainability and are seeking financial solutions that align with environmental goals. Another driver is technological advancements, such as blockchain, artificial intelligence, and mobile banking, which are making green finance more accessible and efficient. Additionally, global investors are prioritizing sustainable finance, providing capital to FinTech start-ups that focus on environmental impact.

Real-World Example: Green FinTech Success in South Africa

A remarkable example of green FinTech in an emerging market is the case of Sun Exchange in South Africa (https://sunexchange.com). Sun Exchange is a blockchain-based platform that allows individuals to invest in solar energy projects.

The platform enables people from around the world to buy solar cells, which are then leased to schools, businesses, and communities in need of clean energy. In return, investors earn passive income from the electricity generated by these solar panels. This model not only promotes renewable energy adoption but also provides financial inclusion by allowing small-scale investors to participate in the green economy.

Sun Exchange has successfully implemented solar projects in schools, hospitals, and businesses across South Africa, reducing reliance on fossil fuels and lowering electricity costs. By combing FinTech with sustainability, Sun Exchange has demonstrated how digital finance can drive positive environmental impact while creating economic opportunities. The success of Sun Exchange highlights the potential of green FinTech in transforming energy access and financial inclusion in emerging markets.

Challenges of Green and Sustainable FinTech in Emerging Markets

One major challenge of green FinTech is the lack of awareness and education about sustainable finance. Many individuals are unfamiliar with green FinTech solutions and how they can benefit from them. Another challenge is regulatory uncertainty, as financial policies related to sustainability are still evolving in many emerging markets. Limited access to technology and digital infrastructure also hinders the adoption of green FinTech, particularly in rural areas. Funding and investment risks present additional challenges. Green FinTech start-ups require capital to develop innovative solutions, however, they often *struggle to attract long-term investors due to concerns about financial returns.*

Future Trends of Green and Sustainable FinTech in Emerging Markets

Green and sustainable FinTech is transforming emerging markets by integrating financial innovation with environmental responsibility. One major trend is the rise of digital green bonds and sustainability-linked loans, allowing businesses to raise capital for environmental projects. The use of blockchain technology is also expected to increase, ensuring transparency and accountability in green investments. Another key trend is the expansion of mobile-based carbon offset platforms, enabling individuals and businesses to track and reduce their carbon footprints.

Artificial intelligence and Big Data will play a significant role in assessing climate risks and providing financial solutions tailored to sustainability goals.

Digital Currencies in Emerging Markets

Digital currencies, including cryptocurrencies and central bank digital currencies (CBDCs), enable faster cross-border transactions and financial inclusion. Digital currencies and FinTech are essential in emerging markets because they provide financial services to underserved populations. Many individuals and businesses struggle to access banking services due to high costs and geographic barriers. Digital currencies help bridge this gap by offering low-cost and borderless financial transactions. Additionally, governments and central banks in emerging markets are exploring the adoption of CBDCs to enhance monetary stability and streamline digital payments. The increased adoption of digital currencies and FinTech solutions is driving innovation, attracting investments, and fostering economic development.

What Is Driving the Growth of Digital Currencies in Emerging Markets?

The growth of digital currencies in emerging markets is driven by a combination of government policies, economic instability, and blockchain technology. Many governments are actively promoting FinTech adoption to modernize financial systems and increase financial inclusion. Countries like China, Nigeria, and India have taken proactive steps by introducing central bank digital currencies (CBDCs) to facilitate faster and more efficient transactions. China's Digital Yuan (e-CNY) is a leading example, designed to provide a state-backed alternative to private cryptocurrencies while ensuring regulatory oversight. These initiatives help expand financial access, reduce reliance on cash, and create a more secure and transparent financial ecosystem.

From the economic instability and inflation perspective, in countries like Argentina, Venezuela, and Turkey, where national currencies have faced extreme devaluation, people increasingly rely on cryptocurrencies and stablecoins such as Bitcoin (BTC) and Tether (USDT) to preserve their wealth. Unlike traditional banks, which often impose withdrawal limits and exchange rate controls, cryptocurrencies provide a decentralized and borderless financial alternative. Many small businesses and freelancers in emerging markets also use stablecoins for cross-border transactions and remittances, reducing transaction fees and bypassing banking restrictions.

Furthermore, the rise of blockchain technology and decentralized finance (DeFi) is also reshaping financial services in emerging economies. DeFi platforms offer lending, borrowing, and payment solutions without the need for traditional banks, increasing financial accessibility. Blockchain-based solutions ensure greater transparency, security, and efficiency, particularly in industries like microfinance, trade finance, and remittances.

Real-World Example: Digital Currency Success in China

A significant example of digital currency adoption in an emerging market is the case of China's digital yuan (e-CNY) (Huang 2024). The Chinese government has developed a central bank digital currency (CBDC) to enhance financial inclusion and improve transaction efficiency. The digital yuan is designed to complement cash payments and reduce reliance on private digital payment platforms such as Alipay and WeChat Pay. The government has conducted pilot programs in several cities, allowing residents to use the digital yuan for everyday transactions, including shopping, transportation, and utility payments. China's experience serves as a model for other countries considering the implementation of central bank digital currencies.

Challenges of Digital Currencies and FinTech in Emerging Markets

One major challenge is regulatory uncertainty. Many governments are still developing policies to regulate digital currencies and cryptocurrencies, leading to inconsistent regulations across different regions. Security concerns also pose a risk, as digital transactions are vulnerable to cyberattacks and fraud. Limited digital literacy among users can slow down adoption, as many people are unfamiliar with using digital financial tools.

Future Trends of Digital Currencies and FinTech in Emerging Markets

The future of digital currencies in emerging markets is promising. One major trend is, as mentioned, the expansion of central bank digital currencies, as more governments explore the benefits of digital currencies for financial stability and inclusion. The integration of blockchain technology will continue to enhance transparency and security in digital transactions. More FinTech companies are expected to develop mobile-based payment solutions to serve unbanked populations. Additionally, the use of decentralized finance will grow, providing alternative financial services without relying on traditional banking institutions. Governments and financial regulators will likely introduce more supportive policies to encourage FinTech innovation while ensuring consumer protection and financial stability.

Insurtech in Emerging Markets

Insurtech, or insurance technology, is transforming the insurance industry. Insurtech helps bridge the gap between uninsured populations and financial security. Traditional insurance services often require lengthy paperwork, in-person visits, and high premiums, which deter many individuals and small businesses from obtaining coverage. Insurtech simplifies the process by offering digital platforms that allow users to compare, purchase, and manage insurance policies through their mobile devices. This accessibility is particularly important in regions where many people rely on informal financial solutions. Additionally, insurtech companies use technology to customize insurance plans, making coverage more affordable and relevant to the needs of individuals and businesses. For example, small farmers can use insurtech solutions to protect their crops against climate-related risks.

What Is Driving the Growth of Insurtech in Emerging Markets?

Several factors are driving the growth of insurtech in emerging markets. One major driver of insurtech's growth is the rise of mobile technology and digital payments. With the increasing penetration of smartphones and mobile wallets, insurers can now offer microinsurance products tailored to low-income individuals. Digital platforms also enable automated claims processing, reducing the complexity and delays associated with traditional insurance policies. Climate change and economic instability are also driving demand for parametric insurance solutions in agriculture, healthcare, and disaster recovery. Insurtech innovations help farmers, gig workers, and small businesses access customized insurance, protecting them against unpredictable financial risks.

Real-World Example: Insurtech Success in China

A remarkable example of insurtech in an emerging market is ZhongAn Insurance in China (Yang n.d.). ZhongAn is China's first online-only insurance company, providing digital insurance products without physical branches. The company leverages artificial intelligence, blockchain, and Big Data to offer highly customized and affordable insurance plans. Customers can purchase policies for travel, health, electronics, and even e-commerce return protection directly through their smartphones.

One of ZhongAn's key innovations is its use of data analytics to assess risk and create personalized insurance solutions. The company has partnered with leading e-commerce platforms, FinTech firms, and healthcare providers to integrate insurance services into digital ecosystems. This approach has significantly increased insurance penetration in China, allowing millions of previously uninsured individuals to access affordable coverage. ZhongAn's success demonstrates how insurtech can revolutionize insurance accessibility and efficiency in emerging markets.

Challenges of Insurtech in Emerging Markets

One major challenge is low insurance awareness and financial literacy. In many emerging markets, insurance is not widely understood or prioritized, as people often rely on informal safety nets. Educating consumers about the benefits of insurance and how digital platforms work remains a significant hurdle. Without adequate awareness, potential customers may be reluctant to adopt insurtech solutions, even if they are accessible and affordable.

Another key issue is regulatory and compliance uncertainty. Insurance is a heavily regulated industry, and in many developing economies, existing regulations are outdated or inconsistent with digital innovations. Insurtech start-ups often struggle with licensing requirements, data protection laws, and evolving government policies, which can slow down market entry and expansion. Moreover, insurtech has enabled microinsurance and low-premium policies, many low-income consumers still struggle with irregular income streams, making premium payments challenging.

Future Trends of Insurtech in Emerging Markets

One major trend of Insurtech is the expansion of microinsurance, offering small and affordable coverage options tailored to low-income populations. The use of artificial intelligence and machine learning will continue to improve risk assessment and fraud detection, making insurance more efficient and secure. Blockchain technology is expected to enhance transparency in claims processing, reducing fraud, and improving customer trust.

Another important trend is the rise of parametric insurance, which provides automatic payouts based on predefined conditions, such as weather data for farmers. This model simplifies claims processing and speeds up payouts, increasing customer satisfaction. Additionally, insurtech companies are expected to form more partnerships with FinTech firms, mobile payment providers, and traditional insurers to expand their reach.

Regtech in Emerging Markets

Regulatory technology, or Regtech, is transforming compliance and regulatory processes in emerging markets by leveraging digital innovation to enhance efficiency and reduce costs. Businesses in these markets often face complex regulatory environments, which can be challenging to navigate due to limited resources and evolving legal frameworks. Regtech solutions help businesses comply with regulations more effectively. By automating compliance processes, Regtech reduces the risk of financial crimes, enhances transparency, and improves operational efficiency.

What Is Driving the Growth of Regtech in Emerging Markets?

The growth of RegTech in emerging markets is being driven by increasing regulatory complexities, rapid digital transformation, and the need for enhanced financial security. As financial ecosystems in these regions expand, governments and financial institutions face mounting challenges in ensuring compliance with evolving regulations while mitigating risks such as fraud, money laundering, and cyber threats. Traditional compliance methods are often slow, costly, and inefficient, making technology-driven solutions essential for streamlining regulatory processes. RegTech leverages artificial intelligence, machine learning, and blockchain to automate compliance, detect anomalies in transactions, and improve risk management, allowing financial institutions to operate more efficiently while maintaining regulatory adherence.

Additionally, the surge in FinTech adoption and the expansion of digital financial services have accelerated the demand for RegTech solutions in emerging markets. With millions of unbanked and underbanked individuals gaining access to digital financial platforms, regulators must implement efficient Know Your Customer (KYC) and Anti-Money Laundering (AML) measures to ensure transparency and security. Many governments are also introducing regulatory sandboxes to encourage innovation while maintaining oversight, fostering a more collaborative regulatory environment. As RegTech continues to evolve, its ability to provide cost-effective, scalable, and real-time compliance solutions makes it a critical driver of financial inclusion and economic stability in emerging markets.

Real-World Example: Regtech Success in Brazil

A good example of Regtech success in an emerging market is Brazil's adoption of digital compliance solutions to improve financial transparency. The Brazilian Central Bank has implemented various initiatives to enhance financial regulations, including the adoption of Open Banking and digital KYC (Know Your Customer) processes. Brazilian Regtech companies such as Quanto and IDwall have played a key role in streamlining compliance for financial institutions by providing AI-driven identity verification and fraud detection solutions.

IDwall (https://idwall.co/pt-BR), for instance, uses artificial intelligence and facial recognition technology to verify customer identities, reducing the risk of fraud and financial crime. By automating the KYC process, IDwall has helped financial institutions in Brazil comply with regulatory requirements more efficiently, reducing onboarding times and improving customer experience. The success of Regtech solutions in Brazil highlights how digital compliance tools can enhance regulatory efficiency and financial inclusion in emerging markets.

Challenges of Regtech in Emerging Markets

One major challenge of Regtech adoption in emerging markets is regulatory inconsistency. Many emerging markets lack uniform regulatory frameworks, making it difficult for businesses to implement standardized compliance solutions. Additionally, some regulatory bodies are slow to adopt digital transformation, creating barriers to Regtech integration.

Another challenge is the cost of implementing Regtech solutions. While Regtech can reduce long-term compliance costs, the initial investment required for adoption can be high, especially for small and medium-sized enterprises (SMEs). Limited digital infrastructure and data security concerns also hinder Regtech adoption. Businesses must ensure that digital compliance solutions are secure and comply with data protection regulations to gain trust from regulators and customers.

Future Trends of Regtech in Emerging Markets

Regtech is transforming compliance processes in emerging markets by leveraging technology to enhance regulatory efficiency and reduce costs. It plays a critical role in financial stability, fraud prevention, and business growth. As a major trend, AI-powered Regtech solutions can analyse large datasets in real-time, identifying compliance risks and ensuring that businesses meet regulatory requirements efficiently. On the other hand, Blockchain technology is also expected to play a significant role in Regtech adoption. Blockchain-based compliance solutions provide secure and transparent transaction records, reducing fraud risks, and enhancing regulatory reporting.

Conclusion

Technology has played a major role in shaping economic systems throughout history. From the early development of writing and record-keeping to modern advancements in digital finance, it has driven significant changes. Financial Technology has transformed how financial services are delivered. Innovations such as AI-driven analytics, decentralized finance, and cryptocurrencies have improved financial efficiency, accessibility, and security. The evolution of FinTech across three phases—FinTech 1.0, FinTech 2.0, and FinTech 3.0—has contributed to these improvements. These advancements have been especially important in emerging markets, where financial inclusion remains a challenge.

In emerging economies, FinTech is bridging gaps left by traditional banking systems. AI-driven financial solutions are improving decision-making, risk assessment, and fraud detection. Mobile payment platforms like Kenya's M-Pesa have changed how people conduct transactions in areas with limited banking access.

Microfinance and lending innovations are supporting small businesses and entrepreneurs, contributing to economic growth. Agri-FinTech is also providing financial access to farmers, which helps improve food security and agricultural productivity.

Sustainable financial solutions have become increasingly important. Green and sustainable FinTech initiatives are promoting environmental responsibility by financing renewable energy projects and supporting climate-friendly economic activities. Platforms like Sun Exchange in South Africa demonstrate how blockchain technology can facilitate investments in solar energy. This benefits both investors and communities.

Regulatory technology has become essential for simplifying compliance in financial services. Digital compliance solutions, AI-driven identity verification, and blockchain-based regulatory reporting are improving financial transparency and security. The adoption of digital currencies, including cryptocurrencies and CBDCs, is further expanding financial innovation. These technologies provide alternatives to traditional monetary systems and enhance cross-border transactions.

The Next Frontier: Quantum Computing and Its Potential Disruptive Impact

FinTech has already transformed financial systems, but quantum computing is poised to disrupt the entire financial and business world in ways previously unimaginable (Leong and Sung 2022). Quantum computing operates on the principles of quantum mechanics, enabling computations at speeds exponentially faster than classical computers. This unprecedented processing power will redefine financial modelling, risk assessment, cybersecurity, and data encryption, leading to a paradigm shift in global financial markets.

In financial services, quantum computing will revolutionize predictive analytics and decision-making. AI-driven financial models will become exponentially more accurate, reshaping market forecasting, fraud detection, and credit risk assessment. The ability to process vast amounts of market data in real-time will allow for ultra-optimized portfolio management, more precise financial planning, and rapid, highly sophisticated high-frequency trading. Traditional economic structures and institutions may struggle to keep pace with these advancements, leading to a fundamental reorganization of financial systems.

The cybersecurity landscape will be profoundly impacted. Although quantum computing offers the potential for stronger encryption, it also threatens current cryptographic methods that secure digital payments and blockchain networks. Widely used security protocols could become obsolete overnight, necessitating the urgent development of quantum-resistant cryptographic systems. If not addressed, this vulnerability could expose financial institutions and digital assets to unprecedented cyber threats, disrupting economies on a global scale.

Quantum computing will also catalyse the next evolution of blockchain and DeFi. With its enhanced computational capabilities, blockchain networks will become significantly more scalable and efficient, reducing transaction costs and energy consumption. Smart contracts will execute more rapidly, enabling real-time automated financial agreements without intermediaries. This could lead to the widespread adoption of decentralized financial systems, challenging traditional banks, insurance providers, and financial intermediaries in ways never seen before.

The Potential Value Creation for Emerging Markets

The disruptive nature of quantum computing will create both challenges and opportunities for emerging markets. Countries that proactively adopt quantum technology will gain a competitive edge, particularly in financial inclusion, economic forecasting, and technological innovation. Quantum-enhanced AI will empower businesses with unprecedented insights, enabling data-driven policymaking, and smarter financial regulations.

For emerging markets, quantum computing presents a unique opportunity to leapfrog outdated financial infrastructures. Quantum-enhanced microfinance platforms can facilitate smarter credit assessments, allowing more individuals and businesses to access financial services. The automation of complex financial processes will enable faster and more secure cross-border transactions, benefiting trade and economic growth. Moreover, emerging economies with strong FinTech ecosystems will attract significant foreign investments, further accelerating their economic progress.

However, the gap between developed and developing economies could widen if emerging markets do not prepare for quantum disruption. Countries lacking quantum-ready infrastructure may face increased cyber risks, financial instability, and economic displacement. Therefore, it is crucial for policymakers, financial institutions, and businesses in these regions to invest in quantum research, collaborate with technology leaders, and establish regulatory frameworks that facilitate responsible quantum adoption.

Final Thoughts: The Future of Financial Innovation in Emerging Markets

Emerging markets will continue to experience significant economic transformation as they integrate advanced financial technologies. FinTech plays a key role in improving financial inclusion, increasing efficiency, and promoting sustainable growth. AI, blockchain, mobile payments, and RegTech will further reinforce the role of digital finance in these regions. However, the disruptive power of quantum computing must not be underestimated—it has the potential to fundamentally reshape global financial systems, creating both unprecedented risks and extraordinary opportunities.

In overall, technology and finance will keep evolving, leading to new opportunities for businesses and individuals worldwide. The development of quantum computing will further accelerate financial transformation, but only those who prepare for its disruptive impact will thrive. Responsible innovation and regulatory cooperation will ensure that financial technology creates a more inclusive, efficient, and resilient global economy.

References

Abebe A, Kegne M (2023) The role of microfinance on women's entrepreneurship development in Western Ethiopia evidence from a structural equation modeling: Non-financial service is the way forward. Cogent Bus Manage 10(3):2256079. https://doi.org/10.1080/23311975.2023.2256079

Huang R (2024, July 15) A 2024 Overview Of The E-CNY, China's Digital Yuan. Forbes. https://www.forbes.com/sites/digital-assets/2024/07/15/a-2024-overview-of-the-e-cny-chinas-digital-yuan/

IFC (2020) MYBank's gender-driven approach to lending. International Finance Corporation

Leong K, Sung A (2018) FinTech (Financial technology): what is it and how to use technologies to create business value in fintech way? Int J Innov Manage Technol 9(2):74–78. https://doi.org/10.18178/ijimt.2018.9.2.791

Leong K, Sung A (2022) What business managers should know about quantum computing? J Interdiscipl Sci 6(2):42–52

Leong K, Sung A (2024) Gender stereotypes in artificial intelligence within the accounting profession using large language models. Human Soc Sci Commun 11(1):1–11. https://doi.org/10.1057/s41599-024-03660-8

Liu S (2016) Will Ant Financial Become Wildly Successful Like Taobao? - CKGSB. CKGSB Knowledge. https://english.ckgsb.edu.cn/knowledge/article/will-ant-financial-become-wildly-successful-like-taobao/

Microsoft (2017, November 7) Digital Agriculture: Farmers in India are using AI to increase crop yields. Microsoft Stories India. https://news.microsoft.com/en-in/features/ai-agriculture-icrisat-upl-india/

Stadler C (2024, August 27) How M-PESA cornered the market in Kenya | News. Warwick Business School. https://www.wbs.ac.uk/news/how-mpesa-cornered-the-market/

The Ant Group (2022) MYbank makes financing more accessible for 45 million SME clients by leveraging digital technology. The Ant Group. https://www.antgroup.com/en/news-media/press-releases/1651219200000

Yang KS (n.d.) ZhongAn Insurance—InsurTech analysis video and research deck. The Digital Insurer. Retrieved January 11, 2025, from https://www.the-digital-insurer.com/dia/zhongan-insurance-insurtech-analysis-video-and-research/

Startup Valuations in Emerging Markets

Kıvılcım Çaylı

What important truth do very few people agree with you on?
—Peter Thiel
I very frequently get the question: "What's going to change in the next 10 years?" And that is a very interesting question; it's a very common one. I almost never get the question: "What's not going to change in the next 10 years?" And I submit to you that that second question is actually the more important of the two — because you can build a business strategy around the things that are stable in time.
—Jeff Bezos

Abstract This chapter focuses on unique challenges in startup valuations in emerging markets and approaches to address them. Each emerging market has distinct characteristics compared to both other emerging markets and developed markets, including but not limited to macroeconomic factors, such as inflation and currency fluctuations, or political instability and company-specific factors caused by a startup's unpredictable nature and their interaction with the market and third parties.

Startup valuation is subjective to some extent, and there is a certain need for a reliable framework to facilitate investment decisions. The author curates 10 startup valuation methods and proposes modifications and adjustments to them, trying to combine them in a startup-specific but practical method in the context of emerging markets.

Additionally, the investor perspective is highly involved in the chapter to give a solid understanding that the valuation practice is a tool to assess an investment and to build an investment decision; it is not an aim itself. And the emerging market startups can provide fruitful investment opportunities for risk-takers.

K. Çaylı (✉)
Ankara, Turkey
e-mail: kivilcim@cayli.org

S. Derindere Köseoğlu, A. Patterson (eds.), *Valuation in Emerging Markets*, Contributions to Finance and Accounting,
https://doi.org/10.1007/978-3-031-93526-8_16

The chapter also discusses important components of the valuation process such as due diligence, performance metrics, qualitative factors, portfolio strategies, exit strategies, and the regulatory scene.

Keywords Acquisition · Deal · Dry Powder · Due Diligence · EBITDA · Enterprise Value · EV · Exit · Fintech · Funding · Investor · IPO · NPV · Private Equity · ROI · Scalability · Venture Capital

Introduction

Both startup valuation and valuation techniques in emerging markets bear unique challenges and issues to be considered. This chapter compares the pros and cons while handling these specific issues, offers methods, and provides "clues" for "surfing the tides of unknown waters." The investor perspective is strongly emphasized.

The initial sections will discuss the definition and characteristics of emerging markets from a startup's perspective, examining their impact on valuation practices. Following this, both the challenges and potential rewards will be evaluated given the context of venture capital and private equity. The determinants of valuation will be analyzed as a chain reaction.

Then, ten startup valuation techniques will be listed and explained with relevant use cases. For each technique, specific emerging market adjustments required from the point of an investor/an analyst will be illustrated.

The quantitative factors and performance metrics affecting valuations, as well as the qualitative factors such as scalability issues and emerging technologies will also be explored in the proceeding sections.

After discussion of the effects of regulatory scene, policies and government incentives, the due diligence efforts which accompany the valuation and are an important part of investment process will be addressed as a solution to problems arising from information asymmetry.

We will also analyze the effects of behavioral economics and psychology over the valuation negotiations and conclude the chapter by looking at the investor's toolbox which consists of portfolio and risk management strategies and exit routes for realization of investment.

A detailed analysis of the components of startup valuation within this specific context will establish a solid framework, enabling analysts to effectively value startups in emerging markets.

Being a Startup in an Emerging Market

Ries (2011) defines a startup as "a human institution designed to create a new product or service under conditions of extreme uncertainty" (p. 8), whereas according to Blank and Dorf (2012), "a startup is not a smaller version of a large company. A startup is a temporary organization in search of a scalable, repeatable, profitable business model" (p. xvii). Words such as "extreme uncertainty" and "temporary" in these broadly accepted definitions connotate volatility and instability: Welcome to emerging markets!

Although there is no universal consensus on which countries qualify as emerging markets, most classifications rely on macroeconomic indicators. However, when defining emerging markets in the context of startups, additional or alternative criteria may be more relevant. These factors include:

- *Total funded amount*: Venture capital funding is typically considered, while private equity investments and M&A transactions involving traditional businesses are often excluded.
- *Average and median deal size*: Both the average and median funding raised for a single company tends to be smaller in emerging markets.
- *Top-quartile investors*: These investors sometimes take part in emerging market transactions, and their participation has a tendency to boost investor demand for that market.
- *Investor type deal allocation*: Angel investors and venture capitalists tend to have a greater percentage of overall funding in emerging markets compared to more conventional investors such as pension funds or funds of funds.
- *Mega-rounds*: Mega-rounds, where more than $100 million is raised, are employed to gauge the maturity of a market. The ratio of mega-rounds to total funding is another key indicator.
- *Number of unicorns and decacorns*: A startup valued at $1 billion is termed a unicorn, and those with more than $10 billion are referred to as decacorns. While emerging markets tend to generate at least a few unicorns, leading developed markets have many more.

Various measures and ratios are derivable from this type of data, typically with macroeconomic figures. "Vertical-based" calculations (a term preferred in venture terminology over "industry-based") are also frequently used. The parameters to be selected rely on the scope of analysis, though investors typically prioritize the factors mentioned above.

An analyst seeking a quantitative approach to classifying markets as developed or emerging can utilize Damodaran's (2025) country-based equity risk premium calculations. They would also work well if used in portfolio management calculations. However, the analyst should keep in mind that the financial models employed in portfolio calculations have drawbacks even in reflecting the performance of portfolios consisting of relatively easily valued assets. Startup valuation introduces significantly greater variability and deviation, often challenging *all* the fundamental assumptions underpinning these models.

Macroeconomic Impacts

In general, startups are more vulnerable to macroeconomic fluctuations than traditional companies. To name a few of the reasons, the first is their life cycle and life span. Often, their contingency budget is very limited (if at all present). Cash flow is widely used for fast growth. Additionally, investor and competitor pressure combined with the ambition of the management team propels the startup forward with an augmented risk appetite. Risk management is not as strict as for conventional companies but widely tolerated and accepted. Internal risk control mechanisms are not robust as they should be. In addition, the product-market fit may not be as strong as that of established competitors. This list is not exhaustive and can be further expanded. Emerging market economies, on the other hand, impose additional macroeconomic forces on these already fragile organizations, these include:

- *Inflation and market interest rates*: It is a fact that inflation affects employment, income distribution, and the growth rates of an economy. An emerging economy faces some other side effects too, often in a rather chaotic way. Pricing behavior shifts, often worsening in a sticky manner. As costs rise, prices surge as well. Decreasing purchasing power forces people to spend more, not save as they would in a stable economy. They believe they won't be able to buy the same product next month, so it's now or never!

  Exaggerated consumption and skyrocketing prices can lead to inflated valuations due to record-high sales figures, or the business may fail due to the same volatility. It is the opposite on the investor side: high interest rates aimed at controlling inflation make the opportunity cost of venture investments extremely high. With the accompanying market risk and volatility, investors tend to park their capital in safe and liquid assets like government bonds, high-interest paying cash accounts, and more stable economies—avoiding venture investments. And as such, decreased demand for startup investments generally leads to deep downticks in valuations. Inflation and interest rates are correlated with currency fluctuations as well, as we discuss below.
- *Currency fluctuations*: Other than the internal economic and political dynamics of emerging markets, inflation and in turn interest rates of the USA, and the major developed economies cause fluctuations in the local currencies of emerging markets. These currency fluctuations affect a startup's valuation in two major ways. The first is that it affects the valuation estimates by changing the parameters in the methods used. Both the cash flows expressed in USD units, while converting from local currency, and the discount rates used are impacted. Subsequently, the Net Present Value (NPV) and Internal Rate of Return (IRR) change as well.

The second point is the shift in the core business of the startup. For example, having a cost structure in local currency and a revenue stream in USD, or vice versa, will have a parallel fluctuation in its financial structure in line with the fluctuation of the currencies; a direct driver of a change in valuation.

- *Political risk*: Emerging markets also in general present similar "volatility" in their political environments as well. Arguably, volatility in the macroeconomic indicators and dynamics is a direct result of the political volatility, since governmental changes, more frequent elections, and major periodical shifts in economic policies contribute a large part of the turbulence. However, we need to keep in mind that volatile markets and the large margins on both sides (positive movements can be as large as the negative ones) in every industry also provide the biggest opportunities for those who know how to surf those waves.

Startup Valuation Challenges and Rewards in the Emerging Market Scene

The unstable characteristics of the markets in emerging markets create extra hurdles on valuation practices for startups. In general terms, valuation practice can be accepted as a mixture of data, predictions, and expectations. That being said, these components bring unique challenges in an emerging market context, which include:

- Reliable data is scarcer. Market players usually do not have access to or are not able to keep *knowledge*-based records. Instead, *information* is available sometimes, but at more superficial levels. Although vastly abundant, regulations do not help much since they are focused primarily on tax purposes and avoiding fraudulent actions. Making precise decisions on a financial basis is not a priority.
- Predictions are often "guesses" or "possibilities," when they shouldn't be. It is also hard to find reliable data for inputs, or solid comparable information or benchmarks.
- In emerging markets, expectations tend to play a bigger role in valuation than they should, especially compared to developed markets. When solid data and strong evidence-based predictions are lacking, these expectations often become the main driver of valuation. But this isn't unique to emerging markets, it's also common in startup valuations worldwide. The real challenge in emerging markets is that the sentiment driving these expectations can be highly volatile, shifting dramatically in short periods.
- The first, agreed, valuation assigned to a startup in these markets—which then sets the stage for future valuations—is usually based on an agreement between the initial investors and the founders. In many cases, this makes it more of a behavioral finance decision than a purely rational financial one. Still, when considering the fundamental risk-reward trade-off in finance, emerging markets can offer strong opportunities.

On the other hand, considering the basic risk-reward structure of financial decision making, emerging markets can provide rewarding investment returns:

- High perceived level of risk justifies investors' expectations for higher returns, and are welcomed.
- The actual level of risk frequently deters major institutional investors, such as pension funds and hedge funds from developed markets, from taking substantial positions, due to their investment mandates. And yet, reduced competition among investors combined with information asymmetry may offer opportunities.
- On the startup side, from an evolutionary point of view, tough circumstances create resilient companies and battle-tested leaders who have endured and excelled in challenging conditions. Indeed, this may be the major ingredient in building unicorns.

An investor who can manage risk well and has the related knowledge would receive high returns. Just keep in mind that some "adjustments" for valuations should be made, which will be considered in the following sections of this book chapter.

How Do Venture Capital and Private Equity Shape Valuations?

From company structures to regulations, from financial modeling to valuation techniques, investors affect the markets in many ways. Furthermore, we can claim that angel investment and then venture capitalists (VCs) and private equity capital (PE) shape not only the valuations, but the standards as well, within the startup space. This is hardly surprising given the fundamental relationship between supply and demand, and emerging markets are no exception.

One of the characteristics of the startup scene in an emerging market is the scarcity of funds despite the often-vast number of startups seeking to raise investor money. Dry powder—committed, but unallocated capital—is limited due to the reasons mentioned above. Hence, VCs and PE are able to set the rules. Universal industry standards are at play, but the adaptation of different strategies to local realities also shapes this unique playbook.

Smaller dry powder leads to smaller cheque sizes, and in turn, issues of scalability. Startups usually do not gain the necessary financial strength. Although the exceptions to return of investments are high, budgets are tight, and the runways are shorter. This is one of the pressure elements over valuations. Frequently, startups cannot scale as easily in emerging markets.

Also, we recall that the first valuation set between the initial investors and the founders is an agreed one. The initial valuation tends to be lower than in developed markets, triggering a chain reaction that reinforces market immaturity (Fig. 1).

Another direct consequence is the increase in the number of pre-seed, seed, and early-stage investments whereas an opposite trend is seen in later-stage investments,

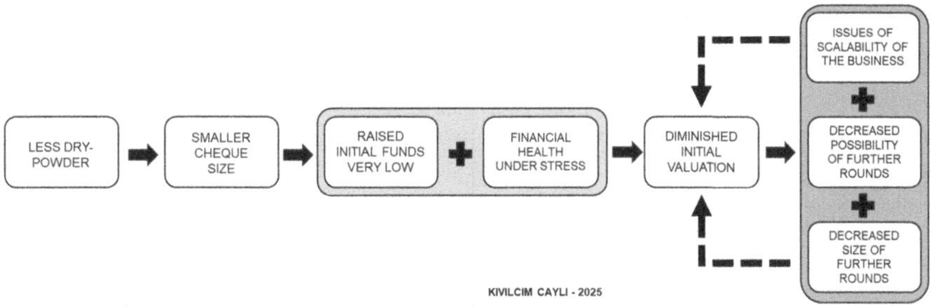

Fig. 1 The chain reaction of startup valuation in emerging markets. Source: Author

for instance the number of Series A+ investments and "mega-rounds" (which in developed markets is often given as funding over $100 million). Typically, the ratio of venture capital invested to private equity deals increases. Additionally, please note that the total amount of private equity deals decreases in size as well. More risk-tolerant investors could potentially seize these opportunities, which we can broadly describe as follows:

- Lower initial valuations may offer "cheaper" deals.
- Valuation multiples kept constant, it is easier to reach the same multiple with smaller initial valuations. For instance, multiplying a $100 M valuation by 5 is more achievable than multiplying a $500 M valuation by the same factor. This phenomenon is significant for fund or portfolio performance calculations and alignments with the mandates of limited partners (LPs).
- Easier-to-reach valuation multiples may allow earlier exits and investment return realization.
- Due to smaller enterprise valuations (EV), IPOs may not be an adequate or accessible option for an exit for most startups. Thus, many emerging markets offer various alternative exit routes such as specialized exchanges with less financial criteria, streamlined IPO processes for tech startups, and crowdfunding platforms. Often, different financial modeling, structuring, valuation techniques, and multipliers are also employed by investors. Valuation techniques are the subject of the next section.

Startup Valuation Techniques in Emerging Markets

Basically, we can list the top 10 valuation techniques for startup valuations as follows in the table below (Fig. 2).

For valuation and investment professionals, it would not be a surprise that the above methods would produce different results even on the same deal. This is because they all focus on the different features and parameters of the startup and most of them are substantially subjective on both sides. This means that both the valuation parameters and the startup's own data are unclear. Additionally, the

METHOD	DEFINITION	HOW?	PROS	CONS	FOR WHOM?
Discounted Cash Flow (DCF)	The widely used technique in corporate finance & investment banking	Calculating the present value of the future cash flows that will be generated by the start-up over a specific period with a discount rate.	Solid, well-understood and most-trusted method	• It depends on predictions, not actual. • Some founders may find it hard-to-use	Works best for revenue-generating startups
Balanced Scorecard	The widely used technique by Angel Investors	Several significant factors are determined and assigned weights. Then, the factors are scored.	• Allows scoring & weighting intangible factors. • Allows comparing startups	Scoring and weighing are subjective	Works best for Angel Investors for deal selection
Venture Capitalist (VC)	The widely used technique by Venture Capitalists, first introduced by Bill Sahlman of Harvard B.S.	An exit multiple and timing are determined. Then, the exit value is discounted to NPV considering the desired ROI, and the valuationis set accordingly.	• Fits well to early-stage high growth startups. • Incorporates return and well-shaped exit	• Totally investor driven and speculative process. • Industries with lower multiples may suffer	Works best for VCs having ROI & timing mandates
Risk Factor Summation	First introduced by Ohio TechAngels, one of the most used methods by Angel Investors	A comparable valuation is set as a base value. Then this value is adjusted against 12 basic risk factors to determine the valuation of the focused startup.	Simple to use, considers risk	• Doesn't consider positives & growth potential. • Doesn't distinguish btw risks & probabilities	Works best for early-stage startups
Market Comparables	Not commonly used for private companies, more suitable for public companies	The transaction valuations for similar startups are determined. Then the average, or weighted average, often adjusted with a specific multiple is used.	Easy to use, doesn't require confidential data	• Comparables are hard-to-find for startups. • Company specific factors aren't considered	Works best with other methods as a benchmark

Fig. 2 Top 10 valuation techniques for startup valuations. Source: Author

First Chicago	Can be counted as a modified or upgraded version of DCF valuation	The present value of the future cash flows that will be generated by the startup are adjusted against risk via bad, good, and base scenarios.	Allows multiple transaction scenarios	• Somewhat subjective • Company specific factors aren't considered	Works best for revenue-generating startups
Multiples Valuation	Not commonly used for private companies, more suitable for public companies	Similar to the market comparables method. Not the transaction value, but a specific metric is preferred this time.	• Easy to use. • Considers industry specific metrics	• Future expectations & potential disregarded • Intangible & intrinsic factors aren't considered	Startups outperforming rivals in a specific metric
Replacement Costs	An asset-based valuation method, which is not commonly used because of some drawbacks	The present values of all the startup's assets are calculated and summed as if they are being purchased again.	Easy to use	• Intangible assets and goodwill are disregarded. • Unreliable results compared to other methods. • Inconvenient for high-tech industries	Asset-intense startups with a large balance sheet
All-Costs-Focused	A costs & expenses-based valuation method, which is rarely used because of some drawbacks	A predetermined valuation and share ratio enough to cover all costs & expenses until the next round. Usually, a goodwill portion is added.	Easy to calculate	• Performance & investor expectations excluded. • Totally subjective & only founder's perspective • Doesn't reflect fair or real value	Best for founders having successful exits in the past
Berkus	The widely used technique by Angel Investors, first introduced by Dave Berkus	Up to 500 K $ is added to the valuation for the presence of each of the 5 significant factors in the startup. The cap is 2.5 M $.	• Remarkably simple to use. • Quick stop-or-go decision	• Totally subjective • Ignores financial metrics, overall performance	Works best for seed stage startups without traction

Fig. 2 (continued)

dynamics of an emerging market are unlikely to offer much assistance in clarifying these uncertainties.

So, what can be done to achieve a reasonable, if not dependable, valuation? It is appropriate to use all applicable methods simultaneously for a deal, and to set a valuation interval, rather than setting an absolute value using a single method. A weighed mixture would also be helpful.

Valuation Adjustments for Emerging Market Startups

It is vital to make adjustments specific to emerging markets carefully and incorporate them into the formulas. Then, the analyst will be able to converge on a more accurate valuation. The following are the essential adjustments for an emerging market depending on the valuation method chosen (Fig. 3).

Quantitative Factors and Performance Metrics in Startup Valuation in an Emerging Market

Classical valuation multiples such as EV/EBITDA, EV/Sales, etc. may not work well for the startups of emerging markets. Two major reasons are:

- Startups, in general, do not have positive EBITDA or Net Earnings figures most of the time, especially in their early years.
- High earnings and sales figures may not reflect the real financial status of the startup because of the inflationist pressures and artificial increases mentioned above.

Hence, to value a startup company in an emerging market, we should conduct a different approach based on real-world performance indicators belonging to that company. For an emerging market investor/analyst, the below metrics may perform well (Fig. 4).

There are tens of other performance metrics that are used in daily practice for measuring a startup's business performance or a fund's/investment portfolio's performance but those are beyond the scope of this chapter.

From Emerging Technologies to Local Dynamics: The Importance of Qualitative Factors

Some other intangible factors also take role in the valuation process. They don't necessarily involve in the startup value directly. Additionally, these factors can be counted as subjective.

METHOD	EMERGING MARKET ADJUSTMENTS
Discounted Cash Flow (DCF)	• Increase the discount rate instead of using the standard rates. Market's actual interest rate, inflation rate, risk free rate, bond interest rate can be employed. • Startup's cash flow predictions may need some tuning as well. But avoid double discounting by using the same indicator.
Balanced Scorecard	Adjustments depend on the parameters chosen initially. For instance, if the addressable market size is a parameter, it may be adjusted by using market-specific purchasing power, extra distribution costs due to the inadequate logistic infrastructure, and so on.
Venture Capitalist (VC)	Adjustments to the DCF should be made. Additionally, the expected ROI should be *decreased* compared to a developed market. It seems contradictory with the risk-reward paradigm of emerging markets, *but* it is not. VCs often predict *lower* ROIs for a startup of an emerging market which is in exactly the same industry and in exactly the same stage and condition for a startup of a developed market. There are no written rules for this, but it is closely related to the perceived survival probability of the startup and the attractiveness of the market. If possible, to find, a similar industry's adjustment ratio may work.
Risk Factor Summation	Since the parameters chosen are all risk-dependent, all should be adjusted with the same approach mentioned in the balanced scorecard method.
Market Comparables	Given the scarcity and quality of reliable data belonging to comparables, plenty of related data from open sources may be derived. For instance, not only the IPO results which are less in size and in number in emerging markets, closed deal statistics, consultancy company reports, crowdfunding benchmark etc. should be involved.
First Chicago	DCF adjustments should be made. Additionally, deviation from the base scenario can be enlarged.
Multiples Valuation	The adjustments proposed above for the market comparables, and VC methods are applicable together.
Replacement Costs	The inflation rate for tangible assets and interest rate for intangible assets should be considered.
All-Costs-Focused	The startup founders in the emerging markets are very prone to a kind of survival bias. As a common pattern, cost projections and calculations are precise and perfect, but revenue forecasts are somewhat sloppy and overestimated. It reflects a tendency to equalize the required fund amount to the round's post money share premiums. Thus, cash flow and income projections should be adjusted with business acumen. "Are there really that number of customers? Is it really an accessible market with that amount of distribution costs? Is this price level sustainable for that long given that competition?", and so on.
Berkus	Since the method itself is highly subjective, any discount for the values of 5 factors would make them more reasonable. A common approach is to apply the same ratio between two compared market's average seed valuations. For example, if the average valuation of the startups at the same stage and in the same industry is double sized in a developed market, the 5 factors of the method can be valued as \$250K rather than \$500K each for the emerging market under consideration.

Fig. 3 Valuation adjustments for EM startups. Source: Author

VALUATION METRIC	DEFINITION	HOW TO APPLY IT?
Runway	It is the number of months that a startup can survive with the cash in hand at the current monthly money burning rate	As a rule of thumb, a funding round provides 12-18 months of runway. So, if a startup needed and raised \$2 M to survive for 15 months in exchange for a 5% post-money share, it is roughly valued at \$40 M.
Annual Recurring Revenue (ARR)	It is the annual revenue coming from the repeating revenue generation cycles such as subscription fees or stock renewing orders. ARR tells more about cash flow than EBITDA, and reflects the startup's business performance much better, even if it is not yet profitable.	Industries and markets have average ARR multiples, and for recent years these are preferred by startup investors for gross deal valuation. For example, a startup can be valued 30 times of its ARR if that is the average for that company stage and industry. Of course, if the figures do not justify this valuation, the possible reasons for the deviation should be carefully considered.
Gross Merchandise Volume (GMV)	It is the total value of the transactions realized on a platform or through a marketplace type business. It reflects the effects of macro trends well in an emerging economy.	It is used as a valuation adjustment factor. The ratio of the current valuation of a competitor to its GMV provides a basis for that market's valuation multiples.

Fig. 4 Real-world performance indicators for startups. Source: Author

- Scalability: There is not a straightforward measurement for scalability of a business. However, the VC game solely depends on multiplying the initial valuation during the exit. As a prerequisite for such expansion in value, the structure and growth potential of the business shall be suitable to be expanded.
- Founder team: Typically seen as a core driver but a hygiene factor in fact, the founders of a startup are under pressure to scale the business quickly. Having a founder with a prior successful exit is appealing to investors, which in turn drives higher valuations. But in emerging markets, there are certain cultures that do not value all types of prior experience as good and may differentiate between success

and failure. Indeed, founders with a past history of failure could be viewed as a bad omen, indicating potential danger.

- Local market size and attractiveness: Contrary to popular belief, real-world observations indicate that the size of a market can actually have a negative effect if it's large and already well-served. In such cases, the startup becomes comfortable within its local market and may not feel the need to expand globally to thrive, a situation known as "hyperlocal." The downside of this is that reliance on just one market leaves the business highly exposed to major, often unpredictable, events—something that's more common in emerging markets.
- Emerging technologies: This can either work in favor of or against a startup as a valuation multiplier. Rapid adoption or the invention of advanced technology can help the startup outpace its competitors almost immediately. However, the same technology also holds the potential to disrupt the startup itself, as competitors have the same opportunity to leverage it. Technological due diligence has to be an essential part of valuation processes.
- Patents and intellectual property rights: Although projected cash flows from that kind of exclusivity may add a premium to the valuation, some investors consider it as a drawback in some emerging markets, as it would be very costly to have legal protection in all major markets, and this would create a heavy burden over the early and tight budgets of the emerging startups. The perceived opportunity cost is about the money that would rather go for growth-related activities.

There are other minor factors, which we can consolidate into the term "incubation factors" which to greater or less degrees can affect the valuations in emerging markets, and the effect may be greater than it would be in a developed market. In short, those are:

- Paying costs in a cheaper currency while earning in a more valuable one may allow a greater distribution margin.
- The city that the startup operates in counts. The abundance of investors, accelerators, tech employees, and universities may provide a competitive edge to scale fast.
- Looser regulations over personal/industrial data and AI usage can enhance the pace of startup growth (which will be discussed in more detail in the following section).

These factors may also be reflected in the valuation parameters being given weights in a much quantitative way just like in the balanced scorecard method.

Case Study: How to Apply in Practice

In this practical case study, the analyst was assigned a valuation study by a VC firm for a seed stage SAAS (Software-As-A-Service) startup recently founded in an emerging market. The firm is planning to invest in the startup and trying to determine

METHOD	SELECTION RATIONALE OF THE METHOD
Berkus	The startup is at the seed stage with very limited performance data available. This method can value some features which would be deemed to be at zero values otherwise. Also, it assigns a reasonable cap for optimistic predictions.
VC	It adds the perspective and expectations of the VC firm, which is a key determinant of the initial valuation of a startup. Expectations include but are not limited to an extremely high ROI and a fruitful valuation which is scalable for future rounds.
DCF	Although heavily dependable on predictions rather than realized performance, DCF provides a basis for the math of the deal. Additionally, a careful eye may spot unrealistic forecasts or inconsistent figures.
Market Comparables	The analyst had knowledge of similar deals within the same industry and at the same stage. Some adjustments are required though, since some of the comparable deals were from developed markets.

Fig. 5 Selected valuation methods. Source: Author

the initial valuation of the deal. Due diligence has already been conducted. The VC firm requires a 90% accuracy for the valuation.

First of all, the analyst picked the relevant methods to use, which are Berkus, VC, DCF, and Market Comparable methods, respectively. Here is the rationale of the selection (Fig. 5):

The analyst proceeds with the calculations and adjustments, as follows:

1. Berkus

   Having the knowledge that the average deal size is 40% lower than the developed markets in that market, the analyst determines the cap of five factors as $300.000 each, instead of $500.000 per factor.

   Then, after evaluation of the five factors by using due diligence report findings the analyst values these as following:

Sound idea	$150.000
Prototype	$300.000
Management team quality	$250.000
Strategic relationships	$300.000
Product rollout or sales	$200.000
TOTAL	$1.200.000

2. VC

   In our example the VC firm generally invests with the expectation of 10X returns in developed markets. In this deal, although riskier, they set a potentially more achievable and more probable 7X target return to be realistic.

   The analyst calculated the expected ARR at the 5th year of the investment from the given financial projections as $1.800.000. In the actual market conditions, similar deals are valued at 5X to 5.5X ARR. Picking 5.25X, the terminal value at the 5th year would be $9.450.000.

To reach this figure with a 7X return expectation, today's valuation should be $1.350.000.

Please note that ROI expectation was not expressed in terms of IRR nor a WACC was not calculated. At the practical level, VCs usually target returns and predict terminal values in multiples.

3. DCF

   To conduct this, the analyst calculated the cash flows for the first five years of the investment, used the same terminal value predicted based on the ARR, and picked the inflation rate as the discount rate:

CF at 1st year	135.000 $
CF at 2nd year	410.000 $
CF at 3rd year	645.000 $
CF at 4th year	880.000 $
CF at 5th year	1.100.000 $
Terminal value	9.450.000 $
Discount rate	40%
DCF valuation	2.230.000 $

In common VC & PE practice, 8% is the widely accepted discount rate in developed markets. However, in emerging markets risk-free rates based on bond interest rates highly differ and might not be priced appropriately for such discount rate usage. Thus, an analyst should use a higher discount rate specific to that emerging market. This may be inflation rate, deposit interest rate, or similar. Often, higher rates are more realistic.

4. Market Comparables

   The analyst was able to find four similar deals. The exercised valuation of two deals from a developed market was discounted by 40% again to account for lower emerging market multiples and higher risks. An exercised valuation from a similar emerging market was converted into USD with that day's local currency rate. This one with the fourth comparable of this startup's market was used directly. The average exercised valuation of these four valuations was found to be $1.700.000.

Please note that Price-to-Book Ratio or Price-to-Earnings Ratios cannot be calculated for a privately held startup at this stage and in turn cannot be used as comparables as in stock valuation practices.

In the next step, the analyst assigned weights for the final values depending on the utilized method (Fig. 6):

METHOD	VALUATION	ASSIGNED WEIGHT
Berkus	$1.200.000	15%
VC	$1.350.000	40%
DCF	$2.230.000	15%
Market Comparables	$1.700.000	30%

Fig. 6 Final valuation values per utilized method. Source: Author

The Rather subjective Berkus and VC methods were assigned lower weights. The market comparables method was given a double times higher weight, since it reflects the fair value and the risk appetite of the market much better. The VC method was given the highest weighting as the investor expectation is the dominant factor for the initial valuation. In addition, it would be likely that the VC firm would be involved in executive and financial management to some extent, which in turn helps push the startup toward the target valuation.

Finally, the analyst calculates the weighted average for the valuation and lower and higher bounds with a 90% confidence interval:

The Weighted Average Valuation: $1.564.500
Lower Bound: $1.083.000
Higher Bound: $2.158.00

Effects of Regulatory Scene, Policies, and Incentives over Valuations

Although policymakers in less liberal emerging markets may have a somewhat higher regulatory appetite, they tend to be cautious when it comes to high-tech industries. This caution creates a space that allows startups to grow quickly in their early stages, free from heavy regulation.

In one real-world example, before a regulatory body was established and authorized in the data sector, some data-tech startups grew rapidly by developing software that utilized unrestricted personal data, without facing significant legal penalties or consequences. However, this is no longer the case. After a stringent regulation has been put in place, it is virtually impossible to use data in a commercially meaningful way.

However, this cautious approach can sometimes backfire. In the same emerging market, restrictions on cryptocurrency transactions held back nearly all blockchain startups for several years. The issue was only recently resolved after regulations were aligned with international standards.

In another real-world example, payment gateways and money transfers were prohibited for fintech companies and challenger banks which were not registered as traditional banks. As a result, hundreds of payment provider fintechs and other tech startups that relied on these channels for revenue did face bankruptcy, many ultimately were unable to survive. Those type of side effects alter valuations by changing the country, industry, or market average multiples and benchmarks, as well as perceived risk of startup investors. On the other hand, the necessity for attracting international investment usually leads the emerging market policy makers to offer advantageous tax regimes, eased financial and legal infrastructure, less stringent governance standards, and of course, subsidies and incentives.

In a recent real-world case, an electrical vehicle producer was given a customs tax exemption worth of 40% in an emerging market, but its competitors from the same country of origin were not. In this market, the customs tax was applied in a cost-plus manner. Thus, the electrical vehicle maker gained the privilege to use an additional 40% gross profit margin which can be employed freely against competition. The bottom-line is if the subsidies and incentives would be considered as liabilities on the balance sheets according to the accounting standards and commercial laws in force for that market. If so, they should be deducted from the calculated company value in most of the valuation techniques.

How to Conduct Due Diligence with this Information Asymmetry Challenge?

Due diligence practice requires a mixture of nuances in emerging markets. As mentioned earlier, reliable data is scarce, and not easy to discover. Let us dissect the process into the subsections below:

- *Financial Due Diligence*: For the confirmation of the valuation, financial statements are examined. Thanks to the adoption of IFRS, "the 3 statements" or equivalents will be available on-site. Multiples and ratios used for the valuation are analyzed. Cash flow forecasts are compared with actual performance. For startups, the three financial statements can be immature and may not reflect the effective valuation though. The reliability of the assumptions used for predictions should also be carefully determined.
- *Legal Due Diligence*: In some emerging markets, legal records may be decentralized over various institutions. Cross-checks should be conducted with all possibly related authorities to mitigate legal risks.
- *Technical (Technological) Due Diligence*: Startup valuations naturally outweigh the technological component of the business since the financial side is weak. This component often consists of deep technology such as AI, blockchain, IoT, and so forth, which probably the financial analyst would not be very familiar with. In such cases, the actual product and its claimed value proposition as well as future development plans and assumptions shall be audited by experts.
- *Sustainability Due Diligence*: Emerging markets may lack the adequate regulatory framework and/or the necessary public budget to meet all international sustainability standards. So, it could be smart to seek compliance with all related parties' criteria and to adhere to the tightest sustainability restrictions possible.

- *Reputation Due Diligence*: The reputation of the founders or the startup is often overlooked, yet it may be low among key stakeholders and the public. The investor may find him/herself in an expensive deal in which the valuation could not be justified in further funding rounds or on a potential exit path. What is ethical or legal in an emerging market may not be so in the investor's country of origin, and vice versa. Analysts shall examine the findings of the due diligence with this point of view on the cross-country valuations and investments.

Portfolio Strategies and Portfolio Risk Management in Emerging Markets

Even thorough due diligence on each investee company may not be sufficient to minimize the overall portfolio risk, given the high-risk nature of emerging markets. Some strategies are brought into play to manage portfolio risks.

Diversification is the prominent buffer for a startup investment portfolio. If the portfolio's investees are predominantly from emerging markets, an additional layer of diversification among several emerging markets, emerging technologies, and industries may work well. Hedging across the markets is also necessary to avoid the hazardous effects of currency fluctuations over the portfolio.

Transferable and scalable businesses provide extra resilience and adaptability for the portfolio as well. This means that if a transferable business that fails in an emerging market for an unavoidable local factor, it could still succeed when positioned in another emerging market, which would enhance overall portfolio success. Valuation swaps are another strategy used across markets in the startup business. After closing an investment round, moving from a market with a lower average multiple for a specific parameter to one with a higher average for that parameter can allow the investor to secure a valuation premium.

Finally, alternative legal structures such as special purpose vehicles and alternative methods such as mezzanine financing may work better to manage overall risk. Many emerging markets offer different financial instruments for startup investing and the startup investor can find more attractive investment methods than traditional investment vehicles.

Behavioral Economics: The Role of Psychology in Determining and Negotiating Valuations

As previously mentioned in preceding sections, the very first valuation is usually a mutually agreed one, not a precisely calculated one. This valuation will be one of the key determinants of further valuations throughout the startup's lifespan. Thus, it can be argued that psychological factors influence the valuations through investors and founders' behaviors during the negotiation process.

Arguably, the basic reason can be the initial conflict of interest. The founder tries to maximize the first valuation to raise the maximum amount of funds in return for the minimum shares outstanding, whereas the investor pursues to lock a "good deal" with the highest possible gains through a minimum amount of investment (there are exceptions as always). Combined with several cognitive and behavioral biases revealed by Kahneman (2011), this initial negotiation is built on a rather irrational basis. According to Gompers et al. (2020) "almost half of the VCs, particularly the early-stage, IT, and smaller VCs, admit to often making gut investment decisions."

Data-driven and fact-based reasoning is recommended to address and challenge these shortcomings. For an effective valuation process, the analyst should:

- Source relevant data,
- Consider the emerging market's unique dynamics,
- Be aware of cognitive biases,
- Conduct a thorough due diligence,
- Consult independent experts if applicable.

Aligned with the Game Theory, if both parties focus solely on maximizing their own benefits, as reflected in their proposed valuations, they will be unable to reach an agreement. Often, undue influence may force one party to accept unfavorable terms in the course of the fundraising process, but my personal experience as an analyst and investor confirms the fact that those types of agreements are usually not executable and are likely to fail. Totally equalized terms would not work either, due to the lack of enough incentives. From this point of view, it can be assumed that the correct initial valuation is the one that enables the startup to move forward, while also maintaining the investor's interest and willingness to continue supporting the company. It is often stated that transparency and honesty can resolve information asymmetry, although it would be naive to assume that these factors would always be on the table during negotiations. As a closing remark: investors sometimes extend negotiations, and this is not always a tactic, as founders always like to believe. Instead, it is often intended to assess the startup's resilience over time amidst the turbulent conditions of an emerging market.

Exit Strategies in Emerging Markets

The exit strategies are generally the same in the emerging markets as developed markets. Depending on the maturity level and volatility of the emerging markets, the chosen exit path may differ, though.

For a startup in an emerging market, the IPO path is, at least locally, a challenging route. Stock exchanges set hard-to-reach financial limits accompanied by strict regulations and red tape. On the other hand, investor pressure (where the IPO is seen as the final exit rather than just another funding round) or a complicated cap table (often resulting from limited early-stage funding, leading to a crowded table with smaller stakes) can prevent an IPO from happening.

A viable exit route may be via acquisitions. Lower valuations of emerging market startups make them attractive for their global or regional competitors. Vertical integration from a global customer or supplier could be expected. Please note that hostile take-overs or buyouts are not as common in emerging market startups, since the fragile nature of the startups usually does not resist the inexistence of the founder team. In addition, cultural factors may make it hard for the markets to accept this kind of acquisition as a formal strategy.

Mergers could be used to raise valuations to a level that meets IPO requirements for access. Secondary buyouts and leveraged buyouts are also challenging paths, as the markets involved may be underdeveloped, capital allocation weaker, and the financial risks post-buyout are more difficult to manage in emerging markets due to the startups' limited debt-servicing capacities.

Crowdfunding can offer an IPO-like financing alternative, though smaller in scale, and with fewer regulations for startups, which make the route more feasible in emerging economies. Additionally, aside from providing financing, crowdfunding is often used to establish the initial valuation with the public, particularly when professional investors are scarcer in the early stages.

Finally, authorities in emerging markets have occasionally sought alternative markets to address market inadequacies. For example, in Turkey, a Private Equity Market was recently established under the stock exchange. In this market, startups can raise funds while proceeding to meet IPO criteria, venture funds can raise LP money from qualified individual investors, and secondary transactions can take place. Valuations must be determined by market makers, accredited consultants, and brokerage firms to ensure fair and reasonable valuations.

Conclusion

Emerging market valuations deviate from developed market valuations in numerous ways because of the differences in major drivers. Even developed markets have a certain level of instability due to inflation, money supply issues, or trade wars. Moreover, startup valuation is not as straightforward as valuing a publicly traded stock or a conventional enterprise. Combining both elements then: emerging market startup valuation is a unique challenge in itself. Both the investors and the founders require a basis for this practice which can help "clear the fog" of uncertainty and subjectivity. Building a reliable framework to assist in this endeavor was the main purpose of the chapter. Obviously, "black swans" (Taleb 2007) in markets and of humankind, along with the unpredictable nature of deep technologies like artificial intelligence or space mining, will introduce additional considerations in startup valuations. Analysts must regularly adapt their methodologies to these emerging paradigms.

Key Terms and Definitions

Crowdfunding: Raising funds from small investors to finance a startup, a project, or a charity similar to an IPO, usually via an online accredited platform in an eased way.

Deal: A transaction or an opportunity for a transaction that involves gaining shares of a startup.

Dry Powder: The reserved money that is not yet invested, kept for follow-up or further investments by an investor, fund, or investment firm.

Due Diligence: The research and audit process aiming to determine the status of a company in a particular function like legal, financial, technological, etc.

Exit: Selling the previously bought shares or conducting a similar financial transaction for them to realize the profits earned.

Fintech: Startups that produce technological products or services in finance, such as payment gateways, challenger banks, online funding, etc.

Initial Public Offering (IPO): The very first selling of the shares of a privately held company to the public and investors over the stock exchanges.

Private Equity (PE): All kinds of equity transactions related to privately held shares of a company or asset including but not limited to VC, risk capital, M&A, IPO, privatization, taking to private, buyout, etc.

Venture Capital(ist) (VC): An investment type/investor which targets to buy minority shares of a promising technology company, expecting to sell the shares in return for a remarkably high gain in future.

Special Purpose Vehicle (SPV): A legal entity founded to execute a particular financial transaction such as an acquisition of a startup, or taking a publicly traded company private.

References

Blank S, Dorf B (2012) The startup owner's manual: the step-by-step guide for building a great company. K&S Ranch Publishing Inc., Pescadero, CA

Damodaran A (2025). https://pages.stern.nyu.edu/~adamodar/

Gompers PA, Gornall W, Kaplan SN, Strebulaev IA (2020) How do venture capitalists make decisions? J Financ Econ 135(1):169–190

Kahneman D (2011) Thinking, fast and slow. Farrar, Straus, and Giroux

Ries E (2011) The lean startup: how today's entrepreneurs use continuous innovation to create radically successful businesses. Crown Business, New York

Taleb NN (2007) The black swan: the impact of the highly improbable. Random House

Startup Valuation Based on a Multivariate Real Options Approach: When the Type of Market Matters

Jesus Cuauhtemoc Tellez and Sinem Derindere Köseoglu

Abstract This chapter applies to a startup valuation an extended version of the Black-Scholes option pricing model named Equity-Linked Exchange Rate Option, which captures the correlation of risk factors and their volatilities. One of the factors is a macroeconomic variable that distinguishes emerging economies while the other one is the prices of assets underlying the expected revenues of the emerging-based startup. Contrary to traditional business valuation in emerging markets where to the expected rate of return (WACC) is added a premium to reflect the characteristics of an emerging market, the Real Options approach based on a multivariate (MV) asset framework allows to "freely" run the level of comovement among risk factors. The MV Real Options (MVRO) approach is compared with the DCF and the original B-S frameworks. Results show that even in worse conditions where the target revenues of the startup survival stage could not be achieved to continue in the project, there is still a value in the startup, the Time Value, which goes beyond its Intrinsic Value. However, the DCF showed that the investor should reject the startup project. In addition, the MVRO framework shows that the startup value increases at a diminishing rate as the volatility of the risk factor increases, and after a certain level of volatility the startup value decreases. This is interpreted as if the venture capitalist would have acclimated to the emerging market environment. After all, attention should be paid to the application of the RO framework since the B-S model was constructed under the market completeness assumption. Thus, the RO approach should be complementary to other valuation methods in the investment decision-taking.

Keywords Valuation · Startups · Real Options · Emerging Markets

---

J. C. Tellez (✉)
Tecnologico de Monterrey, Business School, Monterrey, Mexico
e-mail: cuauhtemoc.tellez@tec.mx

S. D. Köseoglu
Istanbul University, Istanbul, Turkey
e-mail: sderin@istanbul.edu.tr

S. Derindere Köseoğlu, A. Patterson (eds.), *Valuation in Emerging Markets*, Contributions to Finance and Accounting,
https://doi.org/10.1007/978-3-031-93526-8_17

Introduction

Startups can be classified in different ways: three of them are by the type of industry, the business model, and valuation. With respect to industry, the Artificial Intelligence and Big Data, Fintech, and Life sciences and healthcare make up more than 50% of the whole startup industry (Statista, 2024). Related to the business model they can classified by a Business-to-Business (B2B), Business-to-Consumer (B2C), Business-to-Government (B2G), and Consumer-to-Consumer (C2C). Finally, the valuation classification also related to the startup stage, are Cockroach (earlier startup), Ponies (V < \$10 MM), Centaurs (V < \$100 MM), Unicorn (V < \$1 B), Decacorn (V < \$10 B), and Hectocorn (V < \$100 B). Relating to this criteria, North America (Canada, USA, and Mexico) holds the largest share of unicorns with 182, compared to the rest of the world which reaches 132 (Statista, 2024).

However, the global distribution of unicorns does not take into account the macroeconomic factors that influence risk levels across different regions. For example, Canada, the USA, and Mexico are grouped in the same region as of North America, but economic and financial markets conditions between these countries differ substantially. While the sovereign debt credits for Canada and the USA were rated at AA+ Stable as of 2024 (Fitch Ratings) which means *high quality*, Mexico was rated as BBB- Stable which is in the frontier of the upper bound *likely to fulfill obligations, ongoing uncertainty* level. The differences between these countries are likely to influence investors' risk perceptions, leading them to demand higher returns. As a result, a venture capitalist may not view investing in a U.S.-based "cockroach" startup—a startup that is highly resilient, able to survive economic downturns, and operates with lean resources—the same way as investing in a Mexican-based one. Thus, the type of economy and market matters when economic agents face investment decisions. Therefore, companies' valuations may differ when they belong to different economies even if they belong to the same industry. In this case, two types of markets are being considered: a developed and emerging market.

This chapter extends the real options framework illustrated in "A Practical Guide for Startup Valuation: An Analytical Approach" (Derindere 2024) where the Black-Scholes option pricing model is applied for startup valuation. However, in this chapter it is argued based on the importance of common factors that characterize an emerging market which are included in the Black-Scholes model. Specifically, it considers the correlation of the expected cash flows of a startup investment with the critical factors that commonly define an emerging market. In this sense, instead of discussing the amount by which the expected rate of return should increase to capture the emerging market risks and contrary to common approaches of business valuation in emerging markets (James and Koller 2000), within the RO approach it is allowed to "freely" run the correlation of the expected cash flows with those risk factors which capture uncertainty and volatility and which could enhance the vulnerability of an economic agent when investing in a startup of an emerging market.

This chapter is divided as follows. The second section describes the basics and importance of Real Options approach for startup valuation. Then, Section "The Case of Real Options in Emerging Markets" introduces and applies the extended model of Black-Scholes to the emerging market case, which considers the correlation of multiple assets applied to the business case of section two. Finally, the fourth section gives conclusions and recommendations for suitable applications of the extended model in any emerging market.

The Real Options Approach

The real options approach applied to business valuation is based on the theory of financial options, where a financial option is the right to buy or sell an underlying asset at a prespecified price and maturity date named the strike price and expiration date, respectively. The term "real option" was first coined by Myers and Turnbull (1977) and later Trigeorgis (1996) considered it as an approach of collecting embedded options in the capital budgeting process. However, Copeland and Antikarov (2003) give a precise definition of a real option "as a right, but not the obligation, to take an action (e.g., deferring, expanding, contracting or abandoning) at a predetermined cost, called exercise price, for a predetermined period—the life of the option".

In that respect, Fig. 1 represents the payoff of an option to buy a certain asset at a given strike or exercise price and expiration date. It is observed that, under certain market conditions, if the expected price of the underlying asset (S_T) is greater than

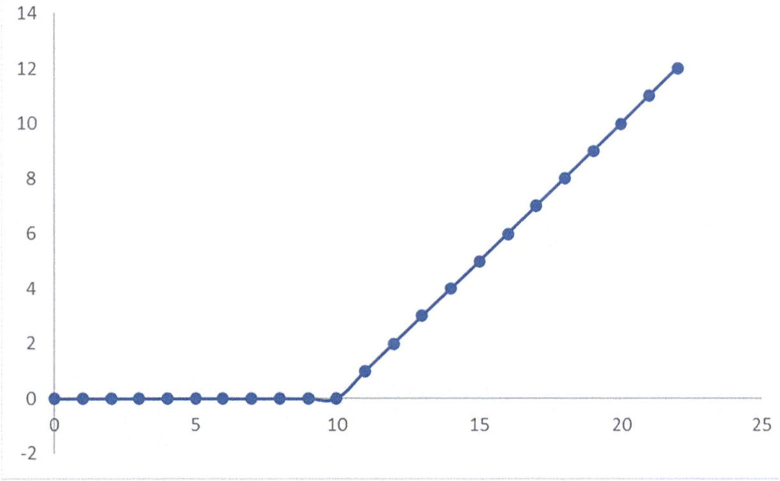

Fig. 1 Profit/Loss (y-axis) profile of a Call option in a long position when K = 10, given expected market prices (*x*-axis) at a certain expiration date. Source: Author's own creation

the strike price (K) at the expiration date then the option to buy the asset can be exercised. In that case, it is said that the option to buy, call option, is in-the-money (ITM). If the expected underlying asset price is equal to the exercise price, then it would be indifferent to the economic agent to exercise the option to buy. On the other hand, if the expected price is less than the strike price, then it would not be feasible to exercise the option buy since in the market it would be "cheaper" to buy the asset than to exercise the option, where in this case it is said that the option is out-of-the-money (OTM).

As an example, when an investor enters into the agreement to buy an underlying asset at K = \$10, if the underlying asset price at the expiration date is $S_T = \$12$, then the investor can exercise the option and would make a profit of \$2 per unit of the underlying asset bought. Otherwise, if the market price were \$8 then the investor may not exercise the option to buy and would prefer to buy the asset outside the agreement at a lower price. In that sense, the terminal value of the call option will be \$0. As a summary, the mathematical expression which describes the optionality of the agreement is stated as $C = max\ (S_T—K,\ 0)$, where S_T is the expected price of the underlying asset at the expiration date, K is the strike price, and C is the expected value of the call option at the expiration date T.

On the other hand, if the option to sell an underlying asset were the case, then it is called a Put Option. Figure 2 depicts the payoff (Profit/Loss profile) of a put option at a given strike price (K) and expiration date. Once at expiration T, if market conditions allow (K > S_T) then the investor may exercise the option to sell the underlying asset at the strike price K. In this case it is said that the put option is in-the-money (ITM). Otherwise, when the agreed price to sell at K is less than the market price S_T, then the investor may not exercise the option and the option value would be zero, where the put option is said to be out-of-the-money (OTM). As an

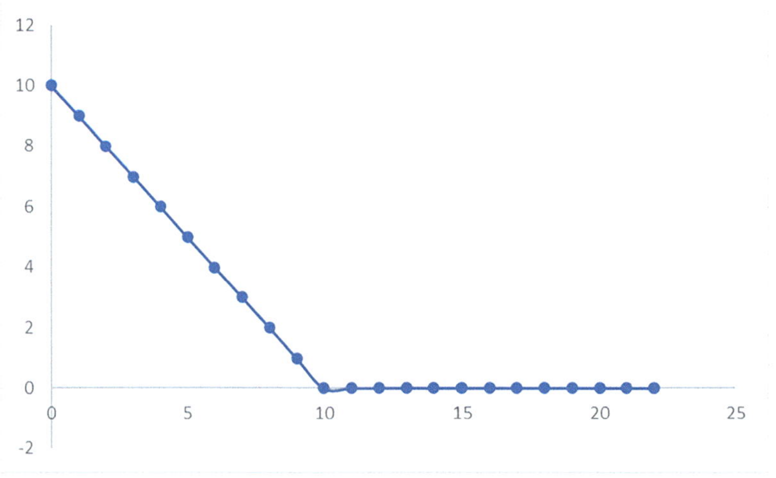

Fig. 2 Profit/Loss (y-axis) profile of a Put option in a long position when K = 10, given expected market prices (x-axis) at expiration date. Source: Author's own creation

Table 1 Properties of options based on the expiration date and strike price

	Value of the option by its type	
Determinant	Call	Put
Contracts with the same expiration date, but different strike prices:	• Increase, as *K*'s are far away from and less than the current S • Decrease, as *K*'s are near from or greater than the current *S*	• Decrease, as *K*'s are far away from and less than the current S • Increase, as *K*'s are near from or greater than the current *S*
Contracts with different expiration dates, but same strike prices:	• Increase, as the expiration date is distant • Decrease, as the expiration date is near	• Increase, as the expiration date is distant • Increase, as the expiration date is near

example, an investor expects that prices will decrease so from now he/she agrees to sell the underlying asset at an exercise price K = $12. Once the put option reaches the expiration date if the market price $S_T = \$10$ is less than the exercise price *K*, then the investor may exercise the option and would make a profit of $2. Under other circumstances the investor may not exercise the option and would sell the asset at the market price, where the put option will have a terminal value of P = $0.

From the point of view of the timing of the exercise, an option is said to be European when the agreement to exercise the option is until its expiration date, while an American option can be exercised at any time during the life of the contract or at the expiration date. Other types of financial options most of them traded in a type of market known as over the counter (OTC), are like Compound, Asian, Binary, Bermudian, Parisian, Barrier, or Double Barrier options. Also, the combination of calls and puts may give rise to investment strategies among others like Bull Spread, Butterfly, Collar, Straddle, or Strangles. An important issue within financial options are properties held when comparing the same type of options but differ in their expiration date and strike price. Table 1 shows a summary of these properties, most of them occurring in an established market like the Chicago Mercantile Exchange (CME).

In that sequence, when the fundamentals and properties of financial options are applied to managerial decisions such as the investment in a project of an ongoing company or a new venture like a startup, then it is said to be the Real Options Approach (ROA). According to Kogut and Kulatilaka (2001), real options are defined as "an investment decision that is characterized by uncertainty, the provision of future managerial discretion to exercise at the appropriate time, and irreversibility". Thus, an investment opportunity could be referred to as a call option, where a firm that wants to invest money or exercise the right to buy (i.e. machinery) has an option to invest now or later.

Following the previous statements, financial options may be addressed by different drivers. However, six major variables may affect the managerial decision to invest (Copeland and Antikarov 2003). The first is related to the value of an asset: if there is an increase in the value of asset, the value of an option also increases. The second is associated with the strike price given the same expiration date (see Table 1). The third factor is related to time, whether the value of an option increases with time (see Table 1). Uncertainty is mainly captured by the volatility of the asset, as a fourth variable, considering that if the managerial decision has flexibility, then the value of an option increases with increasing uncertainty. The fifth is associated with interest rates, when these are high it is observed an increase in the call option value and the put option as well. This occurs because interest rates are associated with the managerial decision carrying cost. The sixth and final variable is related to dividends where an increase in the dividend payout would increase the value of an option, which may happen because dividends are a method to compensate investors when the company or the investment project is funded by equity.

How are these leading drivers considered in the real options approach and their application to a startup valuation case? On one hand, the valuation framework that bridges the gap between a traditional valuation approach and that of the real options is the Discounted Cash Flow (DCF) model. The DCF and consequently the Net Present Value (NPV) of an investment project is a static rigorous criteria framework since only flags the acceptance or rejection of an investment project. However, the real options framework considers the flexibility to postpone, wait, or even enter the project if market conditions may not be favorable (Fabianek et al. 2024) (Vonnegut 2000). This occurs since the options approach deals with the probability of exercising a buy or sell decision if market conditions favor economic agents where this flexibility allows the option value to take its least value at zero. Table 2 shows the relationship between the NPV and RO approaches, where the DCF is an input of the RO approach.

As a second point, recalling the ideas of real options in startup valuation (Derindere 2024), the advantages shown in the RO approach deal primarily with

Table 2 Relationship between NPV and RO approaches

NPV	RO
PVCF: Present Value of Cash Flows	S: current underlying asset price which takes the value of PVCF.
I: Project investment value	K: strike price at which it is agreed to buy or sell the asset, which is the agreed investment in the project.
R: expected rate of return, commonly the WACC.	R_f: the risk-free interest rate, which is the expected rate of return by the investor.
T: the project life.	T: expiration date of the option.
s: Since the NPV is a deterministic approach in which cash flows are generated with certainty, then volatility is zero.	s: even volatility measured by the standard deviation could be considered constant, but the decision is taken under an uncertain environment where probabilities play a key role in the investment decision.
NPV: PVCF—I; if positive then the project is accepted, otherwise it is rejected.	Intrinsic Value: *max (S—K, 0)*; if S > K then it is most probable to exercise the agreed price in the expiration date, otherwise let the contract to expire and buy the asset in the market.

the fact that the option will never take a negative value described by its Intrinsic Value (V), in which mathematical expression for a call option is $V = max(S—K,0)$ while for a put option is $V = max(K—S, 0)$. However, as financial options traded in markets are determined by supply and demand forces, then differences could arise between the market price of the option and its intrinsic value, which is known as the Time Value. Even the Intrinsic Value could be zero which means that the option to buy or sell would not be exercised because the underlying asset price is less than (call option) or greater than (put option) the strike price, but there is still some value within the option related to the timing effect. In other words, although the worst conditions could happen there is still a chance that market conditions may change and that could raise the possibility of exercising the option to buy or sell.

Finally, also taking back the ideas of real options in startup valuation (Derindere 2024), the startup cycle life is segmented into three stages each one with its own level of uncertainty. One of the crucial stages of a startup generating cash flows is during that of Demonstration where cumulative cash flows could reach the highest negative levels known as the Valley of Death (Rencher 2012), as shown in Fig. 3.

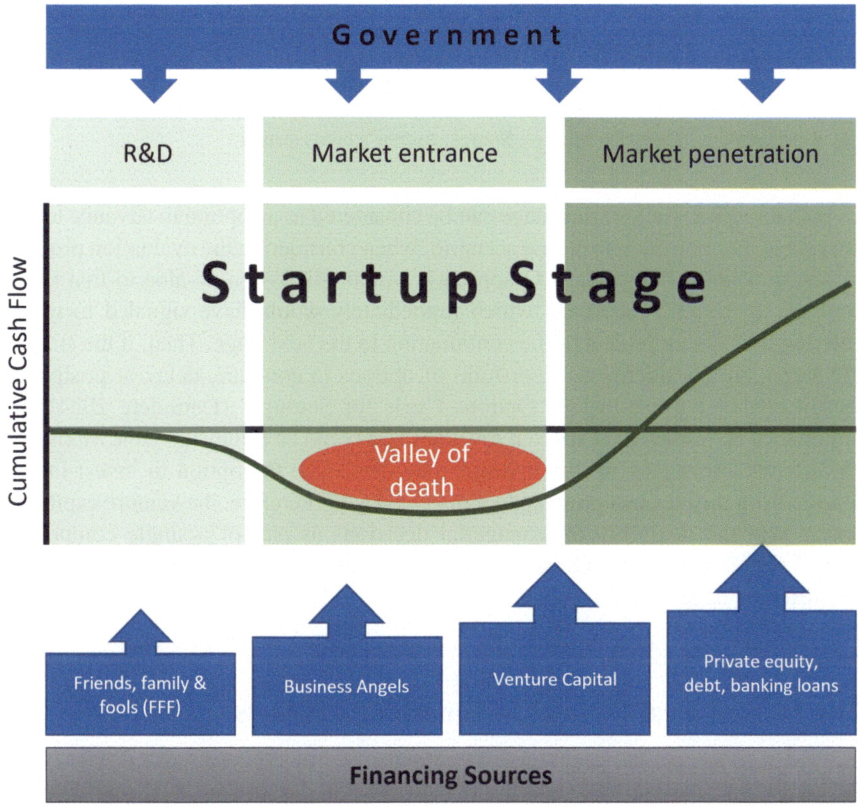

Fig. 3 Startups financing sources. Source: Author's own creation based on Rencher (2012)

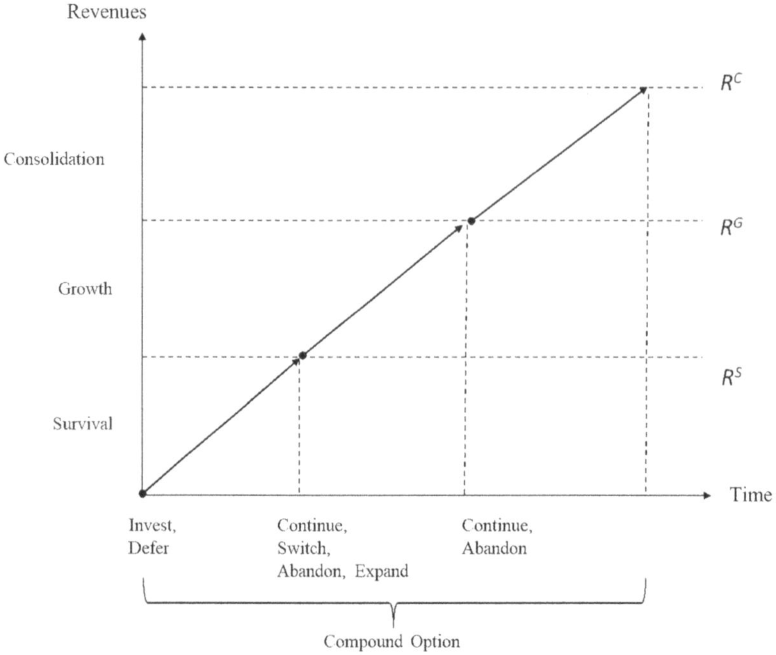

Fig. 4 The Options Cycle for Startups. Source: Author's own creation

In that respect, each startup stage can be considered as an option to advance to the next stage. Even in the worst-case scenario, when considering the evaluation process of investing in a startup, the RO approach would still assign a value to that stage contrary to the DCF approach which immediately would have signaled to reject entering the venture project or the continuation to the next stage. Then, if the startup life stages are considered as a portfolio of options to continue, delay or postpone, then it could give rise to the "Options Cycle for Startups" (Derindere 2024). Its importance is to show the expected revenues that could be achieved by the Startup at its different life stages, so the investor may determine the option to invest in the Startup from the idea inception up to a mature stage. Therefore, the venture capitalist may assess the flexibility of managerial decisions as part of a single compound option, which includes the choices to continue, abandon, switch, expand, or wrap up the different stages (see Fig. 4).

The Case of Real Options in Emerging Markets

Although there are various definitions and methods for categorizing countries as emerging economies based on different characteristics, the concept originates from the 1970s when an emerging economy was simply seen as a less developed economy. As a result, the term "emerging market" emerged to describe economies that

(a) Brazilian Real

(b) Indian Rupee

(c) Mexican Peso

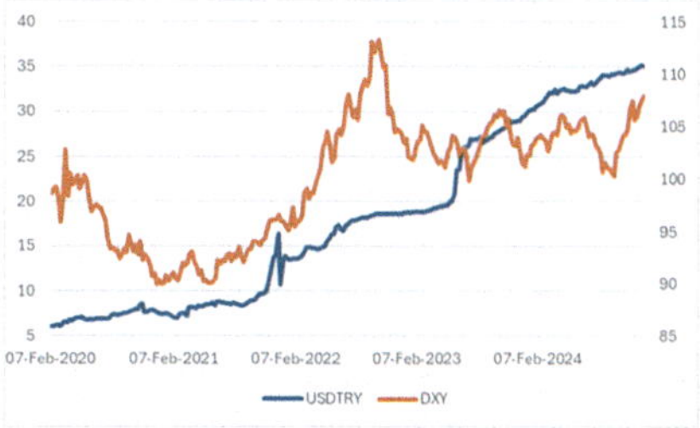

(d) Turkish Lira

Fig. 5 Evolution of four emerging exchange rates against the DXY from February 2020 to December 2024. Source: Author's own creation with data from LSEG

have not yet reached the macroeconomic status of developed countries. Thus, common economic factors may help describe an emerging market, such as high levels of risks, exchange rates fluctuations, inflation, and economic growth (Mardiros and Dicu 2014).

Figure 5 shows the evolution of four emerging market exchange rates from the EM7 (Seven Major Emerging Markets) against the U.S. Dollar Index (DXY) over the period from the COVID-19 pandemic to December 2024, capturing the impact of the public health and geopolitical crises over this period. It is observed that three emerging market currencies experienced significant fluctuations, with the exception of the Turkish Lira, which gradually depreciated until the end of 2021. Indeed, by the end of 2024, the Turkish Lira had depreciated by nearly 300% relative to its value in 2021. Also, the annualized average weekly volatility of the percentage change of the emerging currencies was 16%, whilst that of the Dollar Index was only 7%.

Also, as (high) inflation is considered another common macroeconomic factor of emerging markets, Table 3 depicts the evolution of the previous emerging economies inflation against that of the US. It is observed that the CPI inflation in the US was greater than India and Mexico in 2022 which reached its highest value over the last five years, explained by the consequences of COVID-19 pandemic and supply chain issues. However, the US inflation has been in almost all the time less than the four emerging economies. As an extreme case can be observed in Turkey which peak was also in 2022 but in a double-digit increasing prices environment.

The importance of the common macroeconomic factors that define an emerging market will be considered for the purpose of a startup valuation under the RO

Table 3 Inflation rate (%) of emerging economies and the US from 2018 to 2023

Year	Brazil	India	Mexico	Turkey	USA
2018	3.66	3.94	4.90	16.33	2.44
2019	3.73	3.73	3.64	15.18	1.81
2020	3.21	6.62	3.40	12.28	1.23
2021	8.30	5.13	5.69	19.60	4.70
2022	9.28	6.70	7.90	72.31	8.00
2023	4.59	5.65	5.53	53.86	4.12

Source: Author's own creation with data from FRED (Federal Reserve Bank of St. Louis Economic Data)

Table 4 Net Cash Flows of a startup investment project and economic evaluation criteria in the Survival Stage, when the project is financed with internal sources at 30% expected rate of return

	0	1	2	3
NCF =	(50,000,000.00)	15,000,000.00	20,000,000.00	15,000,000.00
PV =	(50,000,000.00)	11,538,461.54	11,834,319.53	6,827,492.03
PVCF =	30,200,273.10			
NPV =	**(19,799,727)**			
IRR =	**0%**			

approach based on a modified version of the original Black-Scholes model that captures the correlation of risky multiple assets where one of those risky assets could the exchange rate, inflation, or interest rates.

The first scenario involves the startup's valuation using the DCF model under a pessimistic outlook, where the startup is financed solely through internal sources, meaning that the venture capitalist is the exclusive financial supporter of the project.[1] As such, this scenario considers a startup "investment project" when it is 100% financed with internal sources which states that the capital structure could be 100/0. It makes sense since even at the Consolidation stage the Startup could not have generated enough historical financial information or profits that would allow a solid credit rating to enable a significant loan or debt issuance. As illustrated in Figs. 3 and 4, after reaching a certain point in time and achieving the desired revenue levels, the startup gains the potential to initiate a stock issuance process. Table 4 presents the stream of net cash flows and the economic valuation of the startup project during the Survival Stage, which involves an investment of $50,000,000. The expected rate of return is 30%, and the stage is anticipated to expire within the next three years. It is observed that the "startup" project should not be accepted since the present value of the expected cash flows is not able to cover the initial investment (in this case held completely by the investor). In addition, as the project is financed by internal sources then it would be expected to have a higher rate of return since no additional (external) sources are considered that could be benefited by the tax shield.

[1] An extended version of this scenario and other scenarios with their comparison to the RO approach can be revised in Derindere (2024).

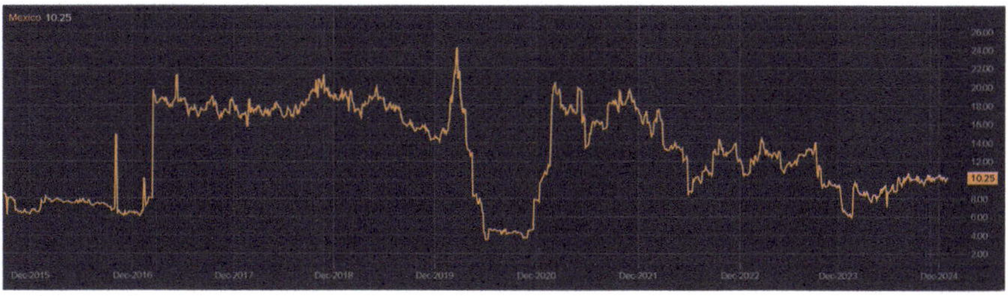

Fig. 6 Evolution of the equity risk premium of Mexico. Source: LSEG

Table 5 Net Cash Flows of an emerging startup investment project and economic evaluation criteria, when the project is financed with internal sources at a 40.23% expected rate of return

	0	1	2	3
NCF =	(50,000,000.00)	15,000,000.00	20,000,000.00	15,000,000.00
PV =	(50,000,000.00)	10,696,712.54	10,170,636.38	5,439,618.69
PVCF =	26,306,967.61			
NPV =	**(23,693,032)**			
IRR =	**0%**			

However, if the startup is based in an emerging economy, a higher return should be considered to reflect and compensate the investor for the additional risks associated with what is termed an "emerging startup" (James and Koller 2000). In that case suppose a Mexican-based startup where the premium to be added is the equity risk premium of 10.23% as of December 2024 (see Fig. 6). Other considerations of the premium to be paid can be reviewed from Damodaran (2025) who illustrates multiple ways to measure country risk.

In that respect, Table 5 shows the Mexican-based emerging startup valuation under a 40.23% rate of return, where it is detected that the NPV worsens. This being so, the venture capitalist would reject investing in the emerging market startup. Also, it is important to recall that the expected cash flows of the startup do not belong to the traditional Free Cash Flows derived from the Income Statement as if it were a going concern, but the cash flows are the startup expected revenues as shown in Figs. 4 and 5 since no historical information is available and the survival of the startup depends heavily on its initial revenues.

The previous scenario shows that under the Net Present Value approach, there may be some rigidity in making investment decisions, as the project should be accepted whenever the NPV is greater than zero, regardless of other factors. Otherwise, the project should be rejected. Nevertheless, how could a managerial decision be supported if the venture capitalist wants to take the risk when startup NPV is negative?

Following the Black-Scholes-Merton (1973) option pricing models (see Appendix 1), let us consider again an investor facing the opportunity to fund a startup business. The investor can assess the investment project from its inception through to a point where the project has achieved the target revenues, which may then allow the investor to decide whether to continue with the investment. In the first Startup cycle stage considered as the Survival stage, the company needs to achieve survival revenues R^S in such a way as to continue to a second stage, the Growth stage. Then, from the beginning the investor could evaluate the option to invest or defer the investment where a crucial variable is the time that would take to reach the Survival Revenues which are those revenues that at least may allow the investor to recover the initial investment.

The RO valuation results for a startup that belongs to a developed market, that is, a 30% rate of return, when volatility of revenues is 15% of a similar startup, are:

- S_t: the present value of revenues,
- K: the initial investment,
- T: time to expiration of the Survival stage,
- R: expected rate of return (opportunity cost)
- σ: volatility of revenues

$$d_1 = \frac{\ln\left(\frac{30{,}200{,}273}{50{,}000{,}000}\right) + \left(0.30 + \frac{1}{2}0.15^2\right)3}{0.15\sqrt{3}} = 1.6534$$

$$d_2 = 1.6534 - 0.15\sqrt{3} = 1.3936$$

$$c_{BS}(S_t, t) = 30{,}200{,}273N(1.6534) - 50{,}000{,}000e^{-0.30(3)}N(1.3936)$$

$$c_{BS}(S_t, t) = 30{,}200{,}273(0.9509) - 50{,}000{,}000e^{-0.30(3)}(0.9183)$$

$$c_{BS}(S_t, t) = 10{,}049{,}460$$

What is going on in this example? Although the target revenues are equal to the initial investment, the startup investment should not be accepted because the NPV is negative. However, the RO valuation gives a positive value of the venture capital investment because of the timing effect implicit in the option to exercise the Survival Stage. In that respect, the intrinsic value of the option to invest in a Startup that could be exercised at the expiration date of the Survival stage is $C = \max(30{,}200{,}273 - 50{,}000{,}000; 0) = \$0$. This means that the present value of the expected level of revenues of $30,200,273 that the Startup could generate during the Survival stage and a target revenue of K = 50,000,000 at the expiration date, the investor would prefer to let the investment expire and not continue to the following stage. This decision was initially suggested by the NPV approach which showed that investing in the Startup may not have been a good decision. However, as the option value considers an intrinsic value and a time value, the real options approach suggests that the project should be taken because over time the Startup may add value.

In another scenario, a venture capitalist has agreed to invest in or acquire a target revenue of K = $50,000,000, which could enable the startup to progress to the next stage or, in a sense, make the investor the future owner of the company. Since the market conditions in which the startup is being valued are not favorable, the present value of the expected revenues is less than the amount of revenues agreed to pay in the future to continue to the next stage. Although the investor faces an unfavorable situation if he/she would like to take the opportunity then he/she should make a down payment to the "startuppers" of $10,049,460 in such a way that the venture capitalist holds the right to buy the "Startup" asset. From both perspectives, the startup company has been priced at a net value of $10,049,460. Even if the NPV would be negative or in the RO approach the intrinsic value would be zero there is a 91% chance, N(d2) = 0.9183, that the option could be exercised in the expiration date T = 3. Since the expiration date is so far from now, this timing effect has a positive impact on the startup value as market conditions may change that would make it quite favorable to continue to the next startup stage.

As time progresses, the venture capitalist could opt to relinquish the decision and transfer the business opportunity to a second investor. The latter could be willing to accept the startup project and pay a $ten million premium to have the right to exercise the investment installment at the revenue lump sum on the survival expiration date. The willingness to pay for a startup which initially would have been rejected is motivated by the fact that revenues during the survival stage could be greater than those expected in the initial evaluation. If the first investor decides to exit the startup project after the initial startup stage and transfers it to a second investor, then this could be an example of an "Abandonment Option", and the estimated net effect for the first investor could be −$40 million. As the second investor is willing to pay a $ten million premium because market conditions may turn better, the first investor is willing to abandon the startup project because market conditions may not be as favorable as the second investor has considered. This first scenario has shown the two sides of the same coin: an initial investor that after making an investment decision in a startup which has shown to be rejected under the NPV scenario, recognizes the opportunity to transfer the startup project and is willing to receive a $ten million premium, despite the net cash flow being -$40 million; and a second investor who is willing to pay $ten million because market conditions may change and get a payback greater than $60 million at the expiration of Survival stage.

Now, consider that the investor facing the Mexican-based startup which needs to assess its decision-making process. In this case, the RO valuation considers the expected rate of return of 40.23%, which results based on the European call B-S formula are as follows:

$$d_1 = \frac{\ln\left(\frac{26{,}306{,}968}{50{,}000{,}000}\right) + \left(0.4023 + \frac{1}{2}0.15^2\right)3}{0.15\sqrt{3}} = 2.3035$$

$$d_2 = 2.3035 - 0.15\sqrt{3} = 2.0437$$

$$c_{BS}(S_t, t) = 26{,}306{,}968 * N(2.3035) - 50{,}000{,}000e^{-0.4023(3)}N(2.0437)$$

$$c_{BS}(S_t, t) = 26{,}306{,}968 * (0.9894) - 50{,}000{,}000e^{-0.4023(3)}(0.9795)$$

$$c_{BS}(S_t, t) = 11{,}377{,}771$$

It is observed that as the expected rate of return increases, so does the value of the option to buy the Survival Stage, assuming volatility remains unchanged. First, the original mathematical relationship between the option to buy and interest rates is positive, known as the Greek letter "rho" (ρ), which measures the sensitiveness of options to changes in interest rates. From a business decision-making perspective, even the present value of the revenue streams (S_t) do not cover the target revenues of K = 50,000,000 in such a way as to continue to the next stage, an increasing rate of return signals a higher opportunity cost which instead of punishing the investment decision as in the NPV approach it compensates the investor giving a higher probability, $N(d_1) = 0.9795$, of exercising the option to continue to the next stage (ceteris paribus, assuming volatility remains unchanged).

However, to capture the risk factors describing an emerging market associated with the expected cash flows, the B-S model is extended to a multiple asset framework where the correlation between the main variable and the risk factor and their variances are captured (see Appendix 2). Consider again the investor with an investment opportunity in a Mexican-based startup, where the expected rate of return is 30%, a correlation between the asset that underlies the stream of revenues with the risk factor (e.g. exchange rate) is 60%, and the annualized volatilities of the revenues' underlying asset and the exchange rate are 15% each one. Then, following the Equity-linked Foreign Exchange Call:

- *K*: the minimum exchange rate at which the investor would convert the startup investment (asset) back to the domestic currency.
- x_0Q_0, the price of the underlying asset, that means the present value of the startup revenues is denominated in the domestic currency, where x_0 is the current exchange rate and Q_0 is the present value of revenues denominated in the foreign currency.
- x_TQ_T, the currency translated value of the startup investment at the expiration of the Survival stage.
- *R*, the expected rate of return in the domestic-denominated currency.
- R_f, the expected rate of return in the foreign-denominated currency, where the following expression based on the purchasing power parity condition is applied to convert a WACC from one currency to another: $WACC_f = [(1 + WACC_d) * (1 + p_f) / (1 + p_d)] - 1$; where p_f and p_d are the expected inflation rates of the foreign and domestic countries, respectively.
- *r*, the correlation between the asset underlying the startup revenues and the exchange rate.
- *s*, the volatility of the asset underlying the startup revenues.

- s, the volatility of the exchange rate.
- T, time to expiration of the Survival stage.

If the Mexican-based startup valuation is done by the end of 2024 where no dividend yield is paid by the asset underlying the revenues, then:

Parameter	Description
$K = 0.047680$	The minimum exchange rate (USD per MXN) showed from 2022 to 2024
$x_0 = 0.049167$	The exchange rate by the end of 2024
$Q_0 = 535{,}057{,}411$	The present value of Mexican pesos-denominated revenues
$x_0Q_0 = 26{,}306{,}968$	The present value of US dollars-denominated revenues
$x_T = 0.045790$	The expected exchange rate at expiration of the Survival stage
$Q_T = 1{,}091{,}941{,}472$	The target revenues at the Survival stage expiration in Mexican pesos
$x_TQ_T = 50{,}000{,}000$	The target revenues denominated in US dollars
$R = 30\%$	Expected rate of return if the investment were in a USA-based startup
$R_f = 32\%$	Expected rate of return when the investment is in a Mexican-based startup, where $p_f = 3.70\%$ and $p_d = 2.5\%$ are the expected inflations in Mexico and USA, respectively
$r = 0.60$	The correlation between the asset prices underlying the startup revenues and the exchange rate
$s = 15\%$	The volatility level measured by the standard deviation of the asset prices underlying the startup revenues
$s = 15\%$	The volatility level measured by the standard deviation of the exchange rate
$T = 3$ *years*	Expiration date of the Survival stage

$$d_1 = \frac{\ln\left(\frac{0.049167}{0.047680}\right) + \left(0.30 - 0.32 + 0.60 * 0.15 * 0.15 + \frac{1}{2}0.15^2\right)3}{0.15\sqrt{3}} = 0.173053$$

$$d_2 = 0.173053 - 0.15\sqrt{3} = -0.086754$$

$$c_{MV} = 26{,}306{,}968 * N(0.173053)$$
$$- (0.047680 * 535{,}057{,}411)e^{-(0.30+0.60*0.15*0.15-0.32)3}N(-0.086754)$$

$$c_{MV} = 26{,}306{,}968 * (0.5687) - 25{,}511{,}537e^{-0.0065(3)}(0.4654)$$

$$c_{MV} = 2{,}852{,}912$$

Results indicate that even if the investor faces an emerging market opportunity, characterized by more volatile macroeconomic variables compared to a developed market, it would require higher compensation to account for the increased risk, the optionality to enter the Survival stage and exercise the target revenues would still create value for the investor. So, instead of the investor paying $11.37 million startup worth, it would only pay $2.85 million. Because of emerging market conditions, the value of the startup has decreased, which has reflected uncertainty levels greater than in a developed market. Although differences between an emerging and developed

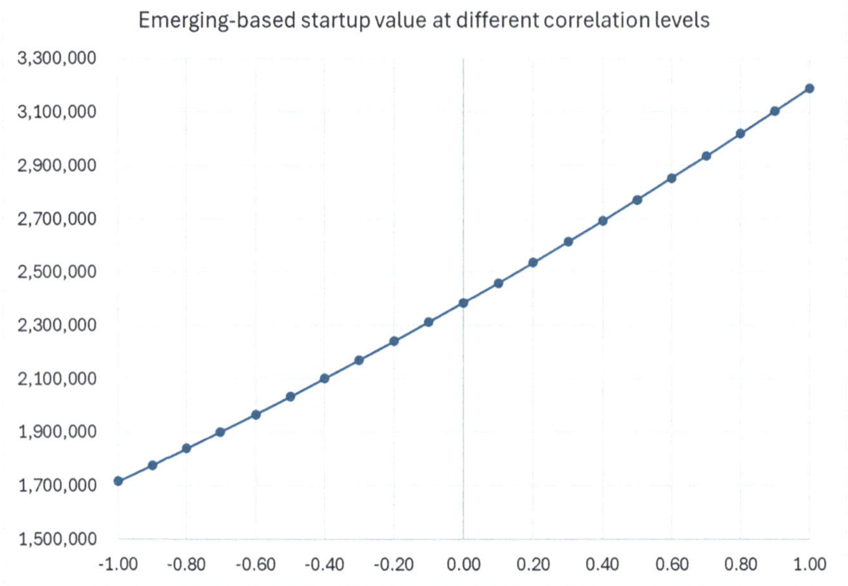

Fig. 7 Sensitivity of the emerging-based startup to correlation between risk factors. Source: Author's own creation

market can arise, the startup keeps a value that shows the probability that market conditions could change during the Survival stage. Thus, the "startupper" and venture capitalist would be willing to receive and pay $2.85 million USD worth of the startup company, respectively.

Figure 7 depicts the sensitivity of the startup value to changes in the correlation between the assets underlying the stream of revenues and the exchange rate. It is observed that there is a positive (and almost linear) relationship between the startup value and the level of correlation. This means that the investor could be willing to pay more for the startup company when the correlation of risk factors increases (ceteris paribus) since the positive comovement of both factors could increase the level of riskiness, but at the same time because of the expiration date far away from now it increases the probability to exercise the option, to maintain in the startup, and continue to the next stage.

On the other hand, when the correlation is fixed at 0.60 but the exchange rate volatility runs within a range of values, it is observed that the value of the startup increases but at a diminishing rate. When the exchange rate volatility changes by 100 basis points, the startup values increase at an increasing rate. But after volatility has reached a peak of 10%, the startup value increases at a diminishing rate (see Fig. 8). Therefore, even if it is observed to have a direct relationship between the startup value and the exchange rate volatility, the startup value becomes less sensitive to an increase in the exchange rate volatility. The business interpretation suggests that while a venture capitalist may be willing to invest a larger amount in a

(a) (b)

Fig. 8 (**a**) The startup value against the exchange rate volatility; (**b**) The startup value change when volatility changes by 1%. Source: Author's own creation

risky decision due to the factors characterizing an emerging market, beyond a certain level of volatility, the investor becomes less sensitive to that risk. This occurs as the investor becomes "acclimated" to the risk environment surrounding the emerging-market startup.

As described above, the investor would need a flexible analytical tool in such a way to determine the option to continue or abandon an investment done in a Startup business. However, the investor faces a greater level of uncertainty when venturing into an emerging market where one of the critical risk factors has been the exchange rate. Once the survival revenues have been achieved, the investor could have the option to abandon or continue, even to switch to another Startup or expand the investment amount in the original. In this case, the Startup has moved from Survival to a Growth stage. However, the investor once again faces the crucial question about the time required to reach a new target revenue known as Growth Revenues R^G which may allow them to move to the third stage. The Growth Revenues are those revenues that may allow the investor to recover the initial investment and any additional installments that permitted an expansion of the original investment.

Finally, as the Startup moves to a Consolidation stage, the investor can evaluate the option to continue or even abandon if the following revenues named Consolidation Revenues may not allow the investor to recover the initial investment. Again, one of the investors' concerns is the time to achieve the Consolidation Revenues in an emerging market environment.

As was noted in this section, the modified version of the B-S model "Equity-linked exchange rate option" allows to capture the volatility of exchange rates and its correlation with the prices of the assets underlying the expected revenues by the emerging-based Startup. If the B-S framework as one of the main and accepted option pricing models is directly applied to the emerging-based case, it was observed that the option value increased whenever the expected rate of return was increasing as the investor needs to be compensated for taking additional risks that characterize an emerging market. This makes sense in two ways. On one hand, the mathematical property of the B-S model states a positive relationship between the option value and interest rates (the reference rate). On the other hand, the business sense would signal that as the opportunity cost increases to move from one asset to another (i.e. the substitution effect of a non-risky asset to a risky asset) implies that the expected return could be achieved with a higher probability. However, this framework does not account for the degree of correlation between the underlying asset and other risk factors, as would be the case in a real-world situation where the venture capitalist faces additional complexities when investing in emerging markets.

As demonstrated in the business case example, the emerging-based startup has a lower value under the multivariate option model compared to the original Black-Scholes model, where the correlation between the risk factors plays a critical role in the startup's valuation. Even market conditions may not be favorable as signaled by the DCF approach (reject to invest in the Survival stage), but the multivariate option as that of the "Equity-linked Foreign Exchange call" shows that besides a high correlation and volatility of the risky asset describing an emerging market the Startup keeps a value (not shown by the DCF) which reflects the probability that those market conditions could change and make the investment get worth.

In conclusion, the Real Options (RO) approach based on a multivariate option model has demonstrated that even though the investor faces a risky project in emerging markets where the NPV would reject it, there is a probability that the investment may get value over Time. Also, it was observed that the NPV is an input of the RO approach. Therefore, both approaches should be complementary tools for managerial business decisions. A key feature in the multivariate RO analysis is the correlation between risky factors where the Startup could generate more value as the degree of association decreases like the diversification principle in investment portfolios. This means, even the venture capitalist would invest in an emerging-based startup, as the risk factors are less correlated the investor could face a better chance to exercise each stage of the startup life cycle.

Conclusions

This chapter applied an Equity-Linked Exchange Rate model which is an extended version of the B-S option pricing model that captures the correlation and volatility of multivariate assets, to value an emerging-based startup company. In that context, the compensation that a venture capitalist may seek for investing in an emerging market is not only captured in the expected rate of return but also in the correlation between the asset underlying the expected revenues of the startup and a risk factor describing an emerging market, and volatilities of both risky assets. The proposed multivariate asset model was fed with different exchange rates values which show market expectations related to the uncertainty of an emerging market. As such, a minimum expected exchange rate, a forward rate, and the current value of the emerging currency allows us to capture the conditions of the emerging economy where in the standpoint of view of international economics they are associated with two other risk factors that describe an emerging economy like inflation rate and interest rates.

The RO approach based on the original B-S model was compared to the DCF when in both cases the expected rate of return was adjusted to reflect the emerging market conditions. In absolute terms, as the expected revenues proposed showed a negative condition of the market, the value of the startup company was highly punished by a rejected flag, which means that the startup was not able to give back to the investor the minimum target revenues to continue to the next stage of the startup life cycle. On the other hand, when the RO was applied it was found that even in the worst case conditions the startup would still create value. This occurs because the Time Value component of the optionality to exercise (i.e. to buy or not to buy) the startup (asset) plays a key role in the managerial decision shown by the probability depicted in the B-S model. In this case, since the time to expiration of the Survival stage is far away from the moment the startup is valued, then there is a greater chance that market conditions could change making them favorable to generate higher revenues than those forecasted.

Nevertheless, the original B-S model does not allow us to capture correlation between risk factors. When applied the extended version as that of a multivariate option model, it was shown that the startup value considerably decreased when the correlation level was fixed at 60%. It was noticed that the startup value and correlation level is keeping a positive relationship. So, even if the correlation could increase to 1, the startup would increase in its value. This implies that the venture capitalist could be willing to pay more for the startup company since it is considered that market conditions may benefit him and would increase the probability to continue to the next Startup stage. Also, it was shown that when the volatility of the exchange rate increases the startup value is the same but at a diminishing rate. The study found a point at which the startup's value reaches its highest level in response to volatility. After surpassing this threshold, further increases in volatility have a weaker effect on value. This implies that investors may adapt to the risks of an emerging market over time, making them less reactive to additional uncertainty. Even so, the startup continues to gain value.

While the real options approach offers flexibility in managerial decisions, it is important to exercise caution. The Black-Scholes model is based on specific assumptions, including a normal probability distribution, rational expectations, constant variance, and, crucially, the concept of complete markets—where both the underlying asset and the financial derivative are tradable securities. However, investment based on a real asset and a startup company are not marketable securities which means that the valuation process is facing a problem of market incompleteness. Therefore, the real options approach should not be viewed as the sole method for making investment decisions in a startup. Instead, it can be used alongside other valuation methodologies to provide a more comprehensive justification for the company's estimated value. Aside from the assumptions on which the RO approach is based that could not fit completely the valuation process of a startup, but it is able to unmask the Intrinsic Value and Time Value of investment decisions.

Appendix 1: An example of the Black-Scholes and Merton (1976) Option Pricing Model

The option pricing formula for a European call option is:

$$c_{BS}(S_t, t) = S_t N(d_1) - Xe^{-R(\tau)} N(d_2), \tag{1}$$

$$d_1 = \frac{\ln\left(\frac{S_t}{X}\right) + \left(R + \frac{1}{2}\sigma^2\right)\tau}{\sigma\sqrt{\tau}}, \tag{2}$$

$$d_2 = d_1 - \sigma\sqrt{\tau} \tag{3}$$

Expression (4) considers the Black-Scholes formula of a European put option:

$$p_{BS}(S_t, t) = Xe^{-R(\tau)} N(-d_2) - S_t N(-d_1), \tag{4}$$

where:

- $c_{BS}(S_t, t)$, is the European call option value as a function of the current underlying asset price S_t at time t.
- $p_{BS}(S_t, t)$, is the European put option value as a function of the current underlying asset price S_t at time t.
- $d_1$and d_2 are standardized random variables.
- $N(d_1)$ and $N(d_2)$, are the Normal Standard Distributions as a function of d_1 and d_2.
- $N(-d_1)$ and $N(-d_2)$, are the Normal Standard Distributions as a function of $-d_1$ and $-d_2$.
- R, is the annual risk-free interest rate.
- τ, the option maturity proportional to a year basis.
- σ^2, the annualized variance of the underlying asset returns, and σ the respective standard deviation (a measure of volatility).

As an example, consider a European call option which expires within 56 days. The agreement states an exercise price of \$45 to buy an asset for which the current market price is \$50 and pays no dividends. The annualized volatility of the asset returns is 15%, the annual reference (risk-free) interest rate is 10%, and the money market convention to be considered is 360 days a year. Then, based on the B-S model, the price of a call option would be:

$$d_1 = \frac{\ln\left(\frac{50}{45}\right) + \left(0.10 + \frac{1}{2}0.15^2\right)0.15}{0.15\sqrt{0.15}} = 2.0734$$

$$d_2 = 2.0734 - 0.15\sqrt{0.15} = 2.0143$$

where $\tau = \frac{56}{360} = 0.15$. Then,

$$c_{BS}(S_t, t) = 50N(2.0734) - 45e^{-0.10(0.15)}N(2.0143)$$

$$c_{BS}(S_t, t) = 50(0.9809) - 45e^{-0.10(0.15)}(0.9780)$$

$$c_{BS}(S_t, t) = 5.72$$

So, a company facing the asset's market risks would agree to hedge its exposure by buying the call option at a price of \$5.72. In this case the company agrees to buy the underlying asset at an exercise price of \$45 that would be exercised within 56 days. If market conditions continue until the expiration date, then the company may exercise its right to buy the asset at \$45. At the expiration date the intrinsic value of the option would be $C = \max(50 - 45, 0) = \$5$, which means that the expected underlying asset at expiration could be \$50. Otherwise, the company could let the option expire and would rather buy the asset at the market price. Finally, the probability that the company may exercise the call option would be 0.9780, and the sensitiveness of the call option to the changes in the underlying asset price is 0.9809, which means that a change in the underlying asset price by 1 unit may outcome a change in the call option price by 0.9809 monetary units.

On the other hand, if the company or investor were the owner of the asset and expects that market prices can fall, then it could buy a Put option. In this case, the company may agree to sell the asset at the exercise price of 45. So, the cost of the hedging strategy using the B-S model would be:

$$p_{BS}(S_{BS}, t) = 45e^{-0.10(0.15)}N(-2.0143) - 50N(-2.0743)$$

$$p_{BS}(S_{BS}, t) = 45e^{-0.10(0.15)}(0.0220) - 45(0.0191)$$

$$p_{BS}(S_t, t) = 0.02$$

If days to expiration would be 90, ceteris paribus, then the value of both options could be,

$$c(S, t) = 6.17,$$

$$p(S, t) = 0.06$$

Results imply that as the expiration date lasts longer, the probability of exercising the call option increases due to the possibility that the expected underlying asset price would eventually be greater than the current asset price given market conditions. This situation would mean that the company or investor pays a greater premium for their hedging or investment strategy. However, a down movement of the expected asset price should also be possible as given by current market conditions, which may imply a greater probability of the Put option to be exercised at the expiration date. So, the company or investor would pay a greater premium to exercise their right to sell the underlying asset.

Appendix 2: The Equity-Linked Exchange Rate Option Model (McDonald 2003)

Equity-Linked Exchange Rate Option

The payoff to protect a variable quantity of currency when K is the minimum expected exchange rate:

$$Q_T x_T + Q_T\, max(0, K - x_T) = Q_T K + Q_T\, max(0, x_T - K) = Q_T K + max(0, Q_T x_T - Q_T K) \quad (5)$$

So, expression (6) is the pricing formula of the payoff in expression (5):

$$C = Q_0 e^{\left(R_f - \delta_Q + \rho\sigma s\right)T}\left[x_0 e^{-\left(R_f - \rho\sigma s\right)T} N(d_1) - e^{-RT} K N(d_2)\right] \quad (6)$$

$$C = x_0 Q_0 e^{-\delta_Q T} N(d_1) - K Q_0 e^{-\left(R + \delta_Q + \rho\sigma s - R_f\right)T} N(d_2) \quad (7)$$

where,

$$d_1 = \frac{ln(x_0/K) + \left(R - R_f + \rho\sigma s + 0.5 s^2\right)T}{s\sqrt{T}} \quad (8)$$

$$d_2 = d_1 - s\sqrt{T} \quad (9)$$

References

Black F, Scholes M (1973) The pricing of options and corporate liabilities. J Polit Econ 81(3): 637–654

Copeland T, Antikarov V (2003) Real options: a practitioner's guide, revised edition. Thomson/Texere, New York

Damodaran, A. (2025). Country default spreads and risk premiums. Retrieved from https://pages.stern.nyu.edu/~adamodar/New_Home_Page/datafile/ctryprem.html

Derindere S (2024) A practical guide for startup valuation: an analytical approach, contributions to finance and accounting. Springer Nature

Fabianek P, Glensk B, Madlener R (2024) A sequential real options analysis for renewable power-to-hydrogen plants for Germany and California. Renew Sust Energ Rev 192:114159

James M, Koller TM (2000) Valuation in emerging markets. McKinsey Q 4. Retrieved from https://people.duke.edu/~charvey/Teaching/BA456_2006/McK00_4.pdf

Kogut B, Kulatilaka N (2001) Capabilities as real options. Organization Science 12(6):744–758.

Mardiros DN, Dicu RM (2014) The Emerging Economies Classification In Terms Of Their Defining, Grouping Criteria And Acronyms Used For This Purpose. Management Strategies Journal, Constantin Brancoveanu University 26(4):311–319

McDonald RL (2003) Derivatives Markets. Addison-Wesley

Myers SC, Turnbull SM (1977) Capital budgeting and the capital asset pricing model: good news and bad news. J Financ 32(2):321–333

Rencher M (2012) Crossing the valley of death: a multi-sited, multi-level ethnographic study of growth startups and entrepreneurial communities in post-industrial Detroit. Wayne State University

Statista (2024) Global startups - statistics & facts. https://www.statista.com

Trigeorgis L (1996) Real options: managerial flexibility and strategy in resource allocation. The MIT Press

Vonnegut A (2000) Real option theories and investment in emerging economies. Emerg Mark Rev 1:82–100

The manufacturer's authorised representative in the EU is Springer Nature Customer Service Centre GmbH, Europaplatz 3, 69115 Heidelberg, Germany. If you have any concerns regarding our products, please contact ProductSafety@springernature.com

Printed and bound by CPI Group (UK) Ltd, Croydon, CR0 4YY
01/10/2026
02225966-0016